Examining Political Violence

Studies of Terrorism, Counterterrorism, and Internal War

Examining Political Violence

Studies of Terrorism, Counterterrorism, and Internal War

Edited by
David Lowe
Austin Turk
Dilip K. Das

International Police Executive Symposium Co-Publication

CRC Press
Taylor & Francis Group
Boca Raton London New York

CRC Press is an imprint of the
Taylor & Francis Group, an **informa** business

CRC Press
Taylor & Francis Group
6000 Broken Sound Parkway NW, Suite 300
Boca Raton, FL 33487-2742

Library of Congress Cataloging-in-Publication Data

Examining political violence : studies of terrorism, counterterrorism, and internal war /
    editors, David Lowe, Austin T. Turk, and Dilip K. Das.
       pages cm
    Includes bibliographical references and index.
    ISBN 978-1-4665-8820-2
    1. Terrorism. 2. Terrorism--Prevention. 3. Police. 4. Political violence. I. Lowe,
David (Lecturer on policing) II. Turk, Austin T., 1934- III. Das, Dilip K., 1941-

HV6431.E945 2014
363.325--dc23   2013021986

Visit the Taylor & Francis Web site at
http://www.taylorandfrancis.com

and the CRC Press Web site at
http://www.crcpress.com

This edited collection of work is dedicated to the memory of two of the contributors, Ayla Schbley and Jean-Paul Brodeur. Not only were they both experts in their fields but also they were pioneers in the study of policing and terrorism, setting the standards for the rest of us to follow.

Contents

Section II

COUNTERING TERRORISM: DEVELOPMENTS FROM 9/11

Section III
POLICING REVOLUTIONARY AND SECESSIONIST VIOLENCE

IPES Preface

The International Police Executive Symposium (IPES) was founded in 1994 to address one major challenge. The two worlds of research and practice remain disconnected even though cooperation between the two is growing. A major reason is that the two groups speak in different languages. The research is published in hard-to-access journals and presented in a manner that is difficult for some to comprehend. On the other hand, police practitioners tend not to mix with researchers and remain secretive about their work. Consequently there is little dialog between the two and almost no attempt to learn from one another. The global dialog among police researchers and practitioners is limited. True, the literature on the police is growing exponentially. But its impact upon day-to-day policing, however, is negligible.

The aims and objectives of the IPES are to provide a forum to foster closer relationships among police researchers and practitioners on a global scale, to facilitate cross-cultural, international and interdisciplinary exchanges for the enrichment of the law enforcement profession, to encourage discussion, and to publish research on challenging and contemporary problems facing the policing profession. One of the most important activities of the IPES is the organization of an annual meeting under the auspices of a police agency or an educational institution. Now in its seventeenth year, the annual meeting, a five-day initiative on specific issues relevant to the policing profession, brings together ministers of interior and justice, police commissioners and chiefs, members of academia representing world-renown institutions, and many more criminal justice elite from over 60 countries. It facilitates interaction and the exchange of ideas and opinions on all aspects of policing. The agenda is structured to encourage dialog in both formal and informal settings.

Another important aspect of the meeting is the publication of the best papers presented, edited by well-known criminal justice scholars and police professionals who attend the meetings. The best papers are selected, thoroughly revised, fully updated, meticulously edited, and published as books based upon the theme of each meeting. This repository of knowledge, under the co-publication imprint of IPES and CRC Press/Taylor & Francis Group, chronicles the important contributions of the International Police Executive Symposium over the last two decades. As a result, in 2011 the United Nations awarded IPES a Special Consultative Status for the Economic and Social Council (ECSOC) honoring its importance in the global security community.

In addition to this book series, the IPES also has a research journal, *Police Practices and Research: An International Journal* (PPR). The *PPR* contains research articles on police issues from practitioners and researchers. It is an international journal in the truest sense of the term and is distributed worldwide. For more information on the *PPR* visit http://www.tandf.co.uk/journals/GPPR.

It is within the IPES ethos that *Examining Political Violence: Studies of Terrorism, Counterterrorism and Internal War* has been published. It is a collection of studies into political violence and terrorism written by academics, practitioners, and former practitioners who are working in academia. A number of the chapters are revised articles that appeared in *Police Practices and Research* along with recent research into the area giving the reader the benefit of seeing how policing of terrorism has developed over the last 10 years. With contributions from writers working in a variety of nations, the book remains within the IPES ethos of propagating good practice at the international level.

IPES advocates, promotes and propagates that POLICING is one of the most basic and essential avenues for improving the quality of life in all nations: rich and poor, modern and traditional, large and small, as well as peaceful and strife-ridden. IPES actively works to drive home to all its office bearers, supporters and admirers that, in order to reach its full potential as an instrument of service to humanity, POLICING must be fully and enthusiastically open to collaboration between research and practice, global exchange of information between police practitioners and academics, universal disseminations and sharing of best practices, generating thinking police leaders and followers, as well as reflecting and writing on the issues challenging to the profession.

Through its annual meetings, hosts, institutional supporters, and publications, IPES reaffirms that POLICING is a moral profession with unflinching adherence to the rule of law and human rights as the embodiment of humane values.

Dilip K. Das
Founding President, International Police Executive Symposium
www.ipes.info

Book Series Editor for Advances in Police Theory and Practice
CRC Press/Taylor & Francis Group

Book Series Editor for Interviews With Global Leaders in
Policing, Courts and Prisons
CRC Press/Taylor & Francis Group

Book Series Editor, PPR Special Issues as Books
Routledge/Taylor & Francis Group

Founding Editor-in-Chief, Police Practice and Research:
An International Journal, PPR
http://www.tandf.co.uk/journals/GPPR

Acknowledgments

The editors would like to thank the writers for their contributions that made this book possible. They would like to thank the CRC Press team at Taylor & Francis for their support in the production of this book, especially Carolyn Spence, senior acquisitions editor, whose patience and advice were invaluable.

Introduction

Since the beginning of 2013, events in North Africa have once again raised the prominence of political violence and terrorism in the minds of world leaders and citizens. The January 2013 siege of the gas facility in Algeria,[1] where the Signed-in Blood Battalion jihadist extremists led by Mokhtar Belmokhtar took the facility's employees hostage, demonstrated the fragility of individuals' security in the region. With a number of the employees coming from Western states, the Algerian gas facility siege no longer became solely an Algerian issue; it was seen as a threat to the security of Western states. This event resulted in U.K. Prime Minister David Cameron becoming the first U.K. prime minister to visit Algeria since its independence in 1961; he held discussions with the Algerian government regarding mutual assistance. The meetings resulted in him saying that it will take decades to minimize the terrorist risk jihadist groups in the Maghreb pose to stability in both North Africa and the West.[2]

Also at this time, France, with U.K. military support, sent troops to Mali to support the Malian government's army fight with a jihadist group linked to Al Qaeda,[3] a conflict that is already turning into a guerrilla war. In this guerrilla war, the Malian and French military have been supported by Chad's armed forces in fighting in the region. Since then there have been reports that Al Qaeda's commander in the Maghreb, Abou Zeid, has been killed.[4] This report was followed by a Chadian military commander claiming that Mokhtar Belmokhtar had also been killed by Chadian forces in northern Mali.[5] A resurgence of jihadist groups targeting Western citizens has been seen not only in the Maghreb or in Mali, but also in northern Nigeria, where jihadist group Boko Harum and the Al Qaeda splinter group Ansaru have been kidnapping Western citizens and holding them hostage, with the Ansaru group recently claiming to have killed the hostages.[6] In just a few short weeks, both France and the United Kingdom have had to send more military personnel to Africa to assist in reducing the threat jihadist groups pose in the region,[7] and this figure could rise in what has the potential to become another Afghanistan. While these events have reminded Western states' governments, if not the world, of the problem jihadist groups pose to national security, it is not just jihadist terrorist groups that pose a threat to national security. Many states have the additional threat of terrorist activity carried out by ethnonational groups, as seen in the United Kingdom with

Ireland, where, at the time of writing, the Irish Republican Army (IRA) deto-
nated a bomb in Belfast, targeting police officers.[8] These events make it very
timely for the publication of this book to assist scholars in the areas of political violence and terrorism.

Covering a number of political violence and terrorist conflicts around
the world, this book will confirm it is not only North Africa where political
violence and terrorism are a problem, and it is not solely jihadist groups who
pose a threat to state security. The book is split into three sections—concepts
of terrorism, countering terrorism, and political violence—and contains a
collection of works, some of which were previously published in the last 10
years as articles in the journal *Police Practice and Research*, many having
been revised and updated specifically for this book. The book also contains
empirical research into terrorism that has not previously been published. In
effect, having taken just over 10 years in the making, this book is unique as
it takes the reader through issues related to political violence and terrorist
acts along with state responses from the 9/11 Al Qaeda attacks on the United
States up to the present period of political violence and terrorism.

Section I: Concepts of Terrorism

Ganor's chapter provides an understanding of what actions amount to acts of
terrorism and the factors that should be taken into account to call a person
a terrorist. Although this is a much-debated area, with many studies struggling to come to a common agreement, Ganor takes us through some considerations on which a common consensus can be found. As Ganor points out,
it is important to differentiate between the goals of a group and the means
used by that group to achieve those goals. What differentiates Ganor's work
from previous work defining terrorism is his study on the differentiation of
guerrilla warfare and terrorism that is pertinent to a number of ongoing terrorist conflicts.

Equally difficult to finding a consensus on defining what amounts to terrorism is finding a consensus on radicalization. Lowe's chapter is a previously
unpublished empirical study on the radicalization of terrorist causes using
the case study of the IRA and its political wing, the 32 County Sovereignty
Movement (32CSM). He demonstrates how radicalization is a complex, multifaceted phenomenon. This is exacerbated with the diverse types of terrorist
activity that are influenced by an equally diverse set of issues and events that
trigger a terror group's cause. In Lowe's examination, he shows how propaganda is used to turn a terror group's activity to raise funds into a cause or, if
there is a death of one of its members, into martyrdom.

One reason it is difficult to define terrorism is due to the various actions
that have been labeled as terrorist activity. This ranges from terrorism by

the state; ethnonationalist groups seeking political and economic freedom for their geographical area, as we see in Ireland or Ingushetia in Russia; and groups driven by religious/philosophical ideology. The last has been predominantly examined with the actions of jihadist groups like Al Qaeda that pose an international threat. Turk's chapter examines the options open to states to deal with religious ideology-based terrorist activity, and focusing on the jihadist threat, Turk raises a contentious issue of recognizing that groups like Al Qaeda are such a special case that to counter their actions requires nonlegal and extralegal measures. Examining psychological profiles of religious terrorism, the late Schbley's chapter can be linked to Turk's assertions as Schbley provides a theoretical framework from which to understand the connections between personal and environmental characteristics and behavioral manifestations that exist in religious-based terror activity that differentiate it from terrorist groups whose actions are based on political and economic grievances.

Section II: Countering Terrorism: Developments from 9/11

The extralegal measures taken to counter the jihadist terrorist threat in particular can be seen in the antiterror legislation states have introduced that provide counterterrorist agencies wider powers to enable them to prevent acts of terrorism. Sloan's chapter examines this, in particular how intelligence is an important factor in preventing acts of terrorism. What is unique in Sloan's chapter is how counterterrorism intelligence is not the sole preserve of national counterterrorism agencies but has pervaded into local policing. Focusing mainly on the United States, Sloan shows how important intelligence gathering is. As a result, every policing agency is involved in intelligence gathering, ranging from a sheriff's department to federal policing agencies. Henry's chapter is closely linked to themes in Sloan's chapter as Henry's study recognizes that to be successful in countering terrorist threats there has to be a coordinated approach at the local police level. Henry was a practitioner, and his chapter highlights how local communities rely on their local police to help keep them safe. Using statistical data, Henry highlights how everyday policing acts such as a motorist document check can help prevent acts of terrorism.

Donnermeyer's chapter builds on this theme. Again focusing mainly on the United States, his study demonstrates the importance of being prepared at the local level for acts of terrorism. A law enforcement officer, Donnermeyer's study explains why a multiagency approach to being prepared for terrorist acts is paramount. Palmer and Whelan's chapter, which is an updated version of an article previously published in *Police Practice and Research*, also looks at the role of other agencies involved in counterterrorism, in particular the private sector security industry. Based on experiences in Australia and how Australian antiterror legislation has incorporated private security into policing this area, examples are given that are found in many other states around the world where private security plays a role in counterterrorism, such as airport security. A key issue they discuss that differentiates this work from previous studies is how accountable these security companies are compared to public policing agencies. Murray's chapter examines how effective a community policing model is in preventing acts of terrorism. As Murray shows, the choice is to maintain a community policing model or adopt a paramilitary one. Murray's analysis demonstrates that community policing offers a more effective model, with the key reason being the community itself trusts community officers. As a result, the community is more likely to impart information to community officers.

This point forms the main argument in Brown's revised chapter that examines how the events of 9/11 had an impact on community policing initiatives in the United States. Brown catalogues how from the late 20th century U.S. policing worked hard to develop community policing to allow a closer relationship between police officers and the community they served. Following the 9/11 attacks on New York and Washington, Brown examines how the demand for more hard-line and pervasive policing to combat terrorist activity confronted and challenged community policing in the United States and updates this to the current situation regarding community policing of a terrorist threat.

Section II concludes with Leman-Langlois and the late Jean-Paul Brodeur's chapter (updated by Leman-Langlois); using Canada as a case study, it examines policing practices of what has been termed old and new terrorism. Their chapter's main points are the following:

1. Efficient counterterrorism necessitates knowledge of the kind of terrorism that is being fought;
2. The knowledge that is needed must support action, and it must be knowledge that can efficiently match core features of terrorist organizations with police response;
3. Persistent terrorism is not caused by structural problems in counterterrorism agencies and therefore does not necessitate organizational reform.

This examination looks at the situation facing the police from the early 21st century until today.

Section III: Policing Revolutionary and Secessionist Violence

Sarma's chapter opens Section III with an examination in the use of informants. His study focuses on one of the most violent and protracted periods of political violence, the 1969–1998 Irish Troubles. Sarma examines issues surrounding the recruitment and handling of informants in groups like the Provisional IRA and the problems policing agencies have handling informants inside terrorist cells. Sarma raises and analyzes a key theoretical issue of police informant handlers allowing their informants to commit crimes/ acts of terrorism while in effect being in the employ of the police and examines how destructive to a terrorist organization informers can be. Although Sarma provides a case study from a former conflict, his study is still relevant as this conflict is reigniting in Ireland, and issues over the British state agencies' use of informants inside terror groups during the Troubles are still emerging, as seen from the 2004 Cory Report, 2007 Ballast Report (Punch, 2012, pp. 136–146), and the currently ongoing Boston College Oral Report on Irish Republican and Loyalist paramilitaries during the Troubles.[9]

Jafa's chapter examines the experiences of Indian policing agencies' investigations into terrorist groups such as the Kashmiri separatists. His chapter looks at how important a cohesive strategy in countering political violence and terrorist organizations is, especially in developing tactics to minimize the risk terrorist cells pose to society. Building on this theme, van de Voorde's chapter on the Liberation Tigers of Tamil Eelam, better known as the Tamil Tigers, is an in-depth study of the organization and tactics deployed by terrorist groups. As Sri Lanka suffered one of the most severe and violent conflicts in terms of political violence, we can link themes and issues raised in previous chapters to examine why it is necessary for there to be a cohesive and coordinated response by the state to combat acts of political violence and terrorism.

Gibbs's chapter is a previously unpublished piece of work that provides a unique and contemporary study examining the targeting of police officers by terrorist groups. Gibbs gives an eloquent and compelling argument why the study of political violence and terrorism should also focus on specific attacks on police officers. Arguing that virtually all of the studies of political violence and terrorism focus mainly on civilian targets, Gibbs gives a unique perspective that the targeting of police officers has evaded most studies and is an action that is more pervasive than originally thought.

James's chapter brings the collection of works on political violence and terrorism to a conclusion. James raises a valid point, which is unique in the study of terrorism, that scholarly commentary on the policing of political violence has been dominated by terrorist organizations' activity. James updated his article published in *Police Practice and Research* for this book; he provides a study on race hate crime fueled by far-right-wing ideology with race hate targeting members of racial groups different from those seen as the perceived indigenous population and religion. Regarding religion, this has included far-right groups targeting Islamic communities, with the far-right groups justifying this as a legitimate response to the actions of jihadist groups on Western citizens.

In effect, this book has taken over 10 years in the making and includes works written in the early part of the 21st century (many of which have been revised and updated) up to previously unpublished studies written in 2013. Emanating from a number of countries in the world, this book offers a study of political violence and terrorism that reveals not only apparent differences but also the many common themes and issues present that apply to the various forms of terrorist and political violent activity around the globe. By examining the issue with studies over such a wide range of time, another advantage of this book is that it shows there are developments in terrorist activity as well as developments in how state agencies are countering that activity. In addition, previously unpublished work in the book reveals there are new issues for states and counterterrorism agencies to contemplate when considering how to deal with political violence and terrorist actions that threaten state security.

Notes

1. BBC News. Algeria hostage crisis: Country by country. http://www.bbc.co.uk/news/world-africa-21116623 (accessed February 8, 2013).
2. BBC News. Cameron in Algeria: PM urges terrorism fight with everything at our disposal. http://www.bbc.co.uk/news/uk-politics-21248277 (accessed February 8, 2013).
3. BBC News. Mali Conflict: "First suicide bombing" in Gao. http://www.bbc.co.uk/news/world-africa-21381379 (accessed February 8, 2013).
4. BBC News. Islamist commander Abou Zeid's death in Mali probable. http://www.bbc.co.uk/news/world-africa-21654190 (accessed March 10, 2013).
5. BBC News. Islamist militant Mokhtar Belmokhtar killed in Mali. http://www.bbc.co.uk/news/world-africa-21645769 (accessed March 10, 2013).
6. BBC News. Nigerian hostage deaths: Ansaru claims backed. http://www.bbc.co.uk/news/world-africa-21645769 (accessed March 10, 2013).
7. BBC News. Mali crisis: 330 UK military personnel sent to West Africa. http://www.bbc.co.uk/news/uk-21240676 (accessed February 8, 2013).
8. BBC News. North Belfast bomb blast: it was attempted murder. http://www.bbc.co.uk/news/uk-northern-ireland-21737624 (accessed March 10, 2013).
9. Updates on the Threat to Oral History Archives. http://bostoncollegesubpoena.wordpress.com/ (accessed March 11, 2013).

Reference

Punch, M. (2012). *State Violence, Collusion and the Troubles.* London: Pluto Press.

The Editors

Dilip K. Das is a professor of criminal justice, former police chief, founding editor in chief of *Police Practice and Research: An International Journal*, Dilip is a human rights consultant to the United Nations. Dilip served in the Indian Police Service for 14 years. After moving the United States he was the founding president of the International Police Executive Symposium and the founding editor of *Police Practice and Research: An International Journal*. Dilip has authored, edited, and coedited more than 30 books and numerous articles, and is human rights consultant to the United Nations. Dilip has received several faculty excellence awards and was a Distinguished Faculty Lecturer.

David Lowe is a principal lecturer at Liverpool John Moores University's Law School. Prior to becoming an academic, he served for 27 years with Merseyside Police in the United Kingdom. Most of his service was as a detective, and most of his detective service was in the United Kingdom's Special Branch Counter-Terrorism Unit. In addition to his recent publications in the area of policing, terrorism, and security, he is regularly used by the television, radio, and print media (particularly the BBC) in the United Kingdom and the rest of Europe for commentary in these areas.

Austin T. Turk is professor of sociology, University of California, Riverside. He is a fellow and former president of the American Society of Criminology and has been a trustee of the Law and Society Association as well as chair of the American Sociological Association's Section on Crime, Law, and Deviance. His research and writing focus primarily on relationships among law, power, and social conflict, with emphasis on the interaction between political policing and political crime. Having long been concerned with terrorism, he is now working mainly on issues in counterterrorism.

The Contributors

Jean-Paul Brodeur was the director of the International Center for Comparative Criminology (Centre international de criminologie comparée) at the University of Montreal, Jean-Paul established himself as a leading figure in Canadian and francophone criminology. His first major published work in this field—a study of the history of commissions of inquiry into police in Canada, 1895–1970—remains a key source on the politics of policing in Canada. He served as research director to many of Canada's most important commissions of inquiry throughout his career and he headed several research projects commissioned by the Law Reform Commission of Canada.

Ben Brown is an associate professor in the Criminal Justice Department at the University of Texas at Brownsville, where he teaches courses on criminological theory, law enforcement, and research methods. His previous research has been published in a number of scholarly journals, such as *Crime and Delinquency, Journal of Criminal Justice,* and *International Journal of Police Science and Management.*

Joseph F. Donnermeyer (PhD, University of Kentucky, 1976) is a professor of rural sociology. His research interests are in the study of rural crime and of changes in Amish communities. He is involved in a number of projects, including an assessment of prevention programs by stakeholders (students, parents, educators, and police officers); an assessment of police executive leadership programs; analyses of rural–urban differences in epidemiologic and etiologic patterns of adolescent substance use; a study of the relationship between community structure and rural crime rates in Australia; and an evaluation of cross-functional problem-solving teams within the Columbus, Ohio Police Department.

Boaz Ganor is an academic who has worked at the International Policy Institute for Counter-Terrorism in Herzlia, Israel. Many of his studies have been on the situation in the Middle East, in particular the Palestinian groups such as Hezbollah and the conflict with Israel.

Jennifer C. Gibbs, PhD, is an assistant professor at Pennsylvania State University at Harrisburg, where she studies terrorism, policing, violence, and victimization, and the scholarship of teaching and learning. Her dissertation,

The Relationship between Legitimacy, Terrorist Attacks, and the Police, completed at the University of Maryland, College Park, won the Homicide Research Working Group 2012 Richard Block Outstanding Dissertation Award.

Vincent E. Henry, CPP, PhD, is associate professor and director of the Homeland Security Management Institute of Long Island University (LIU). He retired from the New York Police Department (NYPD) in 2002 following a 21-year career. In 1989, he became the first American law enforcement officer to be named a Fulbright Scholar and spent a year in Australia studying the cross-cultural patterns of police corruption and reform as a Fulbright Fellow at the Center for Australian Public Sector Management at Griffith University.

Yateendra Singh Jafa was a member of the Indian Police Service at both national and international levels. Since he retired, his work has been extensively published. He has also attended many conferences, delivering his research papers. He has worked at the Jawaharlal Nehru University, New Delhi, India and his main research interests are in policing and terrorism.

Steve James has a BA (Hons), MA, Dip Crim, and PhD from the University of Melbourne. He has been lecturing in criminology at the University of Melbourne since 1987. Between 2004 and 2007, he was associate dean of undergraduate studies for the Faculty of Arts, while teaching later-year subjects in the law enforcement and drugs areas in criminology. He has had long-standing research and policy interests in policing and law enforcement and has conducted work in the areas of police unions, culture, personnel management, police–youth relations, and police crime prevention. He has also been involved in public housing crime prevention policy and practice. In 1995, with Dr. Adam Sutton, he completed the first national evaluation of Australian drug law enforcement.

Stéphane Leman-Langlois is professor of criminology at the School of Social Work, Laval University (Quebec City). He holds the Canada Research Chair in surveillance and the social construction of risk (social-surveillance.com) and is the director of the Terrorism and Counterterrorism Research Group (erta-tcrg.org) at the International Center for Comparative Criminology (University of Montreal). He is also a member of the Quebec Institute of International Studies (Institut québécois des hautes études internationales, HEI, Laval) and of the Raoul Dandurand Chair of Strategic and Diplomatic Studies (Chaire Raoul-Dandurand en études stratégiques et diplomatiques, UQAM). His research has focused on policing, criminal and security intelligence, terrorism, and the new technologies of social control.

John Murray was a police chief in Australia. Following his retirement, he began working in the private sector is an adjunct professor, School of Law, University of Canberra, where his research interests are in policing and terrorism. John has been published in a number of publications in this area.

Darren Palmer is an associate professor at Deakin University in Australia, where he teaches and researches criminal justice topics, mainly criminology, criminal law, policing, psychology, and crime. He is published widely in a number of criminal justice areas and is a leading radio and television expert commentator on policing and criminal justice issues.

Kiran Sarma is a lecturer in psychology at NUI Galway, Ireland. From 2000 to 2004, he worked with An Garda Sicohana (Irish police) as a forensic psychology, crime, and policy analyst. Kiran's main research interests are social forensic psychology and clinical and forensic psychology, and he has a breadth of publications, including in the areas of terrorism, support for terrorism, policing, and victimization.

Ayla Hammond Schbley was a Vietnam veteran and an ex-member of the Delta Force. After 10 years of service, he left the U.S. Army to assist the Drug Enforcement Administration and other intelligence agencies in their counter-narcotics/terrorism efforts. He was an editor of *Terrorism: An International Journal* and published articles on religious terrorism, profiling, threat analyses, hate groups, schizophrenia, and national and international laws and policies. He was a professor of criminal justice at Washburn University in Topeka, Kansas and unfortunately passed away suddenly on July 19, 2005, while hiking the Havasupai Indian Reservation in Arizona with his wife.

Stephen Sloan is a professor of political violence at the University of Oklahoma. He pioneered the development of simulations of terrorist incidents to assist concerned personnel and organizations in the public and private sectors. He has been involved in formulating counterterrorism doctrines for the U.S. military as well as contributing to an evaluation of U.S. policies toward terrorism. In 1986, he was an expert contributor to the vice president's task force on combating terrorism. He also has contributed many publications, including monographs, on terrorism.

Cécile van de Voorde, after publishing the article in *Police Practice and Research* that became her chapter in this book when working at the University of South Florida, has worked at Texas Christian University and the City University of New York, where she was the project director and principal investigator.

Chad Whelan earned a Master of Arts degree in college student development from Appalachian State University. He has six years of professional
experience in the field of student affairs, four of those at the University of
Illinois at Urbana-Champaign. He continued his work in student housing
at the University of South Florida and Western Carolina University prior to
coming to Columbia College.

Terrorism and Counterterrorism

I

Defining Terrorism
Is One Man's Terrorist Another Man's Freedom Fighter?

1

BOAZ GANOR

Contents

Introduction

The terror attacks in the United States on September 11, 2001, and the subsequent efforts by the United States to build a broad-based antiterrorism coalition have thrown into sharp relief the question of what constitutes terrorism. Most researchers tend to believe that an objective and internationally accepted definition of terrorism can never be agreed on; after all, they say, "One man's terrorist is another man's freedom fighter" (Laqueur, 1987, pp. 7, 302). The question of who is a terrorist, according to this school of thought, depends entirely on the subjective outlook of the definer; in any case, such a definition is unnecessary for the international fight against terrorism. In their view, it is sufficient to say that what looks like a terrorist, sounds like a terrorist, and behaves like a terrorist is a terrorist. This position, naturally, contributes nothing to the understanding of an already-difficult issue nor does the attempt to divide terrorism into categories such as "bad and worse terrorism," "internal terrorism and international terrorism," or "tolerable terrorism and intolerable terrorism." All these categories reflect the subjective outlook of whoever is doing the categorizing—and purely subjective categories will not help us to determine who the real terrorists are.

At the same time, there are others who say that a definition of terrorism is necessary, but that such a definition must serve their own political ends (Martha, 1995). States that sponsor terrorism are trying to persuade the international community to define terrorism in such a way that the particular terror groups they sponsor would be outside the definition—thus absolving them from all responsibility for supporting terrorism. Countries such as Syria, Libya, and Iran have lobbied for such a definition, according to which "freedom fighters" would be given carte blanche permission to carry out any kind of attacks they wanted because a just goal can be pursued by all available means. Both these schools of thought are wrong, and both attitudes will make it impossible to fight terrorism effectively. An objective definition of terrorism is not only possible but also indispensable to any serious attempt to combat terrorism. Lacking such a definition, no coordinated fight against international terrorism can ever really get anywhere. A correct and objective definition of terrorism can be based on accepted international laws and principles regarding what behaviors are permitted in conventional wars between nations. These laws are set out in the Geneva and Hague Conventions, which in turn are based on the basic principle that the deliberate harming of soldiers during wartime is a necessary evil, and thus permissible, whereas the deliberate targeting of civilians is absolutely forbidden. These conventions thus differentiate between soldiers who attack a military adversary and war criminals who deliberately attack civilians.

This normative principle relating to a state of war between two countries can be extended without difficulty to a conflict between a nongovernmental organization and a state. This extended version would thus differentiate between guerrilla warfare and terrorism. Exactly in parallel with the distinction between military and civilian targets in war, the extended version would designate as *guerilla warfare* the "deliberate use of violence against military and security personnel to attain political, ideological and religious goals." *Terrorism*, on the other hand, would be defined as "the deliberate use or the threat to use violence against civilians to attain political, ideological, and religious aims" (an attack aimed against government personnel should therefore be defined as terrorism if the target was not in a decision-making position of the state's counterterrorism policy).

What is important in these definitions is the differentiation between the goals and the means used to achieve these goals. The aims of terrorism and guerrilla warfare may well be identical; but they are distinguished from each other by the means used—or more precisely, by the targets of their operations. The guerrilla fighter's targets are military ones, while the terrorist deliberately targets civilians. By this definition, a terrorist organization can no longer claim to be freedom fighters because they are fighting for national liberation or some other worthy goal. Even if its declared ultimate goals are legitimate, an organization that deliberately targets civilians is a terrorist organization. There is no merit or exoneration in fighting for the freedom of one population if in doing so you destroy the rights of another population.

If all the world's civilian populations are not to become pawns in one struggle or another, terrorism—the deliberate targeting of civilians—must be absolutely forbidden, regardless of the legitimacy or justice of its goals. The ends do not justify the means. By carrying out terrorist attacks, the perpetrators make themselves the enemies of all humankind. Only on the basis of an international agreement on the definition of terrorism will it be possible to demand that all nations withhold all support from terrorist organizations. Only on this basis can countries be required to act against terrorists, even when they agree with and support the terrorists' goals.

The worldwide acceptance of this definition of terrorism—and the adoption of international legislation against terrorism and support for terrorism based on this definition—could bring about a change in the cost-benefit calculations of terrorist organizations and their sponsors. At present, terrorist organizations may carry out either terrorist or guerrilla attacks according to their preferences and local conditions only, with no external reason to choose one type of attack over the other. After all, as far as the rest of the world is concerned, the two types of attack are morally equivalent; punishment is identical in both cases. However, should these organizations and their sponsors be made aware that the use of terror will bring them more harm than good, they may opt to focus on guerrilla warfare rather than on terrorism. This would be a great achievement for counterterrorism. Does this definition of terrorism legitimize guerrilla warfare? The definition does make a moral distinction between terrorism and guerrilla warfare. Countries forced to deal with ongoing attacks on their military personnel will obviously perceive these attacks as acts of war, which must be thwarted. These countries cannot expect to enlist the world in a struggle against "legitimate" guerrilla warfare, but they could justifiably demand that the international community assist them were they fighting against terrorism.

Yet another question to be answered is whether countries as well as organizations can be held responsible for carrying out terrorist acts. In effect, this question has already been answered in the form of existing international legislation (United Nations, 1949). The term *terrorism* is superfluous when describing the actions of sovereign states—not because states are on a higher moral level, but because, according to the international conventions, any deliberate attack on civilians in wartime by regular military forces is already defined as a war crime. Should such an attack be carried out during peacetime, the act is defined by convention as a "crime against humanity." In both cases, such acts are already covered by international law, and provisions exist for dealing with the perpetrators. It is when these actions are carried out by politically motivated individuals or groups that the lack of legislation is felt. Ironically, under current international law, organizations are not specifically prohibited from perpetrating actions that are considered illegal and abhorrent when carried out by sovereign states.

There have been previous attempts to address these issues; the U.S. State Department, for example, has put forward a definition according to which terrorism is the deliberate use of violence against noncombatants, whether civilian or not (United States Department of State, 2001). However, this definition of terrorism will not work in practice as it designates attacks on noncombatant military personnel as terrorism. Despite the natural tendency of those who have been harmed by terrorism to adopt this broader definition, terror organizations and their supporters can justly claim that they cannot be expected to attack only military personnel who are armed and ready for battle. If they were held to such a standard, they would lose the element of surprise and be quickly defeated. By narrowing the definition of terrorism to include only deliberate attacks on civilians, we leave room for a "fair fight" between guerrillas and state armies.

Thus, we set a clear moral standard that can be accepted not only by Western countries but also by the Third World and even by some of the terrorist organizations themselves. When such a moral distinction is internationally applied, terrorist organizations will have yet another reason to renounce terrorism in favor of guerrilla actions. The definition of terrorism proposed here can serve as a guide for including or excluding various countries in the international antiterror coalition, as well as for identifying those organizations and countries to be targeted by the coalition. But, its main significance is in the drafting and enforcement of international legislation aimed at forcing states to act against terror organizations operating on their territory. Without an objective and authoritative definition, accepted by all nations, the fight against terrorism will always suffer from "cultural relativism." Without a change in the priorities of all the enlightened countries, and their determination to fight against terrorism apart from any other political or economic interest, it will not be possible to wage an effective war against terrorism. And, without such a unified stand by all nations, the September 11 attacks in the United States will be insignificant compared to the attacks yet to come. The free world must understand that cultural relativism applied to terrorism—whatever the terrorists' goals—will lead only to more terrorism.

Defining Terrorism: The Present Situation

Academics, politicians, security experts, and journalists all use a variety of definitions of terrorism. Some definitions focus on the terrorist organizations' mode of operation. Others emphasize the motivations and characteristics of terrorism, the modus operandi of individual terrorists, and so on. In their book *Political Terrorism*, Schmidt and Jongman (1988) cited 109 different definitions of terrorism, which they obtained in a survey of leading academics in the field. From these definitions, the authors isolated the following recurring elements, in order of their statistical appearance in the definitions: violence, force (appeared in 83.5% of the definitions); political (65%); fear, emphasis on terror (51%); threats (47%); psychological effects and anticipated reactions (41.5%); discrepancy between the targets and the victims (37.5%); intentional, planned, systematic, organized action (32%); and methods of combat, strategy, tactics (30.5%) (Schmidt and Jongman, 1988, p. 5). Respondents were also asked the following question: "What issues in the definition of terrorism remain unresolved?" The following are some of the answers follow (p. 29–30):

1. What is the boundary between terrorism and other forms of political violence?
2. Are government terrorism and resistance terrorism part of the same phenomenon?
3. How is "terrorism" separated from simple criminal acts, from open war between "consenting" groups, and from acts that clearly arise out of mental illness?
4. Is terrorism a subcategory of coercion? Violence? Power? Influence?
5. Can terrorism be legitimate? What gains justify its use?
6. What is the relationship between guerrilla warfare and terrorism?
7. What is the relationship between crime and terrorism?

The following exchange took place between Ned Walker, assistant to the undersecretary for Middle East affairs at the U.S. State Department, and the Hon. Lee Hamilton, chairman of the Subcommittee on Europe and the Middle East—under the auspices of the Committee on Foreign Affairs at the House of Representatives—on the background of talks between the United States and the PLO (Palestine Liberation Organization). The remarks attest to the problems involved in the use of the concept *terrorism*:

Hamilton: Well, how do you define terrorism, do you define it in terms of non-combatance?

Walker: The State Department definition which is included in the terrorism report annually defines it in terms of politically motivated attacks on non-combatant targets.

Hamilton: So an attack on a military unit in Israel will not be terrorism?

Walker: It does not necessarily mean that it would not have a very major impact on whatever we were proposing to do with the PLO.

Hamilton: I understand that, but it would not be terrorism.

Walker: An attack on a military target. Not according to the definition. Now wait a minute; that is not quite correct. You know, attacks can be made on military targets which clearly are terrorism. It depends on the individual circumstances.

Hamilton: Now wait a minute. I thought that you just gave me the State Department definition.

Walker: Non-combatant is the terminology, not military or civilian.

Hamilton: All right. So any attack on a non-combatant could be terrorism?

Walker: That is right.

Hamilton: And a non-combatant could include military?

Walker: Of course.

Hamilton: It certainly would include civilian, right?

Walker: Right.

Hamilton: But an attack on a military unity would not be terrorism?

Walker: It depends on the circumstances.

Hamilton: And what are those circumstances?

Walker: I do not think it will be productive to get into a description of the various terms and conditions under which we are going to define an act by the PLO as terrorism. (Committee on Foreign Affairs, 1989, p. 66).

The prevalent definitions of terrorism entail difficulties, both conceptual and syntactical. It is thus not surprising that alternative concepts with connotations that are more positive—guerrilla movements, underground movements, national liberation movements, commandos, and so on—are often used to describe and characterize the activities of terrorist organizations. Generally, these concepts are used without undue attention to the implications, but at times the use of these definitions is tendentious, grounded in a particular political viewpoint. By resorting to such tendentious definitions of terrorism, terrorist organizations and their supporters seek to gloss over the realities of terrorism, thus establishing their activities on more positive and legitimate foundations. Naturally, terms not opposed to the basic values of liberal democracies, such as "revolutionary violence," "national liberation," and the like, carry fewer negative connotations than the term *terrorism*.

Terrorism or Revolutionary Violence?

Salah Khalef (Abu Iyad) was Yasser Arafat's deputy and one of the leaders of Fatah and Black September. He was responsible for a number of lethal attacks, including the killing of Israeli athletes at the 1972 Munich Olympics. To rationalize such actions, he used the tactic of confounding terrorism with "political violence," stating, "By nature, and even on ideological grounds, I am firmly opposed to political murder and, more generally, to terrorism. Nevertheless, unlike many others, I do not confuse revolutionary violence with terrorism, or operations that constitute political acts with others that do not." (Iyad, 1983, p. 146). Abu Iyad tries to present terrorism and political violence as two different and unconnected phenomena. The implication of this statement is that a political motive makes the activity respectable, and the end justifies the means. I examine this point next.

Terrorism or National Liberation?

A rather widespread attempt to make all definitions of terrorism meaningless is to lump together terrorist activities and the struggle to achieve national liberation. Thus, for instance, the recurrently stated Syrian official position is that Syria does not assist terrorist organizations; rather, it supports national liberation movements. President Hafez el-Assad, in a November 1986 speech to the participants in the 21st Convention of Workers Unions in Syria, said:

> We have always opposed terrorism. But terrorism is one thing and a national struggle against occupation is another. We are against terrorism. ... Nevertheless, we support the struggle against occupation waged by national liberation movements. (Tishrin, 1986)

The attempt to confound the concepts of terrorism and national liberation comes to the fore in various official pronouncements from the Arab world. For instance, the fifth Islamic summit meeting in Kuwait, at the beginning of 1987, stated in its resolutions that:

> The conference reiterates its absolute faith in the need to distinguish the brutal and unlawful terrorist activities perpetrated by individuals, by groups, or by states, from the legitimate struggle of oppressed and subjugated nations against foreign occupation of any kind. This struggle is sanctioned by heavenly law, by human values, and by international conventions. (Al-Anba'a, 1987)

The foreign and interior ministers of the Arab League reiterated this position at their April 1998 meeting in Cairo. In a document titled "Arab

Strategy in the Struggle against Terrorism," they emphasized that belligerent activities aimed at "liberation and self-determination" are not in the category of terrorism, whereas hostile activities against regimes or families of rulers will not be considered political attacks but rather criminal assaults (*Haaretz*, 1998). Here again, we notice an attempt to justify the "means" (terrorism) in terms of the "end" (national liberation). Regardless of the nature of the operation, when we speak of "liberation from the yoke of a foreign occupation," this will not be terrorism but a legitimate and justified activity. This is the source of the cliché, "One man's terrorist is another man's freedom fighter," which stresses that it all depends on the perspective and the worldview of the one doing the defining. The former president of the Soviet Union, Leonid Brezhnev, made the following statement in April 1981, during the visit of the Libyan ruler, Muammar Gadhafi: "Imperialists have no regard either for the will of the people or the laws of history. Liberation struggles cause their indignation. They describe them as terrorism" (Cline and Alexander, 1986, p. 24).

Surprisingly, many in the Western world have accepted the mistaken assumption that terrorism and national liberation are two extremes in the scale of legitimate use of violence. The struggle for national liberation would appear to be the positive and justified end of this sequence, whereas terrorism is the negative and odious one. It is impossible, according to this approach, for any organization to be both a terrorist group and a movement for national liberation at the same time. In failing to understand the difference between these two concepts, many have, in effect, been caught in a semantic trap laid by the terrorist organizations and their allies. They have attempted to contend with the clichés of national liberation by resorting to odd arguments, instead of stating that when a group or organization chooses terrorism as a means, the aim of their struggle cannot be used to justify their actions (see the following discussion). Thus, for instance, Senator Jackson was quoted in Netanyahu's book, *Terrorism: How the West Can Win* (1985, p. 18) as saying:

> The idea that one person's "terrorist" is another's "freedom fighter" cannot be sanctioned. Freedom fighters or revolutionaries don't blow up buses containing non-combatants; terrorist murderers do. Freedom fighters don't set out to capture and slaughter schoolchildren; terrorist murderers do. ... It is a disgrace that democracies would allow the treasured word "freedom" to be associated with acts of terrorists.

Professor Benjamin Netanyahu (1985) also assumed, a priori, that freedom fighters are incapable of perpetrating terrorist acts:

> For in contrast to the terrorist, no freedom fighter has ever deliberately attacked innocents. He has never deliberately killed small children, or passersby in the

street, or foreign visitors, or other civilians who happen to reside in the area of conflict or are merely associated ethnically or religiously with the people of that area. ... The conclusion we must draw from all this is evident. Far from being a bearer of freedom, the terrorist is the carrier of oppression and enslavement. (p. 27)

This approach strengthens the attempt by terrorist organizations to present terrorism and the struggle for liberation as two contradictory concepts. It thus plays into the terrorists' hands by supporting their claim that, since they are struggling to remove someone they consider a foreign occupier, they cannot be considered terrorists. The claim that a freedom fighter cannot be involved in terrorism, murder, and indiscriminate killing is, of course, groundless. A terrorist organization can also be a movement of national liberation, and the concepts of terrorist and freedom fighter are not mutually contradictory.

Targeting "the Innocent"?

Not only terrorists and their allies use the definition of terrorism to promote their own goals and needs, but also politicians in countries affected by terrorism at times make political use of the definition of terrorism by attempting to emphasize its brutality. One of the prevalent ways of illustrating the cruelty and inhumanity of terrorists is to present them as harming "the innocent." Thus, in *Terrorism: How the West Can Win*, Benjamin Netanyahu states that terrorism is "the deliberate and systematic murder, maiming, and menacing of the innocent to inspire fear for political ends" (1985, p. 9). This definition was changed in Netanyahu's third book, *Fighting Terrorism*, when the phrase *the innocent* was replaced by the term *civilians*: "Terrorism is the deliberate and systematic assault on civilians to inspire fear for political ends" (Netanyahu, 1995, p. 8). Innocent (as opposed to civilian) is a subjective concept, influenced by the definer's viewpoint, and therefore must not be the basis for a definition of terrorism. The use of the concept innocent in defining terrorism makes the definition meaningless and turns it into a tool in the political game. The dilemma entailed by the use of the term *innocent* is amply illustrated in this statement by Abu Iyad (1983):

As much as we repudiate any activity that endangers innocent lives, that is, against civilians in countries that are not directly involved in the Arab-Israeli conflict, we feel no remorse concerning attacks against Israeli military and political elements who wage war against the Palestinian people. ... Israeli acts of vengeance usually result in high casualties among Palestinian civilians—particularly when the Israeli Air Force blindly and savagely bombs refugee camps—and it is only natural that we should respond in appropriate ways to deter the enemy from continuing its slaughter of innocent victims. (pp. 78, 155–156)

Abu Iyad here clarifies that innocent victims are civilians in countries that are not directly involved in the Arab-Israeli conflict (implying that civilians in Israel, even children and old people, are not innocent), while he describes Palestinian civilians as innocent victims.

Proposing a Definition of Terrorism

The question is whether it is at all possible to arrive at an exhaustive and objective definition of terrorism that could constitute an accepted and agreed-on foundation for academic research, as well as facilitate operations on an international scale against the perpetrators of terrorist activities. The definition proposed here states that terrorism is the intentional use of, or threat to use, violence against civilians or against civilian targets to attain political aims. This definition is based on three important elements:

1. The essence of the activity—the use of, or threat to use, violence. According to this definition, an activity that does not involve violence or a threat of violence will not be defined as terrorism (including nonviolent protest, e.g., strikes, peaceful demonstrations, tax revolts, etc.).
2. The aim of the activity is always political—namely, the goal is to attain political objectives: changing the regime, changing the people in power, changing social or economic policies, and so on. In the absence of a political aim, the activity in question will not be defined as terrorism. A violent activity against civilians that has no political aim is, at most, an act of criminal delinquency, a felony, or simply an act of insanity unrelated to terrorism. Some scholars tend to add ideological or religious aims to the list of political aims. The advantage of this definition, however, is that it is as short and exhaustive as possible. The concept of "political aim" is sufficiently broad to include these goals as well. The motivation—whether ideological, religious, or something else—behind the political objective is irrelevant for the purpose of defining terrorism. In this context, this statement by Duvall and Stohl deserves mention: "Motives are entirely irrelevant to the concept of political terrorism. Most analysts fail to recognize this and, hence, tend to discuss certain motives as logical or necessary aspects of terrorism. But they are not. At best, they are empirical regularities associated with terrorism. More often they simply confuse analysis" (Schmidt, 1984, p. 100).

3. The targets of terrorism are civilians. Terrorism is thus distinguished from other types of political violence (guerrilla warfare, civil insurrection, etc.). Terrorism exploits the relative vulnerability of the civilian "underbelly"—the tremendous anxiety and the intense media reaction evoked by attacks against civilian targets.

The proposed definition emphasizes that terrorism is not the result of an accidental injury inflicted on a civilian or a group of civilians who stumbled into an area of violent political activity, but stresses that this is an act purposely directed against civilians. Hence, the term *terrorism* should not be ascribed to collateral damage to civilians used as human shields or to cover military activity or installations if such damage is incurred in an attack originally aimed against a military target. In this case, the responsibility for civilian casualties is incumbent on whoever used them as shields.

The proposed definition of terrorism also addresses a lacuna in present international legislation and international conventions to develop a fundamental tool for international cooperation against terrorism. To achieve as wide an accord as possible, this definition must be founded on a system of principles and laws of war, legislated and ratified in many countries. In other words, to reach an accepted definition of terrorism, we must extrapolate from the existing principles of conventional warfare (between countries) to arrive at similar principles for nonconventional warfare (for our purposes, a violent struggle between an organization and a state). Many countries in the world support the view—and have enshrined this in international conventions—that we must differentiate between two types of military personnel who make use of force to attain their aims. On the one hand, there are "soldiers" (members of the military who intentionally target members of rival armies), and on the other, there are "war criminals" (members of the military who intentionally harm civilians).

This normative and accepted attitude toward military personnel operating in a situation of conventional warfare enables us to extrapolate to situations of nonconventional warfare (between an organization and a state), thus allowing us to distinguish terrorism from guerrilla warfare. As noted, terrorism is "a violent struggle intentionally using, or threatening to use, violence against civilians to attain political aims," whereas guerrilla warfare is "a violent struggle using (or threatening to use) violence against military targets, security forces, and the political leadership to attain political aims." Terrorism is thus different from guerrilla warfare in its mode of activity and in the targets chosen by the perpetrators. The only question to be resolved is whether perpetrators choose to attain their aims by targeting civilian or military targets.

Guerrilla Warfare versus Terrorism

Terrorism and guerrilla warfare often serve as alternative designations of the same phenomenon. The term *terrorism*, however, has a far more negative connotation, seemingly requiring one to take a stand, whereas the term *guerrilla warfare* is perceived as neutral and carries a more positive connotation. One of the problems accompanying the use of the concept guerrilla warfare stems from its ambiguity. This nebulousness is cited by Yehoshafat Harkabi (1983, p. 27) in differentiating between guerrilla warfare and guerrilla war. Harkabi (1983) describes guerrilla war as a prolonged war of attrition, with progressively increasing violence, blurred limits, a fluid line of contact, and emphasis on the human factor. In the course of the war, guerrilla combatants become regular military forces until victory is attained and one party is defeated (p. 16).

Similarly, Huntington argues that "guerrilla warfare is a form of warfare by which the strategically weaker side assumes the tactical offensive in selected forms, times and places. Guerrilla warfare is the weapon of the weak" (Laqueur, 1977, p. 392). Harkabi (1983, p. 28) points out that terrorism frequently appears in guerrilla war and indicates that "guerrilla activity is best placed on a sequence, ranging from sporadic terrorist attacks not necessarily against military units, up to sustained guerrilla warfare and confrontation with military forces." Others view guerrilla war and terrorism as two separate points along one sequence dealing with the use of violence (Schmidt, 1984, p. 41). Other scholars, however, choose to draw a clearer distinction between guerrilla warfare and terrorism. Thus, for instance, Walter Laqueur writes: "Urban terrorism is not a new stage in guerrilla war, but differs from it in essential respects, and [that] it is also heir to a different tradition" (1987, p. 1)

The essence of guerrilla warfare is to establish foci, or liberated areas, in the countryside and to set up small military units that will gradually grow in strength, number, and equipment order to fight battles against government troops. In the liberated areas, the guerrillas establish their own institutions, conduct propaganda, and engage in other open political activities. None of this applies to terrorists, whose base of operation is in the cities, who have to operate clandestinely in small units (Laquer, 1987, p. 147). Ehud Sprinzak (1985) sums up this approach: "Guerrilla war is a small war—subject to the same rules that apply to big wars, and on this it differs from terrorism." David Rapaport adds: "The traditional distinguishing characteristic of the terrorist was his explicit refusal to accept the conventional moral limits which defined military and guerrilla action" (cited in Schmidt, 1984, p. 44). As opposed to Laqueur, Paul Wilkinson distinguishes between terrorism and guerrilla warfare by stressing another aspect: harm to civilians:

Guerrillas may fight with small numbers and often inadequate weaponry, but they can and often do fight according to conventions of war, taking and exchanging prisoners and respecting the rights of non-combatants. Terrorists place no limits on means employed and frequently resort to widespread assassination, the waging of "general terror" upon the indigenous civilian population. (cited in Schmidt, 1984, p. 42)

The proposed definition, as noted, distinguishes terrorism from guerrilla activity according to the intended target of attack. The definition states that if an attack deliberately targets civilians, then that attack will be considered a terrorist attack, whereas if it targets military or security personnel, then it will be considered a guerrilla attack. It all depends on who the intended victims are. First and foremost, this definition is meant to answer the need for analyzing and classifying specific events as terrorism or guerrilla activities. This definition is not meant to differentiate between the types of perpetrating organizations. Most organizations resorting to violence for the purpose of attaining political aims have not refrained from harming civilians as well as military personnel. These organizations, then, on the face of it can be defined as both terrorist organizations and guerrilla movements.

Although the proposed definition relates to specific attack, it is still possible to deduce from it whether a particular organization is a terrorist organization or a guerrilla movement. One could, for instance, rely on a quantitative principle—comparing the numbers of terrorist attacks and guerrilla attacks within the total number of violent activities involving the organization. Or, one could rely on a qualitative principle, stating that every organization engaging in attacks against civilian targets is a terrorist organization, and it is irrelevant whether at the same time the same organization was also involved in guerrilla activities. Hence, the claim that every guerrilla organization has also harmed civilians does not affect the proposed definition of terrorism. A situation where organizations are involved simultaneously in terrorism and guerrilla activity is a direct consequence of the lack of an accepted international definition for terrorism and guerrilla warfare. Only a definition agreed on by most countries in the world—and that entails operative action against terrorist groups different from that directed against guerrilla groups—will move these organizations to take "cost-benefit" considerations into account when choosing the mode of activity appropriate to attaining their ends. When the damage incurred by organizations due to their engagement in terrorism is greater than the damage they incur due to their involvement in guerrilla activities, it is plausible to assume that some organizations will choose to focus on guerrilla activities rather than on terrorism. As long as there is no accepted international convention for distinguishing terrorism from guerrilla activity—and as long as such convention is not accompanied by different levels of punitive sanctions—it should come as no surprise that organizations choose to engage in terrorism or in guerrilla activities according to their own operative limitations or circumstances.

The claim that terrorism and guerrilla activities are on one conceptual sequence—to the extent that it has empirical backing—also does not contradict the classification of terrorism and guerrilla activity according to the proposed definition. A situation is certainly possible in which an organization might decide to move from the stage of terrorism to the stage of guerrilla warfare and vice versa, thereby changing its character from one involved only in, or mainly in, terrorism, to one involved mainly in guerrilla warfare.

The Aims of Terrorism and of Guerrilla Warfare

For the purpose of defining terrorism, the type of goal sought is irrelevant (as long as the goal is political). The terrorist and the guerrilla fighter may have the exact same aims, but they choose different means to accomplish them. Among the political aims that different organizations (both terrorist organizations and guerrilla movements) seek to achieve, we might mention national liberation (liberating territory from an occupying power); revolution (changing the government); anarchism (creating chaos); changing the prevalent socioeconomic system, and so on. By characterizing terrorism as a mode of operation directed against civilian targets, as opposed to basing the definition on the goals of the violence, we refute the slogan that one man's terrorist is another man's freedom fighter. This distinction between the target of the attack and its aims shows that the discrepancy between terrorism and freedom fighting is not a subjective difference reflecting the personal viewpoint of the definer. Rather, it constitutes an essential difference, involving a clear distinction between the perpetrators' aims and their mode of operation. As noted, an organization is defined as terrorist because of its mode of operation and its target of attack, whereas calling something a struggle for liberation has to do with the aim that the organization seeks to attain.

Hiding behind the guise of national liberation does not release terrorists from responsibility for their actions. Not only is it untrue that one man's terrorist is another man's freedom fighter, but also it is untrue that "the end justifies the means." The end of national liberation may, in some cases, justify recourse to violence in an attempt to solve the problem that led to the emergence of a particular organization in the first place. Nevertheless, the organization must still act according to the rules of war, directing its activities toward the conquest of military and security targets; in short, it must confine itself to guerrilla activities. When the organization breaks these rules and intentionally targets civilians, it becomes a terrorist organization, according to objective measures and not according to the subjective perception of the definer.

Ends and means in conflicts between an organization and a state. It may be difficult at times to determine whether the victim of an attack was indeed a civilian or whether the attack was intentional. These cases could be placed under the rubric of a "gray area" to be decided in line with the evidence and through the exercise of judicial discretion. The proposed definition may therefore be useful in the legal realm as a criterion for defining and categorizing the perpetrators' activities. In any event, adopting the proposed definition of terrorism will considerably reduce the gray area to a few marginal cases.

Defining States' Involvement in Terrorism

On the basis of this definition of terrorism and guerrilla warfare, how should we define the involvement of states in performing terrorist attacks? Note that violent activities committed by a state against civilians are forbidden by international conventions and are clearly defined as war crimes (in the context of a war situation) and as crimes against humanity (in other situations) (United Nations, 1949, p. 46). Thus, whereas these definitions have led to the international delegitimation of the use of violence against civilians by military personnel and political leaders, a lacuna still exists concerning the use of violence against civilians by organizations or individuals on political grounds. States can be involved in terrorism in various ways: from various levels of general support for terrorist organizations, through operational assistance, initiating or directing attacks, and up to the perpetration of terrorist attacks by official state agencies. All forms of state involvement in terrorism are usually placed "under the general category of terrorist states, or state sponsored terrorism" (Natanyahu, 1980, p. 47). Such a designation has taken on the character of a political weapon; rival states ascribe it to one another, and terrorist organizations use it against states acting against them.

The question of state involvement in terrorist attacks has been extensively discussed in *Countering State-Sponsored Terrorism* (Ganor, 1997). There I suggest the following classification of states according to their level of involvement in terrorism:

4. States supporting terrorism—states that support terrorist organizations, providing financial aid, ideological support, military or operational assistance.
5. States operating terrorism—states that initiate, direct and perform terrorist activities through groups outside their own institutions.
6. States perpetrating terrorism—states perpetrating terrorist acts abroad through their own official bodies—members of its security forces or its intelligence services, or their direct agents. In other

words, states intentionally attacking civilians in other countries in
order to achieve political aims without declaring war. (Ganor, 1997,
p. 7)

As mentioned, according to international conventions (United Nations,
1949), intentional acts of aggression against civilians by official agencies of a
state, either at times of war or in occupied territories, will be considered war
crimes rather than terrorism.

Various countries have engaged in attacks against leading activists of terrorist organizations: planners and initiators of attacks, commanders of operational units, saboteurs, and even the organizations' leaders. On such grounds,
these countries have often been accused of engaging in terrorism themselves.
According to the proposed definition of terrorism (and setting aside questions
bearing on the legitimate confines of a struggle against terrorism and on the
rights of states to fight terrorists in the territory of another sovereign state),
actions by a state against terrorist activists cannot be defined as terrorism
even if only because the latter are not actually civilians. Individuals engaging in terrorist activities, even if not wearing a uniform, exclude themselves
from the civilian community, and rules protecting civilians no longer apply
to them. Thus, just as the definition views decision makers as "legitimate"
targets in guerrilla warfare, so targeting terrorists who head operational,
administrative, or political branches in a terrorist organization should not
itself be considered a terrorist activity since these are the people responsible
for policy formulation and decision making in the organization.

The Importance of Defining Terrorism

As noted, defining terrorism is not only a theoretical issue but also an operative concern of the first order. Terrorism is no longer a local problem of
specific countries but an issue involving a number of international aspects.
Terrorist organizations may perpetrate attacks in a variety of countries; the
victims of attacks can be of different nationalities; the offices, headquarters,
and training camps of terrorist organizations function in various countries;
terrorist organizations receive direct and indirect assistance from different
states, enlist support from different ethnic communities, and secure financial
help throughout the world. Since terrorism is an international phenomenon,
responses to terrorism must also be on an international scale. Developing
an effective international strategy requires agreement on what it is we are
dealing with; in other words, we need a definition of terrorism. International
mobilization against terrorism, such as that which began in the mid-1990s
and culminated in the international conventions in the G-7 countries, the
Sharem el-Sheik Conference, and so on, cannot lead to operational results

as long as the participants cannot agree on a definition. Without answering the question of "What is terrorism?" no responsibility can be imposed on countries supporting terrorism, and steps cannot be taken to combat terrorist organizations and their allies.

Without a definition of terrorism, it is impossible to formulate or enforce international agreements against terrorism. A conspicuous example of the need to define terrorism concerns the extradition of terrorists. Although many countries have signed bilateral and multilateral agreements concerning a variety of crimes, extradition for political offenses is often explicitly excluded, and the background of terrorism is always political. This loophole allows countries to shirk their obligation to extradite individuals wanted for terrorist activities.

In fact, the need for a definition of terrorism can be seen at almost every phase of contending with terrorism (see Figure 3). Such phases include:

1. Legislation and punishment: The laws and regulations enacted to provide security forces with an instrument for combating terrorism. A definition of terrorism is necessary when legislating laws designed to ban terrorism and assistance to terrorism, as well as when setting minimum sentences for terrorists or confiscating their financial resources and supplies. Barring an accepted definition, this legislation has no value. Legislation and punishment must distinguish terrorism from ordinary crime, even when they might actually be identical in practice. The need for a separate legislation and punishment for terrorism stems from the enormous danger that terrorism, due to its political dimension, as opposed to crime, poses to society and its values, to the government in power, and to the public at large.

2. International cooperation: An internationally accepted definition of terrorism is required to strengthen cooperation between countries in the struggle against terrorism and to ensure its effectiveness. This need is particularly obvious in all that concerns the formulation and ratification of international conventions against terrorism—conventions forbidding the perpetration of terrorist acts, assistance to terrorism, transfer of funds to terrorist organizations, state support for terrorist organizations, commercial ties with states sponsoring terrorism—and conventions compelling the extradition of terrorists.

3. States sponsoring terrorism: Modern terrorism is increasingly dependent on the support of nations. States sponsoring terrorism use terrorist organizations as a means to their own ends, while these organizations depend on the assistance they receive from such countries at the economic, military, and operational levels. Some organizations are so closely dependent on the assistance of states that they become "puppets" functioning at the initiative, direction, and

with the complete support of these states. It is impossible to contend
effectively with terrorism without severing the close tie between the
terrorist organizations and the sponsoring states. This tie, however,
cannot be severed without agreeing on a broad definition of terrorism and thus of the states that sponsor it and of the steps to be taken
against them.

4. Offensive action: The state struggling against terrorism must retain
   the initiative. At the same time, attempts must be made to limit, as
   far as possible, the operative capacity of the terrorist organization. To
   attain these aims, a continued offensive must be conducted against
   terrorist organizations. While countries on the defensive naturally
   enjoy the sympathy of others, countries on the offensive are usually censored and criticized by others. To ensure international support for states struggling against terrorism, and perhaps even for a
   joint offensive, an internationally accepted definition of terrorism is
   required that will distinguish freedom fighting (which enjoys a measure of legitimacy among nations) from terrorist activity.

5. Attitudes toward the population supporting terrorism: Terrorist
   organizations often rely on the assistance of a sympathetic civilian
   population. An effective instrument in the limitation of terrorist
   activity is to undermine the ability of the organization to obtain support, assistance, and aid from this population. A definition of terrorism could be helpful here also by determining new rules of the game
   in both the local and the international spheres. Any organization
   contemplating the use of terrorism to attain its political aims will
   have to risk losing its legitimacy, even with the population that supports its aims.

6. Normative scale: A definition that separates terrorism from
   other violent actions will enable the initiation of an international
   campaign designed to undermine the legitimacy of terrorist
   organizations, curtail support for them, and galvanize a united
   international front against them. To undermine the legitimacy of
   terrorist activity (usually stemming from the tendency of various
   countries to identify with some of the aims of terrorist organizations), terrorist activity must be distinguished from guerrilla
   activity as two forms of violent struggle reflecting different levels
   of illegitimacy.

The Attitude of Terrorist Organizations:
Toward the Definition

The definition of terrorism does not require that the terrorist organizations themselves accept it as such. Nevertheless, reaching international agreement will be easier the more objective the definition and the more the definition takes into account the demands and viewpoints of terrorist organizations and their supporters. The proposed definition, as noted, draws a distinction between terrorism and guerrilla warfare at both the conceptual and moral levels. If properly applied, it could challenge organizations that are presently involved in terrorism to abandon it to engage exclusively in guerrilla warfare. As noted, most organizations active today in the national and international arena engage in both terrorist activities and guerrilla warfare; after all, international convention makes no distinction between the two. Hence, there are no rules defining what is forbidden and what is allowed in nonconventional war, and equal punishments are imposed on both terrorists and guerrilla fighters. People perpetrating terrorist attacks or engaging in guerrilla warfare know they can expect the same punishment, whether they attack a military installation or take over a kindergarten. The terrorist attack may be more heavily censored because it involves children, but the legitimacy of these actions will be inferred from their political aims. In these circumstances, why not prefer a terrorist attack that will have far more impact, and will be easier to accomplish, with much less risk?

The international adoption of the proposed definition, with its distinction between terrorism and guerrilla warfare—and its concomitant separation from political aims—could motivate the perpetrators to reconsider their intentions, choosing military targets over civilian targets (guerrilla warfare over terrorism) both because of moral considerations and because of cost-benefit considerations. Regarding the moral consideration, many terrorist organizations are troubled by the moral question bearing on their right to harm civilians, and this concern is reflected in their literature and in interviews with terrorists. Thus, for instance, an activist of the Popular Front for the Liberation of Palestine, Walid Salam, argued in December 1996 that "among activists of the Popular Front, more and more are opposed to military activities against civilians, as the one near Ramallah on Wednesday. They do not say so publicly because of internal discipline and to preserve unity" (*Haaretz*, 1996).

We can also see something of this moral dilemma in Sheik Ahmad Yassin, the leader of Hamas: "According to our religion it is forbidden to kill a woman, a baby, or an old man, but when you kill my sister, and my daughter, and my son, it is my right to defend them" (*Haaretz*, 1997). This concern might explain why, after attacks on civilian targets, organizations such as

Hamas often make public statements proclaiming that they have attacked military targets. The moral dilemma does exist, and the opponents of terrorism must intensify it. When countries acknowledge the principle of relying on guerrilla warfare to attain legitimate political aims and unite in their moral condemnation of terrorism, they increase the moral dilemma that is already prevalent in terrorist organizations.

Regarding the utilitarian consideration, if the perpetrators know that attacking a kindergarten or other civilian target will never be acceptable, that these attacks will turn them into wanted and extraditable terrorists and will undermine the legitimacy of their political goals—and that, when apprehended, they will be punished much more harshly than would guerrilla fighters—they may think twice before choosing terrorism as their modus operandi. Adopting the proposed definition of terrorism, formulating rules of behavior, and setting appropriate punishments in line with the proposed definition will sharpen the cost-benefit considerations of terrorist organizations. One way of encouraging this trend among terrorist organizations is, as noted, to agree on different punishments for those convicted of terrorism and those convicted of guerrilla warfare. Thus, for instance, the possibility should be considered of bringing to criminal trial, under specific charges of terrorism, individuals involved in terrorist activities, while allotting prisoner-of-war status to those accused of involvement in guerrilla activities.

The proposed definition of terrorism may indeed help in the struggle against terrorism at many and varied operative levels. An accepted definition, capable of serving as a basis for international counterterrorist activity, could, above all, bring terrorist organizations to reconsider their actions. They must face the question of whether they will persist in terrorist attacks and risk all that such persistence entails—losing legitimacy, incurring harsh and specific punishments, facing a coordinated international opposition (including military activity), and suffering harm to sources of support and revenue. The international community must encourage the moral and utilitarian dilemmas of terrorist organizations and establish a clear policy accompanied by adequate means of punishment on the basis of an accepted definition.

Summary

We face an essential need to reach a definition of terrorism that will enjoy wide international agreement, thus enabling international operations against terrorist organizations. A definition of this type must rely on the same principles already agreed on regarding conventional wars (between states) and extrapolate from them regarding nonconventional wars (between organization and a state). The definition of terrorism will be the basis and the operational tool for expanding the international community's ability to combat terrorism. It will enable legislation and specific punishments against those perpetrating, involved in, or supporting terrorism and will allow the formulation of a codex of laws and international conventions against terrorism, terrorist organizations, states sponsoring terrorism, and economic firms trading with them. At the same time, the definition of terrorism will hamper the attempts of terrorist organizations to obtain public legitimacy and will erode support among those segments of the population willing to assist them (as opposed to guerrilla activities). Finally, the operative use of the definition of terrorism could motivate terrorist organizations, due to moral or utilitarian considerations, to shift from terrorist activities to alternative courses (such as guerrilla warfare) to attain their aims, thus reducing the scope of international terrorism.

The struggle to define terrorism is sometimes as hard as the struggle against terrorism itself. The present view, claiming it is unnecessary and well-nigh impossible to agree on an objective definition of terrorism, has long established itself as the "politically correct" one. It is the aim of this chapter, however, to demonstrate that an objective, internationally accepted definition of terrorism is a feasible goal, and that an effective struggle against terrorism requires such a definition. The sooner the nations of the world come to this realization, the better.

References

Al-Anba'a. (1987, January 30). *The Fifth Islamic Summit Convention Decisions* [Arabic]. Kuwait.

Cline, Ray S., and Alexander, Yonah. (1986). *Terrorism as State-Sponsored Covert Warfare*. Fairfax, VA: Hero Books.

Committee on Foreign Affairs. (1989). *Hearings and Markup before the Subcommittee on Europe and the Middle East of the Committee on Foreign Affairs, House of Representatives*, 101st Congress, First Session.

Crenshaw, Martha (Ed.). (1995). *Terrorism in Context*. University Park: Pennsylvania State University.

Ganor, Boaz. (1997). *Countering State-Sponsored Terrorism* (ICT Papers). Herzlia, Israel: International Policy Institute for Counter-Terrorism, Interdisciplinary Center.

Haaretz. (1996, December 15). The leader of the PFLP: There is a growing criticism against civilian casualties [Hebrew].

Haaretz. (1997, October 8). Yassin: We will stop the attacks against Israeli civilians when Israel will stop killing Palestinians [Hebrew].

Haaretz. (1998, April 21). Arab League nations sign anti-terror accord [Hebrew]. Retrieved from http://www.ict.org.il/spotlight/det.cfm

Harkabi, Yehoshafat. (1983). *On Guerrilla Warfare* [Hebrew]. Tel-Aviv: Ma'arakhot.

Iyad, Abu. (1983). *Without a Homeland* [Hebrew]. Tel-Aviv: Mifras.

Laqueur, Walter. (1977). *Guerrilla Warfare, a Historical and Critical Study*. London: Weidenfeld & Nicholson.

Laqueur, Walter. (1987). *The Age of Terrorism*. Boston: Little, Brown.

Netanyahu, Benjamin (Ed.). (1980). *International Terrorism: Challenge and Response*. Jerusalem: Jonathan Institute.

Netanyahu, Benjamin. (1985). *Terrorism: How the West Can Win*. New York: Farrar, Strauss and Giroux.

Netanyahu, Benjamin. (1995). *Fighting Terrorism*. New York: Farrar, Strauss and Giroux, New York.

Schmidt, Alex P. (1984). *Political Terrorism*. Amsterdam: SWIDOC and Transaction Books.

Schmidt, Alex P., and Jongman, Albert I. (Eds.). (1988). *Political Terrorism*. Amsterdam: SWIDOC and Transaction Books.

Sprinzak, Ehud. (1985). *Israel and Terrorism*. Lecture at a workshop sponsored by the International Center for the Study of Contemporary Society, Jerusalem.

Tishrin. (1986, November 17). Tishrin [Arabic].Syria.

United Nations. (1949). *Convention Relative to Protection of Civilian Persons in Time of War of 12 August 1949 (Geneva Convention)*. Retrieved from http://www.unog.ch/frames/disarm/distrait/geneva4.pdf

United States Department of State. (2001, April). *Patterns of Global Terrorism 2000*. Washington, DC: Author.

Radicalization of Terrorist Causes
The 32CSM/IRA Threat to U.K. Security

2

DAVID LOWE

Contents

Introduction

Since 2009, the significant increase of violence from Irish dissident groups has broken the relative peace in Northern Ireland brought about by the 1998 Good Friday Agreement (GFA). As the largest and most active of the Irish dissident groups, this chapter focuses on the IRA. The original focus of the research was on the then-largest republican group, the Real IRA (RIRA), and its political wing, the 32 County Sovereignty Movement (32CSM). However, during the data collection period, RIRA amalgamated with another republican dissident group, Republican Action Against Drugs (RAAD), and disaffected former members of the Provisional IRA (PIRA). The increase in size of the group has consequently increased its capability to mount a period of violence in Northern Ireland and, potentially, mainland Britain.[1] As a result, the research focus changed slightly by examining this new IRA group. The danger the 32CSM/IRA pose cannot be understated. The 2012 Northern Ireland Peace Monitoring Report states that as a result of the threat Irish dissident groups in the province pose to U.K. security, the Terrorism Risk Index placed the United Kingdom as at a greater risk than any other Western nation (Nolan, 2012, p. 43).

This chapter focuses on the radicalization process the 32CSM/IRA use to gain support, mainly from Catholic republican/nationalist communities (including recruiting individuals to the IRA). Just as there is difficulty in deriving one agreed definition of what actions amount to an act of terrorism, when examining the empirical work carried out on radicalization, it also contains conflicting findings. This chapter applies radicalization theories to the methods the 32CSM/IRA use to gain support from their use of e-sources, symbols, and ceremonies.

Primary data for this research were obtained from nationalist, republican, and unionist politicians, police officers (mainly the Police Service of Northern Ireland [PSNI] and Ireland's An Garda Siochana), and members of the Catholic community in Northern Ireland (many who had connections with PIRA and Sinn Fein). The analysis of the primary data draws comparisons with the findings of the 2012 Northern Ireland Peace Monitoring Report and the events that led to PIRA's breakaway from the IRA at the start of the 1969–1998 Irish Troubles (now on referred to as the Troubles) to assess if through a radicalization process the 32CSM/IRA can eventually emulate PIRA and Sinn Fein during the Troubles. This research found the IRA is building a capacity to mount a sustained campaign of violence in Northern Ireland, which, through their radicalization of English-based supporters, could expand to carrying out attacks in England. If the IRA achieves this, it would result in the United Kingdom having a terror war on two fronts with Irish and jihadist terror groups.

Background to the Research

The Real IRA

RIRA broke away from PIRA at the time PIRA and Sinn Fein agreed to the GFA in 1998. RIRA announced its opposition to the GFA with the 1999 Omagh bombing, killing 29, making it the worst single atrocity during the Troubles (Vaughan and Kilcommins, 2008, p. 80). Feeling betrayed by PIRA and Sinn Fein for agreeing to the GFA, RIRA viewed the agreement as a concession to an imperial state's (Britain) continuance to govern their country, supported by forces of occupation. Resigning from PIRA's executive, Mickey McKevitt formed a breakaway dissident group, Oglaigh na hEireann (Harden, 2000, p. 311). Oglaigh na hEireann became known as the Real IRA following the staging of illegal roadblocks in 1998, where its members told motorists, "We're from the IRA. The Real IRA" (Harden, 2000, p. 312).

The Northern Ireland Peace Monitoring Report identifies three republican groups: the RIRA, Oglaigh na hEireann, and Continuity IRA (Nolan, 2012, pp. 44–45). This builds on MacDonald's 2008 report on the threat to security in Northern Ireland identifying the same three groups, which at that time had no unified command. My research found the numbers of activists in these groups is higher than those reported by MacDonald. Following a relative lull since 2001, there has been an incremental rise in RIRA attacks in Northern Ireland commencing with the killing of two British Army soldiers at Massereene Barracks in March 2009 in County Antrim,[2] up to 2012 bomb attacks in Derry,[3] and the targeting in early 2013 of PSNI officers.[4] This has included killing PSNI officers,[5] to bombing the U.K. national security service MI5's Belfast headquarters.[6] As the frequency of attacks has increased, at the inception of the research it was important to assess if the RIRA supported by the 32CSM could achieve its main target: to carry out a bombing campaign in England (Nolan, 2012, p. 45).

The "New" IRA

At the end of July 2012, a statement was released by RIRA saying its membership had joined RAAD and other former prominent PIRA members to form a unified structure under a single leadership, thereby increasing their capacity and capability to maintain a sustained campaign of violence.[7] Based predominantly in counties Derry and Tyrone, RAAD was a vigilante group comprised of former PIRA members who carried out punishment beatings on individuals suspected of involvement with drug dealing or drug abuse and antisocial behavior in predominantly Catholic neighborhoods.[8] They operated in a similar fashion to PIRA during the Troubles; to tighten their grip within their community, they regularly gave punishment beatings to those they found stealing or involved in drugs or antisocial behavior, with the punishment often taking the form of shooting the victim's kneecaps (Taylor, 1997, p. 287). This was a natural alliance between both groups as both groups have a similar cause.

Since this alliance, the IRA has carried out a number of attacks. In November 2012, a Maghaberry prison officer, David Black, was killed by the IRA while on his way to work; members of the IRA have been arrested (at the time of writing, they are awaiting trial).[9] In November and December 2012, the PSNI found a number of horizontal mortar bombs across various locations in Northern Ireland; the bombs were capable of piercing the armor of police vehicles. This resulted in an off-duty PSNI officer finding an explosive device under his car on New Year's Eve in 2012.[10] In January 2013, an off-duty PSNI officer saw people at the back of his house, causing him to draw his firearm and shoot at them. The following day a pipe bomb was found at the officer's house.[11] Such incidents have increased from occurring occasionally to what now appears to be a weekly basis. These actions occurring in such a short period demonstrates that the IRA's mission to kill military personnel, police and prison officers, and those who work for the British is no idle threat.

The 32CSM

Parallel to the rise of the IRA is the growth of its political wing, the 32CSM. Formed in December 1997 (Taylor, 1997, p. 328), the 32CSM is not a political party per se and has not stood any candidates in the Northern Ireland Assembly or local elections. Having a political wing associated to a terror group is not unique to Ireland. In Spain, Euskadi ta Askatasuma (Eta) had a political wing, Batasuna, a coalition of leftist national parties containing Eta members among its ranks (Whitaker, 2012, pp. 120–122). The political wings take on the role of legal representatives of terror groups in order to be an avenue of dialogue (Tuman, 2010, p. 20). During the Troubles, Sinn Fein was PIRA's political wing. In 1983, Sinn Fein was led by Gerry Adams, who would neither condone nor condemn PIRA's violent actions (O'Callaghan, 1998, pp. 172–173). Addressing Sinn Fein's ard fhies (party conference) in 1989, Gerry Adams said:

> The history of Ireland and of British colonial involvement throughout the world is that the British government rarely listens to the force of argument. It understands only the argument of force. This is one of the reasons why armed struggle is a fact of life and death in the six counties (1989, p. 2).

From 1983 to the GFA, Sinn Fein adopted a strategy referred to as the "armalite and the ballot box" by which they pursued an electoral strategy alongside PIRA's armed struggle (Taylor, 1997, pp. 281–282). This strategy was successful bringing about the GFA, and Sinn Fein is currently the largest political party from the Catholic community in the Northern Ireland Assembly.

In building a political position from which to defend the nationalist community, rather than having just an armed struggle, Sinn Fein advocated putting more energy into a political solution (Adams, 1996, p. 263). While some observers may spot anomalies in Sinn Fein's assertion, Sinn Fein always claimed to be separate from PIRA (Adams, 2003, p. 46–47). At the time of its inception, the 32CSM leadership attempted to adopt a similar position. Its leader, Bernadette Sands-McKevitt, claimed the 32CSM was a single-issue group with no connection to any paramilitary wing. At the time this assertion was made, two members of the 32CSM Executive were charged with possession of materials for bomb making (Taylor, 1997, p. 358). Three months later, members of the 32CSM were linked to several bombings. The former Royal Ulster Constabulary (RUC) chief constable, Ronnie Flanagan, admitted intelligence reports on the 32CSM revealed its membership included a significant number of dissident elements of PIRA, concluding:

> Undoubtedly people close to the [32CSM] Committee have knowledge, expertise and experience in the terrorist field and probably have access to materials to allow that expertise and experience to be brought to bear in the carrying out of attacks. So I think people close to the [32CSM] Committee pose a very significant threat indeed. (Taylor, 1997, p. 358)

Regarding whether the 32CSM poses a similar threat today, both the PSNI and An Garda Siochana officers interviewed agreed they do, with one officer saying:

> Just look at who the members are. There's Marian Price an ex-Provisional, who is in prison after holding a statement read out by a member of the Real IRA at the 32CSM's commemoration of the Easter Rising in Derry's Creggan cemetery in 2011. Then there's the Duffy's who were in the Provisionals with Colin only recently acquitted at the Massereene Barracks murder trial. I could go on with the names who are members of the 32CSM we suspect are also members of the Real IRA. There isn't even an attempt by the 32CSM to distance themselves from the IRA. The arrests of members of the Real IRA we've made over the last year are all connected to the 32CSM.

Six months after this officer was interviewed, Paul Duffy, Damien Duffy, and Shane Duffy, all members of the RIRA and 32CSM, were charged with the offenses of collecting information likely to be of use to terrorists,[12] conspiracy to murder, and conspiring to cause an explosion.[13] This extremely close relationship between the 32CSM and the IRA shows how dangerous the

32CSM is, not only to peace in Northern Ireland but also to peace in Britain, especially England.

Radicalization

The more one examines radicalization, the more one finds that radicalization is a complex, multifaceted phenomenon (Carpenter, Levitt, and Jacobson, 2009, p. 327). There is no-one-size-fits-all theory to radicalization, as some situations and issues that apply to certain groups will not to others. As a result, no one satisfactory theory exists (Hutson, Long, and Page 2009, p. 18). This may be due to the diverse types of terrorist activity around the world being affected or influenced by a variety of issues and events that triggers their cause. On the danger radicalization poses to the security of its member states, the European Union (EU) states radicalization should be

> viewed as a complex interaction of factors that does not necessarily lead to violence. Since the process can evolve in many different directions, including non-violent ones, radicals can engage in non-violent behaviour without terrorist intent yet still be considered radical. As such, although not every radical becomes a terrorist, every terrorist has gone through a radicalisation process. (OT Institute for Safety, Security, and Crisis Management, 2008, p. 5)

Recognizing the importance of the radicalization process, under a prevention of terrorism strategy, the European Union listed among key priorities the development of a common approach to spot and tackle problem behavior (including misuses of the Internet); the promotion of good governance, democracy, education, and economic prosperity in the European Union; and the development of a media and communication strategy to explain E.U. policies (OT Institute for Safety, Security, and Crisis Management, 2008, p. 61). While the underlying tone of the document is to deal with jihadist extremism, these points also apply to politically motivated terrorism. As the United Kingdom and Ireland are EU member states, this policy also applies to actions by the 32CSM/IRA in the radicalization process.

Coming from the data in this research is the concern that the current economic recession could assist the 32CSM/IRA's cause. Social/economic status has raised differing views in the radicalization process. Examining the processes of jihadist radicalization, Silke states that research has not found a clear link between poverty and deprivation along with membership of extreme organizations. In explaining this, he says because the impoverished are less likely to vote, they are also less likely to become engaged in terrorist organizations (2008, p. 109). Githens-Mazer challenges this and many of the empirical studies that state low income is not a cause of terrorism. He found that an attraction to jihadist violence exists where the individual suffers "difficult" social, political, and *economic* circumstances (2008, p. 27). Githens-Mazer's findings are supported by other studies, certainly in regard to jihadist-based extremism. For example, Hutson, Long, and Page's study found in poverty-stricken areas that economic deprivation was a factor in the radicalization process (2009, p. 21). One agreed finding in most of the empirical studies into radicalization is that where a multisituational position exists, it results in a landscape that is more politically, socially, and economically deprived, making it more fertile to allow a process of radicalization into extremism (Vertigans, 2011, pp. 77–87). Such a landscape Silke recognizes as existing during the Troubles. He says the multisituational position of economic deprivation, educational underperformance, and insufficient representation were important radicalization factors that increased support for Sinn Fein/PIRA from the Catholic community (2008, p. 112). During the Troubles, the radicalized individuals who joined PIRA were not deranged or insane. Punch's study on the Troubles found that while individual members came from a degree of deprivation, they were "resilient, relaxed and stable" (2012, p. 49).

These themes are examined in more detail as the actions of the 32CSM/IRA regarding recruitment and how they get the message of their cause across to a global population are analyzed.

Research Methods Deployed

Sample Size

Apart from examining official data and reports of actions by Irish dissident groups, I visited Northern Ireland to interview republican, nationalist, and unionist politicians (total of 14), police officers (total of 6), and members of the Catholic community (total of 24). The last group included informers I handled as a detective during the Troubles, community leaders, and members of republican organizations. In England, I also interviewed members of Liverpool's Catholic community who were members of republican flute bands. All consented to be interviewed and to have the interview tape-recorded. The interviews took place from June 2012 to October 2012, with most interviews lasting 1 hour.

Research Strategy

In assessing the IRA's capability to mount a sustained campaign that could escalate to Britain, the research was founded on four areas:

1. How active the IRA are;
2. The link between the IRA and 32CSM;

3. Support for the IRA and the 32CSM in Northern Ireland; and

4. Support for the IRA and the 32CSM in Britain.

Research Methods Used

The primary data used in this research emanated from semistructured interviews. To focus the subjects on what the interviews entailed, prior to the interviews I forwarded the subjects a set of topic areas the interview would cover (Bayens & Roberson, 2011, p. 110). The aim of this was to focus the subjects' minds (Baker, 1998, p. 136) on the subject matter to minimize disruption from the interviewer by having to keep the subject discussing solely the topic areas (Baker, 1998, p. 137). The research findings were verified with data from other sources. This is important as Mythen and Walklate state that data from politicians and the police can be discursively shaped because of their involvement in risk definition (2006, p. 389). By passing on the terrorist scare, it can be used as a form of disciplinary control as politicians and police officers harden domestic security objectives (Mythen & Walklate, 2006, p. 330). To minimize any discrediting of the responses, in particular those from the politicians and the police, it was important the validity and reliability of the data were maintained by comparing them to data found in other empirical studies in the topic area.

Ethical Issues

The 2003 Social Research Association's (SRA's) Ethical Guidelines state that social researchers must strive to be aware of the intrusive potential of their work, adding that:

> The advancement of knowledge and the pursuit of information are not themselves sufficient justifications for overriding other social and cultural values. (2003, pp. 25–26)

As Liebling and Stanko point out, "Ethical research is typically defined as that which safeguards the rights and feelings of those who are being researched" (2001, p. 424). The Community Relations Council recently reported a deep-rooted sectarian divide still exists in Northern Ireland.[14] As a result of this divide, Irish dissident groups have a propensity toward violence against those who speak out or who are vehemently opposed to them. It was paramount that whatever was disclosed was dealt with sensitively. This is the reason why the subjects interviewed remained anonymous. A second reason the ethical guidelines were relevant is that it was important that nothing from the data was revealed that could hinder or obstruct any ongoing or recent operations or investigations into the 32CSM/IRA.[15]

Radicalization

Economic Deprivation

Regarding IRA activity within the nationalist communities, a community member who had connections with PIRA summed up a concern many of the politicians and community members had:

> [The IRA] are bigger and more influential in parts of the community than is reported in the papers or on television. I know old hands from my days in the Provisionals are in their ranks and kids who basically have no job, no future and who are bored. As these are hard line fanatics, if things get just a little worse, then god help us.

By "getting a little worse," this respondent referred to the economic recession. Republican and nationalist politicians were concerned that as the U.K. government's austerity measures bite deeper, this could turn disaffected young people to the dissident groups. A Social Democratic Labour Party (SDLP) politician interviewed said:

> Poverty's affected many of my constituents. There's no jobs, cuts in benefits and these are starting to hurt. Some of those I see in my surgery don't see this as a global problem or even an Irish problem. They're blaming the Government in Westminster for making the Irish pay the price. No matter how misinformed it is, this type of thinking only causes further disaffection and if it gets worse there's no doubt in my mind they'll turn to extreme republican groups like the 32CSM and the IRA … in desperation as they get carried away with blaming England.

The U.K. Poverty Site's latest annual survey of hours and earning (updated in December 2010) shows Northern Ireland is not the most economically deprived area of the United Kingdom. It is on a par with Scotland and the midlands area of England, with Wales, the northeast of England, and Yorkshire worse off (Department of Works and Pensions, 2011). There is a similar pattern regarding income inequalities and total weekly income (The Poverty Site, 2011) showing a number of U.K. areas are economically worse off than Northern Ireland. One set of data does supports the concerns poverty is a potential recruitment tool for the 32CSM/IRA. After deducting housing costs, in Northern Ireland 26% of Catholic households are below the median income compared to 16% of Protestant households (Department of Works and Pensions, 2011). The deprivation indicators show the percentage of Catholics suffering is far higher than the percentage of Protestants. For example, 66% of Catholics are behind in one or more household bill compared to 33% of Protestants, and 62% of Catholics are unable to heat the home compared to 31% of Protestants (Nolan, 2012, p. 89).

Suffering worse economic and social conditions compared to their protestant counterparts, in 1968 Catholics aired their grievances through the nonviolent Civil Rights Movement with marches and protests (Coogan, 1995, pp. 60–64). From 1970, Catholics began moving their support from the Civil Rights Movement to PIRA, with the watershed being Bloody Sunday in January 1972. With the state response to their grievances being violence meted out by RUC police officers on civil rights marchers, they felt they were not being listened to (O'Callaghan, 1998, p. 167). Just prior to Bloody Sunday, Coogan said in the *Irish Times*:

> In the North the Catholics have said: we have had enough … the IRA are the hard cutting edge of their grievances and, horrible though many of the deeds which have been done in the North are, the IRA continue to draw support. (1995, p. 133)

After Bloody Sunday, where the British Army's Parachute Regiment opened fire on civil rights marchers in Derry, killing 14 unarmed marchers, support for PIRA from the Catholic community increased to a point that PIRA had more potential recruits than it could cope with (English, 2009, p. 70; Martin 2012, p. 87). English states this situation was not produced by violence alone, "but the cumulative experience of blood stained friction" (2009, p. 71). Underpinning this was Catholics suffering greater poverty compared to Protestants (Taylor, 1997, pp. 38–40). This is not unique to Ireland. Kirby's study of jihadist radicalization found that after the July 7, 2005 London bombing individuals who experience economic and social difficulties in their lives are ripe for radicalization (2007, p. 416).

There are links to an individual's socioeconomic status and susceptibility to radicalization. Kirby, Hutson, Long, and Page found that socioeconomic status plays a role in determining the relationships an individual is able to build (2009, p. 21). Radicalization to violent groups is conceived in the context of local conditions and drivers that vary from case to case (Githens-Mazor, 2008, p. 26). In essence, the empirical studies agree that where socioeconomic status applies to radicalization, the poorer the status, the more likely the radicalization process to extremist groups occurs, whereas the more prosperous democratic societies that respect the rights of their citizens are more resilient and less susceptible to political instability and radicalization. Carpenter et al. explain this is so because "its grievances can be peacefully expressed and mediated through democratic institutions, citizens are less apt to turn to more extreme options" (2009, p. 303). Yet, regarding radicalization to 32CSM/IRA causes, an anomaly exists.

As mentioned, during the Troubles, in addition to economic deprivation, there were two other factors present in the radicalization process: educational underperformance and insufficient political representation (Silke, 2008, p. 112). These last two categories do not currently exist in either the 6 northern or 26 southern counties of Ireland and can explain why the 32CSM remains on the fringes of Irish politics. Post-GFA, the traditional republican/nationalist community does have political representation with Sinn Fein currently the largest party from that community in the Northern Ireland Assembly, with the deputy leader of the Assembly a Sinn Fein MLA. Educational opportunities are equal among both Catholic and Protestant communities. While economic deprivation in the current economic climate applies to both communities, it is the disparity between the Catholic and Protestant communities that is a cause for concern but should be tempered with the absence of the political representation and educational underperformance.

Radicalization through Fund-Raising

When the subjects were asked if the IRA has the financial capability to sustain terror attacks over a prolonged period, the police responses in particular acknowledged there had been an incremental increase in fund-raising capacity by the 32CSM/IRA from April 2011 to May 2012. The politicians agreed with this. One unionist politician said:

> We worked hard for peace in Northern Ireland with both sides ceding some of their ideals to achieve peace. The problem is we never really got rid of the fringe fanatics on both sides. The IRA have the resources to raise enough to finance a terror campaign and lead us back down the slippery slope of sustained violence.

Maintaining a continuous terror campaign is expensive. In 1983, Gerry Adams estimated that for Sinn Fein and PIRA to function at the level of operations at that time cost around £2,000,000 a year (O'Callaghan, 1998, p. 167). The cost to the United Kingdom of the security measures taken during the Troubles was an estimated £9.826 billion (Valino, Buesa, and Baumert, 2010, p. 18). The attack on the World Trade Center and the Pentagon on the 11 September 2001 cost Al Qaeda an estimated US$300,000 (Martin, 2012, p. 520). Martin identifies four main categories where funds are raised to finance terror campaigns:

1. Criminal activity;
2. Personal fortunes;

3. Extortion; and
4. Charities and foundations (2012, p. 521).

   While there is little evidence that PIRA had personal fortunes to tap into, there is evidence PIRA was involved in the other three methods to raise money to fund its activities. During the Troubles, PIRA carried out bank and post office robberies in both the northern 6 and the southern 26 counties of Ireland (O'Callaghan, 1998, pp. 205–207).
   PIRA also used extortion to raise funds. One of their main methods of extortion was targeting wealthy Irish and non-Irish residents in all 32 Irish counties, demanding protection money to prevent them being kidnapped (O'Callaghan, 1998, pp. 166–167). This tactic has been used by other terror groups in different conflicts. Groups like the Colombian Fuerzas Armadas Revolucionaria de Columbia (FARC) and the Filipino Abu Sayyaf have used the threat of kidnapping to raise essential funds. An important element of this tactic is to restrict the number of kidnappings, not only to heighten the fear of being kidnapped, but also to raise the publicity of a terror group's profile when a kidnapping occurs (Vertigans, 2011, p. 113). PIRA also raised a levy on the Falls Taxi Association (each driver contributing £15 a week) and was involved in tax swindles and social security fraud (O'Callaghan, 1998, p. 167). The most well-known PIRA international fund-raising campaign was NORAID (Irish Northern Aid). Founded by Martin Flannery, an IRA veteran in the United States, NORAID raised millions of pounds sterling for PIRA to buy munitions (Taylor, 1997, p. 84). Other forms of PIRA fund-raising were in its drinking clubs, most of which were in Belfast, some raising over £150,000 a year (Taylor, 1997, p. 67).
   Europol's 2012 T-Sat Report states that current IRA criminal activity used to raise funds includes robberies, fraud, extortion, and tobacco and fuel smuggling (Europol, 2012, p. 24). In September 2012, Alan Ryan, an RIRA member (later the IRA), was killed by criminal gangs in Dublin as Ryan was involved in extortion practices to raise funds for the 32CSM/IRA that was part of the IRA's strategy of drug dealing in other parts of Ireland to raise funds (BBC, 2012). Prior to Ryan's murder, 32CSM/IRA were found to be involved in drug dealing to raise funds for their cause in 2010 following the killing of a former RIRA member, Kieran Doherty. Doherty was cultivating a cannabis farm in a house in County Donegal on behalf of RIRA, and after a police raid on the house and it coming to light RIRA was running a cannabis farm, RIRA murdered Doherty on the border of counties Donegal and Derry (BBC, 2010).
   All respondents said the IRA was involved in criminal activity to raise funds. A typical response from one of the republican politicians interviewed was:

You can't discount that robberies are still one way of raising funds but more subtle criminal activity is also being used. I know from the area I represent that social security fraud and Internet fraud is common. Added to that are extortion and protection rackets they run be it through pseudo security companies or plain threats to individuals or criminals involved in drug dealing where the IRA take a cut of their takings.

An example of this type of IRA extortion activity came out during the trial regarding the murder of two drug dealers in Cornwall where two men from Liverpool (England) were tried for the murder. During their trial, under oath, one of the defendants admitted they were working for an Irish republican group based in Liverpool, and their activities were financed by the IRA for fund-raising purposes (Rossington, 2012).[16]

Extortion though the threat of kidnapping was seen by the community members as a possible future IRA action to raise funds, but this action was seen by the respondents in my research as unlikely. A couple of reasons were given. From the community members interviewed, one reason was due to the fact that currently the 32CSM/IRA are not in a position of strength to carry out successful kidnappings. As one of the community members said:

The IRA mightn't have as much muscle the Provos [PIRA] had yet, but they're pretty powerful and that threat's increasing and kidnap's one possibility they could use in the future.

The police officers interviewed were agreed that a main reason why extortion through kidnapping was not a viable option for 32CSM/IRA at the moment is down to the risk involved in kidnapping. These views were summed up by one of the officer's responses:

To raise funds through kidnapping carries a greater risk of detection. Apart from the likes of Internet fraud, a more lucrative form of fund raising is taking on the drug dealers as well as being hypocritical and dealing in drugs themselves.

Irish history shows the IRA in whatever form it takes to prepare for a long war. This is seen from the Irish Republican Brotherhood from the 1860s, with their bombing campaign in London in the 1880s (Bunyan, 1976, pp. 104–111; Staniforth, 2010, p. 79; Vaughan and Kilcommins, 2008, p. 54), to the Troubles themselves. In addition to finances, the ability to maintain a sustained campaign ranges from the strength of republican history and suffering to more mundane but significant momentum provided by organizational dynamics, such as training, fund-raising, commemorations, and organizing structure (English, 2009, p. 74). The IRA has incorporated these dynamics alongside its fund-raising over the last couple of years. An IRA training camp was found in Omagh, where four members were arrested for training IRA members in small arms use.[17] To assist the maintenance of their campaign, the IRA frequently attend marches and assemblies to commemorate Irish republican events to reinforce the history of the Irish struggle against British imperialism, which is a powerful symbol to legitimize their fund-raising from their traditional communities.

Radicalization: The Power of Language and Symbolism to Demonstrate Mutual Empathy

How groups like the 32CSM/IRA use language to raise the profile of their message is important (Taylor, 1997, p. 291). During the Troubles, Sinn Fein referred to prisons like Long Kesh as concentration camps (Adams, 1990, p. 11) and republican prisoners as prisoners of war (Adams, 1990, p. 13). The 32CSM's 2012 New Year statement refers to all republican prisoners detained at Maghaberry and Portlaoise as prisoners of war. An important 32CSM cause is the imprisonment of Marian Price. Price joined PIRA in 1970 (Dillon, 1994, p. 164) and along with her sister, Dolours Price,[18] was imprisoned for the bombing of the Old Bailey courts in London in 1973 (Taylor, 1997, pp. 154–155). She is currently on remand for holding a written statement at the 32CSM/IRA's Easter Rising commemoration at Creggan Cemetery for a masked RIRA member to read out in April 2011 and is facing possible charges related to the 2009 killing of the two soldiers at Massereene Barracks.[19] The 32CSM portrays Price as a victim of British imperial law, referring to her imprisonment as internment. The potency of the 32CSM's message infiltrating mainstream politics is seen in the nationalist SDLP's Alban McGuiness' response to Price's imprisonment, referring to it as *internment*.[20]

Significant in 32CSM's 2012 New Year statement is the rhetoric regarding its position over British sovereignty of Northern Ireland, referring to it as imperialism. Their main cause of supporting the IRA is in intensifying armed conflict because a political discourse for a solution continues to be out of reach, saying:

> The Real IRA are not the cause of conflict in Ireland they are a response to the conditions created by Imperialism in Ireland. The 32CSM believes that there is no room for ambiguity on the issue of resistance.[21]

Similarities to the potency of the language used by 32CSM/IRA to that used by republicans during the Troubles is seen in the language used by Sinn Fein; Sinn Fein also referred to the British as imperialists (Adams, 1996, p. 123), and any initiative taken by the British government in Northern Ireland was perceived as a pogrom against the Catholic community (Adams, 1996, p. 119). Demonstrating mutual empathy during the annual commemoration of the 1916 Easter Rising at Creggan Cemetery in Derry, the 32CSM/IRA demonstrated the lack of ambiguity on the issue of armed resistance to British sovereignty. Although referring to groups in the United States, Vertigans recognizes how items of clothing, badges, and flags used at demonstrations develop mutual empathy among terror organizations and their supporters (Vertigans, 2011, p. 101). Over the last few years, the numbers of supporters/ attendees at Creggan Cemetery in Derry has risen for the Easter Rising commemoration. In 2012, a 32CSM/IRA color party dressed in a black military-style uniform with black berries, on which was the white Easter lily badge, carried the Irish tricolor and the flags of the four districts of Ireland to present them before the republican memorial stone. This was followed by speeches from leading members of the 32CSM. At the 2011 commemoration, the color party consisted of balaclava-wearing IRA members dressed in khaki uniform. In the last few years, a member of the IRA wearing a balaclava appears from the crowd, stands next to the memorial stone, and reads out a statement reiterating what the IRA stands for. In essence, it is that more attacks will be carried out on the police and army as well as those who oppose them.[22]

The Easter Rising commemorations provide a powerful theater for those with republican leanings as they not only project mutual empathy, but also are one of the steps in a radicalization process used for recruitment (Suttmoeller, Chermak, Freilich, and Fitzgerald, 2011, p. 84). With the 32CSM/IRA using these traditional republican symbols, we see two processes at work. First is what Vertigans refers to as "we-ness." Founded on networks based on friendship, camaraderie, similar backgrounds, and beliefs (2011, p. 98), we-ness is a collective effervescence based on shared beliefs, practices, and heightened emotions providing definitions and meaning (Vertigans, 2011, p. 94). The 1916 Easter Rising commemoration is an important commemoration for Irish citizens, and in the Irish Republic, the official commemoration outside the General Post Office Building in Dublin is attended by the Irish president and taoiseach (prime minister).[23] Therefore, the 32CSM/IRA commemoration not only shows Irish solidarity but also can show their commemoration is not in itself subversive and neither is the color party nor the flags displayed as symbols of a proscribed organization. The gold, white, and green tricolor is the internationally recognized flag of the Irish Republic. These symbols together demonstrate the mutual empathy, not only to the 32SCSM and its supporters, but also to republicans in all the 32 counties. This mutual empathy can be linked to an early stage of radicalization the 32CSM/IRA will want to achieve. Demonstrations and symbolic resistance are first steps of radicalization (Horgan 2009, p. 42), and this activity does not have to be violent (Suttmoeller et al., 2011, p. 83). It is worth noting that demonstrations and protests account for 17.2% of the recruitment strategies deployed by violent groups like the IRA (Suttmoeller et al., 2011, p. 92).

The final symbolic gesture demonstrating mutual empathy is the bala-clava-wearing member of the IRA making a statement to the assembly. It is symbolic as the balaclava echoes PIRA's dress code, which illustrates little difference between the two factions. Using the term *Oglaigh na hEireann* is also symbolic. Meaning "soldiers of Ireland," it was used by the original IRA that fought the British in 1918–1921 and is the title of the Irish Republic's Defence Forces.[24] Trying to show there is little difference between them and other Irish republican movements, the main difference is in their threats. Using this difference, the 32CSM/IRA is reinforcing the point that while PIRA may have stopped fighting and decommissioned its weapons in 2005 (Whittaker, 2012, p. 303), in the 32CSM's eyes, the IRA are continuing the war against the British imperialism and traitors who work for them, includ-ing Sinn Fein. This is the self-identification stage part of the radicalization process bringing about personal awareness, resulting in that person explor-ing the ideology of the group (Stottmoeller et al., 2011, p. 84).

On representativeness among the wider nationalist community and if there is mutual empathy toward the 32CSM/IRA, one of the SDLP councilors interviewed said:

> While they hold demonstrations that resonate with members of the nation-alist community, they're not representative at all, but I've noticed a shift in attitude in republican voters towards Sinn Fein. While canvassing in the last elections [May 2011] on the doorstep I came across a lot of disillusioned Sinn Fein supporters. By becoming part of the British establishment in Stormont they see the Shinners [Sinn Fein] as having sold out. That's the danger with the 32CSM, should they ever stand they could take disillusioned Sinn Fein votes.

Being seen as selling out by republican voters is starting to cause alarm in Sinn Fein. One Sinn Fein MLA said:

> They think we've sold them out yet nothing can be further from the truth. ... Republicans now have a voice in Northern Irish politics. The 32CSM's causes are outdated. I've offered to speak to Marian Price but she refuses to see me even though I've criticised her imprisonment in the Assembly and the press, saying it's internment. I know some of the 32CSM members when they were Sinn Fein. Some are good people but they're caught in a time warp.

This particular MLA was asked if he could understand that with Sinn Fein power sharing with the Democratic Unionist Party, coming out in support of the PSNI, and working with a British Northern Ireland Minister why some republicans are disillusioned. His response was:

I've said this before ... these people are living in the past. Their efforts to turn the clock back are futile. They want to return to the days of armed struggle and the misery this will cause.

During the interview with this MLA, it was pointed out in 1986 he said that Sinn Fein was

a socialist republican movement, a movement that supports the use of armed struggle in the six counties and the establishment of a socialist republic in the thirty-two counties of Ireland. (English 2009, p. 88)

When asked what the difference was between this message and the message given by the 32CSM/IRA, his response was:

At that time Sinn Fein was fighting for rights for the nationalist community ... we were in a struggle with the British having to fight their violent and vicious pogrom. Republican voters should look at what we've done not at what we haven't. ... What I said in 1986 was in a different Ireland to what we have now.

The demonstration of mutual empathy is a powerful strand of radicalization as the Easter Rising commemoration is a powerful piece of theatre, one that for the 32CSM/IRA cannot be criticized for holding in Ireland as similar commemorations are run all over the 32 Irish counties. The rhetoric used in the speeches and proclamations of the 32CSM/IRA is also powerful in demonstrating mutual empathy that is close to Sinn Fein policies. It can be difficult for some members of the traditional republican/nationalist community to differentiate between the two. The 32CSM/IRA are stealing the symbols of legitimate events commemorating those that sacrificed their lives to establish an Irish state that promotes the values of democracy and peace. The 32CSM/IRA are replacing those values with the promotion of murder, extortion, and other forms of criminality. This view was mentioned by some of the other subjects, especially from the republican politicians and community members. A response from one of the community encapsulates the sentiments given by the subjects on this topic:

Being a republican party Sinn Fein still have the desire that all thirty-two counties are unified under the rule of the Dail, Dublin. The difference is how they go about it. Sinn Fein want to use the political process like a referendum. I can't say the 32CSM want to continue with the armalite and ballot box approach. As they won't stand at elections that tells me that supporting IRA violence is the only way to achieve this goal.

Radicalization via the Internet

Terror groups and their political wings need to gain support not only from the community they claim to represent but also from the global community. The use of the Internet and social media is an important source for a wider audience garnering sympathy for or at least a measure of understanding of their cause. If terrorist groups use the Internet, they can successfully achieve the spread of their message (Martin, 2012, p. 45). Focused on jihadist terrorism, Sageman's work in this area demonstrates how the Internet is a useful, inexpensive tool to send a group's message quickly to potentially billions of people (Sageman, 2008, Chapter 7). This returns us to Vertigans' we-ness as the Internet provides terror groups with new opportunities to gain potential recruits (2011, p. 80). With the Internet producing 27.9% and 38.7% of its membership for both violent and nonviolent groups, respectively, the Internet is an important recruitment tool (Stottmoeller, 2011, p. 92).

The 32CSM/IRA have used e-sources as a platform to create a dialogue with a global audience that has triggered Irish mainstream political responses. Now a Dail Techta Dala (TD),[25] Gerry Adams is looking to help Irish dissident groups by offering to hold talks in an attempt to bring about a cessation of their violence. In response to widening their message via e-sources, in May 2012 the Northern Irish Assembly Deputy Leader Martin McGuiness told the Sinn Fein ard fheis the war with the British is over, and groups like the IRA's actions are pathetic and futile attempts to turn back the clock.[26] Concerned the 32CSM/IRA message was getting through to the nationalist community, he did not dismiss the possibility of a united Ireland, believing it could be brought about by peaceful means, not through an armed struggle. Extolling the peace process for allowing a national reconciliation with unionists that he saw as necessary for constitutional change, he said, "A peaceful and democratic path to a united Ireland is there" (DeBreadun, 2012). Sinn Fein TD Martin Lewis called on Sinn Fein to renew its commitment to the unification of the 32 counties by campaigning to the Irish government to commission a Green Paper on unity (Moriarty, 2012). It appears that the concern that disaffected republican voters turning away from Sinn Fein with the corresponding increase in support for the 32CSM regarding its main aims of a united Ireland has forced Sinn Fein to respond.

To date, the 32CSM/IRA are some way off in emulating PIRA and Sinn Fein during the Troubles in achieving widespread mutual empathy with nationalist communities and a global audience. One example is seen with the use of social media to oppose the IRA and the impact the 32CSM hoped to achieve following the IRA's killing of a Catholic PSNI officer in 2011. With a Facebook protest group "not in my name" set up, it showed the IRA it did not achieve its aim of intimidating Catholics from joining the PSNI or even getting the message across that it is fighting in their cause. A week after being set up, this Facebook group organized a protest that resulted in thousands of people assembling on the streets of Omagh to demonstrate against the IRA's killing of the police officer, Ronan Kerr.[27]

While the IRA does not use any social media or Internet websites as it would reveal the details of its members, the 32CSM overtly spread the IRA's message through their websites and social media pages. Regionalized, but all carrying the same message, the 32CSM websites have been effective in raising international awareness of its cause. This included organizing a protest in Canada on 22 May 2012 for the release of Marian Price[28] and seven arrested IRA suspects.[29] A report written by U.S. 32CSM/IRA sympathizers refers to the imprisonment of IRA suspects as internment, with the suspects being called prisoners of war.[30]

While this use of the Internet appears to have some impact, it is not replicated among the grassroots feelings of the politicians and community members who were interviewed. One of the republican politicians said:

> Apart from wanting a united Ireland free of British rule it's hard to associate with their cause. I know that's what many of my constituents think. Political movements like 32CSM or Irish Socialist Republican Party or Republican Sinn Fein are a minor voice in Ireland. They don't stand at elections as they wouldn't get many votes because the majority's not interested in their message.

Recruitment to Causes via Social Media

Another advantage in the use of social media such as Facebook, Twitter, and YouTube is terror groups are offered opportunities to demystify their opponents to bring in new supporters and prevent current supporters from drifting away by focusing them into more constructive pursuits (Seib, 2012, p. 69). Through the 32CSM's use of social media, we see Sageman's radicalization model operating. Radicalization is not a specified linear process for him. He states there are four prongs to radicalization:

1. Moral outrage;
2. Interpretation;
3. Resonance with personal experience; and
4. Mobilization through networks that interact with each other (Sageman, 2008, pp. 57–62).

The 32CSM's Free Marion Price Facebook page,[31] set up to create a moral outrage, has 3,519 supporters.[32] Although not a large amount of support compared to other Facebook protest pages, it was successful in mobilizing over 1,000 protesters gathering in Belfast on 27 May 2012 to raise wider public support for the Free Marian Price campaign. Regardless of the high numbers this rally attracted, it was not reported in the U.K. mainstream news media, including Ulster TV and BBC news Northern Ireland. This includes the print media, with the U.K. newspapers, including the Northern Ireland-based *Belfast Telegraph,* failing to report on the event. Coverage of the rally can only be found on Internet sites linked to the 32CSM.[33] On the same weekend of the 32CSM's rally, the Marian Price cause did result in increasing more pressure on Sinn Fein, with one of their MLAs, Raymond McCartney, calling for the release of Price at its ard fhies (Moriarty, 2012).

Marian Price's imprisonment has not totally evaded the U.K. media. In January 2012, Eamonn McCann reported in *The Guardian* on Price's imprisonment, referring to it as a "scandal." McCann commented that Price is not being held for any crime other than the belief the United Kingdom would be better off without her, interpreting her imprisonment as internment (McCann, 2012). A reason why this has evaded mainstream U.K. media could be linked to what Tuman found. Examining media reporting on terrorist-related activity, he states that key to what was reported lay with the media's public relations experts and media consultants who help decide what is and what is not covered (Tuman, 2010, p. 166).

The 32CSM-related Facebook page with the most supporters is the Long Kesh Facebook group,[34] with over 4,910 supporters. It has already posted on its wall pictures and support for the Duffy brothers (referred to in the section on the 32CSM), who they refer to as the "Duffy 3." Once more, we see a moral outrage mobilizing support. Soon after their arrest, details of a meeting in the Cock Inn, Euston Station, London, were posted on the Long Kesh page, accompanied by an arrangement for fly posting (the indiscriminate pasting of posters on buildings) in London to raise awareness of the Duffy brothers' imprisonment.

Another social media source used to good effect by both the 32CSM and the IRA in the radicalization process is YouTube. A 32CSM recruitment video, posted on 1 June 2011, attracted 2,119 views,[35] with an earlier video, posted on 14 June 2008, "The 32CSM—Who We Are," attracting 11,452 views. A video posted on YouTube raising awareness and support for Marian Price posted in December 2011 has attracted 2,457 views.[36] The RIRA has also been active in posting video clips on YouTube. One posted in November 2007 showing RIRA operatives on maneuvers accompanied by a soundtrack of Irish rebel songs has been successful in attracting over 167,329 views.[37]

While using social media to promote their causes, the 32CSM/IRA are quick to denounce those who also use social media with a critical voice to their actions. In June 2011, a Scottish journalist, David Leggatt, reported that the 32CSM was linked to RIRA. In a strongly worded response, the 32CSM repudiated Leggat's claim, saying they only support republican prisoners of war (the likes of Marian Price, a convicted PIRA bomber; and Campbell, a convicted RIRA terrorist).[38] In January 2013, I also have been victim of the

32CSM's vitriol, with veiled threats to those like me who deign to associate them with the IRA. Based on the research covered in this chapter, a lecture I delivered to my students was filmed and placed on YouTube. Following a prolonged e-mail exchange with the 32CSM that questioned my findings, as there was no initial backing down from me to retract my findings, the 32CSM threatened to protest outside my university and accost students attending the degree program I run. As a result, the lecture was removed from YouTube, accompanied by a polite e-mail from me to the 32CSM. I can understand my university's fears of having 32SCSM/IRA members outside the campus building as the clip referenced in the notes indicates the type of person who protests in the 32CSM and how threatening a body it is.[39]

E-media demonstrates the potential for increasing support and recruits to their cause. Having Facebook "likes" or "friends" or views on YouTube in the thousands demonstrates how successful the fringe political voice of the 32CSM has been in using social media to attract individuals to their causes. As Seib (2012) points out, no doubt a situation will develop that, through the use of this relatively cheap and accessible media, new followers will be recruited to their cause as the 32CSM/IRA attempt to demystify their message. The potential danger is it can attract British supporters, who may want to go further than declaring their support for the 32CSM/IRA by clicking the Facebook like button to physically helping IRA operatives on the British mainland to carry out bombing attacks.

Loyalist Paramilitary Violence: Fueling and Legitimizing the Fire of 32CSM/IRA's Cause?

An issue that came out of the research was how 32CSM/IRA activity could provoke a violent response from loyalist paramilitary groups like the Ulster Volunteer Force (UVF). The impact that the rise of UVF activity can have on peace in Northern Ireland should not be underestimated. Many accounts claim the Troubles were ignited by loyalist politicking that encouraged UVF activity (Bamford, 2005, p. 582). Coogan records the activities of the Reverend Ian Paisley (former leader of the Democratic Unionist Party and the Northern Ireland Assembly) in stirring up the loyalist community at the start of the Troubles. He states this led to loyalist demonstrations and attacks on Catholics, resulting in the killing of prominent republicans (1995, pp. 47–50; Taylor, 1997, p. 30). As one of the police officers interviewed said:

> One knock on effect of the rise in republican dissident activity is an escalation of loyalist dissident group activity. As well as an increase in UVF activity, there's been the emergence of a small group, the Real Ulster Volunteer Force, which we believe to be a response by loyalists to the emergence of the Real IRA. Our intelligence states they came about following discontent with the

lack of reaction by the UVF to the killing of the officers in Lurgan and Omagh along with the bombings carried out by the Real IRA over the last few years.

Should Loyalist dissident groups carry out attacks against republicans, it would play into the hands of the 32CSM/IRA. Nolan states the UVF in 2007 pursued a nonmilitarized role, but by 2010, the UVF returned to violence, including murders of Catholics (Nolan, 2012, p. 46). The UVF's political wing, the Progressive Unionist Party, failed in gaining electoral success in the 2011 elections, leading to a resurgence of UVF street activity and a significant increase in gable-end street murals depicting UVF men (Nolan, 2012, p. 47). Any increase in UVF violence will result in RIRA's equally violent responses under the cause of protecting the nationalist community. During the Troubles, PIRA saw itself as the main protector of the Catholic community, which included violence against loyalist groups (Bamford, 2005, p. 583). The 32CSM/IRA are likely to adopt a similar strategy.

The community members interviewed were concerned about UVF violence. A former PIRA operative who now works for Sinn Fein said:

> It's unlikely in (names location) the UVF will do anything, but in districts in Belfast like Short Strand and areas where there's a small nationalist community like Antrim is where the damage can be done. All it'll take is a few shootings of Catholics and the IRA will claim the PSNI can't or won't protect the Catholic community because the PSNI is the RUC[40] in disguise. Some will fall for this bullshit, some possibly joining the IRA.

This danger has become a reality. Since December 2012 and up to the time of writing in January 2013, Loyalists organized by the UVF have held regular violent protests against the decision of Belfast City Council's decision to only fly the Union flag on certain days, not 365 days a year.[41] In addition to injuring a number of PSNI officers in the riots that followed the demonstrations, Loyalists have attacked republican, nationalist, and Alliance Party premises; a police car with a police officer inside was petrol bombed; and violence escalated in other cities and towns in Northern Ireland. including the Catholic-populated Short Strand area of Belfast, which led to a conflict between the Loyalists and the Catholic residents of Short Strand.[42]

In addition to an increase in Loyalist violence that has echoes of the mid-1960s Loyalist violence against republican and nationalist targets, for the 32CSM/IRA to have greater success in getting their message across in Ireland and globally, it only takes the economic and social conditions in Ireland to worsen or another event in which republicans suffer violence to inflame a situation. One of the republican councilors summed the current situation in Northern Ireland:

You don't take a naked flame into a room full of petrol. Even if it's a match that's running low it can be enough to ignite it. That's the north of Ireland at the moment.'

Conclusion: Radicalizing Support of Individuals in Britain to the 32CSM/IIRA Cause

Background to British Support for Irish Republican Groups

Throughout the various Irish wars, Irish dissident groups have received support from Irish communities living in Britain. During the Irish war of independence, when the founder of the IRA, Michael Collins, arrived in England in 1919 he received support from the Liverpool Irish republican volunteer unit (Mackay, 1996, p. 136). In early 1939, the IRA sent an ultimatum to the British prime minister demanding the British leave Northern Ireland. Not receiving a reply, the IRA bombed English cities with assistance from Liverpool Irish republican supporters (Hewitt, 2008, pp. 14–15). During the Troubles, O'Callaghan, an active PIRA operative, describes the help he received from Liverpool Irish republican sympathizers when he was sent to England on a bombing mission (O'Callaghan, 1998, pp. 149–151). During the Troubles, Liverpool was never attacked by PIRA's English Department. The main reason for this is the large ethnic Irish Catholic community in the city, a number of whom had sympathies for Sinn Fein and PIRA. In fact, it went beyond sympathy to actual physical support for PIRA's English Department and PIRA cells' attacks in England. In Liverpool and the wider Merseyside area, PIRA had a number of safe houses and quartermasters and activists who were Liverpool-born Catholics descended from Irish immigrants as far back as the 1840s (Dillon, 1994, pp. 283–286). O'Callaghan is adamant that one reason for the success of PIRA's English Department was the support it received from British-based sympathizers, those based in Liverpool in particular (O'Callaghan, 1998, pp. 112–115).

The 32CSM/IRA and British Republican Flute Bands

The influence of the 32CSM/IRA's use of social media and websites present in Britain can be seen in the 32CSM England, Alba, and Cymru website.[43] Its 2013 New Year message reinforces the opposition to British rule in Northern Ireland,[44] and the website contains links to support for Marian Price[45] and the IRA, including one of the web pages dedicated to the recently killed IRA member Alan Ryan, where the video link has been removed.[46]

Nowhere near the scale of Northern Ireland, sectarianism is present in Liverpool and can be traced from the 1840s when Liverpool's Catholic Irish émigrés built a community in the north of the city around Scotland

Road and Everton with the subsequent support for the Orange order from
the Protestant community. There is strong support for the republican flute
bands, the largest being the Liverpool Irish Patriots Republican Flute Band
(rfb). A spokesperson for the band was interviewed and said:

> We don't support the 32CSM or the Real IRA. We support Sinn Fein and never
> had any connection with the Provo's. … While celebrating Irishness and Irish
> music, we're a socialist movement supporting the working class here in Liverpool
> and in Ireland. … In Liverpool it's the likes of the James Larkin Republican Flue
> Band that supports the 32CSM. We have no connections with them.

Founded in 1996, the James Larkin rfb openly supports the 32CSM
and the RIRA. No one from the James Larkin rfb agreed to be interviewed
for this research. Taking its name from a Liverpool-born socialist of Irish
Catholic parents, Larkin was active in organizing the trade union movement in Liverpool and Ireland. By introducing industrial dispute into mainstream Irish history, Larkin created a positive view of enabling strike tactics
into a moral struggle linked to the armed struggle for Irish independence
(O'Connor, 2002, p. 102). Showing no alignment to the trade union movement, in the James Larkin rfb's Liverpool address is a reaffirmation of the
32CSM/IRA's politics and actions:

> The Anglo Irish conflict is not resolved. The British Parliament and Crown
> still maintains a sovereign claim over part of Ireland. Acts of insurgency
> against this claim continue. Irish POW's remain incarcerated. No amount of
> emotional rhetoric or flawed references to democracy can mask these blatant
> truths. … The starting point for democracy in Ireland is an immediate British
> withdrawal. The terms for a just peace must begin with self-determination for
> the Irish people. Every generation has asserted these rights. Acts of the British
> Parliament can have no place in the sovereign affairs of the Irish people. …
> The claims of British neutrality toward the Six Counties are a sham.[47]

The James Larkin rfb has joined the West of Scotland Band Alliance,
which is also aligned to the 32CSM. One of the largest members of the alliance is the Glasgow-based Parkhead rfb, also aligned to the 32CSM, which
march in commemoration parades organized by the 32CSM. As one of the
Liverpool community members interviewed said:

> It's groups like that [James Larkin and Parkhead rfb] that can turn young
> heads on the mainland to get caught up in the romance of fighting for a uni-
> fied thirty-two county Ireland. They're surrounded by the tricolour, hear
> heroic tales of the Troubles, learn the rebel songs and so on. It only needs a few
> of them to help the IRA in England. Just one successful attack will tell Britain

and the world the IRA is back. ... There are times I look at some individuals and know they'd assist an IRA mission.

The James Larkin rfb's own website[47] and its Facebook page[48] make it clear that the band supports the 32CSM. The James Larkin rfb Facebook page, which is kept more up to date than the website, supports the "Irish prisoners of war" like Marian Price, the end of British rule over the six northern Irish counties, and the IRA, including Alan Ryan. This is all part of the radicalization via e-sources showing mutual empathy discussed previously. The danger is that all it takes is for a few supporters based on the British mainland to make arrangements for the IRA to bomb targets in England.

How Extortion and Murder Have Become a Romanticized 32CSM/IRA Cause

The propaganda the 32CSM/IRA produce on both sides of the Irish Sea to radicalize individuals show how they have portrayed extortion and RIRA member Alan Ryan's murder to martyrdom to the 32CSM/IRA cause. Among the most potent case studies that demonstrates the threat the 32CSM/IRA poses is the portrayal of Ryan as a martyr. Ryan was based in Dublin and ran a security company that was involved in extortion, including violence and threats to drug gangs to raise money for the 32CSM/IRA (shortly before his death, he was admonished by the senior commanders of the IRA for pocketing some of the money for his personal use) (BBC, 2012). In September 2012, after upsetting too many criminal gangs in Dublin, a hit man was hired to kill Ryan. The week after his death, Ryan was given a full IRA paramilitary funeral in his hometown district of Donaghmade that included a volley of shots fired over his coffin by an IRA color party. The murder and particularly the funeral caused outrage among Irish citizens and politicians (*Irish Independent*, 2012). The report of the murder and the funeral of Alan Ryan in the *Irish Independent* sums up the outrage encapsulating the points found and raised in my research. Describing Ryan as an "extortionist and a killer," the *Irish Independent* is critical of how the 32CSM/IRA choreographed Ryan's funeral as they turned him into a martyr for republicanism who was fighting drug barons on behalf of the downtrodden working class, with the report saying that 32CSM/IRA now have their equivalent of Bobby Sands. The report exposes how the 32CSM tutored its members regarding what to say publically to media outlets and how certain members of the 32CSM/IRA were selected as spokespersons.[49] The article sums up the events and the dangerous consequences of such 32CSM/IRA actions and portrayal of events like those surrounding Ryan, saying:

The Special Branch has already established an intricate network or informants in the RIRA camp and the gang responsible. ... Meanwhile the RIRA will not seek vengeance for a while. The godfathers will manage it as carefully as they did the funeral. They see this as an opportunity to make inroads into hard-pressed communities and recruit a new generation of gullible kids. (*Irish Independent,* 2012)

This is why the 32CSM/IRA cannot be taken lightly. Europol's 2012 TE-SAT report states, as well as building support, the IRA has had continued success in the deployment of improvised explosive devices, which is a cause for concern as it shows that in the past 2 years the IRA has improved their engineering and technical capabilities (Europol, 2012, p. 24). Not only does the 32CSM/IRA pose a security threat to Northern Ireland, they are increasing their capability to pose a security threat in England. IRA activity is a classic example of the communal terrorism model (Martin, 2012, p. 11). Not often commanding international headlines but deeply rooted in cultural memories of conflict against the British and Irish Protestants, communal terrorism is vicious and intractable (Martin, 2012, pp. 119–120). As 3,284 people died during the Troubles (Martin, 2012, p. 121), to avoid a repeat of this it is paramount that a political and policing effort against the 32CSM/IRA is a top priority. As PIRA's Brighton bomber, Brian Magee, who targeted the British Prime Minister in 1984 poignantly stated, the security services have to be lucky all of the time, while the IRA only have to be lucky once (Taylor, 1997, p. 253).

Notes

1. BBC News. (July 27, 2012). *NI's dissident groups to unite under IRA banner.* Retrieved from HYPERLINK "http://www.bbc.co.uk/news/uk-northern-ireland-19009272"http://www.bbc.co.uk/news/uk-northern-ireland-19009272 [accessed August 5, 2012].
2. BBC. (March 8, 2009). *News Two Soldiers killed at Massereene Barracks.* Retrieved from HYPERLINK "http://news.bbc.co.uk/1/hi/northern_ireland/7930837.stm"http://news.bbc.co.uk/1/hi/northern_ireland/7930837.stm [accessed May 15, 2012].
3. BBC News. (January 20, 2012). *Real IRA bomb attacks.* Retrieved from HYPERLINK "http://www.bbc.co.uk/news/uk-northern-ireland-16645604"http://www.bbc.co.uk/news/uk-northern-ireland-16645604 [accessed May 15, 2012].
4. BBC News. (January 29, 2013). *Omagh police bomb incident was attempted murder.* Retrieved from HYPERLINK "http://www.bbc.co.uk/news/uk-northern-ireland-21247711"http://www.bbc.co.uk/news/uk-northern-ireland-21247711 [accessed January 30, 2013].

5. BBC News. (April 7, 2011). *PSNI Officer, Ronan Kerr killed by Real IRA.* Retrieved from HYPERLINK "http://www.bbc.co.uk/news/uk-northern-ireland-13001728"http://www.bbc.co.uk/news/uk-northern-ireland-13001728 [accessed May 15, 2012].

6. BBC. (April 28, 2011). *News Bombing of MI5 HQ at Palace Barracks, Belfast.* Retrieved from HYPERLINK "http://www.bbc.co.uk/news/uk-northern-ireland-13223966"http://www.bbc.co.uk/news/uk-northern-ireland-13223966 [accessed May 15, 2012].

7. BBC News. (July 27, 2012). *What does dissident republican "merger" statement mean?* Retrieved from HYPERLINK "http://www.bbc.co.uk/news/uk-northern-ireland-19014981"http://www.bbc.co.uk/news/uk-northern-ireland-19014981 [accessed September 6, 2012].

8. BBC News. (August 23, 2010). *Who are the dissident republicans?* Retrieved from HYPERLINK "http://www.bbc.co.uk/news/uk-northern-ireland-10732264"http://www.bbc.co.uk/news/uk-northern-ireland-10732264 [accessed September 6, 2012].

9. BBC News. (November 1, 2012). *Prison officer murdered on NI motorway.* Retrieved from HYPERLINK "http://www.bbc.co.uk/news/uk-20164563"http://www.bbc.co.uk/news/uk-20164563 [accessed January 7, 2013].

10. BBC News. (November 1, 2012). *Dissident republicans "remain determined to kill."* Retrieved from HYPERLINK "http://www.bbc.co.uk/news/uk-20164563"http://www.bbc.co.uk/news/uk-20164563 [accessed January 7, 2013].

11. BBC News. (January 29, 2013). *Omagh Bomb incidents: assembly member believes police officer was targeted.* Retrieved from HYPERLINK "http://www.bbc.co.uk/news/uk-northern-ireland-21247711"http://www.bbc.co.uk/news/uk-northern-ireland-21247711 [accessed January 30, 2013].

12. UK anti-terror legislation, Section 58 Terrorism Act 2000.

13. BBC News. (May 19, 2012). *Duffy relatives on terror charges.* Retrieved from HYPERLINK "http://www.bbc.co.uk/news/uk-northern-ireland-18128778" http://www.bbc.co.uk/news/uk-northern-ireland-18128778 [accessed May 28, 2012].

14. BBC News. (May 15, 2012). Sectarian division still deeply rooted in NI. Retrieved from HYPERLINK "http://www.bbc.co.uk/news/uk-northern-ireland-18076231"http://www.bbc.co.uk/news/uk-northern-ireland-18076231 [accessed May 15, 2012].

15. A draft of this article has been approved by Special Branch Counter-Terrorism Unit.

16. BBC News. (January 13, 2012). *Cornwall shooting death men "worked for IRA drug gang."* Retrieved from HYPERLINK "http://www.bbc.co.uk/news/uk-england-16543286"http://www.bbc.co.uk/news/uk-england-16543286 [accessed January 20, 2013].

17. BBC News. (May 19, 2012). *Four remanded over "terror training camp" near Omagh.* Retrieved from HYPERLINK "http://www.bbc.co.uk/news/uk-northern-ireland-18130609"http://www.bbc.co.uk/news/uk-northern-ireland-18130609 [accessed May 28, 2012].

18. (January 24, 2013). Dolours Price died peacefully in her Dublin home in December 2012 and has become another "martyr" to the 32CSM/IRA cause. Retrieved from HYPERLINK "http://www.32csm.net/" \l "!/2013/01/32csm-condolences-to-family-of-late.html"http://www.32csm.net/#!/2013/01/32csm-condolences-to-family-of-late.html [accessed January 30, 2013].

19. BBC News. (May 10, 2012). *Derry Terrorist Easter rally charges dismissed.* Retrieved from HYPERLINK "http://www.bbc.co.uk/news/uk-northern-ireland-18022527"http://www.bbc.co.uk/news/uk-northern-ireland-18022527 [accessed May 24, 2012].

20. BBC News. (May 13, 2012). *Marian Price being interned says SDLP's Alban McGuiness.* Retrieved from HYPERLINK "http://www.bbc.co.uk/news/uk-northern-ireland-18049635"http://www.bbc.co.uk/news/uk-northern-ireland-18049635 [accessed May 16, 2012].

21. 32CSM 2012 website.

22. TV. (April 9, 2012). 32CSM's *Easter Rising commemoration.* Retrieved from HYPERLINK "http://www.u.tv/News/Six-held-after-RIRA-threatens-police/4dda6662-5c13-4949-b287-102c977cb25c"http://www.u.tv/News/Six-held-after-RIRA-threatens-police/4dda6662-5c13-4949-b287-102c977cb25c [accessed May 30, 2012].

23. 1916 Easter rising Commemoration Ceremony, Dublin. (2012). Retrieved from HYPERLINK "http://www.youtube.com/watch?v=c76-K_ZsNuo"http://www.youtube.com/watch?v=c76-K_ZsNuo [accessed May 26, 2012].

24. Oglaigh na hEireann: Defence forces Ireland website Retrieved from HYPERLINK "http://www.military.ie/"http://www.military.ie/ [accessed May 28, 2012].

25. Irish Member of Parliament.

26. BBC News. (May 27, 2012). *Gerry Adams says dissident republican talks offer is genuine.* Retrieved from HYPERLINK "http://www.bbc.co.uk/news/uk-northern-ireland-18225884"http://www.bbc.co.uk/news/uk-northern-ireland-18225884 [accessed May 28, 2012].

27. BBC News. (April 10, 2011). *Omagh remembers murdered policeman at rally.* Retrieved from HYPERLINK "http://www.bbc.co.uk/news/uk-13029286"http://www.bbc.co.uk/news/uk-13029286 [accessed April 4, 2012].

28. BBC News. (May 10, 2012). *Derry Terrorist Easter rally charges dismissed.* Retrieved from HYPERLINK "http://www.bbc.co.uk/news/uk-northern-ireland-18022527"http://www.bbc.co.uk/news/uk-northern-ireland-18022527 [accessed May 24, 2012].

29. John Bonnar. (May 23, 2012). Toronto group demands immediate release of Irish republican political prisoner. *Online newsletter for activists.* Retrieved from HYPERLINK "http://rabble.ca/blogs/bloggers/johnbon/2012/05/toronto-group-demands-immediate-release-irish-republican-political-pr"http://rabble.ca/blogs/bloggers/johnbon/2012/05/toronto-group-demands-immediate-release-irish-republican-political-pr [accessed May 28, 2012].

30. 32CSM Derry website. The Irish Republican Immersion Experience – Perspective from America. Retrieved from HYPERLINK "http://www.derry32csm.com/" \l "!/2012/05/irish-republican-immersion-experience.html"http://www.derry32csm.com/#!/2012/05/irish-republican-immersion-experience.html [accessed May 24, 2012].

31. 32CSM Tyrone website. Retrieved from HYPERLINK "http://www.facebook.com/search/results.php?q=32+County+Sovereignty+movement+Tyrone&init=quick&tas=0.5166589089280618" \l "!/FreeMarianPriceNOW"http://www.facebook.com/search/results.php?q=32+County+Sovereignty+movement+Tyrone&init=quick&tas=0.5166589089280618#!/FreeMarianPriceNOW [accessed May 28, 2012].

32. Free Marian Price NOW website. Retrieved from HYPERLINK "http://www.facebook.com/author.davidlowe" \l "!/FreeMarianPriceNOW?fref=ts"http://www.facebook.com/author.davidlowe#!/FreeMarianPriceNOW?fref=ts [accessed January 30, 2013].

33. 32CSM Tyrone website. Retrieved from HYPERLINK "http://www.facebook.com/search/results.php?q=32+County+Sovereignty+movement+Tyrone&init=quick&tas=0.5166589089280618" \l "!/FreeMarianPriceNOW"http://www.facebook.com/search/results.php?q=32+County+Sovereignty+movement+Tyrone&init=quick&tas=0.5166589089280618#!/FreeMarianPriceNOW [accessed May 28, 2012].

34. 32CSM Tyrone website. Retrieved from HYPERLINK "http://www.facebook.com/search/results.php?q=32+County+Sovereignty+movement+Tyrone&init=quick&tas=0.5166589089280618" \l "!/profile.php?id=100002091740429"http://www.facebook.com/search/results.php?q=32+County+Sovereignty+movement+Tyrone&init=quick&tas=0.5166589089280618#!/profile.php?id=100002091740429 [accessed January 30, 2013].

35. YouTube. Join the 32 County Sovereignty Movement. Retrieved from HYPERLINK "http://www.youtube.com/watch?v=ss3j0wTyMs4"http://www.youtube.com/watch?v=ss3j0wTyMs4 [accessed January 30, 2013].

36. YouTube. Free Marian Price. Retrieved from HYPERLINK "http://www.youtube.com/watch?v=MUqivvLi6Ws"http://www.youtube.com/watch?v=MUqivvLi6Ws [accessed January 30, 2013].

37. YouTube. Oglaigh na hEireann Real Irish Republican Army News Report. Retrieved from HYPERLINK "http://www.youtube.com/watch?v=7zx-bafKRtA&feature=related"http://www.youtube.com/watch?v=7zx-bafKRtA&feature=related [accessed January 30, 2013].

38. 32CSM website. Retrieved from HYPERLINK "http://32csmscot.blogspot.co.uk/2011/06/leggat-claims-repudiated.html" \l "comment-form"http://32csmscot.blogspot.co.uk/2011/06/leggat-claims-repudiated.html#comment-form [accessed January 30, 2013].

39. HYPERLINK "http://www.youtube.com/watch?v=ur96ylrWphI"http://www.youtube.com/watch?v=ur96ylrWphI [accessed January 30, 2013].

40. The Royal Ulster Constabulary.

41. BBC News. (January 7, 2013). *Timeline of attacks in Northern Ireland political parties*. Retrieved from HYPERLINK "http://www.bbc.co.uk/news/uk-northern-ireland-20720406"http://www.bbc.co.uk/news/uk-northern-ireland-20720406 [accessed January 29, 2013].

42 BBC News. (December 11, 2012). *Police car petrol bombed near MP Naomi Long's office*. Retrieved from HYPERLINK "http://www.bbc.co.uk/news/uk-northern-ireland-20676315"http://www.bbc.co.uk/news/uk-northern-ireland-20676315 [accessed January 29, 2013].

43 Gaughan Stagg Cumann blog. Retrieved from HYPERLINK "http://gaughanstagg-cumann.blogspot.co.uk/?view=magazine" \l "!/"http://gaughanstaggcumann.blogspot.co.uk/?view=magazine#!/ [accessed January 30, 2013].

44. Gaughan Stagg Cumann blog. Retrieved from HYPERLINK "http://gaughanstagg-cumann.blogspot.co.uk/?view=magazine" \l "!/2012/12/32-county-sover-eignty-movement-new-year.html"http://gaughanstaggcumann.blogspot.co.uk/?view=magazine#!/2012/12/32-county-sovereignty-movement-new-year.html [accessed January 30, 2013].

45. Gaughan Stagg Cumann blog. Retrieved from HYPERLINK "http://gaughanstaggcumann.blogspot.co.uk/?view=magazine" \l "!/2012/12/wher-ever-there-is-conflict-women-must.html"http://gaughanstaggcumann.blogspot.co.uk/?view=magazine#!/2012/12/wherever-there-is-conflict-women-must.html [accessed January 30, 2013].

46. Gaughan Stagg Cumann blog. Retrieved from HYPERLINK "http://gaughanstagg-cumann.blogspot.co.uk/?view=magazine" \l "!/2012/11/ballad-of-alan-ryan.html"http://gaughanstaggcumann.blogspot.co.uk/?view=magazine#!/2012/11/ballad-of-alan-ryan.html [accessed January 30, 2013] and The Ballad of 43. Alan Ryan. Retrieved from HYPERLINK "http://www.youtube.com/watch?v=Bs-YkfXdtCo"http://www.youtube.com/watch?v=Bs-YkfXdtCo [accessed January 30, 2013].

47. James Larkin Republican Flute Band Blogspot. (January 11, 2011). Retrieved from HYPERLINK "http://jimlarkinrfb.blogspot.co.uk/"http://jimlarkinrfb.blogspot.co.uk/ [accessed January 30, 2013].

48. James Larkin Facebook page. Retrieved from HYPERLINK "http://www.face-book.com/people/James-Larkin-Rfb/100001306623263"http://www.facebook.com/people/James-Larkin-Rfb/100001306623263 [accessed January 30, 2013].

49. To support this hear the interview by Ireland's Ocean Radio with Paul Stewart of the 32CSM on Ryan and his funeral. (September 13, 2012). Retrieved from HYPERLINK "http://www.youtube.com/watch?v=FwZkvLuBk-g"http://www.youtube.com/watch?v=FwZkvLuBk-g [accessed January 30, 2013].

References

Adams, G. (1989, February 2). Presidential address to Sinn Fein's January 1989 Ard Fheis. *An Phoblacht/Republican News*, 2.

Adams, G. (1990). *Cage Eleven*. Dingle, Ireland: Brandon Book.

Adams, G. (1996). *Before the Dawn*. London: Heinemann.

Adams, G. (2003). *A Farther Shore: Ireland's Long Road to Peace*. New York: Random House.

Baker, C. (1998). Membership categorization and interview accounts. In David Silverman (Ed.), *Qualitative Research: Theory, Method and Practice*. London: Sage, pp. 130–143.

Bamford, B.W.C. (2005). The role and effectiveness of intelligence in Northern Ireland. *Intelligence and National Security, 20*(4), 581–607.

Bayens, G.J., and Roberson, C. (2011). *Criminal Justice Research Methods: Theory and Practice*. Boca Raton, FL: CRC Press.

BBC. (2010). *Real IRA admits to border killing.* Retrieved from http://news.bbc. co.uk/1/hi/northern_ireland/foyle_and_west/8535731.stm (accessed January 30, 2013).

BBC. (2012, October 30). *BBC spotlight: Irish Republicans and the drugs war.* Retrieved from http://www.youtube.com/watch?v=mVYcacfwook (accessed January 29, 2013).

Bunyan, T. (1976). *The History and Practice of the Political Police in Britain.* London: Friedman.

Carpenter, J.S., Levitt, M., and Jacobson, M. (2009). Confronting the ideology of radical extremism. *Journal of National Security Law & Policy, 3,* 301–327.

Coogan, T.P. (1995). *The Troubles: Ireland's Ordeal 1965–1956 and the Search for Peace.* London: Hutchinson.

DeBreadun, D. (2012, May 25). McGuiness outlines SF vision. *The Irish Times.*

Department of Work and Pensions. (2011). *Family Resources Survey.* Retrieved from http://www.research.dwp..gov.uk/asd/frs/ (accessed March 31, 2012).

English, R. (2009). *Terrorism: How to Respond.* Oxford, UK: Oxford University Press.

Europol. (2012). *EU Terrorism Situation and Trend Report TE-SAT 2012* Hague, Denmark: Europol.

Githens-Mazer, J. (2008). Causes of jihadi terrorism: Beyond paintballing and social exclusion. *Criminal Justice Matters, 73*(1), 26–28.

Harden, T. (2000). *Bandit Country: The IRA and South Armagh.* London: Hodder and Stoughton.

Hewitt, S. (2008). *The British War on Terror.* London: Continuum Books.

Horgan, J. (2009). *Walking Away from Terrorism.* London: Routledge.

Hutson, R., Long, T., and Page, M (2009). Pathways to violent radicalisation in the Middle East: A model for future studies of transnational jihad. *Rusi Journal, 154*(2), 18–26.

Irish Independent. (2012, September 15). The truth about Alan Ryan and his funeral. *Irish Independent.* Retrieved from http://www.independent.ie/national-news/ the-truth-about-alan-ryan-and-his-funeral-3229680.html (accessed January 30, 2013).

Kirby, A. (2007). London bombers as self-starters: A case study in indigenous radicalisation and the emergence of autonomous cliques. *Studies in Conflict and Terrorism, 30*(Winter), 415–428.

Liebling, A., and Stanko, B. (2001). Allegiance and ambivalence: Some Dilemmas in researching disorder and violence. *British Journal of Criminology, 41*(3), 421–430.

MacDonald, S. (2008, July 28). MI5 targets dissidents as Irish terror threat grows. *The Guardian.*

Mackay, J. (1996). *Michael Collins: A Life.* Edinburgh: Mainstream.

Martin, M. (2012). *Understanding Terrorism: Challenges, Perspectives, and Issues* (4th ed.). London: Sage.

McCann, E. (2012, January 18). The detention of IRA veteran Marian Price harks back to internment. *The Guardian.*

Moriarty, G. (2012, May 26). Now is the time to "forge new friendships." *The Irish Times.*

Mythen, G., and Walklate, S. (2006). Criminology and terrorism: Which thesis risk society or governmentality? *British Journal of Criminology, 46*(3), 379–398.

Nolan, P. (2012). *Northern Ireland Peace Monitoring Report.* Belfast: Community Relations Council.

O'Callaghan, S. (1998). *The Informer.* London: Transworld.

O'Connor, E. (2002). *James Larkin.* Cork, Ireland: Cork University Press.

OT Institute for Safety, Security and Crisis Management. (2008). *Radicalisation, Recruitment and the EU Counter-radicalisation Strategy.* Brussels: European Commission.

Punch, M. (2012). *State Violence, Collusion and the Troubles: Counter Insurgency, Government Deviance and Northern Ireland.* London: Pluto Press.

Rossington, B. (2012, January 28). Souse/IRA gang ran massive drug trade across the UK, Bebington boxer Brett Flounery trial told. *Liverpool Echo.* Retrieved from http://www.liverpoolecho.co.uk/liverpool-news/local-news/2012/01/28/scouse-ira-gang-ran-massive-drug-trade-across-the-uk-bebington-boxer-brett-flournoy-murder-trial-told-100252–30214775/ (accessed January 30, 2013).

Sageman, M. (2008). *Leaderless Jihad: Terror Networks in the Twenty-First Century.* Philadelphia: University of Philadelphia Press.

Seib, P. (2012). Public diplomacy versus terrorism. In D. Freedman and D. Kishan Thussu (Eds.), *Media and Terrorism.* London: Sage, pp. 63–76.

Silke, A. (2008). Holy warriors: Exploring the psychological processes of jihadi radicalisation. *European Journal of Criminology, 5*(1) 99–123.

Social Research Association (2003). *Social Research Association's Ethical Guidelines.* Retrieved from http://www.the-sra.org.uk (accessed January 11, 2012).

Staniforth, A. (2010). Blackstone's Counter-terrorism Handbook (2nd edition). Oxford: Oxford University Press.

Suttmoeller, M., Chermak, S., Freilich, J.D., and Fitzgerald, S. (2011). Radicalisation and risk assessment. In L.W. Kennedy and E.F. McGarrell (Eds.), *Crime and Terrorism Risk: Studies in Criminology and Criminal Justice.* London: Routledge, pp. 78–96.

Taylor, P. (1997). *Provos, the IRA and Sinn Fein.* London: Bloomsbury.

The Poverty Site. (2011). *Annual Survey of Hours and Earnings 2010.* Retrieved from http://www.poverty.org.uk (accessed March 31, 2012).

Tuman, J.S. (2010). *Communicating Terror: The Rhetorical Dimensions of Terrorism* (2nd ed.). London: Sage.

Valino, A., Buesa, M., and Baumert, T. (2010). The economics of terrorism: An overview of theory and applied studies. In M. Buesa and T. Baumert (Eds.), *The Economic Repercussions of Terrorism.* Oxford, UK: Oxford University Press, pp. 3–35.

Vaughan, B., and Kilcommins, S. (2008). *Terrorism, Rights and the Rule of Law.* Cullompton, UK: Willan.

Vertigans, S. (2011). *The Sociology of Terrorism: People, Places and Processes.* London: Routledge.

Whittaker, D. (2012). *The Terrorism Reader* (4th ed.). London: Routledge.

Policing International Terrorism
Options

3

AUSTIN T. TURK

Contents

Introduction

Before considering issues and options in policing terrorism, it must be recognized that terrorism is a social construction, not a clearly defined "object" out there somewhere (Turk, 2002). The word gives a political meaning to destructive acts that might as readily be seen as criminal or maniacal without political significance. It is the historical context of a particular struggle over power that is invoked when enemies use words such as oppressor and terrorist to characterize one another. To focus on terrorism requires deciding which struggles and which parties are of specific concern.

Political resistance to governmental authority is today increasingly likely to be called terrorism by officials and their supporters. Violent resistance is almost certain to be so termed, but nonviolent challenges may also be portrayed as merely tactical supplements to opposition violence ("the political wing" at work). A fairly new angle is for governments engaged in the suppression of any organized armed resistance to define their operations as counter-terrorism, part of the American-led "war" against terrorism. Local issues and insurgencies are thus rhetorically transformed into international ones, with opponents defined as participants in the global terrorist campaign against civilization itself. Not only does this imagery encourage the demonization of those opposing even the most brutal and exploitative governments, but also it promotes the notion that such governmental repression deserves international financial and other support.

The United States and its allies are indeed confronting a serious threat to wreak as much devastation as possible on the people, institutions, and material resources of the most economically developed and democratic countries. We should focus on that threat, specifically the Al Qaeda network and its supporters. We should not be led merely by claims of "fighting terrorism" to support diplomatically, financially, or militarily the military and intelligence operations of governments against their internal enemies. Neither should we accept the often self-serving and uncorroborated intelligence offerings from external sources as the basis for decisions on where and whom to attack. As the lapses of our own intelligence bureaucracies have demonstrated, even our own presumably objective self-defensive efforts to prevent and curtail terrorism against us do not always guarantee good intelligence or timely use of it. If in-house intelligence is not necessarily accurate or usable, there is an even greater potential for mistakes and disinformation in intelligence produced by other parties with their own interests.

Given that our focus is on Al Qaeda and its supporters, and that our own intelligence sources and analyses constitute the most trustworthy basis for operations against them, what are the key issues facing us, and what are our options?

The Limitations of Individualized Justice

As Wilkinson (1979) pointed out decades ago, liberal democracies are especially vulnerable to terrorism because of the openness that defines them and the legal institutions by which citizen freedom from tyranny is ensured. Written or unwritten, the constitutions of the democracies enshrine the principle that each individual has worth, with rights to "life, liberty, and the pursuit of happiness." Rights to speak freely, to accept or reject religious beliefs, to assemble peaceably, to change employment and residence, and a host of other expressions of independence are spelled out in the legal codes and judicial decisions of the democracies. When disputes over such rights arise, legal proceedings to resolve them define the issues in reference to the liabilities and immunities, powers, and duties of specific individuals or classes of individuals. Even when corporate entities are involved, they are treated as "legal persons" with equivalent rights. The legal system is oriented to individualized justice, seeking to adjust outcomes to the unique features of each party involved in each case. In principle, without probative grounds specified in law, no party can be subjected to targeting by investigative and enforcement agencies.

However, individualized justice has limited effectiveness when the security of citizens and their social institutions is threatened by criminal organizations and conspiratorial networks. Internally, legal adjustments have been made to deal with organized political crime (especially in time of war) and with the depredations of large-scale economic outlaws (organized crime, corporate villains). In the United States and other democracies, individual rights have many times been curtailed in the name of national security (Kittrie and Wedlock, 1998). The corpus of "white-collar crime" law has developed largely in response to the demonstrated shortcomings of individualized justice in controlling organizational deviance (Stone, 1991). When the regulatory emphasis of such laws has inhibited effective law enforcement, conspiracy law has been broadened to provide more leeway, the most notable example in recent times being the 1970 Racketeer Influenced and Corrupt Organizations (RICO) statute. Used successfully against both America's organized crime families and domestic extremist groups such as the Ku Klux Klan, the RICO statute has proven to be an inadequate tool for dealing with international terrorism (Smith, Damphousse, Jackson, Freedom, and Sellers, 2002). The basic issue in the war against international terrorism is how far individualized justice can be stretched without irretrievable loss of citizen rights.

There are three options: (a) to continue trying to apply the standards of individualized justice to operations against global enemy organizations, networks, and movements; (b) to treat the enemy as if it were a nation at war against us, which means operating according to the internationally recognized rules of war; or (c) to recognize the nature of the enemy as a special case requiring exceptional nonlegal and extralegal measures. Regarding the first option, it seems clear by now that the agents and supporters of Al Qaeda cannot be accorded the same rights as citizens of a democracy, not even adjustments created to deal with internal organized threats can be used effectively against such a global enemy network. As for the second option, despite widespread demands that detainees apprehended in Afghanistan and elsewhere be treated as prisoners of war, the need to interrogate them must have priority over conventions that assume the conflict is an instance of war between nations. The third option will be unacceptable to those in America and elsewhere for whom established legal norms have absolute value and priority. Nonetheless, we are indeed facing a different kind and severity of threat than ever before in human history. Of course, terrorism is not new, but the level of resources and the enormity of the destructive potential of Al Qaeda put it in a new class of terrorist threat. For the first time, a terrorist enemy has the capacity to acquire and use weapons of mass destruction.

To treat such an enemy as an ordinary criminal or a combatant in an internation war is to ignore at our peril the distinctiveness of global terrorism. The economically and politically advanced nations are threatened by an implacable enemy whose hatred for everything we are and value can be satisfied only by our destruction. This is not an enemy intent on material gain or political dominance; this foe is dedicated to our cultural extermination and is willing to kill all of us unless those of us who survive accept rule by a barbarous regime of alien and theologically primitive religious absolutists. The Al Qaeda terrorists see themselves as "holy warriors" engaged in a "cosmic war" against the satanic forces of modernism and secularism threatening true Islam (Juergensmeyer, 2000). Extraordinary measures are needed, both to stop the terrorists of today and to make sure they have no successors.

Stopping Terrorists and Uprooting Terrorism

Among the options for stopping international terrorists are monitoring, confiscation, extradition, extraction, assassination, and war. All have been tried under the constraints of domestic and international laws, with some success but so far without demonstrable progress toward the goal of ending the threat. What might be done if legal constraints were modified or ignored? What are the likely consequences?

Monitoring (surveillance) is limited by such requirements as having to obtain bureaucratic and judicial approvals that delimit who, what, when, and where surveillance may be undertaken. Such requirements can be modified to give responsible agencies "wartime" emergency powers to monitor anyone suspected of terrorist activities, including fund-raising and transmission of messages. Intelligence oversight committees would, as at present, be provided with confidential reports on surveillance targeting and the results of such monitoring. There would be sacrifice of privacy rights—which technological innovations are already undermining (Marx, 1988)—and of the right to challenge surveillance decisions and findings in court. And, there would be a risk of unjustifiable profiling, which could be minimized by agency and oversight committee reviews of the selection of targets and the fruits of profiling. If, for example, terrorists are found to be disproportionately of particular ethnic origins, then it would be entirely reasonable to target at least for initial screening people whose appearance, names, itineraries, or other characteristics suggest they have such origins.

Confiscation of bank funds, freezing of accounts, and other tactics depriving global terrorists of resources cannot be successful without the cooperation of foreign governments and economic institutions—and some of the major havens and pipelines have so far been off limits because of diplomatic and military considerations. Efforts to track financial and other logistical transactions should be maximized to deny resources to terrorists as far as possible. Although diplomatic and strategic military concerns have to be taken into account, it would also have to be recognized by those in control of the havens and pipelines that their immunity is not unlimited. The American government, in particular, may well have to deliver—secretly if not openly—demands, with appropriate and credible threats, that such havens and pipelines be eliminated with no subterfuge. Erstwhile friendly as well as unfriendly nations can no longer be allowed to play both sides in the global conflict.

Extradition is dependent on whether treaties exist and whether governments consider extraditing suspects to be in their own interest. Countries unfriendly to the democracies have often harbored suspected terrorists, sometimes delaying justice for years even in the rare instances when suspects are finally given up for trial—as when Libya eventually handed over the Lockerbie bombers. And, even friendly governments such as Canada have refused to extradite unless their courts are provided with detailed evidence supporting the request, evidence that is often sensitive concerning intelligence operations and sources. Given the long history of governmental reluctance to extradite political offenders (Ingraham, 1979), as well as strong opposition in many nations to extradite anyone who might be given a death sentence, it follows that extradition is an option of little use in stopping international terrorists.

The obvious alternative to extradition is extraction, capturing and bringing suspects back for investigation and trial. But, extraction is problematic in that many, within and outside the United States, consider it virtually synonymous with kidnapping even when official agents (much less bounty hunters) cooperating with local authorities make the arrest. Although the Federal Bureau of Investigation is now authorized to investigate cases anywhere in the world and to apprehend and bring back suspects, the legal status of agents is at best ambiguous in many countries. Nonetheless, unpublicized extraction is likely to be an effective tactic for bringing suspects to secure places where they can be interrogated and their fates decided. Targeting decisions for extraction would be made and reviewed as in monitoring.

Where there is already overwhelming evidence of guilt, assassination may be preferable to extraction. Despite legal prohibitions and general abhorrence of political murder, assassination has for centuries been at least tacitly accepted by governments and their enemies as an option. The option is most likely to be adopted when the opposition has proven to be especially and increasingly dangerous, when legal or logistical obstructions block or delay preemptive action in the face of imminent attack, when postattack survivors demand retaliation, and when specific key figures in the opposition can be identified. The conflict with Al Qaeda and supporters meets all these conditions. Apart from legal objections, there are significant risks of diplomatic crises when assassinations are carried out in foreign settings. If assassins are captured by local authorities, the crisis potential is even greater. Further, there is some risk of mistakes in the identification of targets, as occurred at Lillehamer, Norway, during the Israeli extermination campaign against those responsible for the Munich Olympics massacre (Jonas, 1984). To minimize the risks if the assassination option is used, the policy decision should be secret and plausibly deniable; each targeting decision and operation should be based on firm intelligence, and oversight should be limited by the strictest "need-to-know" criterion.

War is decisive insofar as a concentration of enemy forces and facilities can be targeted. As we have seen in Afghanistan, the military option is effective as long as the enemy is contained, but decreasingly so when combatants are able to scatter and find escape routes. Still, terrorists do have to meet at least in small groups for training and planning. Wherever group facilities are located, they should be targeted for destruction by special forces trained in assassination and demolition techniques (see Rivers, 1986, for detailed recommendations based on personal experience). Any war involves military casualties, mistakes, and collateral damage, but such negatives are far outweighed by the need to make sure that Al Qaeda can never again establish the kind of bases they had in Afghanistan, Sudan, and elsewhere. Much progress has been made toward optimal international cooperation to destroy the terrorist network, and among the democracies, commitment to that goal seems to be firm. However, because of internal weakness, fear, sympathy, or corruption, in many nations the potential exists for Al Qaeda and its supporters to regroup in new sites. Every effort should be made to persuade governments not to help the enemy either actively or passively, with appropriate blends of threatened punishments and promised rewards.

We should understand that Al Qaeda and cooperative organizations such as Hamas and Hezbollah have long been operating inside the United States as well as in scores of other countries (Emerson, 2002). It follows that the war against international terrorism includes any cells or individual agents operating in this country. They are exceptional enemies and must be treated as such. The civil liberties of American citizens cannot be accorded those whose intent is to destroy American society. Consequently, agents such as Jose Padilla should be treated as enemy combatants, on the predicate that they have forfeited the right to be treated as an ordinary citizen or conventional criminal. If a new category of offender must be created in law, then the government should move speedily to make clear that anyone joining the international terrorist movement will not enjoy the rights of due process available to others. All who join or directly assist international terrorists should be put on notice that they face indefinite detention, open-ended interrogation, and isolation from both external contacts and other prisoners.

The immediate goal of stopping terrorists has obvious priority, but the ultimately more important goal is to uproot terrorism. Ideologically and economically as well as militarily and diplomatically, the democracies must go on the offensive. This does not mean public relations campaigns that merely extol the virtues of "our way of life." Instead, it means seeking ways to promote alternatives to the archaic totalitarian beliefs that fuel terrorism.

Diplomatic initiatives have so far concentrated on stopping terrorists, with relatively little attention to uprooting terrorism. What is first needed is a concerted effort by the democracies to establish an international force ready to intervene wherever international terrorists congregate. Ideally, such a force will assist as necessary the local government's suppression of terrorist gatherings or bases. Where the local government is unwilling or unable to move effectively, the international force should be free unilaterally to attack the terrorists.

Second, the united democracies should create—through the United Nations as far as possible—an institutional framework for promoting democratic values. On the ideological front, the democracies would agree to facilitate such programs as educational exchanges, public discussions and debates, and media reviews of the historical disasters resulting from ideological fanaticism. Moderate and progressive social movements would be enlisted in the "democracy campaign" and given tangible support insofar as they demonstrated commitment to the nonviolent advancement of all their nations' people.

Without real economic development, no counterterrorism strategy will succeed. In the name of development, the International Monetary Fund and other agencies have long promoted "free market" capitalism as the solution to the growing divide between the rich and the wretched of the world. Exporters and the local compradors who profit with them have historically acceded to political rule by the most tyrannical elites, and the corruption and exploitation that sustain them, on the premise that business interests can be kept separate from political concerns (Herman, 1982). This is certainly no longer a defensible view. Ironically, the drive to televise the world for profit has provided the ideologists of terrorism with ammunition, images exaggerating the affluence of the advanced nations in callous disregard of the severely limited life chances of most people. Even scions of the elites, such as the Saudis who constituted the majority of the pilots and bombers of the September 11, 2001, attack, are reinforced in their hatred of democracy by firsthand observation of the superficial materialism, racism, and "arrogance of power" rampant in the upper circles of the United States and other democracies. Aid to developing countries will have to be a real investment in their development, not subject to control for profit by exporters or local elites. Investment in democratization, not in securing profitable markets, will have to be the priority concern in decisions on where and how capital will be allocated.

Obviously, there will be resistance to democratization. From within, liberal relativists can be expected to see aggressive support for democracy in undemocratic nations as illegally imposing value judgments, while geopolitical "realists" will likely object to such interference in other people's affairs as dangerous adventurism. From without, the elites who profit from maintaining archaic social institutions or merely exploitative systems will undoubtedly invoke international law to condemn such interference in their "domestic affairs." In either case, the answer is that there is a clear and present danger to the survival of civilization, which supersedes existing international understandings about the rights and immunities of states. As necessary, international law would have to be modified to recognize that harboring or sponsoring international terrorism against democracy constitutes a crime against humanity. Negotiation to terminate such conduct would be limited to an offer of assistance if the government in question pleaded either ignorance or inability to stop the threat. Attempting to prolong the negotiation would be considered an act of defiance, warranting whatever degree of intervention was deemed necessary to end the threat.

What has been said may strike many as extremist and provocative. Regardless of how it is received, the message is that the threat is horrendous and necessitates exceptional measures to deal with it. Few will argue that we must stop the terrorists who are already committed to our destruction, and most will probably agree that new procedural rules on the treatment of international terrorists will have to be instituted. A considerable outcry is to be anticipated in reaction to the call for an aggressive campaign to promote democracy, especially to the idea of military intervention by an international force wherever and for whatever reason local governments do not stamp out terrorist operations. But, most controversial is likely to be the idea that the cultural assumptions and social institutions of the democracies must themselves be reformed.

If the threat of international terrorism is to be ended, the democracies will have to demonstrate beyond question that they are transcending materialism and racism and are helping the peoples of the earth toward more hopeful futures. As long as gross inequities persist within the democracies, and between them and the rest of the world, there can be no end to terrorism. The roots of terrorism are the inequities that spark resentment among the disadvantaged and give credence to the accusations of those who blame the values and institutions of democracy for the failings of their own systems. We ourselves must show that democracy really works and promote it relentlessly against all who reject the premise that all people should have the right to life, liberty, and the peaceful pursuit of happiness.

The Long Struggle Ahead

It is clear that the struggle against international terrorism will not be soon or clearly ended. Even as we hunt down terrorists, we know that they are being replaced. Until the roots of terrorism are eliminated, there will be no safety. What will be far more difficult than stopping terrorists is uprooting terrorism because it will require changing our own societies as well as those of others. As our own history shows, democratization is a long, torturous process that works against great resistance and with great confusion. The war against terrorism will last as long we fall short of achieving the once-noble goal of "making the world safe for democracy." Because defending democracy cannot ultimately succeed unless there is real democracy to be defended, the long struggle to promote democracy has to be waged at home as well as abroad.

References

Emerson, Steven. (2002). *American Jihad: The Terrorists Living Among Us*. Free Press, New York.

Herman, Edward S. (1982). *The Real Terror Network: Terrorism in Fact and Propaganda*. South End Press, Boston.

Ingraham, Barton L. (1979). *Political Crime in Europe: A Comparative Study of France, Germany and England*. University of California Press, Berkeley.

Jonas, George. (1984). *Vengeance*. Lester & Orpen Dennys/Collins, New York.

Juergensmeyer, Mark. (2000). *Terror in the Mind of God: The Global Rise of Religious Violence*. University of California Press, Berkeley.

Kittrie, Nicholas N., and Wedlock, Eldon D., Jr. (Eds.). (1998). *The Tree of Liberty: A Documentary History of Rebellion and Political Crime in America* (Rev. ed.). Johns Hopkins University Press, Baltimore.

Marx, Gary T. (1988). *Undercover: Police Surveillance in America*. University of California Press, Berkeley.

Rivers, Gayle. (1986). *The War Against the Terrorists: How to Win It*. Stein & Day, New York.

Smith, Brent, Damphousse, Kelly R., Jackson, Freedom, and Sellers, Amy. (2002). The prosecution and punishment of international terrorists in federal courts: 1980–1998. *Criminology & Public Policy, 1*(3), 311–338.

Stone, Christopher D. (1991). *Where the Law Ends: The Social Control of Corporate Behavior*. Waveland Press, Prospect Heights, IL.

Turk, Austin T. (2002). *Terrorism. The Encyclopaedia of Crime and Justice* (Vol. 4, 2nd ed., pp. 1549–1556). Macmillan Reference USA, New York.

Wilkinson, Paul. (1979). *Terrorism and the Liberal State*. New York University Press, New York.

Toward a Common Profile of Religious Terrorism

Some Psychosocial Determinants of Christian and Islamic Terrorists

4

AYLA HAMMOND SCHBLEY

Contents

Introduction

This study contributes to the literature investigating the connections between factors leading terrorists to kill others and themselves in the name of deities. Specifically, by examining the psychosocial commonalities between representative Christian and Muslim terrorists with strong ethnoreligious identities,

this chapter offers a first step toward a common profile of this type of terrorist. It follows on previous research by Schbley (n.d.), extending his profile for
Islamists to contemporary Christian extremists. Schbley's work showed no
important differences between Islamist Shi'a terrorists and Islamists living
in Western Europe "when their self-reports of impulse-control, personality disorders, depression, propensity to violence, and self-immolation were
compared" (n.d.).[1] The central hypothesis of this chapter is that there should
be essentially no difference between these extreme believers and similarly
extreme Christian zealots.

Theoretical Foundations for Profiling Religious Terrorists

Profiling is an amalgamation of forensic psychology and psychodynamical[2]
orientation skills and cognizance of the detriments of psychosocial functioning. It is founded on researchers' abilities to compartmentalize behavioral
patterns when supplemented by viable psychodynamically oriented theoretical concepts to postulate connections between personal and environmental
characteristics and behavioral manifestations. Thus, psychological dynamics, personal characteristics, and behavioral patterns of Islamist terrorists are
constructed through the use of

1. Nomothetic and idiographic approaches;
2. Direct observation and interviews of victims of terrorism and terrorists
   already condemned and at large for their successful or failed terrorism;
3. Quantitative psychometrics;
4. Psychiatric nosology and direct engagement;
5. Case and document studies; and
6. Discriminant analytical statistics systematically collected and compartmentalized to empower the field with needed data.

Group profiling, like that of individuals, is also grounded in psychody-
namics theory as governed by the psychological determination of a human
behavior paradigm. Even so, it remains based on the precept that any behavior may be interpreted as the outcome of an interaction between personality
and circumstantial conditions. The transition from one person's profile into
that of a group or groups requires the employment of additional theoretical
models, such as the coercion and cultural transmission of deviance theories,
to explain the dynamics of inter- and intragroup behaviors.

The coercion theory and the cultural transmission of deviance theory
supplement the explanation power of the psychodynamic theory and illuminate the continuity and interconnectedness between an individual's psychodynamic behavior and those of groups (Hull, 1935; Richer, 1988). By

connecting the culting processes[3] to training and indoctrination on how to hate and inflict violence with impunity, these theories are viable to explain the behaviors of terror cells and organizations (McCord, 1995; Sellin, 1938). They explain not only how terror groups are able to maintain cohesion but also how terror groups sustain themselves across time, culture, and nations.

According to Sellin (1938) and more recently Patterson (in McCord, 1995), when a group adopts an ideology that is disapproved of by the dominant culture, the stage is set for criminal behavior. Sellin (1938) was also able to demonstrate that the more criminal the behavior is, the stronger group cohesion and allegiance is to the subculture than to the dominant culture or conventional society. Therefore, terror groups are expected and have been observed to have the strongest cohesion and allegiance possible for they are united by the most heinous of criminal acts—terrorism.

These situations of strong cohesion within groups of criminals are the consequences of operational conditions of specific personality traits (Baron & Kenny, 1986). Thus, cohesion within and among terror groups infers commonalities of psychosocial moderator–mediator variables that, once identified, can be compartmentalized into a profile. Hence, profiling Islamist terrorists is a process of translating subjective sectarian, biopsychosocial, and culture-specific attributes and experiences into objective and universal lists of symptoms that fit into codified primer profiles. Henceforth, the transmission of deviance theory explains not only the factors behind the expected and observed strong cohesion within terror groups and the reasons why these cohesions have and will unite terror groups across culture, time, and nations but also the existence of biopsychosocial universal commonalities within and among these groups that make profiling possible (Lester, Yang, & Lindsay, 2004; Mahrer, 1985; Schbley, 2003).

Inherent Legal, Conceptual, and Theoretical Limitations

This cross-cultural, cross-national, cross-sectarian comparative analysis of the profiles of Muslim and Christian terrorists is an attempt to identify common[4] personality and character disorders and dogmatic toxic ideologies[5] that are most effective in rendering individuals from various cultures and beliefs susceptible to self-immolation and the killing of unknown others.[6] Like other forms of categorization and classification, this profiling approach is geared to summarize information, define conceptual categories in ways that would give structure to research and communication among researchers, decipher character signals, and facilitate the explanation of terror events (Hoffman & McCormick, 2004). It shall not become a viable and court-admissible science until it satisfies *Daubert* and Federal Rules of Evidence.[7] This can only be satisfied with replication of studies, collection of psychiatric history and premorbid functioning data on studies' participants, and falsification of new precepts able to break the circularity embedded in the logic of profiling (Bell, 1976; Schbley, n.d.).

In addition, and despite the scientific rigors and replications these theoretical foundations of profiling have undergone in studies by Douglas and Olshaker (1998), Holmes (1998), Hull (1935), Schbley (2003), and Turvey (1999) (to name but a few), one of profiling's primary theoretical precepts remains problematic. This conceptual problem derives from the circularity within the theoretical bases of profiling.

In explanation, profiling research is designed to test hypotheses whose main aim is to confirm or disconfirm biopsychosocial dynamic theoretical propositions, which in turn provide the empirical basis for the testing of such hypotheses. This inherent circularity that is intrinsic to the logic of profiling, going from the findings to the theoretical proposition and from there to the network of theoretical assumptions, is "a serious problem" that limits the scientific rigor when testing such hypotheses (Brodbeck & Feigl, 1968, p. 17).

This circularity embedded in the logic of profiling, which can be attributed by sceptics to our societal technological determinism (Bell, 1976), limits not only the latter's theoretical generalizability but also its viability. This viability is also limited by the lack of psychiatric history and premorbid functioning data on most profiled terrorists and those who have self-reported propensity to violence. Therefore, primer profiles are not to be relied on to the exclusion of other alternatives. They are a means of last resort; therefore, their primary purpose must be limited to providing leads and refocusing investigations or resources only.

Henceforth, primer profiles must be viewed for what they are: educated guesses when time restraints are prohibitive. They are tools intended to empower law enforcement, decision and policy makers, and intelligence and counterterrorism experts with an effective yet limited approach to preempting crimes against humanity.

Probable Implications of Inherent Limitations

Before one considers the proposed outcomes of this study's observations and reviews, one must consider the various implications of the following three inherent limitations of this and any profile:

1. *Fundamental Attribution Errors*: Negative dispositional factors when performing causal or isomorphic attribution, or disconfirming communication and identity, moral exclusion, or relational dissimilarity, do cause attribution errors (Gudykunst, 1998).
2. *Outliers*: Outliers are cases outside the realm and the scope of any profile for they are the by-product of several intervening and

uncontrolled-for variables. Thus, the character and personality attributes of outliers would not superimpose a good fit to those isolated by this study's profile.[8]

3. *Abuse*: Although profiling is a tool designed to assist in decision making, reallocation of limited resources, and time management only, its programmatic abuse is the third inherent limitation because the human improvident propensity is to alleviate, avoid, or eliminate probable and even possible threats. Such human propensity to alleviate dissonance may be equated with a high probability for disparagement, derision, and discrimination against individuals or groups.

Field Applications

The Federal Bureau of Investigation (FBI) Behavioral Science Unit (BSU), based in their Training Division at Quantico, Virginia, is the world's leading center in the development, research, and provision of training programs on profiling. Even though profiling has yet to satisfy *Daubert* and Federal Rules of Evidence and become a court-admissible science,[9] the FBI's BSU deduces profiles because citizen's classifications are allowed if they are "narrowly tailored" to a "compelling governmental interest" and therefore they are "not prohibited by the Equal Protection Clause, Title VI, or §1981" when employed in public interest according to the Supreme Court's rulings in response to polemics in *Terry v. Ohio* (1968) and more recently *Grutter v. Bollinger* (2003).

   Backed by such edicts, forensic psychologists associated with the FBI's National Center for the Analysis of Violent Crime (NCAVC), a component of BSU, developed the *Crime Classification Manual* (Douglas, Burgess, Burgess, & Ressler, 1997) that describes the ideal criminal-profiling process. These processes are neither formulated nor implemented to promote a "cult of expertise and professionalism" (Said, 1993) but to produce a major work on the characteristics of violent offenders, as stated in the following definition of *offender profiling*:

> Offender profiling is a method of identifying the perpetrator of a crime based on an analysis of the nature of the offense and the manner in which it was committed. Various aspects of the criminal's personality makeup are determined from his or her choice of actions before, during, and after the crime. This information is combined with other pertinent details and physical evidence, and then compared with the characteristics of known personality types and mental abnormalities to develop a practical working description of the offender. (Douglas et al., 1997, p. 21)

Even though the FBI, law enforcement, and intelligence agencies world-wide employ profiling, its validity as a tool to identify prospective terrorists and predict the likelihood of their violence is based not only on the statistical significance of profiling (Douglas et al., 1997)[10] but also on its use by Islamist terror organizations for recruitment and to signal their characters (Hoffman & McCormick, 2004).

It is irrefutable that religious terror organizations have been employing profiling to solicit efficiently and effectively the right person to commit not only self-immolation but also the killing of unknowns in the name of God. In a program, *The Mind of a Suicide Bomber*,[11] Abul Nasser Issa, a Hamas bomb maker and recruiter, was interviewed in an Israeli prison. When asked, "How do you know who is qualified to become a shaheed. How do you convince one to blow himself up?" Issa responded:

> You will see it in his eyes. ... A shaheed[12] has to have the motivation to become a martyr, to have faith. It is an ideological, religious, and also patriotic motivation, because this kind of a job requires a strong will and persistence.'[13,14]

Thus, and just like this study's profile, the eyes as well as the motivations of prospective religious terrorists inform their recruiters of their propensity to terrorism and self-immolation.[15]

However, Hamas recruiters are not the only ones who employ profiling in the selection of prospective homicide/suicide bombers. Hezbullah organizations have selection committees staffed by psychologists who review each Istishhadee's[16] application prior to its approval and sanction.[17]

These uncontroverted observations were also made by Kramer (1996) when he stated, "We realize that while self-martyrs sacrificed themselves, they were also sacrificed by others. They were selected, prepared, and guided toward their self-martyrdom" (p. 235). Hence, if profiling is effective in empowering terror organizations with a tool to identify prospective religious terrorists and communicate such characteristics, then the rationale is that it must be effective in empowering antiterror organizations with a tool to receive such signals, reidentify such personality and character traits, and preempt their mayhem.

Ethnographic and Dogmatic Mandates when Profiling Religious Terrorists

Notwithstanding, familiarity with forensic psychology and psychiatry, political science, criminology and sociology, qualitative and quantitative research methodologies, and statistics is not sufficient to deduce a cross-cultural, cross-national profile of religious terrorists. What is of utmost importance is a working knowledge of the dogmatic canons and historical traditions of such sects and religious movements. In addition to the ability to tune out intentional misinformation, profilers must be proficient ethnographers to deduce proper comparative analyses. This in-depth knowledge is needed to weed out intentional misinformation or idiosyncratic misunderstandings.

Anthology of Observations

Toward Profiling Christian Religious Terrorism

The 950-plus homicide/suicide bombings committed against humanity in 14 countries by Islamic religious terrorists made profiling said terrorists simple.[18] However, such simplicity was denied this research when it endeavored to profile the psychosocial attributes of Christian religious terrorists.

Typology of Observations

Profiling Abortion Clinic Bombers

The task of profiling Christian religious terrorists was begun by interviewing abortion clinic protestors in Wichita, Kansas. However, after 9 years of observations and over 250 interviews, I found that the dominant majority of abortion clinic protestors in Wichita, Kansas, were Catholics over the retirement age. The overwhelming majority were passive resisters who opted to fill their postretirement free time by expressing their religious beliefs and freedom of speech by standing outside a known abortionist church or clinic with a sign or a banner.

Nonetheless, since 2000 some American, Australian, and Canadian abortion clinics and staff have endured several bombings, shootings, and murders. So far, nine abortion clinic staff and obstetricians have been killed. All nine killings have been attributed to males between the ages of 21 and 43. The following are some examples: (a) John Slavi III, who was convicted on two counts of first-degree murder in Illinois; (b) Peter James Knight, who was convicted of the killing of an obstetrician in Melbourne, Australia; (c) Eric Robert Rudolph, who has been convicted for three bombings (including that in 1996 at the Atlanta, Georgia, downtown Olympic Park), the murder of a police officer and an abortion clinic staff member, and the wounding of 147 additional symbolic victims; and (d) James Kopp, who has been convicted for the murder of Dr. Barnett Slepian, has been charged in the nonfatal shooting of an abortion doctor in Canada, and is a suspect in three other shootings of abortion providers.

Although all the attacks on obstetricians and abortion clinics are acts of terrorism because they are violent assaults against symbolic victims (Schbley,

2003) and have been legally identified as such in court documents,[19] they were performed by individuals without a cell or organizational structure. Even though the manifesto of an organization called Army of God has been found buried in the backyard of a woman charged in the nonfatal shooting of an abortion doctor in Wichita, Kansas, none of the convicted felons has claimed organizational affiliations, cell membership, or terror networking.[20]

Notwithstanding that these acts of religious terrorism are deprived of formal or informal organizational structures, their perpetrators do share common psychosocial commonalties with terrorists who are organized and structured. In the court files of the *People State of New York v. James Kopp* (2003), a 1-day bench proceeding, James Kopp (nicknamed Atomic Dog) pleaded to and was found guilty of second-degree murder for the fatal shooting of Dr. Barnett Slepian.[21] Bruce A. Barket, Kopp's attorney, introduced several medical reports diagnosing his client as suffering from acute clinical depression aggravated by dogma-induced "episodic psychoses" that forced his client to kill out of "depraved indifference to human life." This defense, also unsuccessful, has been presented in all the prior cases and therefore permits the stipulation that abortion clinic bombers do share most of the psychosocial pathologies that have been identified by this study as moderator–mediator variables in Muslim terrorism. This insanity defense has also been employed in justifying the unjustifiable hate and killings by Buford O'Neal Furrow, Walter Eliyah Thody, and others who are members of the Phineas Priesthood (PP).[22]

Although these defense claims of personality and character disorders were supported by numerous defense and court-appointed psychologists' and psychiatrists' reports, this study's attempt to confirm such claims instigated its repetitive requests of James Kopp, Buford Furrow, Walter Thody, John Slavi III, Peter Knight, Eric Rudolph, and several other abortion clinic protestors in Wichita, Kansas, to take the Minnesota Multiphasic Personality Inventory (MMPI 543 item),[23] the Global Personality Inventory (GPI 300 item),[24] and the CES-D (Center for Epidemiological Studies–Depression Scale) 24-item scale (Radloff, 1977) tests to assess the validity of their claims. Most have refused due to pending appeals, and a few have requested excessive fees that were way beyond the limited budget of this research.

Therefore, in its final analysis and conclusion this study incorporates the psychological profiles of James Kopp, Buford Furrow, Walter Thody, John Slavi III, Peter Knight, and Eric Rudolph as delineated by court-appointed psychologists. However, this is not to be considered a setback in this search for a common profile for almost all contemporary Christian terrorism, spanning the spectrum of affiliations from the IRA to the PP, may be labeled as racism or political terrorism[25] committed by a group with a strong ethnoreligious identity because their goals are not to bear witness against dogmatic antagonism or despotism but to consciously and forcibly redress a policy or political grievance.[26]

All contemporary Christian terrorism may not be labeled as organized religious terrorism except for the following group of monks, who were well organized and funded to terrorize due to perceived canonic antagonism; therefore, this organization merits its placement among other infamous religious terror organizations, such as Hezbullah, Islamic Brotherhood, or Islamic Jihad. This Christian terror organization is the Order of Maronite Monks.

Backgrounds of Contemporary Christian Terrorism

The search for the only true contemporary Christian terror organization that is unconscious of the maliciousness embedded in its acts and was formed to protect against a perceived threat to religious ideology unfortunately took this research back to Lebanon. Thus, in addition to its label as the birthplace of civilization,[27] Lebanon permitted not only the formation of an Islamist core terror organization—Hezbullah[28]—but also the formation of another organization with actions that are equally heinous: the Order of Maronite Monks. This Christian terror organization was modeled after the seventh-century Tautomic Crusaders, was staffed by Maronite monks, and was created for the sole purpose of preemptive terror activities.

Who Are the Maronites? The Maronites are an indigenous Lebanese Christian Rite and one of 22 rites within the Catholic Church. They originated as an ecclesiastical grouping of Catholic Christians, who assembled around the hermit monk, Maron, in Homs, Syria, in the late fourth century. By 1850, because of persecution from other Antiochian and Greek Orthodox Christians, Druze, and Muslims, they withdrew into the mountainous land of Lebanon, where they are its most dominant and deprived inhabitants.

Who Are the Order of Maronite Monks? The Maronite Monastic Order, the owners of a sizable portion of Lebanon's mountainous land, has sought to safeguard the rights of Christians during Lebanon's uncivil war by providing financial and political support to its militia (the Lebanese Forces) and by commissioning the formation of the Order of Maronite Monks. This Order of Maronite Monks consisted of 200 well-armed and trained priests who were housed in four monasteries and four minor seminaries.

Thus, this Christian terror organization, unconscious of the malice embedded in its acts, was created by two Maronite monks, Father Charbel Oassis and Father Bulus Na'aman. To create this terror organization in the name of God, both monks used a personality profile to solicit and recruit 200 Maronite monks. Religious terrorism profiles were reemployed to reselect 100 of these monks for a special assignment.

Around August 1982, Father Bulus Na'aman, then the new head of the order, used psychological profiling techniques to identify and recruit 100

monks for the task of exterminating Palestinians in two Beirut refugee
camps, Sabra and Shatila.[29] Around 8 p.m. on September 16, 1982, the 100
monks from the Order of Maronite Monks, supported by 50 of the Lebanese
Forces under the command of Elie Hobeika, entered the camps and executed
most men, women, and children.[30]

The zeal of this short-lived[31] Christian Order of Maronite Monks was
not limited to the provision of moral and manpower support to Lebanese
Christian forces combating Muslim encroachments and exterminating
future threats but also included the manufacture,[32] sale, and distribution of
heroin. On May 7, 1985, Gabriel Rizk, one of the 100 monks who participated
in the Sabra and Shatila massacres, was arrested with 4 kilos of heroin in
Austin, Texas.[33] His participation in the Sabra and Shatila massacres and his
role as a Maronite monk and as a member of the Order of Maronite Monks
was attested to by a Drug Enforcement Administration undercover agent,
whose investigation led to the arrest and conviction of Rizk. This information and the process of his selection for the terror operation were reiterated
during this study's interview.

Profiling a Maronite Terrorist   On their 13th birthday, Gabriel Rizk and
another member of the Order of Maronite Monks[34] were bequeathed[35] by
their families to the Monastery of Mar Elyshaa in Bsharry, Lebanon.[36] Rizk's
family believed that he was possessed by the devil for torturing animals.[37]
After 5 years of seminary training at Ayn Saadah, *Rahib* (Monk) Rizk was
assigned by his monsigneur to the Order of Maronite Monks.[38] Around
August 1982, he was summoned to the presence of Father Bulus Na'aman,
who had just been appointed to the leadership of the order. Once there, he
was asked to join a select group within the order that had been given the task
of executing the order's "most important mission." He was informed that his
psychological profile indicated that he possessed needed special attributes
and tendencies.

This study's interview of Rizk began by administering to him the MMPI
543-item,[39] the GPI 300-item,[40] and the CES-D 24-item scales (Radloff, 1977).
Collectively, these scales permitted Rizk to self-report symptoms of several
mental disorders, such as depressive, acute stress and other anxiety, intermittent explosive and other impulse control, and paranoid and antisocial personality disorders. When asked in English, "Did you kill any child, and if so,
how would your Christian faith justify this killing?" he responded by saying:

> We had all the weapons we needed. Most of us entered the camps with hatch-
> ets and knifes. ... We [sic] done so, to give them the opportunity to fight us off
> ... or kill us. I did want to die, because, I would have been killed for my God
> and my people ... and yes, I killed some children ... maybe 30 or 40 ... because
> they are the future killers of my people, worshipers of my God. By God's will I

entered the camps ... to deliver my church from their wrath. It was God's will
that we did it.[41]

When asked, "How could you justify your actions when the Bible
instructs you to turn your right cheek if you were hit on your left cheek?" His
response was given with an unyielding conviction:

I am my brother's keeper. ... I have been instructed by God to guard over my
church. I did not murder any one. I just prohibited them from murdering my
faith. ... It is God's will, and for which I am grateful. ... God will protect the
innocent and will glorify them in heavens. ... So, if I, a servant of God, made
a mistake and murdered in his name, God would have not permitted me and
would have saved the innocent from my unintentional mistake.[42]

This perceived divine message that justified the unconscious killing of children[43] was reconfirmed in Hatem's (1999) account of his experiences as
the bodyguard of the commander of the Lebanese Forces, Elie Hobeika.[44]
Although this by-product of hate and fear created by Lebanon's 15-year civil
war was short-lived, it left its mark on humanity and social consciousness.

What warrants equal notice and inference is the fact that most of Rizk's
self-reported symptoms and attributes of depressive, acute stress and anxiety, intermittent explosive and impulse control, and paranoid and antisocial
personality disorders are identical to those assessed by the defense and court-
appointed psychologists for James Kopp, Buford Furrow, Walter Thody, John
Slavi III, Peter Knight, and Eric Rudolph.

Discussion

Even though this study's one interview and seven[45] profiles of Christian religious terrorists would not in the best of circumstances permit this study to
deduce generalizable observations, it does confirm that this research is on
the right track toward a common profile. From the analysis of Gabriel Rizk's
profile and those provided by court-appointed psychologists and psychiatrists in their evaluation of abortion clinic and PP killers, we may confidently
conclude that, just like Muslim terrorists, Christians suffering from one or
more mental disorders, including, but not limited to, oppositional defiant,
impulse control, antisocial, and other personality disorders, when aggravated
by dogma-induced critical/psychotic depression, may transition from zealots
to self-immolating terrorists. Thus, psychosocial moderator–mediator variables may be causal factors in the transition of Christians and Muslims from
zealots to self-immolating terrorists (see the profile in the "Appendix" to this
chapter).

Not only are the religiosity levels of the PP members and Maronite monks self-evident, but also the level of their commitment and determination may be inferred from their willingness to sacrifice their lives and those of others. Just like their Islamic counterparts, court psychiatrists, psychometric measures, and I found these Christian terrorists to be equally unconscious of the malice embedded in their acts of terror.

What is equally striking is the adoption of antithetical ideology to Christianity by Christian zealots. Just like their Muslim counterparts, Maronite monks' gestalt from reason was made possible by hate and indoctrination—in monasteries—to believe that (a) their death and the death of their symbolic victims would only be temporal, (b) they were collectively chosen by God to be his tool, (c) they were prophets of his message, and (d) for their sacrifice they would all (victim and terrorists alike) be eternally alive in the heavens.

These Christian zealots' adoption of an ideology that is antithetical to their fundamental dogmatic and canonic Christian beliefs can be explained by the cultural transmission of deviance theory. Again, this theory postulates that fear, not reason, creates hate and promulgates violence. Thus, religious terrorism may not be as much about the toxic ideology (e.g., Islamist Jihadist) for the protection or defense of religious canons as it is about the grouping of individuals with psychosocial anomalies, disorders, and anomies[46] in an environment of hate and fear. It may be this nurturing of hate in such individuals, that is, the culting process, that is leading to the adoption of such ideology that is disapproved by the dominant culture or religious canons and that in turn sets the stage for criminal behavior and terrorism (Sellin, 1938).

Future research may explore the latter possibility and that toxic ideologies, such as Islamic Jihad, once held as an indicator of commitment and faith,[47] may attract individuals with certain psychosocial pathologies or suicidal tendencies and justify their self-immolation. Religious faith is built on martyrs' corpses, whose spilled blood nurtures faith's growth and ossifies the infrastructures of future commitments and devotion to its dogma and canons.

These proposed explanations and future research topics are intended to stimulate discussions and address a lacuna. The outcomes of this study permit me to infer that Christian and Muslim religious terrorists may be afflicted with common psychosocial commonalities (see "Appendix"). Therefore, I call on future research to test the latter's applicability to terrorists with these and other ethnoreligious identities and to confirm or disconfirm the viability of the proposed 30 moderator–mediator variables, for once a common profile is identified, measures may be implemented to preempt religious terrorists' impediments to our global security and peace.

Notes

1. Schbley's (n.d.) cross-cultural, cross-national, cross-sectarian comparative analysis of 722 Islamist citizens of 30 countries now residents of 8 European countries deduced that Islamist Jihadist toxic and deterministic ideology that has infected Shi'a Hezbullah Islamist terrorists has equally infected Muslims of various sects.

2. *Psychodynamic* means active mind. Simply put, when a person is enduring a mental struggle, readjustment and understanding are sought by probing his or her unconscious mind through the use of psychoanalytic theories as developed by Freud (iceberg model), Jung, Adler, Erikson, Klein, Lacan, and others.

3. Terror organizations are intentionally unknowable to outsiders. Their understanding requires indoctrination via a culting process. It is a four-stage process: (a) Seduction: In this phase, the concentration is on seducing rather than openly persuading prospective recruits. (b) Disorientation: A recruit undergoes an overstimulation or understimulation campaign for the purpose of decreasing reasoning abilities and increasing suggestibility. (c) Snapping: This is identified by sudden personality change and shift in belief system. (d) Maintenance: This is the process of maintaining the new belief system (Hammer & Van Zandt, 1997).

4. Although individuals possess unique self-concept contents, the overall structure of a self-concept (i.e., self-immolation in the name of a deity) may be common among many individuals (Gordon, 1968, p. 457).

5. This chapter infers the probability that toxic ideology (Islamic Jihad) may force those who have adopted it to self-sacrifice and sacrifice others for it to propagate, in comparison to the genetic determinism process by which the lancet fluke reproduces and propagates (Dennett, 2003).

   The genetic determinism of this parasite, which is called *Dicrocoelium dendriticum*, forces it to self-sacrifice and sacrifices others to propagate. In explanation, the genetic determinism of the lancet fluke requires the first intermediate host (usually a snail) to consume its first generation, which will asexually divide inside the snail and excrete the fluke's second generation with certain pheromones that attract ants. Once consumed by an ant, the lancet's second generation afflicts its host's nervous system and causes it to change its behavior, and, atypically, climb up plant stems to be eaten by grazing mammals, where its third generation is nurtured into adult stage and is able to sexually reproduce and propagate. Therefore, to reproduce and promulgate, the lancet fluke's genetic determinism forces it to self-sacrifice in two generations so that it can reproduce and propagate in the third generation.

6. However, this process of cross-sectarian profiling would require the mixing of multidisciplinary approaches, the detailed explanation of which is given in the work of Schbley (n.d.).

7. The *Daubert* rule of evidence identifies the two touchstones for court-admissibility, which are reliability and relevancy and which can be achieved through hypothesis testing and peer reviews [*Daubert v. Merrell Dow Pharmaceuticals, Inc.*, 509 U.S. 579, 113 S.Ct. 2786, 125 L.Ed.2d 469 (1993)]. The Federal Rules of Evidence provide that "[i]f scientific, technical, or other specialized knowledge will assist the truer of fact to understand the evidence or to determine a fact in issue, a witness qualified as an expert by knowledge, skill, experience, training, or education, may testify thereto in the form of an opinion or otherwise" [*United*

States v. Harvard, 260 F. 3d 597, 601 (7th Cir. 2001) (Fed. R. Evid. 702); retrieved May 22, 2004, from http://www.forensic-evidence.com/site/ID/ID_palmprint. html).

8. During an interview at one of Israel's top-security prisons, Hassan Salameh and Mohammed Abou-Wardy, two of Hamas's suicide bomber cell leaders, confessed to a *60 Minutes* reporter on videotape that they gave several of their first cousins 30 minutes to accept or decline suicide missions. In one such mission, Majdy Abou-Wardy, while a student at a vocational school in the occupied territories, was given 30 minutes by his cousin Mohammed Abou-Wardy to decide and accept a suicide bombing. He accepted, and his homicide bombing mission killed 17 Israeli teens in a shopping mall in the name of Allah. This episode of American Broadcast Journal's *60 Minutes* was produced by Michael Gashon and Bill Curtis as a *48 Hours* investigation.

9. See Note 7.

10. The Israeli airline El Al Security Services attributes the fact that they have not had any hijacking since 1968, in spite of Israel's ongoing conflict with Palestinians, Arabs, and Islamists worldwide, primarily because since then they have relentlessly implemented profiling in singling prospective terrorists (e.g., Islamists, Arabs, and Palestinians) for extensive search procedures.

11. It was aired on MSNBC on April 26, 2003, and was hosted by John Seigenthaler. However, Dan Setton originally produced it under the title *Shaheed: The Making of a Suicide Bomber*.

12. (a) Hamas homicide/suicide Islamic terrorists identify themselves as shaheed (i.e., martyr). They are called Istishhadi, which means "self-chosen martyrdom in the name of Allah and the Islamic cause" (Juergensmeyer, 2000, p. 72). They refuse to acknowledge that self-immolation perpetrated by a suicide bomber is suicide. Instead, they believe that self-immolation is an act of martyrdom or Istishhad—death during Jihad. "Do not believe that those who were killed in the path of Allah—during Jihad—are dead, but alive with God" (the Quran, Sourat Repentance, 10, 3). Thus, a suicide bomber is called an Istishhadi and is believed by Muslims to be eternally alive in the Janna—heavens. (b) Hezbullah members (Shi'a Muslim religious terrorists) also identify themselves as Istishhadeen.

13. See Note 8.

14. Although the producer of this program did provide English translations to the interviewee's Arabic statements, I made a few corrections to properly capture the meaning and contents of the interviewee's message.

15. Appleby (2000) describes a Hamas recruitment of a teen for a suicide bombing as follows: "In a courtyard set back from a side street in Israeli-occupied Gaza City, the teenager stands at the center of a circle of Palestinian Arab youths who are chanting in unison, 'Islam called, the Qu'rab called: Who will answer the call?' Without hesitation the boy/man who is the hero of this particular ritualized drama answers, 'Here am I! At your service!' With the camera rolling and his fellow Hamas recruits chanting 'Kill me, rend me, drown me in your blood'—a line from a song popular among the members of the radical Palestinian Muslim movement—the new Lion of Hamas lowers himself into a

makeshift coffin as he recites verses from the Qu'ran. ... He will join the ranks of the holy martyrs. ... With the first drop of his blood, the martyr is said to go straight to Paradise, his past sins wiped clean from the book of his life" (p. 25).

16. Lebanon, ancient Phoenicia, is one cradle of documented civilization. It is one of the first nations to be known to have communicated by a language, established a state and trading practices, set out to sea, and sowed the seeds of civilization throughout the Mediterranean region.

17. A prospective Hezbullah homicide/suicide bomber must apply to commit self-immolation. Secret committees made up of clerics, intelligence and security officers, and psychologists or psychiatrists review each application, solicit proper permissions from the prospective martyr's family, and endorse or disapprove the operation. Once an operation is approved, funds for the Istishadee's family are disbursed and held in trust by a martyrs' association. In Lebanon, the name of the Hezbullah's Martyr's Association trustee is Kassem Aleyk.

18. Data from the web pages of the National Memorial Institute for the Prevention of Terrorism's (MIPT's) comprehensive databank of global terrorist incidents and organizations—Terrorism Knowledge Base; from the International Policy Institute for Counter-Terrorism (ICT); and from the National Security Studies Center at the University of Haifa (Weinberg, Pedahzur, & Canetti-Nisim, 2003). Retrieved February 11, 2003, from http://www.tkb.org/Home.jsp and http://www.ict.org.il

19. "This amounted to an assassination for religious reasons," said Joseph J. Marusak, the deputy district attorney in Erie County, New York, who prosecuted James Kopp for the murder of Dr. Barnett A. Slepian, a Buffalo obstetrician. "That's terrorism" (*New York Times*, Metropolitan Desk, March 12, 2003, p. 1).

20. The importance of organizational structures to the identification and manufacturing of terrorists was stressed during a panel discussion chaired by Professor Merari and reported by the *Washington Post*. Dr. Merari (a psychologist at Tel Aviv University in Israel who has puzzled over the psychological makeup of the September 11 hijackers and has spent years studying suicide attacks around the world) stated, "Suicide candidates, when they are chosen by an organization, enter into one end of a production process and in the other end they come out as complete, ready suicides" (*Washington Post*, 2001). From Peer pressure spurs terrorists, psychologists say: Attackers unlike usual suicide bombers, October, 1. Retrieved January 2, 2002, from http://www.psychminded.co.uk/news/news2001/1001/10terror.htm

21. A bullet that pierced the doctor's kitchen window as he returned home with his wife and four sons from a synagogue was fired from a Russian assault rifle of the type employed by terrorists worldwide.

22. Similar beliefs (Christian identity) were shared by the short-lived group, the Covenant, Sword, and Arm of the Lord (CSAL) in northwestern Arkansas. This group also used a similar insanity defense in their trial.

23. MMPI was the only personality self-report inventory used. Cattell, Meyers-Briggs, and Beck's Inventories were not employed. MMPI was first developed in 1943. Its current version, the MMPI-2, published in 1989 and composed of 16 scales, was used to assess Rizk's psychopathy and propensity to violence. MMPI-2 scales most relevant to this study are Psychopathic deviate (Pd), which measured Rizk's antisocial tendencies, impulsiveness, authority conflicts, and shallow attachments; the F-scale, which assessed the extent of his psychopathology; Schizophrenia (Sc), which measured his propensity to bizarre thinking;

and the Over-Controlled Hostility (Oh) scale and Hypomania (Ma) scale were useful in confirming prior and predicting future propensity for uncommonly violent acts and propensity for delinquency.

24. GPI is ideal for practitioners and researchers doing cross-cultural work by transporting personality inventories developed in one country to another country of interest. It was developed with cross-cultural input from psychologists from 11 countries and 10 languages, including Arabic (Schmit, Kihm, & Robie, 2000).

25. Political terrorism may be distinguished from religious terrorism for the latter is perpetrated to communicate a perceived divine message by zealots who are unconscious of the maliciousness of their terrorism.

26. Although many terror and ethnic-cleansing operations were carried out by organizations with Christian ethnoreligious identities in Albania, Kosovo, Macedonia, and Serbia, on April 2, 2004, the 27 members of Foreign Ministers of the NATO–Russia Council (NRC, comprised of NATO representatives and ministers from Russia, Bulgaria, Estonia, Latvia, Lithuania, Romania, Slovenia, and Slovakia, who met in Brussels) labeled said activities as state sponsored and relieved over 450 paramilitants from their individual culpabilities. The authority of the NRC was bestowed by U.N. Security Council Resolution 1244, under which KFOR (the Kosovo Force—a NATO-led peacekeeping force) and UNMIK (the United Nations Interim Administration Mission in Kosovo) presently occupy Kosovo. Retrieved May 10, 2004, from http://belgrade.usembassy. gov/current/040406b.html, http://www.usoffice-pristina.rpo.at/galls/photos4.htm, and http://emperors-clothes.com/articles/jared/nocrime.htm

27. See Note 16.

28. Hezbullah is one of two Islamist core terror organizations synergizing the ongoing unification of all Islamist terror organizations into a Netwar of International Islamization Terrorism (IIT). The second core organization that is equally toxic to world peace is the Islamic Brotherhood. This latter organization is the umbrella and birth mother to Al Qaeda and most other Islamist terror organizations worldwide (Schbley, 2004). As for IIT, it is a concept coined by Schbley (2003) to describe an ongoing unification phenomenon that will dwarf Commintern in scope, dimension, population, polarization capabilities, willingness to wage war and die, threat to international and human security, and U.S. hegemony. From Chechnya, Uzbekistan, Tajikistan, Afghanistan, Pakistan, Iran, Iraq, Turkey, on to Morocco, 45 nations that are Islamic, nuclear, and volatile are being unified under the banner of Islam and as an Islamic theocracy that amasses twice the population and land mass as the former Soviet Union, with socioeconomic and political ideology (Islamist Jihadist) that by the most conservative of estimates transcends in intensity, commitment, determination, and willingness to wage war, those accorded to the Soviet Union and NATO combined.

29. According to two sources: (1) this study's interviewee, Gabriel Rizk; and (2) Hatem (1999).

30. According to the International Red Cross, over 2,750 Muslim Palestinians were killed.

31. According to Gabriel Rizk, Pope John Paul II ordered the immediate disband-ment of the order shortly after the massacres in Sabra and Shatila became public.

32. At Rizk's trial, the assistant U.S. Attorney, Carl Pierce, commented that "The Order of Maronite Monks has taken control of a pharmaceutical manufactur-ing company in Ayn Saadah ... and are employing French chemists to produce pharmaceutical quality heroin ... and the confiscated 4 kilos of heroin are the purest, most concentrated, most potent form ever smuggled into the United states" (*U.S. v. Gabriel Antone Rizk*, 1985).

33. Rizk was released in 2000 after serving a term of 15 years in a federal penitentiary and was deported back to Lebanon. Rizk is presently a resident in Amsterdam, Holland, where I was able to secure an interview on December 29, 2002.

34. Michelle Khoury, another monk from the Order of Maronite Monks, was also indicted for trafficking narcotics in New York City. However, Khoury jumped bail before his trial date. Although an interview was scheduled with him in Rome, Italy, to be conducted on December 23, 2002, he opted to cancel due to unexplained reasons. The familial, friendship, and fellowship ties between Khoury and Rizk and their coconspiracy in narcoterrorism affirm the third and fourth traits of this study's proposed psychosocial profile.

35. Poor Lebanese Meronite families, unable to support their monasteries with financial tithing or in-kind donations, traditionally bequeathed one of their children as a payment in lieu of their financial obligation to the monastery. This bequeathal of one child guaranteed the poor Maronites divine protection for their remaining children.

36. Rizk's age, gender, social, and economic status conform to the proposed Muslim religious terrorists' traits identified in this study's profile by numbers 4, 12–15, and 19.

37. There is only one overlapping and primary behavioral criterion that is com-mon to diagnoses with sociopathy, psychopathy, dyssocial personality disorder, and antisocial personality disorder: the cruelty to animals criterion (Douglas, Ressler, Burgess, & Hartman, 1986; Pinizzotto, 1984). "Of the 365 serial killers thus far studied, ... almost all have a documented history of cruelty to animals" (Fox & Levin, 1994, p. 71). Hence, Rizk's history of cruelty to animals affirms this study's proposed psychosocial profile's 28th trait.

38. Rizk's status as a monk implies his strong religious identity and training in reli-giolegal and theological matters and conforms to this study's proposed 2nd, 17th, and 27th traits.

39. See Note 21.

40. See Note 22.

41. These statements affirm the compatibility of several of Rizk's psychosocial pro-pensities and attributes to the Muslim terrorists' traits identified in this study's proposed profile by numbers 9, 10, 23, 24, and 26.

42. These statements also affirm the conformity of Rizk's psychosocial attributes of the following traits identified by numbers 11, 16, 18, 20–23, 29, and 30.

43. This perceived divine message is common among Muslim terrorists and affirms the probable universality of this study's proposed psychosocial profile's first attribute.

44. Hobeika was recently assassinated in a car bomb in a suburb of Beirut, Lebanon.

45. Rizk's profile was deduced by this study, and the other six were assessed by defense and court-appointed psychologists.

46. "When the ends of action become contradictory, inaccessible or insignificant, a condition of anomie arises, characterized by critical depression, a general loss of orientation, and accompanied by feelings of emptiness and apathy" (Powell, 1958, p. 132).
47. See Note 31.

Appendix: Profile of Islamist Terrorists

The following profile is proposed in an effort to explain and deduce a theoretical model of the development and evolution of religious terrorism (Schbley, n.d.):

1. Religious terrorism is a method of forcefully communicating a perceived divine message/command.
2. Religious terrorism is performed by elements with strong religious identity.
3. Most religious terrorist cells are made up of four to eight members who are interconnected through the cells' stem elements only.
4. A religious terrorist is recruited by and from the concentric circles of the family, friendship, or fellowship of its stem element who is the first among equals.
5. In most cases, cell members themselves choose the symbolic target for their terrorism to maintain cell security and operational integrity. The stem element secures operational provisions, funds, and technical and intelligence support.
6. Each cell member is constantly under other cell members' observation or control. The culting process of religious terrorism restricts or discourages the unchaperoned contact of cell elements with outsiders to sustain their indoctrination and maintain their commitment.
7. Once a cell member commits self-immolation, most other members will commit the same act.
8. Most religious terrorists choose to commit self-immolation around religiously significant anniversaries.
9. Religious terrorism is not restricted to the influence of governmental decision making.
10. Most religious terrorists prefer "theocratic to democratic practices" (Appleby, 2000).
11. Most are willing to "subordinate secular laws to sacred epistemology" (Appleby, 2000).
12. Most religious terrorists who have committed or are willing to commit suicide missions are between the ages of 13 and 27, are from poor families, have one or more siblings, and are geoculturally immobile.
13. While there have been a few females, paid mercenaries, and married men with children among the ranks of religious terrorists, these cells have been the exceptions.
14. Most religious terrorists who are not from poor families or refugee camps are the by-products of the migration of middle-/lower-middle-class college-bound high achievers into economically stagnant urban slums (Ansari, 1984).
15. The inconsistency of prospective religious terrorists' educational status with that of their parents (who are illiterate or have up to a fifth-grade education), employment opportunities, imposed restrictions based on ethnoreligious identities, and a sense of inequity synergizes their affinity for fundamentalism.

16. Most religious terrorists are "absolutist in orientation" (Appleby, 2000).

17. Most Muslim religious terrorists are "poorly trained, mediocrities in religio-legal and theological matters" (Appleby, 2000).

18. Most religious terrorists' beliefs are based on the interpretations of charismatic religious leadership.

19. A religious terrorist's affinity for self-immolation is inversely related to his or her wealth.

20. Religious terrorism is mostly executed for fulfilling personal salvation by answering a perceived divine message/will or following directives from charismatic religious leaderships.

21. Terrorism provides some religious zealots with profound spiritual satisfaction and fulfillment. It is perceived as a measurable indicator of their dedication, the upper limit of which is the extent of their willingness to commit self-immolation.

22. To a religious terrorist, perceived religious obligations or divine messages transcend social consciousness and social obligations.

23. Non-self-defensive acts of violence distinguish religious terrorism from those acts committed to fighting for religious freedom.

24. The potential religious terrorist has an affinity for martyrdom, is not averse to risk, and is a risk taker.

25. As a religious terrorist becomes committed to the act of self-immolation, he or she exhibits signs of serene disengagement (SD). These signs of snapping or detachment from their secular milieu are marked by a faint smile, distant look, lack of eye contact with the interviewers, disciplined or submissive body posture, and what appears to be a contentment or inner peace with imminent fate.

26. Religious terrorists committed to self-immolation would attempt to follow strict dogmatic rules of conduct to maintain their perceived purity and qualification for heavenly admissions. They would speak in the plural, refrain from vulgarity, perform all religious and secular obligations, and pay all legal debts.

27. Before their self-immolation, a religious terrorist would not indulge in earthly pleasures (e.g., sex, gambling, liquor, and dance).

28. A religious terrorist most often may suffer from one or more mental disorders, including, but not limited to, oppositional defiant, impulse control, antisocial, or other personality disorders. These disengaging characteristics and personality disorders, when aggravated by dogma-induced critical/psychotic depression, may be causal factors in the transition from zealotry to terrorism and self-immolation.

29. A religious terrorist's target would most likely be well defined and limited in scope and dimension and would not transcend a concentric target zone.

30. Religious terrorists' psychosocial attributes may be distinguished from those of political terrorists not only by the prior 29 traits, but also by their unconscious awareness of the maliciousness of their terrorism. This gestalt from reason is made possible by indoctrinating them to believe that (a) their death and the death of their symbolic victims will only be temporal, (b) they are collectively chosen by deity to be his tool, (c) they are prophets of his message, and (d) for their sacrifice they will all (victims and terrorists alike) be eternally alive in the heavens.

References

Ansari, H. (1984). The Islamic militants in Egyptian politics. *International Journal of Middle East Studies, 16*(1), 123–144.

Appleby, S. (2000). *The ambivalence of the sacred: Religion, violence, and reconciliation.* New York: Rowman and Littlefield.

Baron, R., & Kenny, D. (1986). The moderator-mediator variable distinction in social psychology research: Conceptual, strategic, and statistical considerations. *Journal of Personality and Social Psychology, 51,* 1173–1182.

Bell, D. (1976). *The cultural contradictions of capitalism.* New York: Basic Books.

Brodbeck, M., & Feigl, H. (1968). *Readings in the philosophy of the social sciences.* New York: Macmillan.

Dennett, D. (2003). *Freedom evolves.* New York: Viking Penguin.

Douglas, J., Burgess, W., Burgess, A., & Ressler, R. (1997). *Crime classification manual: A standard system for investigating and classifying violent crimes.* Hoboken, NJ: Jossey-Bass.

Douglas, J., & Olshaker, M. (1998). *Obsession.* New York: Pocket Books.

Douglas, J. E., Ressler, R. K., Burgess, A. W., & Hartman, C. R. (1986). Criminal profiling from crime scene analysis. *Behavioral Sciences and The Law, 4*(4), 401–421.

Fox, J. A., & Levin, J. (1994). *Overkill: Mass murder and serial killing exposed.* New York: Plenum Press.

Gordon, C. (1968). Self-conceptions: Configurations of content. In C. Gordon & K. T. Gergen (Eds.), *The self in social interaction* (pp. 115–136). New York: Wiley.

Grutter v. Bollinger, 539 U.S. 306 (2003).

Gudykunst, W. (1998). *Bridging differences: Effective intergroup communication* (3rd ed.). Thousand Oaks, CA: Sage.

Hatem, R. (1999). *From Israel to Damascus: The painful road of blood, betrayal and deception.* Beirut, Lebanon: Pride International.

Hoffman, B., & McCormick, G. (2004). Terrorism, signaling, and suicide attack. *Studies in Conflict and Terrorism, 27*(4), 243–281.

Holmes, R. (1998). Sequential predation. In R. Holmes & S. Holmes (Eds.), *Contemporary perspectives on serial murder* (pp. 101–112). Thousand Oaks, CA: Sage.

Hull, C. (1935). The conflicting psychologies of learning—A way out. *Psychological Review, 42,* 491–516.

Juergensmeyer, M. (2000). *Terror in the mind of God: The global rise of religious violence.* Los Angeles: University of California Press.

Kramer, M. (1996). Sacrifice and self-martyrdom in Shi'ite Lebanon. In M. Kramer, *Arab awakening and Islamic revival* (pp. 231–243). New Brunswick, NJ: Transaction. (First published in *Terrorism and Political Violence, 3*(3), 30–47, 1991.)

Lester, D., Yang, B., & Lindsay, M. (2004). Suicide bombers: Are psychological profiles possible? *Studies in Conflict and Terrorism, 27*(4), 283–295.

Mahrer, A. (1985). *Psychotherapeutic change: An alternative approach to meaning and measurement.* New York: Norton.

McCord, J. (Ed.). (1995). *Coercion and punishment in long-term perspectives.* New York: Cambridge University Press.

People State of New York v. James Kopp, Indictment No. 98-2555-S01, County Court of New York, Erie County, Case decided on May 9, 2003.

Pinizzotto, A. (1984). Forensic psychology: Criminal personality profiling. *Journal of Police Science and Administration, 12*(1), 32–40.

Radloff, L. (1977). The CES-D Scale: A self-report depression scale for research in the general population. *Applied Psychosocial Measurement, 1,* 385–401.

Richer, B. (1988). *The social learning theory revisited.* Ottawa, Canada: Livre Publique.

Said, E. (1993). *Culture AND imperialism.* New York: Knopf.

Schbley, A. (2003). Defining religious terrorism: A causal and anthological profile. *Studies in Conflict and Terrorism, 26*(2), 105–134.

Schbley, A. (2004). Religious terrorism, the media, and international Islamization terrorism: Justifying the unjustifiable. *Studies in Conflict and Terrorism, 27*(3), 207–233.

Schbley, A. (n.d.). Toward a common profile of religious terrorism: Some psychosocial determinants of Islamists profile. *Studies in Conflict and Terrorism* (under review).

Schmit, M., Kihm, J., & Robie, C. (2000). Development of a global measure of personality. *Personnel Psychology, 53*(1), 153–185.

Sellin, T. (1938). *Culture conflict and crime.* New York: Social Science Research Council.

Terry v. Ohio, 392 U.S. 1 (1968).

Turvey, B. (1999). *Criminal profiling.* San Diego, CA: Academic Press.

Weinberg, L., Pedahzur, A., & Canetti-Nisim, D. (2003). The social and religious characteristics of suicide bombers and their victims. *Terrorism and Political Violence, 15*(3), 139–153.

Countering Terrorism

II

Developments from 9/11

Meeting the Terrorist Threat

The Localization of Counterterrorism Intelligence

5

STEPHEN SLOAN

Contents

Introduction

The tragic events of September 11, 2001, affirmed the grim reality that terrorists now have the intentions and capabilities to engage in acts of mass destruction. The Al Qaeda network and other terrorist groups motivated by religious extremism have made nonnegotiable demands on the United States. In addition, such cults as Aum Shinrikyo served earlier notice that there were those who would utilize weapons of mass destruction (WMD) when it attacked the Tokyo subway system with sarin gas on March 20, 1995. Unlike terrorist groups in the past concerned with avoiding acts that would totally alienate public opinion in a targeted country and concomitantly would justify public support for draconian measures against them, today's terrorists include those groups who do not have any constraints in their resort to indiscriminate mass terrorism. Furthermore, the perpetrators of the acts, as in the case of the suicide bombers, may personally not be concerned about temporal affairs since by their actions they believe they will achieve their goals as they enter paradise. Moreover, as in the case of Aum Shinrikyo, there are now groups of what can be called technoanarchists who increasingly have the potential capability to attempt and achieve their ultimate objective: the destruction of the exiting social, political, and economic order.

The capabilities to either acquire or fabricate chemical, biological, and nuclear weapons have been accelerated as a result of three factors. First, with the breakup of the Soviet Union there are readily available stocks of weapons of "superterrorism" that are neither effectively secured nor accounted for. Second, there is a growing global criminal enterprise, perhaps best personified by the Russian Mafia, who will be willing to sell either the weapons or the materials of mass destruction to the highest bidder. Third, there are increasingly unemployed or underemployed scientists and technicians who have not realized their career goals and by economic necessity will offer their services both directly and indirectly to those who would engage in developing, deploying, and using a new generation of lethal weapon systems. These scientists are joined by those who are probably even more dangerous, alienated individuals who find the support of terrorist weapon development attractive because of religious or ideological motivation. They are the young men and women in many Third World countries who have not only failed to realize their career goals but also have rejected what they regard to be the secular and material values of the West in particular and other postindustrial societies in general. But, while they may reject the values, they may be more than willing to use their technological skills as a contribution to their version of a holy war fueled by fundamentalist beliefs that lead to extremism and violence.

Despite the impressive gains in developing first-responder capabilities on the state, local, and national levels, the national trauma created by limited anthrax attacks serves to underscore how even an individual whose agenda and identity are still to be known engaged in a very effective psychological campaign of terrorism. Given the response to those attacks, it is sobering to consider what the public's reaction would be to an incident or campaign involving the use of WMD. When one then considers both the physical and psychological cost of the events of September 11, it is a sobering fact to recognize that irrespective of the level of training and valor of those who would respond to future incidents of mass terrorism, they in all probability would be quickly overwhelmed in what for all intents and purposes would not be a form of crisis or emergency management or consequence management but an exercise in the physical, psychological, organizational damage control and physical and organizational triage.

Despite the establishment of the Department of Homeland Security and its funding of a wide variety of what are essentially necessary, but reactive, programs, the fact remains that irrespective of the scenario building and training, governments and citizens could be quickly overwhelmed by either a single attack or coordinated attacks of mass terrorism utilizing the plethora of new and increasingly lethal forms of substances and delivery systems. Unquestionably, developing the techniques of response at all levels of national, state, and local government is vital and can ultimately save lives and help governmental activities be reconstituted after a major attack, the fact is there never can be a totally secure environment. How many September 11ths could the United States endure as a people, a nation, and a government? What therefore must be addressed is the vital need to move away and beyond a reactive "gate and key," static and defensive mentality and increasingly develop an offensive and preemptive capability to seize the initiative against those who have by their own words declared a total war against the United States. The following observations, of course, do not offer a silver bullet to an enduring and growing threat or address the very questionable challenges associated with eliminating the root causes of terrorism. I caution that even if one could identify and act on root causes, violence and terrorism take on their own dynamics by which primal causes may no longer be significant or, even worse, be used as a means to justify any number of acts of carnage.

The Key Role of Intelligence and the Problem of Different Interpretations and Functions

At a conference at the Rand Corporation on terrorism in 1976, a leading Israeli counterterrorism advisor made an observation, which was valid then and even more important now in the age of potential mass destruction (personal note, 1980). He noted that in the Israeli case, if there was an incident, there was a 90% failure in his country's counterterrorism policies, doctrine, and capabilities, with that 90% failure potentially being defined as a failure of intelligence. Certainly, the Israeli case has its own unique problems, and clearly the resort to suicide bombing has greatly intensified the demand for effective counterterrorism abilities. But, if anything, it reinforces the vital need for effective intelligence to prevent highly dedicated terrorists who have an incredibly rich target environment since they have declared total war on an entire nation's population.

An understanding of the key role of intelligence, particularly by the population at large and the law enforcement community, is unfortunately not clearly appreciated as a major technique in fighting crime, much less terrorism. To the average state or local police officer, intelligence is often equated with clandestine and covert operations that fit within the perception that intelligence is first and foremost a form of spying, a perception that has been greatly enhanced in the popular culture. But, intelligence has always been far more than the art of spying or "trade craft," which is traditionally viewed as an aspect of, but not the major function of, intelligence. An understanding of this reality is important if intelligence in general and more specifically police intelligence are to become a major weapon in the continuing battle against both domestic and international terrorism.

There are any number of definitions of intelligence, but the following one perhaps best encapsulates the major objectives, functions, and goals of intelligence:

> In the American context intelligence connotes information needed or desired by the Government in pursuance of its national interests. It includes the process of obtaining, evaluating, protecting and eventually exploiting information. But that is not all. Intelligence encompasses the defense of US institutions from penetration and harm by hostile intelligence services. The term is also used to describe the mechanism or mechanism and the bureaucracy, which accomplish these activities. Hence, US intelligence, or the intelligence community. Its four major disciplines (analysis, collection, counterintelligence, covert action) are interdependent. Success in any of the four is related to the effectiveness achieved in the others. (Godson, 1983)

It is not the purpose of this chapter to discuss all aspects of the elements of intelligence as they relate to countering terrorism, but this definition is particularly useful for it addresses how intelligence is often viewed, particularly on the national level as contrasted to the state and local levels and especially as intelligence requirements relate to the law enforcement function. A more succinct definition provides the base point to understand the difference between intelligence as it relates to national security and police intelligence:

> Strictly speaking intelligence can be defined as the "product resulting from the collection, evaluation, analysis, integration and interpretation of all available information which concerns one or more aspects of foreign nations or areas of operation which is immediately or potentially significant for planning." (Richelson, 1989, p. 1)

This definition provides a useful basis to understand the disconnects that often exist on the conduct of intelligence at all levels. In the first place, this definition focuses on those agencies within the intelligence community that are primarily concerned with the impact of international developments on national security. This focus stands in contrast to intelligence as it relates to law enforcement, for which the emphasis is on utilizing intelligence to primarily prevent or prosecute crime within the United States. Certainly, the lines between domestic law enforcement and national security requirements are being blurred in a world where foreign and domestic threats are increasingly related and, concomitantly, domestic law enforcement agencies, most notably the Federal Bureau of Investigation (FBI), have international responsibilities, but the division of labor remains. In the second place, intelligence related to national security is primarily concerned with providing information for "planning"; that is, it is essentially intended to assist the national government in developing the diplomatic, economic, and military policies and strategies to defend or enhance the international objectives of the United States. This stands in contrast to the major goal of police intelligence, which is the collection of evidence to be utilized in the administration of justice. As a result, the collection of national intelligence does not have the constraints faced by domestic intelligence since the latter must meet the more rigorous requirements of providing evidence in court in contrast to information for planning. It is one thing, for example, to have the flexibility to protect an intelligence source from exposure in the conduct of foreign intelligence; it is quite another thing to have that source compromised in legal proceedings that may require the source to be revealed.

In the second place, one can contend that national intelligence in the realm of foreign collection and operations need not essentially be reactive. Those involved may indeed take the offensive for positive intelligence instead of emphasizing the function of counterintelligence. In contrast, domestic intelligence, as in the case of the law enforcement, in general must be essentially defensive and reactive. To take the offensive, as in the case of "preventive detention," a practice where countries are faced with on-going terrorist campaigns, taking offensive action such as "preventative detention" raises very serious constitutional issues of due process that conflicts with democratic principles and governance.

In the third place, intelligence on the national level associated with national security in the international arena can and must ultimately be strategic in nature. Ideally, it must ascertain longer-term trends in the global environment as a means of anticipating and developing policies and measures to anticipate, lessen, or eliminate potential threats before they can become a reality. In addition, the utilization of a strategic approach can enable the country to take an offensive posture instead of primarily reacting to both long- and short-term developments. In contrast, domestic law enforcement is understandably primarily tactical in nature. Those who are involved in this vital function are primarily concerned with providing their departments or agencies with the guidance that can help them respond to or prevent more or less immediate threats to the public order. The so-called big picture is left to the intelligence community, although even at that level, the challenges relating to immediate threats can and do act as a barrier to the development of strategic intelligence, as for example, related to long-term terrorist threats.

If the differences between international, national security, and strategic intelligence as contrasted to domestic, law enforcement, and tactical intelligence create difficulties in developing a unity of purpose and action to meet the terrorist threat through effective intelligence, the organizational and bureaucratic factors that are central in guiding the operations on the national, state, and local levels act as yet another impediment to effectively employing intelligence on the forefront of the U.S. counterterrorism effort.

The problem of sharing intelligence on the national level is further complicated by the understandable different role of the FBI in collecting intelligence as contrasted to the collection of intelligence by state and local departments and agencies. Under the auspices of the Department of Justice, the bureau's major concern in the past has been the collection of information to be used as evidence in a domestic court of law. However, it should be noted that the line is being blurred as even before September 11, Congress mandated that the FBI be heavily involved in conducting investigations of incidents of terrorism overseas that led to the killing and wounding of American citizens as well as impressive extraterritorial "snatch operations" against indicted war criminals and those who have engaged in drug trafficking and other criminal activities. This has placed a major strain on the ability of the FBI to carry out its new responsibilities while involved in working with state and local departments in reference to such federal laws associated with the apprehension and prosecution of bank robbers.

However, despite the growing and very necessary recognition that there is a need for the sharing of information on all levels, it is still difficult to change the organizational culture of a large bureaucracy. Despite the need for more cooperation, there is still an apparent disconnect between the federal law enforcement agencies, particularly the FBI and state and local law enforcement. Despite the calls for a partnership, local police still perceive that the sharing of intelligence is not a two-way street, and that the bureau takes information from them without fully reciprocating in kind. In part, this is justified by not wishing to expose what is viewed as sensitive information, but this may also be a manifestation of a cult of exclusiveness and elitism that in the past characterized the FBI's organizational culture. Whether it is valid or not, the perception, in part based on past experience, has acted as an impediment for meaningful cooperation. The current administration is now addressing the need to more meaningfully share intelligence with the state and local authorities. The questions associated with the best ways to operationalize the process and accompanying recommendations need to be considered.

The Changing Threat Environment: The Need for Cooperation and the Localization of Intelligence

As a result of the events of September 11, there is a tragic confirmation that terrorist groups have the capacity and will engage in long-term surveillances of potential targets. Certainly, the skyjacking teams that conducted the sophisticated coordinated attacks against the World Trade Center and the Pentagon illustrated that directly and indirectly through their support mechanism. The terrorists were able to survey potential targets, obtain the necessary flight training, and carry out multifaceted operations. Given this reality and the fact that the bar to the resort to mass terrorism has been lifted, it is imperative that law enforcement at all levels identify and apprehend terrorists before they become tactical (i.e., begin their movement to the targets). It is important to emphasize that once the operational phase begins, despite the physical security and associated measures that may be taken, the terrorists have for all intent and purposes seized the initiative since they can be selective against a whole constellation of potential targets, whereas the authorities are in an essentially reactive and defensive position in which one lapse in security may lead to an operational success by the terrorists.

Therefore, effective counterterrorism intelligence should focus on identifying and apprehending terrorists before they go mobile. Moreover, this is the phase they are often most vulnerable to capture since they must come out of their clandestine environment to move beyond preoperational planning to full-scale preparation for an attack. Therefore, while it will be imperative that federal law enforcement agencies collect evidence on terrorist groups as well as information, it will become an essential requirement that state and local law enforcement agencies and departments be given the legal mandate and funding to be adequately brought into the intelligence cycle of "planning and direction, collection, processing, production and analysis and dissemination" (Richelson, 1989, p. 4).

To this end, they must be involved in the intelligence loop and not only acquire a solid knowledge of terrorists' tactics, strategies, and goals but also learn the basic techniques of the intelligence cycle. How, for example, can a local agency, department, or sheriff's office become aware of and develop and apply the necessary analytical skills to select potential targets (i.e., potential or actual terrorist groups) for collection? The requirements for collection and analysis are clearly related to the need for an equitable sharing of data and information with the federal level. In addition, the demand to analyze increasingly burdensome amounts of information associated with false leads, hoaxes, and real targets needs to be shared to develop the capabilities of local law enforcement and their federal counterparts to acquire the analytical skill to separate the "noise from the signal" and especially on the local level apply what they have acquired to the unique threat environment of their own community.

The ability to collect, analyze, and disseminate data and information does not require a fundamental transformation of the skills already acquired by those who engage in police intelligence on the local level. In effect, a collection process is already used in regard to gangs, drug cartels, and other forms of organized crime that could be applied to terrorists, their cells, and networks. But, beyond this consideration, who better than local law enforcement to be knowledgeable of what is happening in their community. Moreover, the need for the localization of intelligence is increasing in rural areas, where there may be softer and therefore more attractive targets of opportunity for terrorists, ranging from pipelines to corporate headquarters, or the opportunity to engage in agroterrorism. In addition, by engaging in local counterterrorism intelligence, the law enforcement community can mobilize the public through the modification of existing crime watch programs that could identify potential terrorist activities—what could be called crime watch with muscle. The same public awareness that could lead to the discovery of a meth lab could also apply to a bomb factory or a safe house.

To achieve a level of integration between the federal, state, and local levels, there have been positive steps that have already been taken in reference to training. For example, former Attorney General Ashcroft stated the following in a memorandum to all U.S. attorney generals on the state level:

> I have previously directed that guidance on the implementation of the USA PATRIOT ACT, including the sharing of information with the intelligence community, be incorporated into the training of all Anti-Terrorists Coordinators within the U.S. Attorney's Offices. The first national training session of Anti-Terrorism Coordinators will occur on November 13–15, 2001. (But perhaps of Greater significance is the following.) ... to insure that such training is more accessible to local law enforcement ... I hereby direct that, by January 15, 2001, training similar to that of the Anti-Terrorism Coordinators be made available to local law enforcement participants in the Anti-Terrorism Task Forces either at the National Advocacy Training Center in Columbia, South Carolina, or through remote training at the 94 United States Attorneys' Offices. Each district should determine whether chiefs of police or other local law enforcement officers should also receive such training. (Ashcroft, 2001; italics added)

But, beyond the training, there is also the requirement to strengthen the capability of state and local agencies and departments to develop their own counterterrorism intelligence capabilities and therefore become more equal partners in the intelligence "war against terrorism." While there is no single model that needs to be applied, one can modify existing organizational structures to meet the task. In Oklahoma, we have seen the use of an existing agency to act as a state clearinghouse for counterterrorism intelligence: the Oklahoma State Bureau of Investigation (OSBI).

By Statute 150.21A Crimes Information Unit (Oklahoma Statute, 1966), "The Director of the Oklahoma Bureau of Investigation may establish a criminal information unit within the Bureau." Among its responsibilities are the following:

1. Investigate organized crime, criminal conspiracies, and the threat of violent crimes;

2. Collect information concerning the activity and identity of individuals reasonably believed to be engaged in organized crime, criminal conspiracies, or threatening violent crime;
3. Analyze collected information and disseminate such information to other law enforcement agencies for the purposes of criminal investigation and crime prevention;
4. Coordinate the effort of this state with local, state, and federal agencies to protect its citizens against organized crime, criminal conspiracies, and threats of violent crime by creating a clearinghouse of crime-related information for use by state, local, and federal law enforcement agencies; and
5. Provide training to peace officers of this state concerning the legal collection, preservation, and dissemination of crime-related information.

The statute in effect provides a clearinghouse for the collection and dissemination of criminal intelligence that, it is hoped, can through adequate funding be adjusted and applied to meeting the requirements of counterterrorism intelligence. Moreover, using existing law and organization has other benefits. The OSBI has among its agents many who have worked in local law enforcement. In addition, the bureau has worked closely with state and local police on a routine basis and is quite knowledgeable about their needs and concerns. As a consequence, they have established a pattern of mutual respect.

The use of an existing state bureau or agency is certainly one of the steps in the right direction, but it requires that there be a pool of trained personnel on the local level who can assist the statewide organization in carrying out its intelligence function. (An example of this training involving more than 100 sheriffs and other law enforcement personnel took place in a program, Community Response to Terrorism, under the auspices of the Oklahoma Sheriffs Association, the Oklahoma Association of Chiefs of Police, and the Regional Community Policing Institute, October 2002.) This does not mean to imply that all jurisdictions, some very small, need to have their own capabilities. Rather, depending on the size of the county or counties, a designated representative for a number of the smaller departments or sheriff's officers can be trained to act in liaison with the state entity in conjunction with larger, often urban, departments that may have their own intelligence office. These designated individuals should meet regularly and continually engage in the sharing of information through an institutionalized disseminating process that goes beyond that of a traditional "good old boy network." (The problem with the latter is as follows: If you are not part of the informal network, you may not obtain the necessary information.)

The statewide counterorganization would not compete with existing task forces. It would, as in the past, participate in their activities. But, by having its own capabilities, the statewide organization would increasingly have the leverage to more effectively require the federal agencies to share information since the state would have its own important assets on the local level.

In seeking to achieve integration of the local, state, and federal levels, there will be a need to consider moving away from the classic ladder hierarchy of command and control emanating from the top, and there is a temptation for micromanagement. In addition, such a change would be a move away from traditional bureaucratic structures that have all too often unfortunately encouraged "stovepiping," which has led to the failure to either vertically or laterally share information among agencies. It should also be noted that the expansion of the capabilities of an existing state agency is preferable to the creation of yet one more layer of bureaucracy that could act as a barrier to achieve necessary unity of effort. Finally, following an incident it is hoped that through decentralization first responders will be at the forefront of engaging in counterterrorism intelligence in their jurisdiction.

Conclusion

Clearly, the development of the "localization of intelligence" requires an innovative approach to meeting the coordinated and yet decentralized organizational doctrine of modern terrorist cells and organizations. Moreover, there must be recognition that the collection of counterterrorism intelligence at the local level walks a fine line between developing necessary awareness and paranoia. The local effort must constantly be sensitive to the requirement to balance the rights to privacy and due process with the requirements dictated by national security at all levels. Oversight is vital. But, despite the challenges, in the long term the events of September 11 underscore the need for effective counterterrorism intelligence on the state and local levels. This approach recognizes a basic fact in reference to both domestic and international terrorism: To modify the words of the late Speaker of the House Tip O'Neill, "All terrorism is local."

References

Ashcroft, John. (2001, November 12). *Memorandum to All United States Attorneys, From: The Attorney General: Subject: Cooperation with State and Local Officials, November 14, 2001.*
Godson, Roy. (1983). Editorial. In Roy Godson, *Intelligence Requirements for the 1980s: Elements of Intelligence* (Vol. 5, Rev. ed.). New Brunswick, NJ: Transaction Books.
Oklahoma Statute. (1966). Crime Information Unit, 150:21A, Effective November 1, 23.

Personal note. (1980). Statement made at the workshop of an International Conference on Terrorism and Low Level Conflict, sponsored by the Rand Corporation, September 8–12.

Richelson, Jeffrey. (1989). *The U.S. Intelligence Community* (2nd ed.). Cambridge, MA: Ballinger.

The Need for a Coordinated and Strategic Local Police Approach to Terrorism
A Practitioner's Perspective

6

VINCENT E. HENRY

Contents

Introduction

The September 11, 2001, terrorist attacks on the World Trade Center and the Pentagon have forever changed the face of American policing. The repercussions and long-term impact of the attacks are far ranging and have yet to be fully understood or comprehended, but it is certain that these terrorist acts will continue to resonate in American policing and in American society. The attacks have had, and will continue to have, a profound effect on the way police, law enforcement, and other public safety agencies do business, ultimately requiring that these agencies substantially alter their traditional policies, training, operations, and interactions with other agencies as well as with the communities they serve. It is a safe assertion that no other historic event has so fundamentally and so radically transformed American society and culture, American domestic and foreign policy, and American policing.

The suddenness and magnitude of these attacks, perhaps especially the attack against the World Trade Center with its massive casualties and devastating property damage, bring the issues of terrorism and the police response to terrorism into substantially sharper focus. Issues and problems that previously garnered relatively little attention within American police agencies are now at the fore, and police agencies across the nation are struggling to quickly adapt to the new realities of a post–September 11 environment. Within police management circles, one of the most important—and most troubling—impacts of the September 11 attacks is the realization that large-scale terrorist events can be (and have been) launched against the American people by foreign terrorist groups. This is not to say that American policing or the American public has been entirely ignorant of this possibility, but that for many sectors of the population and for many police officials, the actuality of this devastating attack and the massive casualties it involved have moved the possibility of terrorist activity out of the realm of abstraction. The actuality of the September 11 attacks has shaken American policing, placing the potential for future terrorist attacks squarely within the realm of distinct probability. Indeed, the current consensus among terrorism experts and knowledgeable government officials seems to be that it is not a question of whether additional terrorist attacks will take place, but rather where and when they will take place (Shenon and Stout, 2002).

Further, as more attention is focused on terrorism, there is an emerging recognition in American society and American policing that future attacks may not be confined to major cities: If terrorists can so effectively strike New York and Washington, D.C.—cities that have a history of smaller terrorist acts and whose police and public safety agencies are relatively well prepared to prevent, detect, and respond to terrorist events—they can strike in smaller and less-prepared municipalities as well. The September 11 attacks made clear the chilling fact that the potential for future terrorist activity exists across the broad spectrum of American policing (Yim, 2002).

Notwithstanding previous successful attacks by domestic and foreign terrorist groups in the United States (the 1993 World Trade Center bombing by Islamic extremists in New York City and the 1994 bombing of the Alfred P. Murrah Federal Building in Oklahoma City by right-wing domestic terrorists, for example) and a number of foiled terrorist plots by foreign groups (including a 1993 conspiracy to destroy the United Nations Building and two tunnels in New York City, a 1997 Brooklyn subway bombing plot, and the planned millennium bombing of Los Angeles International Airport), until recently the prospect of terrorist activity had not fully penetrated the American psyche. Before the September 11 attacks, terrorism was, for many Americans, something that happened overseas or in large cities. The American public, protected as it was by thousands of miles of oceanic moats, by its borders with friendly northern and southern neighbors, and by a seemingly strong and effective intelligence community, regarded itself as largely immune from the threat of large-scale international terrorism. September 11 changed all that.

Even the 1993 World Trade Center and 1994 Oklahoma City bombings—devastating as they were in terms of injuries, lives lost, and their economic and psychological impact—pale in comparison to the overall impact of the September 2001 Pentagon and World Trade Center attacks. Almost 3,000 lives were lost on September 11, billions in property losses accrued, and an already-shrinking economy was significantly weakened. The United States and its allied nations began prosecuting a full-scale war in Afghanistan and other terrorist strongholds throughout the world, and billions were poured into homeland defense and domestic preparedness initiatives. The psychological trauma experienced during and after the attacks—trauma that affects not only the immediate survivors of the event and the public safety rescue workers who responded to it, but also individuals across the nation and around the world—is incalculable. Americans' sense of security and safety has been fundamentally and perhaps irreparably shattered.

As they have in the past—especially in times of crisis—Americans justifiably expect that local law enforcement and public safety agencies will help restore some sense of safety and security to the nation. The public expects local police and public safety agencies to focus their resources on the prevention and deterrence of terrorism, to respond effectively and decisively to terrorist events, and to thoroughly investigate terrorist acts and bring those responsible to justice. These expectations are not altogether unreasonable; despite the significance of the threat, the magnitude of the public concern about it, and the tremendous scope of the problems this issue engenders, American law enforcement and public safety agencies have always operated under the mandate to protect the public and, as important, to maintain the public's perception of safety and security.

In line with the recognition that future acts of terrorism are now a distinct possibility or perhaps even a probability, Americans must also come to grips with the difficult fact that future terrorist acts may well occur in smaller jurisdictions that are less prepared to effectively prevent, deter, respond to, or deal with such acts. Big cities on the East and West Coasts have so far been the primary targets of terrorist groups—and they certainly remain potential targets—but the possibility of attacks in outlying suburban areas and even in medium and small cities in the American heartland by foreign extremists cannot be discounted. When we add to this equation the threat posed by right-wing militias and other radical domestic terrorist groups and consider the impact of the 1994 Oklahoma City bombing, the unsettling threat to public security looms even larger.

If we pause to consider some of the goals common to many terrorist groups—to create public fear through violence, to gain recognition and publicity for their cause, to cause overreaction by government, and to reduce the public's sense of security by taxing law enforcement and public safety resources—we can begin to glimpse the potent effect a significant attack or a coordinated series of significant attacks in the heartland could have. Such attacks would reify, reinforce, and extend, in very powerful ways, the tremendous fear Americans felt when New York City and Washington, D.C. were attacked: It would truly communicate the frightening message that terrorists can strike anywhere at any time.

At the risk of sounding alarmist, we can no longer conceptualize terrorism as a problem that only affects major cities, just as we can no longer afford for police in smaller jurisdictions to remain less than fully prepared to deal with terrorism and terrorist acts. If the institution of American policing is to fulfill its role and protect lives and property, it must take a highly coordinated and strategic approach to terrorism—a decisive and committed approach that involves law enforcement and public safety agencies throughout the nation and at every level of government. The sudden and shocking public realization that foreign terrorism is a bona fide threat along with the profound expectations placed on American police and public safety agencies raise a number of issues and problems that will test the mettle of local law enforcement and local public safety organizations. How quickly and how effectively these institutions can adapt to these issues and overcome these problems remains uncertain, but the stakes are undeniably high: To a large extent, the recognition of terrorism as a bona fide threat will determine a host of law enforcement policies and operations, which will in turn determine the American public's level of actual safety as well as their ongoing faith in public safety institutions. If the threat remains unrecognized or if the preventive measures implemented in response to a recognized threat are inadequate, the probability of additional attacks and additional casualties increases. In other words, the police and public safety response to the realities of a post–September 11 world will influence both the likelihood and the effectiveness of additional future attacks and ultimately whether terrorists succeed in achieving their goals. Preparedness is a deterrent to terrorism.

The issues and problems facing the institution of policing are complex, but for the sake of conceptual clarity, we can see that they fall within three primary categories. First, the public expectation and mandate that law enforcement will prevent and deter terrorist acts highlights the compelling need for effective intelligence gathering and analysis, for more sophisticated and realistic dissemination of intelligence information, and for a coordinated proactive intelligence capability that spans local, state, and federal law enforcement boundaries.

Second, demands for an effective public safety response to actual crisis events illuminate the need for better, more coordinated, and more sophisticated operational policies and practices that involve a much broader range of agencies and institutions. To be effective, agencies must work together cooperatively, and their personnel must be properly equipped and properly trained to quickly assess and react to crisis situations in a strategic and flexible way. The lessons learned from earlier terrorist events provide a useful template for understanding and preparing for future events, but the fact that terrorists also learn from their experience and improve on past operations demands that police and public safety agencies take a flexible and adaptive approach.

Finally, demands for swift and certain identification and prosecution of those responsible for terrorist acts are in large measure dependent on the efficacy of law enforcement's response to the first two categories; at minimum, they require that local, state, and federal agencies ignore or overcome some of the traditional organizational boundaries and rivalries that have previously separated them, instead working together to conduct coordinated investigations. Considered as a whole, these demands can be summarized as militating for better coordination, better definition of roles and responsibilities, and more effective utilization of resources across the landscape of American law enforcement.

The prospect of achieving these goals is complicated by a variety of constraints and impediments. Bearing in mind the tremendous breadth and size of American law enforcement—there are more than 16,600 separate and relatively autonomous local police agencies, state police agencies, and sheriff's departments in the United States, ranging in size from agencies with a single part-time officer to an agency with almost 40,000 sworn members (Hickman and Reaves, 2001)—the prospect of quickly developing the capacity for highly coordinated and highly focused response by all or even most of these agencies in each of these three areas is unquestionably daunting.

A host of organizational, logistic, legal, and funding issues will inevitably operate to frustrate attempts to better coordinate law enforcement activities, as will the likely emergence of turf wars and inter- and intraagency politics that have always inhibited the effective achievement of law enforcement's mission and goals. These petty quarrels have no place in post–September 11 policing, however, and the new realities require nothing less than a thorough and comprehensive initiative to defeat such shallow disputes.

Given the functional autonomy of these law enforcement agencies and the highly decentralized nature of American policing, both of which are fundamental to our system of government and ultimately to the protection of liberty, coordination cannot be ensured through legislation or executive action alone. It is certainly not suggested that all local police agencies unilaterally engage in extensive overt or covert surveillance, that they proactively investigate "suspicious" persons or organizations, or that they entirely take on the responsibility for counterintelligence operations. These activities require specific resources and a particular expertise, and to ensure the proper balance between civil liberties and public safety is not compromised, they also require a level of superceding administrative and judicial supervision that is probably not possible in any but a handful of the largest local law enforcement entities. It is suggested, however, that the myriad impediments to basic communication between law enforcement agencies must be reduced to permit more effective use of resources and legitimately gathered information. Simply stated, American law enforcement as a whole currently lacks the formal communications infrastructure and the resolve to effectively share critical intelligence information to the agencies that have the resources and responsibility to properly act on the information (Yim, 2002).

Legislation at the federal, state, and local levels can do a great deal to facilitate the necessary interaction and cooperation (just as it can function to impede the realization of these goals), but legislation cannot hope to compel the development of truly effective relationships between and among agencies. Rather, the political will to forge closer relationships between agencies, to coordinate their activities, and to better define their respective roles and responsibilities with regard to terrorism and other public safety crises must arise among law enforcement officials and political leaders. Members of the executive and legislative branches must give their unqualified support and encouragement to these initiatives, but committed federal, state, and local law enforcement officials must play the primary role in creating workable partnerships.

This chapter examines each of the three constellations of issues and goals identified, highlighting some of the constraints that operate to frustrate their achievement as well as some of the opportunities that exist to facilitate them. It should be well noted that as this chapter went to press the first time (Henry, 2002), less than 10 months have elapsed since American policing heard its September 11 wake-up call. The process of evolving and integrating new policies, new structures, and new mind-sets throughout law enforcement is—and under optimal circumstances should be—a relatively gradual and deliberate one. For many, the pace of this process to date has undoubtedly been excruciatingly slow, and the perception may be that rather little substantive progress has been made. It is difficult to empirically examine the accuracy of this perception since fairly little systematic analysis of organizational and policy change in American policing has been made publicly available in the preceding months, but some police agencies certainly seem to be pursuing practical and practicable strategies designed to address this constellation of issues. The New York City Police Department (NYPD) is one such agency, and because a great many of the organizational and policy changes it effected have become public knowledge, this chapter focuses on the NYPD's activities and initiatives.

Terrorism Prevention and Coordinated Intelligence

In the broadest sense, the primary mission of law enforcement is the prevention of crime, and this mission ultimately extends to the prevention of terrorist crimes. We have noted that there are about 16,600 autonomous local police, state police, and sheriff's agencies in the United States, and the almost 678,000 full-time officers who comprise these agencies (Hickman and Reaves, 2001) must certainly have contact with literally millions of individuals on a daily basis. Police contacts with the public run the gamut from the most casual or mundane interactions between the cop on the beat and the law-abiding citizen to enforcement situations resulting in arrest for serious criminal offenses. These contacts represent a potential wellspring of basic criminal intelligence: No matter the context in which the interaction occurs, local police officers are exceptionally well situated to gather basic intelligence information. To date, however, this nascent intelligence resource remains essentially untapped. To whatever limited extent this intelligence resource is currently exploited, the emphasis is primarily on responding to traditional crime rather than to preventing terrorist crime.

In point of fact, most police officers assigned to patrol or enforcement duties informally gather, analyze, and disseminate basic criminal intelligence on a daily basis. They interact with the public, casually or actively obtaining information about the community and the people who inhabit it, and they typically conduct some sort of rudimentary analysis to achieve a better understanding of the community and its crime problems. In many cases, they share this basic intelligence with other members of their agency to prevent, deter, and solve crimes. In some instances, most notably when officers recognize the significance or importance of some item of information, they take pains to ensure that other officers and, often, other agencies are formally apprised of it. All too often, though, the importance of crime intelligence becomes apparent after the fact: Once police are aware that a particular crime has occurred, they recognize the value of particular items of information they already possess, and, it is hoped, they pass that information along to those responsible for retrospectively investigating the offense. Intuition and experience suggest that basic criminal intelligence is much less frequently used proactively to prevent and deter crime than to solve crimes that have already taken place. In other words, information that might have been preventive intelligence for police instead becomes investigative or prosecutive evidence.

In many agencies, gathering criminal intelligence is part of a fairly informal or even haphazard system—after some informal culling and rudimentary analysis by supervisors, field reports and crime complaints prepared by patrol officers may become the subject of daily roll call briefings or may be posted at some sort of crime information center for officers' casual perusal. Such informal systems depend greatly on the capacity of the patrol officer and the reviewing supervisor to recognize the potential value of the basic intelligence the reports contain, and again the focus tends to be on traditional crime. In other agencies, operational policies may formally require that certain types of intelligence are memorialized in reports that are forwarded to detectives or crime analysts for further action, but here again the focus has traditionally been on hard criminal intelligence. Virtually without regard to the size or the complexity of the agency, though, we can see that police practice invariably involves some form of formal or informal criminal intelligence system even if the relative sophistication and effectiveness of these crime intelligence systems vary tremendously from agency to agency. Police officers are not, generally speaking, formally trained in intelligence gathering and analysis.

These rudimentary systems in American policing are certainly a far cry from the type of dynamic and sophisticated intelligence systems required to adequately prevent and deter terrorism. As noted, police are typically oriented toward recognizing particular types of crime intelligence, but they are less attuned to other types of information and less apt to recognize its potential value. Because the police mandate has always emphasized crime control, and because police are schooled in the subtleties and nuances of criminal behavior, officers are generally likely to recognize and act on crime-related intelligence. Since the police mandate has not previously placed a great emphasis on terrorism, and since police are not likely to be well acquainted with the kind of subtle behaviors or cues that may indicate potential terrorist activity, they are not apt to even recognize the significance of some information and therefore not apt to ensure that it is brought to the attention of others.

Officers may not recognize that certain types of criminal information—for example, that a motorist who was cited for a traffic infraction possessed a forged out-of-state driver's license—may have significant intelligence value. Unless officers have been trained to recognize forged documents, unless they are aware of the importance of forged identification for terrorists, and unless they recognize that such documents are often produced by sophisticated rings, the officer or agency may not take appropriate action. Even assuming that the officer recognizes the license as a forgery, the agency may treat the information as simply part of a conventional crime and neglect to pass the intelligence on to appropriate parties or to authorities in the other state. Even if the out-of-state driver does not appear to be a potential terrorist, this intelligence should be passed along because an investigation may lead to the forgery ring's closure and perhaps even to the identification of actual terrorists. An effective intelligence system thus depends on the intelligence gatherer's capacity to recognize the value of certain information, the intelligence analyst's capacity to integrate disparate items of information, and a structure or system that facilitates two-way communication between the gatherer and the analyst.

Because forged documents are important tools for terrorists as well as criminals, the NYPD has been training all its patrol officers in forged document recognition. It has also formed investigative task forces involving other local agencies and the Department of Motor Vehicles to conduct investigations and sting operations aimed at uncovering and eliminating forgery rings. Enhanced training, better intelligence-gathering and intelligence-sharing protocols, and improved investigations have increased the likelihood of detecting and deterring terrorist activities as well as such traditional crimes as insurance fraud.

Two key elements in successfully exploiting the vast repository of intelligence information that resides in American police agencies, then, are shifting the police mind-set to include the notion of fighting terrorism and educating police officers about terrorist practices, methods, and activities. Currently, both elements are lacking. This is not to say that every American law enforcement officer must become a terrorism expert—that is another daunting and perhaps unachievable task—but that there exists a great need for more and better education about terrorism in American policing. Only when police agencies recognize that the post–September 11 public safety mandate now includes protecting the public from terrorism and begin to educate their officers about terrorism will the mind-set begin to change. As the mind-set changes, and as awareness of terrorist activity increases, the quantity and quality of valuable intelligence available to law enforcement will also increase.

To this end, some local police agencies (especially the larger ones) have developed and incorporated new first-responder training curricula. The NYPD's In-Tac training program for patrol officers, for example, consists of one training day of practical and realistic tactical role-play scenarios followed by one training day of classroom instruction. The instructors selected to present this popular training are all seasoned street cops, and the realistic but flexible nature of the interactive scenarios—which are adapted from actual tactical scenarios NYPD cops have encountered in the field—add to the program's credibility and appeal. Following the September 11 attacks, an "Introduction to Counter-Terrorism" curriculum was introduced through In-Tac training: Officers spend the first day enacting the kind of everyday tactical situations in which they might encounter potential terrorists or potential terrorist activities (e.g., car stops, suspicious person calls, and bomb threats) and part of the second day critiquing their tactical response. The second day's curriculum also provides additional information about the history and activities of various terrorist groups as well as the tactical and cognitive knowledge officers need to recognize and thwart such incidents as bombings, weapons of mass destruction (WMD), and nuclear, chemical, and biological (NBC) incidents. Besides providing cognitive knowledge and insight into these topics, the training emphasizes officer safety as well as the agency's response protocols.

As part of a comprehensive training package, In-Tac is making a difference in terms of developing an awareness mind-set. Other elements of the training package include a series of videos officers watch in their weekly in-service training, various bulletins and messages presented at daily roll calls, Terrorism Awareness Bulletins (described more fully further in the chapter), and informational cards officers are required to carry in their memo books while on patrol.

Communications Structures

Another key element in achieving a coordinated intelligence capability to help detect and deter terrorism involves fundamentally changing the structure of communications within and between law enforcement agencies. Even if an agency develops information, it has little value unless and until it is subjected to preliminary analysis, evaluated for its intelligence potential, and passed along to other officers and other agencies where it can be further evaluated and incorporated with the intelligence data they have collected. If the information proves useful and leads to the development of hard intelligence, the hard intelligence must also be disseminated upward and downward to the agencies and officers who can make use of it. Only when operational police officers are made aware of the specific threats and activities they should be looking for, though, can their talents at intelligence gathering be fully utilized.

The NYPD, for example, has added an intelligence component to its basic recruit training curriculum. The Police Academy's intelligence officer maintains liaison with other intelligence officers and units throughout the agency, reviews news and media coverage of terrorism activities and world affairs (i.e., open-source intelligence), and prepares daily intelligence briefings that are disseminated to recruits through their instructors. Instructors lead discussions of these specific and general topics, and recruits are orally quizzed about how this information and these skills can be applied in everyday police activities. The rationale and purpose behind this component is to get young officers thinking about the way national and world affairs affect their work, to create an analytic mind-set in which officers will actively seek and use information, and to instill the kind of analytical habits that foster good intelligence gathering. In addition, the NYPD regularly disseminates Terrorism Awareness Bulletins throughout the agency. These timely bulletins advise officers of current threats and provide information to help recognize potential terrorist activities. For example, a Terrorism Awareness Bulletin explaining the activities of radical Islamic suicide bombers might advise that, for religious reasons, suicide bombers typically remove all or most of their body hair and may wear perfume immediately prior to the attack—information that can potentially help cops recognize and prevent a suicide bombing. Other Terrorism Awareness Bulletins might describe the various odors that may indicate the presence of an airborne chemical agent. The continual flow of terrorism-related information and knowledge fosters a mind-set of awareness to one's surroundings and encourages dialogue about these issues.

In a similar vein, other police agencies can ensure that officers are kept informed through daily roll call briefings that provide the same type of information. In addition to current national and world events, these briefings might include updates on agency policies as well as local issues and events that potentially involve criminal or terrorist activities. Are any poisonous chemicals manufactured or stored in quantity anywhere in the agency's jurisdiction? If so, what type of security is in place, and what facts should officers responding to the location be aware of? The key is to get American police officers to be well informed; to think critically about what they see, hear, and do; and to share the information they gather with other officers and other entities.

Overcoming Communications Barriers

American policing was never designed to facilitate the free flow of intelligence information between and among law enforcement agencies, and significant barriers to communication often exist between them. In particular, the flow of information and intelligence between agencies at different levels of government has been especially problematic.

The tortuously named Uniting and Strengthening America by Providing Appropriate Tools Required to Intercept and Obstruct Terrorism (USA PATRIOT) Act of 2001, passed by Congress on October 25, 2001, and signed into law by President Bush on the following day, represented a single opportunity for the federal legislative branch to enhance the flow of intelligence across the three levels of American government. This 342-page bill was a synthesis off four separate proposed bills submitted in the House of Representatives and Senate that amended at least 15 different federal statutes and instituted a wide variety of changes to federal criminal procedure rules. Despite a host of supporting testimony from leading American municipal police officials, Congress ultimately chose not to mandate that federal agencies share intelligence with state and local agencies.

The act's final provisions did require that federal law enforcement and intelligence agencies share some limited terrorist intelligence between themselves, but after rather little public debate or discussion, Congress removed language in earlier drafts that would have brought state and local agencies into the intelligence loop. By removing this language, Congress missed the opportunity to develop a highly effective and broad-based intelligence collection and dissemination system that would maximize the resources available to the intelligence community. Congress also indirectly facilitated the emergence of inter- and intraagency turf wars and disputes over the control and use of information—turf wars that have historically interfered with local law enforcement's ability to ensure public safety (Oates, 2001).

Historically, there has been a great reluctance on the part of federal law enforcement agencies to share intelligence information, especially with state and local agencies. A great deal of this reluctance seems based on a fundamental, long-standing, and self-interested distrust of local law enforcement. While concerns for intelligence leaks or the misuse of information might at first glance seem to justify some of the suspicion, these concerns should also be considered in light of the compelling need to enlist the personnel and other resources of local law enforcement in the fight against terrorism. The competition for budgets, for resources, and for public credit between the 16 federal agencies charged with intelligence gathering and analysis responsibilities may also underlie some of this bureaucratic resistance.

Since knowledgeable and informed local law enforcement agencies can and should play an important role in intelligence work—especially in terms of deterring and preventing terrorist acts—it seems reasonable to expect that layers of effective safeguards could be built into the intelligence collection and dissemination system to adequately protect confidential sources and data. Congress, however, ultimately opted not to compel federal agencies to share intelligence with state and local law enforcement. Intuition and an understanding of the essential role coordinated intelligence systems should play in combating terrorism suggest that in the rush to quickly enact legislation, the USA PATRIOT Act's failure to create a more inclusive intelligence loop was a faulty and disappointing legislative decision that may ultimately operate to the detriment of public safety.

There currently exist few established mechanisms for the widespread formal dissemination of raw, soft, or hard intelligence among local police agencies, and this fact imputes the need for the creation of regional intelligence networks. Perhaps operating under the aegis of state government or in cooperation with state law enforcement entities, representatives of local law enforcement agencies could meet regularly to share intelligence.

Heather MacDonald (2001), writing in *The City Journal*, makes precisely this point. MacDonald (2001) outlines the intrinsic difficulties faced in collecting and sharing intelligence across agency lines, noting that many major cities have joint terrorist task forces (JTTFs) operating under the leadership of the FBI. By agreement, the FBI has exclusive jurisdiction over local terrorist investigations in jurisdictions where JTTFs operate. Insofar as the JTTFs include seconded local and state law enforcement personnel, they would seem to be part of an effective intelligence system: Local law enforcement officials typically have better sources of information in the communities that might harbor terrorists. In New York City, for example, the JTTF includes some of the best detectives in the NYPD—highly experienced detectives with unparalleled knowledge of the city and its criminal networks—but the same detectives who collect and provide intelligence to the FBI are often precluded from sharing the same information with their own agency. One of the dilatory tactics federal law enforcement agencies have employed to limit the transmission of intelligence information to local law enforcement executives is to delay their required security clearances. It is an ironic reality that local law enforcement officers can be legally forbidden from sharing information with their own chief executive until the chief receives an FBI security clearance—a process that can take months or years. MacDonald (2001) cites this and a variety of additional sources and evidence to make the case that turf wars and federal law enforcement's penchant for secrecy have severely hampered terrorist investigations.

MacDonald (2001) calls for the creation of an intelligence system similar in form and structure to the NYPD's Compstat system—a crime intelligence and accountability management system that many credit with bringing about New York's tremendous reduction in crime since 1994. The NYPD's Compstat meetings facilitate accountability and diminish turf wars in part by bringing the commanders of various units together and requiring them to share information with commanders of other units and with the agency's top executives. Department executives question precinct commanders intensely about the number, type, and distribution of crimes within their precincts as well as about the strategies the commanders are employing to reduce crime. Commanders are held highly accountable—the intensity of the meetings help executives to quickly and accurately identify the strengths and weaknesses of individual commanders, and commanders whose skills and abilities are lacking are replaced with more competent managers. The meetings also permit executives to identify those commanders who are team players and those who are not (Henry, 2002).

MacDonald (2001) suggests that biweekly "Fedstat" meetings should be convened in major American cities, to be chaired by the FBI special agent in charge with all other relevant law enforcement agency heads attending. The purpose of these meetings would be twofold: to ensure that every agency is aggressively pursuing its investigations and to ensure that intelligence is being shared among and within the agencies. Security concerns would be addressed by requiring agency heads to obtain FBI security clearances—a highly subjective process that could, at the FBI's discretion, be easily expedited.

In other areas and regions of the nation without JTTFs, local law enforcement agencies could organize their own regularly scheduled intelligence-sharing meetings. The specific structures and constellations of the agencies involved are less important to this analysis than the fact that some sort of intelligence network is required. If Congress and federal law enforcement are unwilling to sponsor, fund, and nurture these coordinating networks, the burden to organize them necessarily falls on state and local agencies.

Some of the measures implemented by the NYPD prove illustrative of the kind of steps other local law enforcement agencies can take, albeit on a smaller scale, to enhance their ability to deal more effectively with terrorist threats. Since taking office in January 2002, NYPD Police Commissioner Raymond Kelly has undertaken several initiatives to strengthen and improve the department's intelligence and counterterrorism functions, and they include assembling a highly experienced team of executives and advisors as well as modifying the organizational structure.

For example, Kelly created a new Intelligence Bureau that subsumed the former Intelligence Division, increasing its personnel to approximately 700 investigators. About half of the bureau's workload is now devoted to gathering, analyzing, and disseminating intelligence on foreign and domestic terrorist groups, with the remainder of the workload focusing on more traditional gang, organized crime, and criminal enterprise intelligence. The Intelligence Bureau's shift from what was primarily a criminal intelligence unit necessitated the development of new skill sets and new methods of conducting intelligence work. To enhance its use of open-source intelligence and other intelligence methods, the bureau recruited experienced officers with an expertise and background in military intelligence. The department also recruited and retained a highly experienced intelligence expert to head the bureau: Kelly appointed David Cohen, a retired 35-year official of the Central Intelligence Agency (CIA) and that agency's former director of operations for the newly created position of deputy commissioner of intelligence ("Ex-C.I.A. Spy Chief," 2002; Levitt, 2002).

On the counterterrorism front, Kelly appointed Marine Corps Lieutenant General Frank Libutti, former commander of Marine Corps Forces in the Pacific and former special assistant for homeland security at the United States Department of Defense, to the newly created position of deputy commissioner for counterterrorism (City of New York, 2002). The new Counter-Terrorism Bureau includes the approximately 100 detectives assigned to the FBI-NYPD JTTF and another hundred or so officers involved in ongoing training of the agency's personnel, ongoing assessment of New York City's vulnerability to various kinds of terrorist attacks, and ongoing evaluation of the agency's resources, procedures, and overall capacity to prevent, deter, and respond to terrorism (Kelly, 2002).

Because both these officials work closely together, and because both report directly to the police commissioner, the NYPD has created a tight organizational structure with exceptionally short lines of communication—the type of structure that fosters a rapid and effective strategic response to emerging issues and concerns. Because both executives are essentially "outsiders" to the NYPD who nevertheless possess a wealth of "insider" experience and knowledge about dealing with the federal sector, many of the communications problems, mutual distrust issues, and agency rivalries that typically plague interactions between local and federal law enforcement can easily be ameliorated or overcome.

Other NYPD initiatives involve establishing formal liaison with the intelligence and counterterrorism entities of friendly foreign nations around the globe and sending officers to observe, train with, and learn from agencies with far greater experience in these matters. Officers from the NYPD have visited Israel to study that country's intelligence and counterterrorism operations (Associated Press, 2002; O'Shaughnessy, 2002), and operational, training, and intelligence officers have visited the Garda Siochana, the Police Service of Northern Ireland, and the London Metropolitan Police Service to learn from the experience of their Special Branch and Anti-Terrorism squads. A small team of NYPD intelligence officers was even sent to Afghanistan (Marzulli, 2002). A host of other outreach initiatives have strengthened relationships between the NYPD.

Given the tremendous importance of coordination and cooperation between police and other public safety agencies, New York's police and fire commissioners have jointly instituted a host of initiatives to improve communications and coordinate policies. The initiatives include conducting more joint training exercises, integrating radio systems, utilizing police helicopters as a platform for Fire Department of New York (FDNY) officials to direct fire operations, and assigning command-level personnel as full-time liaison (Rashbaum, 2002).

The NYPD has also forged an unprecedented number of formal and informal relationships with private security management organizations, the health care sector, transportation associations, local colleges and universities, and other entities with resources necessary in the fight against terrorism. Through mutual dialogue, planning, and training, these organizations play an important advisory role in determining the policy of the NYPD and the city of New York. By the same token, keeping these entities informed about terrorism helps ensure both the perception and the reality of safety throughout the city, and they can also form an important link in the intelligence chain. The NYPD sponsored a seminar for 250 landlords and real estate executives, for example, to brief them on improving building security, recognizing forged identity documents, and other information obtained from Al Qaeda manuals about the type of apartments terrorists might favor (Fries, 2002).

Certainly, few American local law enforcement agencies could devote resources and personnel at the same proportion as the NYPD, but smaller agencies can nevertheless emulate some of the principles illustrated in the NYPD's approach. Many smaller agencies could, for example, easily nominate an intelligence/counterterrorism officer with the responsibility to prepare weekly (or, preferably, daily) intelligence briefings collected from open-source materials and from other law enforcement agencies. One of the intelligence/ counterterrorism officer's roles should be to generate a mind-set of awareness and preparedness by disseminating and collecting information and by establishing a fairly high level of discourse about terrorism and tactical response to it. Not every agency can retain a former ranking CIA official or a Marine Corps lieutenant general to beef up its capabilities, but many police chiefs could establish closer liaison with local active and reserve military units and draw on their expertise and resources. Police chiefs could also establish advisory groups comprised of active, retired, or reserve military officers; health care officials and administrators; scientists from local colleges and universities; and the heads of various professional organizations. These and other initiatives represent a relatively inexpensive yet highly effective way for local law enforcement to ensure preparedness for a potential terrorist event.

Coordinated Response to Terrorist Acts

As noted, well-orchestrated mass casualty attacks in large urban areas are by no means the only potential terrorist threat faced by American law enforcement and public safety agencies. Large urban agencies represent only a fraction of total law enforcement personnel and resources, and agencies in smaller suburban and rural areas must also become better prepared to deal with terrorist threats and terrorist events. At first glance, mass casualty attacks and the potential use of WMD may seem best suited to densely populated areas, but we must recognize that a well-coordinated series of smaller attacks in less-prepared jurisdictions could have just as devastating an impact on American society as an attack against a major city. Such attacks could, in other words, just as easily advance the terrorist agenda. The possibility of coordinated multiple attacks illuminates the need for coordinated cross-jurisdictional command-and-control systems as well as for coordinated cross-jurisdictional training and response protocols.

Bearing in mind that terrorist goals typically include the creation of widespread public fear, we can see that media attention brings attention to the terrorist group's activities and objectives, eroding public faith in government and in government agencies charged with the responsibility for public safety. Attacks in the American heartland would therefore seem quite attractive to foreign and domestic terrorists. Extensive target hardening initiatives have taken place in large municipalities since September 11, including more effective security measures at international airports as well as at bridges, tunnels, and public transportation hubs. Because their police departments and public safety agencies typically have greater resources and generally higher levels of preparedness, big cities may have a degree of resilience to terrorist actions that is absent in smaller municipalities.

We must bear in mind that terrorists are, in a sense, criminals of opportunity: They can be expected to identify and exploit vulnerabilities and to take the path of least resistance as long as that path leads to the attainment of their goals. If target hardening, enhanced terrorism awareness, and augmented security measures in urban areas are successful—that is, if they make terrorist activities more difficult to carry out in big cities—terrorists may shift their attention to less-prepared smaller jurisdictions. American policing must therefore not exclude or discount the potential for attacks in less densely populated areas and perhaps especially the potential for a coordinated series of multiple attacks that would severely deplete local public safety resources.

A coordinated series of multiple attacks against soft targets in the American heartland would certainly add a new dimension of public fear and would severely tax law enforcement and public safety resources. Smaller law enforcement and public safety agencies typically rely on mutual aid arrangements to deal with disasters and with the major crime events they encounter, but intuition and experience suggest that relatively few public safety agencies have developed extensive contingency plans to deal with major events other than traditional crimes and natural calamities. Although police agencies generally have some historic knowledge of how they should deal with disasters and major crime events, that knowledge may not be directly applicable to the special circumstances surrounding terrorist actions. Contingency plans for evacuating the public from a coastal area in the event of a hurricane, for example, might assume that bridges will be intact, that roads will be generally passable, and that adequate warning of an impending storm will be given. This plan might be of absolutely no use if a sudden terrorist attack includes damaging bridges and other routes of egress.

A series of small simultaneous attacks in several adjoining suburban jurisdictions—several small bombings or arson attacks, for example, or a sudden rash of highly dispersed bomb threats at sensitive installations across several geographically large but thinly populated jurisdictions—would severely limit the number of law enforcement personnel available to respond to any given location. Quite simply, agencies might be spread too thinly and be too preoccupied with their own local events to respond to another agency's call for mutual aid.

This and other scenarios highlight the compelling need for cross-jurisdictional training and development of cross-jurisdictional response protocols, as well as the need for more expansive thinking, better planning, greater interaction between agencies, and more cooperation with the private security industry. To avoid additional confusion in the chaotic aftermath of a terrorist event, police officers and agencies responding to a mutual assistance call must be generally aware of the policies and protocols operating within the affected jurisdiction. By way of example, a predetermined response plan would clearly establish the roles and responsibilities of each agency and clarify the number and type of public safety personnel available for deployment. Among other things, the response plan—which should be flexible enough to adapt to unforeseen exigencies—would identify installations that are likely targets, specifying emergency response and public evacuation routes as well as predesignated staging areas.

A critical issue at the scene of many disasters and large-scale emergencies is exactly which agency will take operational command. In some municipal policy jurisdictions, the fire chief or some other emergency management official is the designated commander. Particularly in smaller jurisdictions, there may be no existing municipal policy to guide this essential decision, resulting in significant operational delays and additional chaos.

Other troublesome issues include the interoperability of radio and other communication systems as well as the specific roles personnel from outside agencies will play. In a hostage situation, for example, should negotiators or SWAT (special weapons and tactics) team members from another jurisdiction take an active role as part of the operational team, or should they be deployed in some other support capacity? If they are to take part in the operation, have they trained with the local negotiators or SWAT team members to an extent that they will be an asset rather than a liability? A host of logistical, legal, and liability issues will certainly shape these decisions, which must be resolved prior to the onset of the emergency.

Similar issues exist with regard to interactions with the private security industry and the use of private security's resources for a public purpose. Private security personnel should certainly not be expected to fulfill the role of trained police officers, but they can assume a great many ancillary and support functions in a time of crisis if adequate preparation, planning, and training have taken place. If a potential terrorist event—a bomb threat or a hostage situation, for example—takes place on a local college campus or at a suburban shopping mall, private security forces might be mobilized to divert traffic, to assist in evacuation efforts, or to establish a secure outer perimeter. While private security forces typically operate only on private property, the most expedient strategy in times of crisis might be to dispatch uniformed security guards to off-site traffic posts so that better-trained police officers can focus their attentions and energies on the immediate threat. These and other strategies will, of course, require specific kinds of preevent planning and training as well as a set of agreements outlining specific roles and responsibilities among the entities involved.

None of these activities can take place unless law enforcement and public safety agencies meet with each other (and with private security directors) to creatively identify the possible threat scenarios they face, to construct coherent response plans, to consider logistics issues, and to iron out viable protocols in which all of the players know their own roles as well as the roles others will play. Beyond this planning process, these entities must also conduct regular joint mobilization drills to ensure that the plans and protocols are workable and practicable. Simply developing a paper plan is insufficient, and abstract tabletop exercises cannot hope to capture the situational exigencies and human errors that inevitably occur in the real world to confound even the best-laid plans. Tabletop exercises and joint command drills are an excellent way to identify some types of conflicts in interagency protocols, to define appropriate roles, and to streamline procedures, but they cannot account for the equipment malfunctions, communications snafus, and human foibles and misjudgments that inevitably plague first responders during real crises. First responders must also play an active part in the exercises if planning and training for major events are to be successful.

Strategic–Tactical Response

Prior to September 11, 2001, American policing as a whole was largely ignorant of terrorism, of terrorist groups, and of terrorist methods and operations. As noted, though, many or most American police officers and police agencies are generally effective in terms of dealing with traditional crime. Police are keenly aware that the seemingly ordinary situations they encounter can quickly evolve into dangerous criminal events, and most police adapt to this reality by using effective strategies and tactics in even their most routine interactions with the public.

The same cannot be said for most police officers in terms of their preparedness for terrorist events. In fact, intuition and experience suggest that the vast majority of American police officers lack specific knowledge and training to recognize the cues that may indicate terrorist activity, and many probably lack the mind-set and repertoire of specific skills necessary to respond safely and effectively to actual events. What proportion of officers, called to a residence to resolve a landlord–tenant dispute, would recognize the presence of equipment and materials used to manufacture explosives or to breed biological agents?

How many officers, responding to a call that several people have fallen ill during an outdoor park concert, would have the foresight to look around for the carcasses of birds and small animals as they approach the scene? The presence of dead birds or dead animals may indicate the presence of a toxic airborne agent. If the officers do observe this cue, should they enter the area and become possible victims themselves, or should they stay a safe distance from the victims and simply disperse the crowd? Should the crowd be scattered or moved a safe distance away to await decontamination? What is a "safe distance" from the site? Who should be permitted to treat the victims, and what kind of personal protective equipment should they put on before approaching the victims?

The point here is that the knowledge, skills, and attitudes that have traditionally served the police officer well in terms of fighting crime are entirely inadequate to deal with many kinds of terrorist acts. Police and public safety personnel must be prepared for a different range and quality of threats in a post–September 11 world, and that preparation includes developing an entirely new and entirely different set of terrorist-related knowledge, skills, and attitudes.

Without further belaboring the point, the knowledge, skills, and attitudes in this regard are largely lacking at the local level of law enforcement, and municipalities must immediately take affirmative steps to address this problem. In line with the observations made previously in this chapter, American local law enforcement must develop and implement strategies that build partnerships and maximize the effectiveness of available resources.

Coordinated Investigations

Many of the principles and points outlined apply to the proactive investigation of extremist groups and potential terrorist activities as well as the retrospective investigation of terrorist actions. Such investigations require a very high level of sophistication, extensive knowledge of specific terrorist groups and methods, and tremendous cooperation that typically spans organizational boundaries. Whether prospective or retrospective, successful terrorist investigations rely greatly on intelligence systems, and we have seen that these systems are lacking in American law enforcement. Indeed, many other structural and organizational frailties of American law enforcement can also complicate and inhibit effective terrorist investigations.

It is important to recognize that the responsibility for investigating virtually all bombings and terrorist attacks lies with federal law enforcement. The state or local agency may be called on to assist the investigation in various collateral ways, but the role of that agency will certainly not be that of the primary investigative agency. Given the history of friction between federal and local law enforcement, the tendency for petty jealousies and misunderstandings to escalate into full-blown turf wars, and the tremendous media attention and public pressure that will inevitably accompany the investigation, it is also doubtful that a given terrorist investigation will proceed quickly and smoothly. Conflicts are practically unavoidable in the current law enforcement climate. Local law enforcement officials may not have the sophisticated expertise and the logistic and support resources required to conduct these investigations, but they generally possess better lines of communication with the local community and better sources of local information than federal agencies. Local law enforcement's formal and informal intelligence systems will thus take on a critical importance, again pointing to the need to develop stronger intelligence capacities at the local level.

The prospect of a major terrorist investigation also indicates the *a priori* need for better relationships between local law enforcement and public safety agencies, better planning, and better response protocols. Another intrinsic element is the ongoing cultivation of viable relationships between law enforcement, public safety agencies, and private security within a region. When cooperative relationships already exist, and when personnel have previously developed contacts and knowledge of the other entities' operations, the organizational boundaries that might ordinarily inhibit an investigation are significantly diminished.

Summary and Conclusion

If American police and public safety agencies are to face and overcome the threat of terrorist activities, they must dramatically change their policies, their training, their operational practices, and their relationships with each other. The specter of terrorism, as demonstrated in the September 11 attacks on the World Trade Center and the Pentagon, has ushered in a new reality for American policing—a reality that the institution of policing is largely unprepared to face.

This chapter has attempted to set forth some of the difficulties and challenges American policing is likely to face in relation to the emerging terrorist threat. One of the most daunting challenges involves coming to grips with the notion that future acts of terrorism, if and when they occur, may not take place in large urban areas. The terrorist threat should not be conceived of narrowly or in terms of earlier terrorist acts and attempted terrorist acts; while the potential for terrorism involving mass casualty attacks in big cities remains real, the potential for different kinds of terrorist activity also exists in smaller urban, suburban, or even rural jurisdictions. In particular, a coordinated series of attacks on targeted sites in the American heartland seems tailor made for extending the terrorist agenda and achieving terrorist goals. Whether or not those threats ever come to fruition, American police agencies in smaller jurisdictions must be prepared to take up the challenge of combating terrorism.

In light of the terrorist threat, American policing must find new ways to preserve its decentralized system while achieving greater coordination of efforts and resources across organizational boundaries. If American police are to continue deterring, preventing, and responding to events that threaten lives and property, as well as maintaining the public's sense of safety and security, significant operational and policy changes must take place. These include developing more cooperative relationships between law enforcement and public safety agencies at all levels of government and developing the kind of attitudes, skills, and knowledge American police need to be as effective in combating terrorism as they are in combating traditional crime.

This cooperation and coordination entails greater and more effective threat identification, better planning for potential terrorist events, and a relaxation of organizational boundaries. It also requires more effective, efficient, and sophisticated intelligence systems—especially at the state and local levels of law enforcement—and better systems for communicating intelligence within, between, and among agencies. Finally, the realities of post–September 11 policing call for a host of new training initiatives that will equip police officers and other public safety personnel with the wherewithal to effectively identify and respond to terrorist threats.

References

Associated Press. (2002, May 19). Five from NYPD in Israel studying suicide bombers. Retrieved from http:/www.newsday.com/news/local/newyork/ny-bc-ny–nypd-israel0519may19.story

City of New York, Office of the Mayor. (2002, January 16). *Mayor Michael R. Bloomberg and Police Commissioner Raymond W. Kelly Appoint United States Marine Lieutenant General Frank Libutti in Newly-Created Post of Deputy Commissioner of Counterterrorism.* Press Release 012-02. New York: Author.

Ex-C.I.A. spy chief to run NYC police intelligence. (2002, January 25). *New York Times,* p. B1.

Fries, Jacob. (2002, June 4). City landlords get a primer for spotting terrorist tenants. *New York Times,* p. B1.

Henry, V.E. (2002). The need for a coordinated and strategic local police approach to terrorism: A practitioner's perspective. *Police Practice & Research* 3(4), pp. 319–336.

Henry, Vincent E. (2002). *The Compstat Paradigm: Management Accountability in Policing, Business and the Public Sector.* Flushing, NY: Looseleaf Law.

Hickman, Matthew H., and Reaves, Brian A. (2001). *Local Police Departments, 1999.* NCJ 186478. Washington, DC: Bureau of Justice Statistics.

Kelly, Raymond W. (2002). *Police Commissioner Raymond Kelly's Statement Before the City Council Public Safety Committee, February 21, 2002.* Retrieved from http://www.gothamgazette.com/iotw/security/transcript.shtml

Levitt, Leonard. (2002, January 25). Kelly hires CIA exec. *Newsday.* Retrieved from http://www.newsday.com/news/local/newyork/ny-nyint252564805jan25.htm

MacDonald, Heather. (2001, Autumn). Keeping New York safe from terrorists. *City Journal,* pp. 58–68.

Marzulli, John. (2002, January 11). N.Y. cops to tackle Taliban. *New York Daily News,* p. 3.

Oates, Daniel J. (2001, November 5). The FBI can't do it alone. *New York Times*, p. A31.

O'Shaughnessy, Patrice. (2002, May 19). NYPD in Israel for suicide attack prep: Learning methods of detection, strategy. *New York Daily News*.

Rashbaum, William K. (2002, May 24). Commissioners seek closer ties for Fire Dept. and the police. *New York Times*, p. B1.

Shenon, Philip, and Stout, David. (2002, May 21). Rumsfeld says terrorists will use weapons of mass destruction. *New York Times*, p. A1.

Yim, Randall A. (2002). National Preparedness: Integration of Federal, State, Local and Private Sector Efforts is Critical to an Effective National Security Strategy for Homeland Security. General Accounting Office, Washington DC, (GAO-02-0621T), Testimony before the House of Representatives' Committee on Transportation and Infrastructure, Subcommittee on Economic Development, Public Buildings, and Emergency Management, April 11.

Suggested Reading

Van Natta, Don, and Johnston, David. (2002, June 2). Wary of risk, slow to adapt, FBI stumbles in terror war. *New York Times*, p. A1.

Local Preparedness for Terrorism

A View from Law Enforcement*

7

JOSEPH F. DONNERMEYER

Contents

Introduction

This chapter examines the views of the law enforcement community concerning critical issues related to local preparedness for possible terrorist incidents. Information is derived from a statewide conference held on domestic preparedness in Ohio. Representatives from law enforcement agencies located in all 88 counties of the state attended the conference and determined a set of top five priority issues in response to four discussion questions: (a) critical equipment needs; (b) critical training needs; (c) critical internal issues; and (d) critical external issues.

Since September 11, 2001, media portrayals of the New York City Police Department have been quite prominent and very positive. The public has learned that the police are "first responders" to the scene of tragedies and are frequently placed at great risk.

* Support for the statewide conference was provided by the Office of the Lieutenant Governor in cooperation with the Ohio Emergency Management Agency, the Ohio Highway Patrol, the Ohio Department of Rehabilitation and Corrections, the Ohio Office of Criminal Justice Services, the Public Utilities Commission of Ohio, and The Ohio State University.

Beyond the media hype, however, is a different story. It is neither the glamorous tale of heroic rescue efforts nor the tragic depictions of officers who lose their lives in the line of duty. This story is more mundane. It is about local preparedness by the police in communities both large and small to respond to incidents of terrorism. It is about how the police define the probability of terrorism occurring in their community in relation to the cost of preparation.

The purpose of this chapter is to examine preparedness issues from the point of view of the police. Information for this article comes from a series of group discussion sessions attended by police officers who examined various dimensions of local preparedness for terrorism. These sessions occurred at a statewide conference held on that subject in Ohio in June 2000. This conference also included concurrent sessions for other first responders (i.e., fire, emergency medical, health officials, etc.) and community leaders concerned about issues related to terrorism (Office of the Lieutenant Governor, 2000). Clearly, timing is important, and any conference focused on the issue of terrorism is chronologically defined in relation to September 11. Would police perceptions be different if the conference were held in October 2001 rather than in June 2000? Are the views of the police more valid today than before September 11, 2001? Perhaps, but perhaps not. I argue that general issues related to local preparedness for terrorism should be discussed without the rush of recent events and instead tempered by the everyday issues confronting the police in communities across the country.

Community and Policing in the United States

The context of policing in the United States can best be described as a complex system (Whisenand and Ferguson, 2002). Federal and state legislation empower local communities to establish their own police agencies and services. These legislative bodies also define the parameters in which police powers are exercised in the United States, specifically through laws that put limits on who can be a police officer; minimum requirements for basic or entry-level training, plus requirements for recertification and advanced training; certification of training programs and facilities; laws defining police powers of arrests; costly penalties for crimes committed against police officers; appropriate police practices in relation to citizens' rights; and the internal management of police departments, including budgeting and conformance of personnel to agency policies and procedures, among a host of other managerial functions.

Within the parameters set by federal and state governments, each local community is relatively autonomous in terms of how its police agencies are set up and run. There are nearly 17,000 local law enforcement agencies in the

United States, from as small as 1 officer (or sworn personnel) to as large as more than 39,000 officers (Hickman and Reaves, 2001). Size adds complexity to the way a police agency is administered and variety to the ways the agency relates to the community in terms of how sworn personnel respond to calls for service and how the police department develops collaborative arrangements with other public service agencies in the community (Palone, Myers, and Worden, 2000; Weisheit, Falcone, and Wells, 1999).

Also influencing the complex fabric of policing in the United States is the way in which police agencies are organized and integrated into the bureaucratic structure of local community services. In some communities, the head of the police department has nearly complete overlapping jurisdictions and missions (Geller, 1985; Hickman and Reaves, 2001; Whisenand and Ferguson, 2002) and autonomy to do whatever he or she likes. Other communities require much more accountability of the police agency, such as through periodic updates of police activities and crime statistics and routinized auditing of police budgets. Political arrangements of local communities vary as well. In some communities, the head of the police agency reports to a single person, such as a mayor or city manager. In other communities, accountability is directly to an elected assembly, such as a city council, county commissioners, or township trustees. Some communities add an extra layer to their bureaucratic structures by hiring a "safety director," to whom the head of the police agency (and other local first-responder agencies) is directly accountable (Geller, 1985; Whisenand and Ferguson, 2002).

Further complicating the patchwork quilt arrangements of policing in the United States is the fact that local police agencies can overlap in their jurisdictions. For example, local units of government include both counties (or county equivalents) and incorporated places, such as cities, towns, and villages. Usually, the status of city is reserved for incorporated places with large populations, the status of town for populations smaller than cities, and the status of village for the smallest populations. State-level laws specify these statuses, and each of the 50 states will have a different arrangement for the relationship between population size and the status of an incorporated place. The unincorporated areas of counties in many states are subdivided into townships. All three—counties, townships, and incorporated places—can establish police agencies. Plus, in many localities, the jurisdictions of these police agencies can overlap. For example, there are over 3,000 countywide sheriff's departments (Hickman and Reaves, 2001). These police agencies can have jurisdiction over the whole county, including all townships and incorporated places located within the boundaries of the county. In some states, sheriff's departments are restricted to serving arrest warrants and subpoenas for people to appear in court, with a separate countywide police department. In other states, sheriff's departments are full-service police agencies, matching the same breadth of mission and array of functions as police agencies of townships and incorporated places.

There is another dimension to the complexity of policing in the United States. It is the presence of specialized police agencies authorized by the constitutions and bylaws of state governments. These agencies, which often have far-ranging jurisdictions and police powers, can include a statewide police or police devoted to servicing highways (i.e., highway patrol), public housing (i.e., metropolitan housing authority), parks and recreation areas (i.e., park police or park rangers), and public transit (i.e., metropolitan subway or transit system police).

The locality-specific nature of policing is complicated by one more dimension: the nature of community itself (Sharp, 2001; Wilkinson, 1970). By definition, community has both a geographic referent and an organizational referent. Typically, a *community* is defined as a place where members have common ties. As a place, most communities have boundaries, frequently defined by geography (i.e., rivers, mountains, valleys, etc.); political jurisdictions (i.e., counties, townships, incorporated places); or both. Communities vary by the amount of cohesion exhibited by the individuals and groups who reside and act within the boundaries. In other words, in some communities, there is strong identity with the community and strong ties among community members. In other communities, identity is weak among most members, ties are not very strong, and there is little social capital on which collective action can be built (Sharp, 2001). Commonly, it has been assumed that smaller communities represent the former type, and larger, more urban-like communities represent the latter. However, that is not always so. Some rural communities are not very cohesive, and many large, urban communities exhibit an amazing degree of cohesion among their members.

The community context is an important influence on the organizational behavior of the police. Not only do the heads of police agencies have to deal with administration of the agency itself, but also they must contend with the ever-shifting and often-competing interests of different constituencies within the community (Geller, 1985; Palone et al., 2000). Beyond calls for service, police agencies and police response to crime are shaped at the local level by politicians, civic and volunteer groups, activists, local media, religious groups, youth and youth-related groups, and a host of other individuals and organizations. A community's relative intolerance of deviance and the values and political attitudes of its citizens partly determine which laws are enforced aggressively and which laws are not.

Nearly all communities in the United States have politically defined boundaries. As such, they are authorized to provide various services and collect taxes. The police represent one type of service considered basic or vital to the general welfare and safety of the populace. However, there are others who also are considered first responders. In most communities, these other first responders would include firefighting and emergency medical services (EMS) personnel. Sometimes, fire departments provide EMS, or these services may be provided by a specialized group within the fire department.

Beyond first responders, there are other local groups involved in issues related to safety and security, including an agency responsible for responding to large emergencies, such as natural and human-made disasters. Most often referred to as an emergency management agency, local offices are integrated with the state office of emergency management through various administrative arrangements and procedures that seek to ensure rapid response when situations arise. Also, at the local level, there are public health agencies of various sorts that are concerned with medical issues, including the early detection and treatment of disease.

One measure of a community's cohesion is the extent to which these various agencies, including the police, cooperate with each other when emergency situations occur. For example, tornadoes are frequent in the Midwestern states and can cause massive devastation. Rapid and effective response requires coordination among all of these agencies. Even public health agencies become involved because natural disasters have the potential to contaminate water and food sources.

Community theorists define cohesion along two dimensions: vertical and horizontal (Garkovich, 1989; Sharp, 2001; Wilkinson, 1970). Vertical integration refers to the strength of relationships between an individual or group at the local level and various individuals and groups beyond the immediate boundaries of the community. For example, a police agency's vertically integrated relationships would include memberships in professional police associations, relationships with statewide police organizations (such as the state police), and relationships with various criminal justice agencies, such as the state attorney general's office or a state forensics lab. Some of these vertically integrated relationships are mandated by federal and state laws, while others are arrangements developed through contacts initiated by a local police agency with an outside agency to acquire additional resources and expertise.

Horizontal integration refers to the strength of relationships between individuals and groups within the immediate boundaries of the community. For example, there are various degrees of both cooperation and competition between a police agency and a fire department. On the one hand, both are first responders who have responsibility for incidents involving public safety. At the scene of a fire, fire department personnel are responsible for suppression of the blaze and the rescue of individuals from the burning structure. The police are responsible for securing the area so that fire department personnel can perform their duties without interruption and so that onlookers are not endangered. On the other hand, the respective heads of police and fire agencies must frequently compete with each other for funding from the same local elected officials and vie for support from the same community at large and the various constituency groups within it.

In most communities of the United States, volunteers (i.e., nonpaid personnel) help staff both police agencies and fire departments, creating situations in which the two groups must competitively recruit from the same pool of citizens (Whisenand and Ferguson, 2002). Among law enforcement, these volunteers frequently are called "police reserves," who can be called to duty in emergency situations or when large events are held, such as festivals or concerts, that require additional personnel. In many communities of the United States, fire departments are staffed almost completely by volunteers. Even the fire chief may serve part time and is a volunteer. Fire departments become more than merely agencies responsible for responding to calls for service; they become a focal point for various social activities (and the political center for local politics), such as a place for volunteers to congregate and gossip, and as a group raising money to purchase fire protection equipment.

Similar relationships exist between the police and other local agencies in the community responsible for issues of health and safety. It is into this complex network of overlapping jurisdictions and varying degrees of interagency collaboration and competition that the issue of preparedness for terrorism has now confronted every police agency in the United States.

The State of Ohio Conference on Terrorism

During the 1990s, a series of incidents raised grave concerns about the possibility that terrorism would become a growing reality in the United States. These incidents included events occurring both inside and outside the country. Conflicts around the world made headlines nearly every day in the United States, from such places as far away as Northern Ireland, Sri Lanka, Israel and Palestine, and the Basque region of Spain and from groups within countries formed after the breakup of Yugoslavia, among others. Plus, U.S. citizens and property in other countries (i.e., embassies, ships, and military installations) have been the frequent targets for attacks by terrorists. Within the United States, there were many events as well, including incidents of terrorism by right-wing and antigovernment groups, extremist groups promoting various environmental and animal rights issues, and groups opposed to the globalization of the economy, the practices and policies of international corporations, free-trade summits by world leaders, and so on. As well, race relations within U.S. society have been and will continue to be a possible domestic source for terrorism. In the past, civil rights groups and leaders of predominantly black churches have been the targets of violence.

In particular, one incident served to change the mind-set of many elected officials, especially at the state and federal levels. This was April 19, 1995, when Timothy McVeigh and accomplices bombed the federal building in Oklahoma City, Oklahoma. Over 160 people were killed. This incident had important symbolic value for these state and federal leaders. First, it occurred in the midwestern region of the United States. A common assumption prior to that time was that terrorism only occurred in large cities on the East and West Coasts of the country. Second, the perpetrator was a citizen of the United States and was a military veteran. But third, and most important, the ability of first-responder agencies in the community (and surrounding communities) of Oklahoma City was put severely to the test. Their ability to coordinate rescue and investigatory efforts was vital to the recovery process of victims' families and friends and the ability of police investigators to uncover clues and apprehend the terrorists.

Yet, public opinion about terrorism continued to be weak after Oklahoma City insofar as most people believed that the likelihood of an incident occurring in their community was almost nil. Although public attention was jolted by the World Trade Center and Pentagon events of September 11, 2001, when citizens consider terrorism in reference to their own communities, they have maintained the belief that the chances are very small. To quote one U.S. citizen from the medium-size midwestern town ("September 11, 6 Months Later," 2002): "You have to get to the airport early, and you have to take off your shoes. ... Besides that, what's changed?"

Methodology

The Oklahoma City bombing set in motion the idea that terrorism could occur in the "heartland" or midwestern states of the United States. In Ohio, a statewide conference on domestic preparedness was organized. The conference was cosponsored by the Office of the Lieutenant Governor and the Ohio Department of Public Safety plus the Ohio Emergency Management Agency. A number of other state-level institutions also assisted with the conference, including the Ohio State University (OSU). The role of the OSU team (which I led) was to record the proceedings, including observations and note taking at each of the plenary and concurrent sessions (Office of the Lieutenant Governor, 2000).

Altogether, slightly more than 900 persons attended the 2-day conference, which was held on June 5–6, 2000. Ohio is subdivided into 88 counties, and representatives of various local agencies who are important to the "horizontal integration" of the community were invited. These included locally based representatives from (a) police agencies; (b) firefighting agencies; (c) EMS; (d) emergency management agencies; (e) public health officials; (f) the medical community, including local doctors, hospital personnel, and the coroner; and (g) local elected officials.

The 88 counties in Ohio vary greatly in population size and composition. The most rural county in Ohio has fewer than 13,000 residents, while the largest includes 1.4 million people. Ohio is a state that includes three metropolitan areas of more than 1 million (Cincinnati, Cleveland, and Columbus) and 13 smaller metropolitan areas. As well, within its borders are many suburban communities, communities located on the fringe between urbanized areas and rural areas, a large number of small towns, and areas that are exclusively rural. The U.S. Bureau of the Census (2002) indicates that 2.8 million of Ohio's approximately 11 million residents live in small towns and unincorporated areas. Local stakeholders to the conference reflected the diversity of these community environments, which indicates that the law enforcement representatives and those of the other groups brought with them experiences reflective of the overlapping jurisdictions and missions of their own agencies and of issues related to both vertical and horizontal integration of their communities.

A significant portion of the conference was devoted to breakout sessions in which each of these seven "stakeholder" groups considered a set of four questions with reference to the major theme or focus of the conference: domestic preparedness. The four questions were as follows: (a) What are the most critical equipment issues? (b) What are the most critical training issues? (c) What are the most critical internal issues? and (d) What are the most critical external issues?

Since a member of each stakeholder group was invited from each of the 88 counties in the state, the size of the stakeholder groups was quite large. A team of four trained facilitators guided each of the concurrent sessions in which the police and the other six stakeholder groups independently discussed the four issues and developed their short lists of priorities. The facilitators introduced the topics and supervised the discussion. Facilitators recorded issues on flip chart paper. Anyone could enter an issue on the list. Then, participants were handed discussion sheets. On these sheets, they were asked to first write up to 10 critical issues in reference to the question under consideration. Through discussion and debate, guided by the facilitators, the list was reduced to five and a final vote was taken. Despite the best efforts of facilitators, however, some of the groups, depending on the question under consideration, did not conform to the principle of listing only five priorities. On occasion, as many as seven and as few as three priorities were listed. The priorities were reported by the facilitation team leader at the general closing session of the conference.

In this chapter, the critical issues related to preparedness as prioritized by representatives from police agencies across the state of Ohio are presented. In addition, their priorities are compared to the other stakeholder groups.

Results

The first question regarded critical equipment issues. Table 8.1 includes a summary of the five priority issues of law enforcement on each of the four questions. Also included are issues identified by the other six stakeholder groups, but not by the police.

For law enforcement, the five critical equipment issues were as follows: (a) communications equipment; (b) personal protective equipment (PPE); (c) detection equipment (hazmat); (d) funding for the first-time purchase of equipment; and (e) funding for the maintenance of equipment. Based on the notes of the observers in the law enforcement session, the police defined critical equipment issues in terms of improving their inventories, with most indicating that their agencies have little or none of the equipment necessary to respond adequately to an incident of terrorism or to protect police officers and others who must respond to such incidents. At the same time, the police representatives at the conference recognized that equipment purchases for possible incidents of terrorism (to assist with rescue, to gather evidence, or to detect bombs, dangerous chemicals, and other weapons of mass destruction) require special funding beyond discretionary monies already available for patrol cars, weapons, vests, and other police paraphernalia.

All seven stakeholder groups were in agreement that communications equipment was one of the top five critical equipment issues. In addition, four of the other six groups indicated that the purchase of PPE and hazmat equipment was a top priority. Working independently, the police and fire groups had nearly identical equipment priority lists. Of particular note is that both the police and the firefighter groups were the only stakeholder groups to list funding of equipment among their top five critical equipment issues. Three priorities not identified by the police but listed by two or more of the other six groups included (a) equipment necessary to establish a command center; (b) software containing reference material information about weapons of mass destruction and other pertinent information in response to critical incidents; and (c) decontamination equipment.

It was possible that if there were no agreement among the seven stakeholder groups, the list of critical equipment issues in Table 7.1 would include about 35 different items. In fact, there were only 34 critical equipment issues identified (although the firefighter group listed 2 extra, the medical community group identified only 3, and the local EMA (emergency management agency) stakeholders identified only 4). However, the list was less than half that size, indicating only 15 discrete equipment issues. In other words, for every equipment issue identified, there were 2.4 votes; that is, an average of 2.4 stakeholders groups identified each issue as a high priority. This indicates a moderate amount of agreement among each of the seven local stakeholder groups. In addition, the top five priorities listed by representatives from local

Table 7.1 Priorities of Law Enforcement and Other Stakeholder Groups

Critical Equipment Needs	Critical Training Issues	Critical Internal Issues	Critical External Issues
	Top Five Priorities of Law Enforcement		
Communications equipment (P, F, EMS, MED, PHO, EMA, EO)	Certification of training (P, F, EMS, PHO, EO)	Intraagency policies and procedures for response to incidents and communication (P, F, EMS, MED, PHO, EO)	Ongoing interagency coordination (P, F, PHO, EO)
Personal protective equipment (PPE) (P, F, EMS, PHO, EO)	Resource guide of certified trainers and training sites (P, F)	Personal retention (P)	Political support (local and state) (P, F, PHO, EO)
Funding for first-time equipment purchases (P, F)	Incident command training (P)	Command staff training (P, EMS)	Media relations (P, PHO, EO)
Funding for equipment maintenance (P, F)	Funding of certified training sites (P)	Training in use of equipment (PPE, hazmat, etc.) (P, EMS)	Mutual aid agreements (P, MED)
	Top Five Priorities of Other Stakeholder Groups		
Command center equipment (EMA, EO)	Conduct of mock disaster exercises (EMS, PHO, EO)	Funding (F, EMS, EMA, EO)	Public awareness and public education (F, PHO, EO)
Reference materials software (PHO, EMA)	Certification of instructors (F, EMS, EMA)	Adequate and qualified staff (EMS, MED, PHO, EMA)	Incident command/ chain of command (EMS, EMA)
Decontamination equipment (F, EMS)	Continuous training on preparedness for terrorism (MED, EMA)	Commitment of personnel (F, MED)	Interagency/ cross-agency training (F)
Response vehicles (EMS)	Training funds for local agencies (F, MED)	Support from the general and state agencies (MED, EMA)	Intelligence (F)
Emergency generators (EO)	Media/public information (PHO, EO)	Assessing needs within the agency (F)	External communication (from local to state level) (EO)

(Continued)

Table 7.1 Priorities of Law Enforcement and Other Stakeholder Groups (Continued)

Critical Equipment Needs	Critical Training Issues	Critical Internal Issues	Critical External Issues
Crash cart (MED)	Interagency roles in critical incidents (PHO)	Conflict with other duties in mission of agency (F)	State guidelines for training and equipment (MED)
On-site portable computers (PHO)	ID of weapons of mass destruction (PHO)	Funding for development of mission in relation to terrorism (EMA)	Information on national standards for training and equipment (EMS)
Identification of high-priority equipment (MED)	Using computer software (PHO)	Administrative management of emergency response (MED)	Coordination of health care professional training needs (MED)
Antidotes (F)	Using personal protective equipment (EMS)	Standardized emergency response plan across all agencies (PHO)	Integrate public health standards into critical standards (PHO)
	Unified interagency training on issues related to terrorism (F)	Critical incident training (PHO)	Funding for replacement of used equipment (F)
	Finding ways to effectively train busy people (MED)	Security for public officials (EO)	Finding ways to effectively train busy people (MED)
	Appropriate training for personnel from utility companies (EO)	Media relations (EO)	Federal and state assistance for intervention (EO)
	Appropriate training for elected officials (EO)	Promotion of emergency management agencies (EMA)	
	Assessing training needs and priorities (EMA)	Unforeseeable circumstances (EO)	
	Evaluating trainers and training programs (EMA)		

Abbreviations: P, police; F, fire; EMS, emergency medical services; MED, medical community (doctors and hospital administrators); PHO, public health officials; EMA, local emergency management agency workers; EO, elected officials.

law enforcement were also listed 16 of the remaining 29 times by the other six groups, indicating that the priority issues of the police were largely the same priorities of the other stakeholder groups.

The second question concerned critical training issues. In contrast to the results in Table 8.1, perceptions of critical training issues among the seven stakeholder groups were much more divergent. There were 21 different priorities listed of 33 possible, or 1.57 votes per priority training issue identified. The discrepancy from 35 possible priorities was due to the fact that only 3 priorities were listed by the medical community, 4 by EMA representatives, and 6 by elected officials.

The law enforcement stakeholder group was very much concerned about the issue of certification. Three of their top five priority issues expressed this concern, including certification of training about how to respond to terrorist incidents, a resource guide of certified trainers and training sites, and funding of sites where certified training can be conducted. These priorities reflected the environment in which police training on many other issues is conducted. Observer notes from this session indicated that the participants were concerned that the funding for terrorism training will create a number of "overnight experts" who do not meet standards. The police representatives also recognized that training budgets for police agencies, large and small, were already stretched to the limit, and that if the police are expected to increase their preparedness for possible incidents of terrorism, then state and federal governments must be prepared to provide the monies necessary to fund the training sites.

The police response to this question was quite logical given the context of policing in the United States. Federal and state laws define the standards for police training and retraining and who (trainers and training sites) is eligible to conduct this training. It was perfectly logical for the police stakeholder group to consider critical training issues about terrorism in the same terms as their other training.

In addition to issues related to certification, the police identified two other training needs. The first was basic training for first responders (the police plus fire and EMS). Observer notes indicated that a number of the police participants had knowledge of the police experience from Oklahoma City, where a coordinated effort with other first responders was considered relatively effective. Therefore, they expressed the need that basic training was necessary for all three groups, not merely the police. Likewise, the other critical issue identified as a top five priority by the police stakeholder group was incident command training. Again, those who expressed the need for this kind of training frequently referred to the experience of Oklahoma City, where the chain of command had been predetermined through mutual aid agreements of the police department and other first-responding groups.

Police priorities did not always agree with the other six stakeholder groups. Issues identified by two or more of these other groups included (a) the conduct of mock disaster exercises; (b) certification of trainers; (c) continuous training on preparedness for terrorism; (d) training funds for local agencies; and (e) media relations/public information training.

Critical internal issues were the topic of the third question. Thirty-four priorities were identified by the seven stakeholder groups in regard to the question of critical internal issues. Public health officials listed only four priorities. Altogether, 18 different issues were identified, or 1.9 votes per issue. Among the top five priority issues of the law enforcement stakeholder group, three related to training, including training on how the police should respond to critical incidents, command staff training, and training in the use of equipment (PPE, hazmat, etc.). These three issues reflected priorities previously expressed in response to questions about critical issues relative to both equipment and training.

There were two other internal issues in the top five priority list identified by the police. The first was the concern among a number of the participants in the police stakeholder group for the need to establish agency policy and guidelines about how to respond to incidents of terrorism. This priority reflects the culture of police agencies in the United States insofar as standardization of procedures is a prominent concern. One of the primary duties of the chief executive officer (CEO) of a police agency is to review and reformulate the procedure "manual" of the police agency. These procedures reflect not only various federal and state guidelines that define the mission of policing but also agreements between management and unionized officers and procedures established to avoid lawsuits through inappropriate actions or the negligent behavior of sworn personnel. Concern about policies and procedures was also the most frequently mentioned issue, making the top five priority list for four of the seven stakeholder groups.

Also considered important by the law enforcement representatives was the issue of personnel retention. They were the only group to rank this issue as a top priority. Observer notes indicated that the concern centered on the high turnover rate among patrol officers due to transfer from one agency to another, resignations, and retirements. Every personnel change requires learning new policies and regulations, given the relative autonomy of each agency to develop its own set of rules.

Three of the top five priorities of the law enforcement stakeholder group overlapped with the EMS stakeholder group, namely, training on how to respond to critical incidents, command staff training, and training in the use of equipment. Elected officials also listed critical incident training among their top five internal issues.

There were two issues rated high by at least four stakeholder groups that did not make the top five priority list of law enforcement. These were "funding" and "adequate and qualified staff." Funding was a high-priority internal issue for firefighters, EMS personnel, local EMA personnel, and local elected officials. Adequate and qualified staff were a priority for EMS personnel, local representatives of the medical community, public health officials, and local EMA personnel. Both reflect the belief of representatives of these agencies that they are underfunded and understaffed in general; hence, their capacity to be responsive to any kind of incident involving multiple victims would be difficult.

The fourth and final question asked the police and the other six stakeholder groups to consider critical external issues. Two of the top-priority issues of the police involved their relationship with other agencies in the community (i.e., horizontal integration). These were ongoing interagency coordination and communication and mutual aid agreements. With both priority issues, the law enforcement group realized that interagency coordination and communication in their community was rarely very good, although they qualified their statements by noting that most first-responding agencies were able to cooperate sufficiently to respond to incidents when necessary. However, a terrorist incident would be at an entirely different level, something never experienced before by anyone in the community, and would require a new, heightened level of coordination. For this reason, mutual aid agreements become extremely important, and several of the law enforcement representatives saw a parallel between the critical internal issue of intraagency policies and procedures and the external issue of mutual aid agreements that spell out policies and procedures between agencies.

Two other top-five police priority issues included dimensions of both vertical and horizontal integration. These were political support (local and state) and media relations. The discussion centered mostly on local political support for the financial cost of preparedness and the fact that local elected officials "take their cue" (to quote one of the participants) directly from voters. However, the discussion also included the importance of political support from state leaders so that local political leaders feel the pressure to be equally supportive. Plus, state political support is necessary for proper levels of funding to come about (also a top five priority issue). Overall, the police representatives were skeptical of the sustainability of political support for domestic preparedness, believing that it will wane because the public's attention span, vis-à-vis the media's attention span, is rather short. Obviously, this discussion occurred before the events of September 11, but as the *USA Today* quotation cited previously aptly demonstrated ("September 11, 6 months later," 2002), public attention to terrorism has already begun to decline.

In regard to media relations, observers' notes indicated that the discussion by the police included both local and national media, with the police representatives realizing that any local incident of terrorism would bring media from around the country and the world to their community. They recognized that mutual aid agreements have to include which first responder or other community agency (or coordination thereof) will be responsible for clearing information for public release. They also discussed the problems of keeping the media away from the scene where evidence must be collected without restricting the rights of a free press. Finally, another part of the discussion of the media centered on media bias toward the police and the accuracy of media reports of other incidents involving the police. In essence, part of the reason that the police consider media relations a high-priority external issue is prior skepticism and animosity toward the press.

There were 20 different priority issues listed by all seven stakeholder groups. Altogether, there were 36 votes on critical external issues, with every group identifying five priorities, except the medical community, which listed six priorities. There were 1.8 votes by stakeholder groups per issue.

All but one of the other six stakeholder groups (namely, local EMA representatives) agreed with the police that ongoing interagency coordination and communication was a priority issue. Three others agreed with the police that political support was critical. In addition, two other stakeholder groups lined up with the police on the importance of funding and media relations. Two external issues considered important by two or more of the other six stakeholder groups were (a) public awareness and public education relative to terrorism and to local preparedness; and (b) establishment of chain of command in response to critical incidents.

Summary and Conclusion

The purpose of this chapter was to examine issues related to domestic preparedness from the point of view of the police, based on a statewide conference held in Ohio in June 2000. Information was derived from a formal process, guided by facilitators, of developing priority issues in response to four questions about preparedness and from the notes of observers to the discussion sessions. Comparisons of police priorities of the critical issues were made with six other stakeholder groups consisting of local representatives from throughout the state. These included firefighters, EMS personnel, the medical community, public health officials, local EMA personnel, and elected officials. In large part, the other six stakeholder groups agreed with the assessment of domestic preparedness as formulated by the police. Despite this, it was often the case that top five priorities among all seven stakeholder groups varied due to the unique perspectives and special interests of each.

When examining the various priority issues raised specifically by the police to the four questions, three patterns emerge. First, the police indicated a high priority for equipment necessary to respond effectively to terrorism and for equipment that would protect them while at the scene of the incidents. Recognizing that current police budgets are not sufficient to purchase and maintain this equipment, they also identified funding as a high priority for both initial purchases and for maintenance of the equipment so that it can be used when the time comes. However, without local and state political support, they felt that such funding is not likely to occur.

Second, the police identified certified training as a high priority. This included training in the use of equipment and in the chain of command within the police agency and between other agencies when incidents occur. Training must meet minimum standards as specified by a certification process that includes both trainers and training sites, and these must be listed in a resource guide so that local police agencies can access the right kinds of training, trainers, and training sites. Like equipment, training includes a maintenance dimension because of personnel turnover in the police ranks. Of course, as with equipment purchase and maintenance, current police budgets are insufficient to fund training for domestic preparedness. Local and state political support becomes essential.

Third, policies and procedures must be established proactively so that the police agency and its personnel know what to do should an incident of terrorism occur. Likewise, interagency coordination and communication during a time of crisis requires prior development of mutual aid agreements, especially among first-responder agencies within the same community.

The nature of policing at the local, community level is clearly evident in police perceptions of critical issues that need to be addressed to prepare for incidents of terrorism. The officers felt that assistance from the outside (vertical integration) must come in the form of funding, political support, and an infrastructure of certified training sites and trainers. Further, the officers recognized that their relationship to other service groups in the community, including other first responders, was critical to an effective response (horizontal integration).

Policing in America is conditioned by the locality-specific nature of the U.S. federated system of governance (federal, state, and local) and by a culture that values local community autonomy. In turn, these broad social structural and cultural parameters condition the response of the police (and the other stakeholder groups) to an issue like domestic preparedness. For example, none of the notes of observers recorded a comment by an officer indicating that domestic preparedness for terrorism should be under the sole jurisdiction of a statewide agency. Yet, nearly every participant, at one time or another, believed that outside assistance (funding, certification standards, and political support) was essential for preparedness within their communities. Likewise, when they considered coordination and communication issues with other first responders, the issue was always discussed as a local, community-level issue and not as a state or federal issue.

References

Garkovich, Lorraine E. (1989). Local organizations and leadership in community development. In James A. Christenson and Jerry W. Robinson (Eds.), *Community Development in Perspective* (pp. 196–218). Ames: Iowa State University Press.

Geller, William A. (Ed.). (1985). *Police Leadership in America: Crisis and Opportunity.* New York: Praeger.

Hickman, Matthew J., and Reaves, Brian A. (2001). *Local Police Departments, 1999.* NCJ 186478. Washington, DC: U.S. Department of Justice, Bureau of Justice Statistics.

Office of the Lieutenant Governor. (2000). *Terrorism 2000: State of Ohio Conference on Terrorism and Domestic Preparedness.* Columbus, OH: Office of the Lieutenant Governor.

Palone, Eugene A., Myers, Stephanie M., and Worden, Robert E. (2000). Police culture, individuals, and community policing: Evidence from two police departments. *Justice Quarterly, 17*(3), 575–605.

September 11, 6 months later. (2002, March 7). *USA Today*, p. 1.

Sharp, Jeff S. (2001). Locating the community field: A study of inter-organizational network structure and capacity for community action. *Rural Sociology, 66*(3), 403–424.

U.S. Bureau of the Census. (2002). *State and County Quick Facts.* Retrieved from http://quickfacts.census.gov/qfd/states/39000.html

Weisheit, Ralph A., Falcone, David N., and Wells, L. Edward (1999). *Crime and Policing in Rural and Smalltown America.* Prospect Heights, IL: Waveland Press.

Whisenand, Paul M., and Ferguson, R. Fred. (2002). *The Managing of Police Organizations* (5th ed.). Upper Saddle River, NJ: Prentice-Hall.

Wilkinson, Kenneth P. (1970). The community as a social field. *Social Forces, 48,* 311–322.

Policing and Networks in the Field of Counterterrorism[1]

8

DARREN PALMER
CHAD WHELAN

Contents

Introduction

Since the terrorist attacks of 2001, policing has undergone considerable structural change. At the theoretical level, considerable international intellectual effort has been directed at rethinking the concept of policing (Johnston and Shearing, 2003; Palmer, 2009; Palmer and Whelan, 2007); the organization of policing (Bayley and Shearing, 2001; Jones and Newburn, 1998); and the conceptual delineation between different forms of policing (Jones and Newburn, 1999, 2002; Rigakos, 2005). In this chapter, we focus on how counterterrorism is shaping different ways of governing *through* policing in its many forms and practices. More specifically, the chapter examines recent developments in counterterrorism policing in Australia at national and subnational levels to enhance our understanding of how counterterrorism responses are reshaping the policing and security field and raises policy issues concerning the location of responsibility for counterterrorism practices and the accountabilities related to such decision making. We also link Australian developments with similarities at the international level.

In response to the terrorist attacks of September 11, 2001, in the United States and the subsequent "war on terror," the Australian commonwealth government launched its new program of counterterrorism with three distinct "documents": the National Counterterrorism Plan (NCTP); new law enforcement legislation (specifically the Security Legislation Amendment (Terrorism) Act 2002 and the Australian Security Intelligence Organization (ASIO) (Amendment) Act 2003 and associated legislation); and a public awareness campaign, "Let's look out for Australia." Further substantial legal reforms were introduced in late 2005, such as the Anti-Terrorism Act (No. 2) 2002, which, as identified in this chapter, further confirms our analysis. At the subnational level (state and territory governments), the organization of counterterrorism policing largely, although not totally, mirrors these developments through supporting legislation and administrative programs. This level needs to be taken into account because the Australian constitution divides responsibilities for criminal justice in a way that means each of the six states, the two territories, and the commonwealth have their own criminal justice framework, including police agencies. The exception to this is the Australian Capital Territory, which employs the commonwealth police—the Australian Federal Police—under contract to provide basic police services (James, 2005). Unlike the United States, for instance, Australia does not have city or municipal police or the regional or county forces found in the United Kingdom. Further, the size of the police agencies varies considerably. Nationally, Australia has 59,821 operational police and 6,693 nonoperational staff (as of June 2011). The largest is in New South Wales and consists of 17,033 operational staff, while the smallest is the Australian Capital Territory, with just 858 operational police (Australian Productivity Commission, 2012, Table 6.1, p. 6.5). This does not include the Australian Federal Police national duties, which has 2,463 sworn officers and 836 protective service officers (guarding public buildings and protection of dignitaries; see Australian Federal Police, 2012, Table C3, p. 8).

There are several key features in these planning, legislative, and media initiatives: the "new federalism" that they entail; the introduction of offenses specifically defined as terrorism; the "responsibilization" of citizens and corporate entities (O'Malley and Palmer, 1996); and the networking of policing across state and nonstate sectors, or what one of us refers to as "security networks" (Whelan, 2012). While each of these is addressed, the main focus here is on the loose coupling of state and nonstate policing across counterterrorism security networks. It is argued that in ways not yet fully addressed, counterterrorism adds a new layer of complexity to the "extended policing family" (Johnston, 2003) in terms of how the networks are formed, the cooperation and integration of different policing agents, and the different forms of operationalizing accountability (accountability for prevention of and reaction to terrorism, as well as for public or democratic accountability).

While Australian opposition to many of these measures was intense (Senate Legal and Constitutional Committee, 2002; Senate Legal and Constitutional References Committee, 2002), most particularly the ASIO Amendment Bill (many of the more punitive elements were scaled back in the final legislation), the counterterrorism program contains within it both new governmental categories—terrorists, people with information about terrorism, people funding terrorist organizations, and so on—and new ways of governing. These new categories and new techniques point toward a broader shift in "re-imagining policing" (Cooley, 2005), "securitization" (Loader, 2002), and "wider reconfiguration of contemporary governance" (Johnston and Shearing, 2003, p. 12) in contemporary Australia. It is a program that is unfolding in an everyday sense.

Introducing the "Terrorist"

Australia has a history of events that would today be labeled terrorism, but prior to September 11, 2001, only one Australian jurisdiction had used the criminal law to label specific acts as "terrorism." The Northern Territory (1983) had introduced terrorist offenses to its criminal code (Section 50). In other jurisdictions, what is now called terrorism was partly covered by the term *politically motivated violence*, which is the term used in the ASIO Act 1979 (Section 4). It is true to say "partly" because the new categories of terrorist and terrorism extend in significant ways beyond politically motivated violence.

In 2002, the commonwealth passed the Security Legislation Amendment (Terrorism) Act, which introduced terrorism as an element of key offenses in the Criminal Code—Part 5.3 Terrorism. The NCTP paraphrases the legislated definition (Commonwealth Criminal Code, Section 100.1) of terrorism in the following terms (in the same way as done in 2004):

> A "terrorist act" is an action or threat intended to advance a political, ideological or religious cause by coercing or intimidating an Australian or foreign government or the public, by causing serious harm to people or property, endangering life, creating a serious risk to the health and safety of the public or seriously disrupting trade, critical infrastructure or electronic systems. (National Counterterrorism Committee, 2012, p. 4 (15))

Legal definitions of terrorism are problematic (Golder and Williams, 2004) and were explicitly rejected in the responses to an earlier incident of politically motivated violence in 1978 (the Hilton hotel bombing, which is discussed further in the chapter). For instance, as O'Neill, Rice, and Douglas (2004) point out, there are a number of value statements in the definition of terrorism that will require case law judgments specific to terrorist acts for clarification, such as "coercing," "intimidating," "serious harm," and "serious risk." Others, such as Tham (2004, p. 520), argue that the counterterrorism legislation was introduced with "indecent haste" and was based on "misrepresentations" of existing laws and government powers (pp. 523–524) and in a manner that stifled public deliberation (p. 526). For Tham (2004), the outcome was a stream of poorly developed legislation that further entrenched the potential "lawlessness" of the ASIO, the key security agency granted significantly increased powers of surveillance and interrogation, and made it difficult to hold it accountable (Michaelsen, 2005; Tham, 2004, pp. 529–530). In other words, the key features of the counterterrorism measures were elements of "securitization": the dramatization of the threats to the extent that they challenge "our way of life" and framing this dramatization in a manner that creates imperatives, making change "both urgent and inevitable" (Loader, 2002, p. 135).

If not eliminated by the management of risk associated with terrorism, the "root causes" approach to the elimination of politically motivated violence has at least ceded ground. This is not to suggest that overt disciplinary and punitive measures have been eliminated, but rather that there has been significant movement away from causation to association of "risky" subjects and behaviors (O'Malley, 2004). Where, however, much of the literature on "actuarial justice" and "risk management" highlights the shift away from criminal law toward the use of less-moralized forms of administration (Valverde and Cirak, 2003), in the domain of counterterrorism the criminal law is revalorized as the tool to address terrorists and their associated entities and behaviors (financing, associating, and supporting statements). Thus, the new criminal law provisions are not simply limited to specific forms of terrorism conjured in the public imagination such as suicide bombings and the like, but rather extend to include related behaviors and problems: It is an offense not only to engage in terrorist violence or attempt to do so but also to make a donation to organizations that are politically defined as "terrorist organizations" or to have any information that law enforcement authorities believe would assist them in the prevention and control of terrorism. In other words, the governmental reach is extended to the array of risk factors that might ultimately lead to a terrorist incident rather than being limited to the incident or planning of the incident itself.

This is no small issue, for as we discuss in this chapter, the emergent governmental framework extends into what is now referred to as *critical infrastructure*, a term that covers activities as diverse as transport systems; communication systems; educational facilities; finance systems; commercial assets; hazardous materials (chemicals, fuels); health services;

manufacturing; and "human assets" (community leaders and subject matter experts) (Commonwealth Government, 2004a). Furthermore, the framework for the protection of critical infrastructure adopts an "all-hazards" approach, of which terrorism is but one of the potential threats, and involves agencies or organizations regardless of any defining boundary of state or nonstate ownership or involvement. However, the form of ownership—public or private—is of some significance in terms of governmental practices: In Australia, 90% of critical infrastructure is privately owned (Commonwealth Government, 2004a); in the United States, private ownership constitutes 85% (National Commission on Terrorist Attacks upon the United States, 2004, p. 317); and in the United Kingdom, the "majority" of critical infrastructure is privately owned (National Infrastructure Security Co-ordination Centre, 2006; changed in 2007 to the Centre for the Protection of National Infrastructure). Thus, the perennial policing problems of communication, information sharing, and coordination are magnified as the subject of intervention moves from state-owned to privately owned entities.

The New Federalism

While there is some evidence of evolutionary change in vesting greater powers in the commonwealth or national government, the distinctiveness of current developments suggest a "new federalism," or what one journalist labeled "feral Federalism" (Shanahan, 2003). Historically, in the division of criminal justice powers, states and territories have been responsible for internal security and the commonwealth government for external matters. This is complicated in detail. For example, commonwealth criminal jurisdiction covers federal offenses occurring within state and territory boundaries (for instance, the Commonwealth Crimes Act 1901 as amended), and particular commonwealth zones such as airports or commonwealth buildings are located within state and territory boundaries. Since 1993, however, following the introduction of the Federal Police in 1979 (although a more limited form of federal police existed before this date), and the responses to organized crime such as the introduction of the National Crime Authority in 1984 (since replaced by the Australian Crime Commission in 2003), there has been a steady trend toward the commonwealth assuming greater policing and law enforcement responsibility. The former development represented increased federal prominence in Australian policing, while the latter meant a significant shift away from state-based policing by the introduction of specialized agencies to deal with organized crime, as well as corporate regulation through the National Company and Securities Commission in 1981, which was replaced by the Australian Securities Commission in 1991 and then the Australian Securities and Investment Commission in 1998. In both instances, the perceived threat of criminal conduct beyond the boundaries, and therefore capacities, of states and territories was viewed as necessitating a redrawing of state-commonwealth relations that had remained largely stable since federation in 1901.

When counterterrorism measures are viewed from this perspective, what at first glance seem to be largely arcane constitutional provisions in the terrorism legislation become on closer examination a matter of ceding state powers to the commonwealth. In effect, state and territory legislation (for example, the Terrorism [Commonwealth Powers] Act 2003, Victoria) refers to the commonwealth the power to make and amend legislation related to terrorism. Following the passing of these forms of state and territory legislation, the commonwealth introduced a new Part 5.3 into the Criminal Code Amendment (Terrorism) Act 2003 to incorporate the new powers of the commonwealth. Centrally, the commonwealth is able to make amendments to terrorist-related offenses, subject to the approval of a majority of the states and territories (O'Neill et al., 2004, pp. 252–253). In the general climate of the "war on terror," there would need to be compelling arguments for a state or territory to deny commonwealth actions, particularly given the political risk of being portrayed as "soft on terrorism," which would be likely to stifle any jurisdictional bravado.[2]

The key issue here is that while the increased law enforcement role of the commonwealth is not new to counterterrorism policing, in the post-9/11 period it was certainly more far reaching than the corporate and organized crime policing that preceded it. Of particular interest is the "return" of organized crime as a key focus and the use of terrorism laws as a model for new policing (and punishment) techniques. This is particularly noteworthy in the various efforts to act against "outlaw motorcycle clubs" (see Bartels, 2010). For example, we have seen some states attempt to introduce laws prescribing "criminal organizations," which have been directed toward outlaw motorcycle clubs, as well as even introduce "control orders" and seek to apply them to individual members of these clubs. A number of motorcycle clubs have—and continue to—challenged the validity of these laws with some success.

While things have undoubtedly changed since 9/11, there is a specific event that is directly related to terrorism and the new federalism. As Hocking (2004) argues in her detailed study of the history of counterterrorism laws in Australia, the bombing of the Hilton hotel during the 1978 Commonwealth Heads of Government meeting in Sydney represented a significant historical shift in two ways. First, the actions of the commonwealth government in taking over authority for responding to the bombing and subsequent security arrangements represented a "significant historical shift in the balance of power between the Commonwealth and the states regarding domestic violence in favour of the Commonwealth" (2004, p. 93). Second, the use of the armed forces was based on treating a terrorist act as different from normal law-and-order issues to be addressed by civil police. Terrorism became a new form of violence politically, legally, and administratively (although not a legally defined act until 2002) that now warranted the use of the military to protect nationhood or sovereignty (2004, pp. 93–94).

It can be argued that current counterterrorism mechanisms such as the NCTP and associated terrorism legislation build politically, administratively, and legally on the trend toward greater commonwealth powers. Yet, the introduction of state police counterterrorism units and the paramilitarization of state policing generally (McCulloch, 2001) suggest recourse to the use of the military will be dependent on the scale of the terrorist act(s). It was during the post-Hilton reviews of policing and security that the recommendations to form the Federal Police were made. More recent developments have clarified and cemented the powers of the commonwealth to use the military to protect commonwealth interests during peacetime, without obtaining formal agreement from the states (Defence Legislation Amendment [Aid to Civilian Authorities] Act 2000) (Hocking, 2004, p. 98). Further, the Council of Australian Governments (COAG) agreed in September 2005 to conduct a review of Part III of the Defense Act 1903 to "enhance and clarify the arrangements for calling out the Australian Defence Force to assist civilian authorities" (COAG, 2005, p.3).

We previously suggested that "only a response to a real event will determine the exact nature of the new federalism" and the extent to which the states and territories will "accept an increasing role for the Commonwealth in civil or domestic order." Since then, several cases have highlighted the increased role of the commonwealth acting within states and territories. One example is the Australian Federal Police and Victoria Police raids conducted in Melbourne (and simultaneously the Federal Police with the New South Wales Police in Sydney) in 2005. These raids targeted a group of 17 men led by Abdul Nacer Benbrika, who was charged and convicted of being a leader of a "terrorist organization." More controversial was the involvement of the Australian Federal Police in Queensland in 2007 with the arrest and continued detention of Dr. Mohamed Haneef on suspicion of supporting terrorist acts related to the failed bombing of Glasgow airport that year. The Haneef case has many dimensions beyond the scope of this chapter (see the Clarke, 2008; Pickering and McCulloch, 2010; Rix, 2009). However, key questions have been raised concerning the decision of the Australian Federal Police to continually detain and subsequently charge Haneef with providing support to a terrorist organization seemingly in the face of statements from other relevant agencies, including the ASIO, that Haneef was not a security threat. This was made worse by the decision of then Immigration Minister Chris Andrews to cancel Haneef's visa on "character grounds," a decision that was later overturned by the federal court. Haneef was later cleared of all charges and financially compensated by the Australian government. These two examples highlight the veracity of our original argument, namely, that terrorism has heralded an increasing role of federal agencies in criminal justice in a manner that highlights the "new federalism."

Responsibilization

Central to counterterrorism is the construction of rational choice actors and an active citizenry enrolled in the fight against terrorism. In recent years, such governmental strategies seeking to make citizens, communities, and various organizations responsible for the management of their own risks have been referred to as "responsibilization" strategies (O'Malley and Palmer, 1996). However, much of the literature on responsibilization has focused on the general public (the macro level) and not discussed how this mentality can also operate on and through the corporate sector (micro levels).

At a macro level, all Australian citizens are enrolled in counterterrorism through the governmental instruction to "be alert but not alarmed." On this measure, the federal government mailed to all Australian households a terrorism information kit, "Let's look out for Australia" (Commonwealth Government, 2002), that included instructions on what to look for and a refrigerator magnet with a terrorism hotline telephone number. The aim was to put national security and the threat of terrorism into "rational perspective," linking national security measures to "protecting the Australian way of life from a possible terrorist threat" (Commonwealth Government, 2003, p. 5). In the accompanying photomontage, there were iconic pictures of Australians at the beach or standing around a barbecue and of a group of children from a range of ethnic backgrounds. The overall image was a "friendly, decent, democratic people" portraying a message of why "the way of life we all value so highly must go on" (Commonwealth Government, 2003, p. 5).

At the micro level, policing or security networks, which include special police units, together with subspecialties such as transport, information technology, energy, or health, are engaged in a process of shaping the responsible management of risk within their particular locations. This is more than merely target hardening of particular sites, as it extends into the creation of responsible risk management practices, particularly in those sites deemed as essential services and critical infrastructure, that require enhanced prevention and responses to terrorism and other threats, such as natural disasters. Any site that is declared an essential service is required to develop a risk management and security plan (see, for instance, the Terrorism Community Protection Act, Part 6).

Special police units in the areas of counterterrorism and emergency management work with these sites to develop and assess plans. For critical infrastructure, the sites are more numerous and are assessed in terms of key sites that are of importance to the nation on social, economic, and defense and security grounds. In 2004, the commonwealth developed a National Critical Infrastructure Strategy (now called the Critical Infrastructure Resilience Strategy, CIRS), with the states of New South Wales and Queensland relatively quickly following, and immediately started working on the identification of sites that fit within the strategy and the levels of protection needed. Victoria, on the other hand, first focused on identifying critical infrastructure and prioritizing through the Victoria Police state community assets, commercial assets, hazardous materials assets, human assets, and state gatherings. Formally titled the Victorian Framework for Critical Infrastructure Protection from Terrorism, its strategy was released in 2007. It is at this level that potential "leakage" occurs as the subnational level determines sites of state and territory critical infrastructure that are not covered by the National Critical Infrastructure Strategy (sites may be critical to both or may be critical only to a state or territory). For instance, on the eastern seaboard where states are connected to the national power grid, some energy nodes are deemed nationally significant, but other power sites might be of importance only at the state level. There are also "sites within sites" or what are referred to as "critical" nodes. For example, within a petrol refinery, critical nodes might include tank storage areas or power plants. With state police assistance, information is developed to identify critical nodes with a view to developing an information database that can be made available to key selected authorities, although information is understandably closely guarded and released only on a need-to-know basis.

Since responsibilization for the management of risk is not unilaterally imposed on owners and operators of critical infrastructure, it would be a mistake to assume that states and territories exercise sovereign authority in a disciplinary sense, although this can occur with such matters as essential services. To do so could cause unwanted effects. First, it would place much of the burden for the protection of private assets on the public sector. Cost recovery could go some way to recouping the expense of such measures, but it raises the possibility of resistance from the owners of private facilities who may not want police intervention or who may be wary of carrying the financial burden of state-imposed security measures. This concern has already been strongly stated in the aviation sector (Yates, 2005). For example, Sir John Wheeler's review into airport policing and security in 2005, which resulted from general concerns about security protection against potential terrorist activities as well as more specific concerns identified in mid-2005 about organized criminal activities at airports, examined this issue. Wheeler found that the private sector recognized some need to fund security as part of the cost of doing business, but questioned government imposition of additional security requirements without "serious consultation" and without government absorbing "more of that cost" (2005, p. 35). Wheeler had found similar limitations in security arrangements in his earlier review of airport security in the United Kingdom (Wheeler, 2002). The United States Critical Infrastructure Protection Program (2006, p. 2) had similarly discovered that the significant involvement of the private sector and the absence of a single authority and responsibility for the management of security made the task of protecting critical infrastructure daunting.

Similarly, a review of aviation and maritime security by the Parliamentary Joint Committee on Law Enforcement (2011, p. 7) found ongoing problems with "information sharing arrangements between law enforcement agencies and private sector organizations in the aviation and maritime sectors," subsequently addressed at the federal level by the Crimes Legislation Amendment (Power and Offenses) Act 2012 and Australian Crime Commission Amendment Regulation 2012 (No. 1). These amendments were designed to allow the key criminal intelligence-gathering agency, the Australian Crime Commission, to more easily share intelligence and to share it with more agencies and the private sector as part of the development of a broader National Criminal Intelligence Management Strategy. Part of the justification for these changes, in line with our analysis of a deepening responsibilization of the private sector, is that it is "better equipping industry to implement its own measures" (Australian Government, 2012).

At the state level, recent evidence of the ongoing difficulties of ensuring responsibilization in the private sector is found in a Victorian auditor general's (2010, p. ix) report on water and transport critical infrastructure; the auditor general concluded that, "[n]one of the operators [reviewed] were fully compliant with the risk management requirements of the Terrorism (Community Protection) Act 2003." Overall, we can see that the task of protecting critical infrastructure is one of trying to respect the autonomy of the private sector while managing the risk of terrorism.

Risk management procedures are being shaped largely through expert advice and information and governance by audit to ensure plans are in place and workable. The underlying logic is that once owners and operators of essential services and critical infrastructure are informed of the risks and the requirements for prevention and response, they will fully cooperate with risk management protocols. In other words, the governmental objective is to achieve voluntary acceptance of risk avoidance measures rather than their imposition by the state. So, rather than being passive recipients of governmental directions, corporate entities actively adopt security measures through industry representatives and through site-by-site negotiation of the content of the governmental programs. What is at play concerns the extent to which liberal government can shape conduct at a distance while maintaining the freedom of the corporate sector. Yet, when it comes to security of the state against terrorism or the protection of state assets, regardless of legal ownership, residual state powers to compel the adoption of proper security measures influence the freedom of choice to adopt security and risk management plans.

All of this indicates that the "multilateralization" of policing (Bayley and Shearing, 2001) is not so much a response to the incapacities of state-based policing as it is recognition of the private ownership of critical infrastructure. It is a task of engendering enhanced responsibilization in the private sector, and it requires considerable effort, sometimes through sovereign control techniques such as apply to legally determined essential services but, more generally, through administrative mechanisms that strengthen risk management capacities in the private sector. Still, as Yates (2005) points out and Wheeler (2005) documents, just how far the private sector is willing to employ the security and risk management processes demanded, and to absorb the associated costs, remains to be seen. If the ongoing debate over airport security is any indicator, it is likely that cost sharing is at least part of the solution to the security of critical infrastructure and public safety generally. Finally, by aligning security measures to state counterterrorism measures, the corporate entities are able to "augment their security programmes by instrumentalizing the coercive power of the state" (Hutchinson and O'Connor, 2005, p. 132), combining private property and contract law "rights" with state authority and resources to govern privately owned, publicly used sites.

Networked Policing

Responsibilization of the private sector intersects with the important organizational changes in policing associated with the emergence of networked policing or what is more broadly referred to as "security networks" (Brodeur and Dupont, 2006; Dupont, 2004; Gill, 2006; Whelan, 2011, 2012). We can understand *networks* as groups of organizations (referred to as "actors" or "nodes") that have formed relationships (or "ties") to work together to achieve not only their own goals but also a collective or shared goal. Networks are increasing in number and in importance in a range of areas to the extent that some argue they are becoming more dominant than traditional hierarchical approaches to coordination (Raab and Kenis, 2009). Networks are now regularly used as a means to manage "wicked" problems (known as those that cross the boundaries of individual organizations and cannot be divided in "neat" parts and allocated to single organizations), of which terrorism is a clear example (Whelan, 2012). In the case of policing and security, the organizations that participate in these networks can be incredibly diverse, including local, institutional, and communal actors (Dupont, 2004). Security networks exist at the local, regional, and international levels and cross the public, private, and "communitarian" sectors (Gill, 2006).

Networks display at least two important dynamics: structural and relational. Networks can be highly structured, whereby all forms of interaction can be brokered through a central actor, or loosely structured, making it difficult to coordinate a network and creating uncertainty concerning the roles and responsibilities of network participants. In terms of relational dynamics, networks are defined by relationships that take place within and between network members. These relationships need to be based on high levels of trust and cooperation to minimize the negative effects of power relations, competition, and conflict, which if unchecked significantly undermine the effectiveness of networks and the "collective goods" in the form of benefits to all individuals and agencies involved in the network (Brodeur and Dupont, 2006). Traditional concerns with such relationships include cultural differences between organizations, something that has been of significant concern in the field of national security (Whelan, 2012). Further, on top of the difficulties with identifying responsibilities within networks, networks can transcend traditional forms of democratic accountability, suggesting other types of frameworks need to be established to monitor and evaluate policing networks (Hermer, Kempa, Shearing, Stenning, and Wood, 2005; Loader, 2000). In what follows, we concentrate on two examples of networked policing as a portent of future developments: policing critical infrastructure and police-private security partnerships. The two necessarily overlap to some extent, but for our purposes we treat them as discrete developments.

Policing Critical Infrastructure

We mentioned the detailed arrangements that have developed to protect critical infrastructure, whether from terrorism or from other forces such as natural disasters. These measures were discussed in terms of broader processes of responsibilization of owners and operators of critical infrastructure, where the security practices are shaped by the expert advice and information provided by state police. These sites of national and subnational significance involve state and nonstate actors and interests, creating further complexity for the issues of information sharing, divided responsibility, and coordination of effort (National Commission on Terrorist Attacks upon the United States, 2004; Wheeler 2002, 2005).

To address these problems in the area of critical infrastructure, the Australian government declared that the fostering of "effective partnerships with state and territory governments and the private sector" is central to protecting critical infrastructure (Commonwealth Government, 2004b, p. 32), a point further reinforced in the more recent Australian government's CIRS (2010). To facilitate these partnerships, the government formed the Trusted Information Sharing Network (TISN) for Critical Infrastructure Protection.

The TISN was and remains a forum for owners and operators of critical infrastructure to exchange information on matters related to security. It has a critical infrastructure advisory council (CIAC) to advise the attorney general on matters relating to critical infrastructure protection. The CIAC has representatives from infrastructure assurance advisory groups (IAAGs), expert advisory groups, each of the states and territories, relevant agencies of the commonwealth government, and the National Counterterrorism Committee (the committee responsible for coordinating counterterrorism arrangements nationwide). Thus, not only does TISN enable communication between business and government on matters pertaining to the protection of critical infrastructure, but also through the CIAC it has a direct link to high-level policy makers on matters of security (Commonwealth Government, 2004a, now the National Critical Infrastructure Resilience Committee). The TISN thus was and remains a form of security network that cuts across state and nonstate boundaries to shape security risk awareness. As the assistant secretary of the Critical Infrastructure Protection Branch has indicated, risk assessment tasks for the owners and operators of critical infrastructure include the need to understand the nature of risks and vulnerabilities and to identify precisely where the responsibility for protection and remedies resides (Rothery, 2005).

In 2007, the Australian government conducted a comprehensive review of the critical infrastructure program, which found that "the term 'critical infrastructure protection' did not adequately reflect the Program's all-hazards approach instead implying a protective security focus" and "recommended that the Program be shifted to resilience" (Australian Government's CIRS, 2010). This focus on resilience was further enhanced in 2008 in Ric Smith's Homeland and Border Security Review, which stated that "resilience is an underlying element of the CIP [critical infrastructure protection] and should be promoted" and "incorporated into the title of relevant committees" (Australian Government's CIRS, 2010). Following this, the COAG conducted a further review of national critical infrastructure protection in 2009. It found that "protective security measures alone" cannot protect all critical infrastructure "given the broad range of potential threats and hazards" and argued "CIR [critical infrastructure resilience] is therefore a more suitable approach, and organising principle, for activities in response to all hazards" (Australian Government's CIRS, 2010). In terms of the threat of terrorism, the Homeland and Border Security Review recommended that "the protection of critical infrastructure should remain a discrete body of work over sighted by the National Counterterrorism Committee," but there was a need for "a whole-of-nation resilience-based approach to disaster management" (Australian Government's CIRS, 2010), which in turn led to the development of the new National Emergency Management Committee (NEMC). The NEMC produced the CIRS, which, following from the National Security Statement delivered by the then-prime minster on December 4, 2008, broadened the focus of national security from concerns with terrorism "to include non-traditional threats such as organized crime, natural disasters and pandemics," which "necessitates a broader approach to risk management which is achievable through a resilience paradigm" (Rudd, 2008).

While TISN also transcends the national and subnational divide, a key role in critical infrastructure protection and resilience is carried out by state and territorial police organizations. This function was generally undertaken by what is referred to as counterterrorism units, a development taking place across subnational police organizations designed to improve the coordination of counterterrorism activities. In Victoria, this activity was performed by the Counterterrorism Coordination Unit (CTCU), which is now broadly structured under "emergency management" as part of a further shift toward an all-hazards approach to risk and security management. The primary task of the CTCU was to identify critical infrastructure within its jurisdiction. As previously discussed, while this may overlap with infrastructure deemed to be of national importance, it allows states and territories to shape their understanding of critical infrastructure in important ways. For example, the national strategy did not include educational sites as critical infrastructure, but Victoria was initially extending the national guidelines to include education as a state asset (Anderson, 2005). Therefore, even within the centralization of the new federalism, states such as Victoria retain significant scope to shape the implementation of national guidelines. This remains the case following the 2010 CIRS; the Minister stated that "[e]ach State and Territory government has their own approach to critical infrastructure in their jurisdiction" and that the Australian Government is committed to "working with owners and operators and State and Territory governments to achieve complementary and mutually beneficial outcomes" (Australian Government's CIRS, 2010).

Counterterrorism—or emergency management—units and their members are key nodes in policing networks designed to protect critical infrastructure. The types of critical infrastructure were initially placed into categories and each allocated an individual agent from the CTCU as its principal contact. Conceptually, the units became "security nodes," advising owners and operators of critical infrastructure how to best secure their assets and meet the relevant standards and emergency management requirements imposed on them. In the case of Victoria, the CTCU was involved in establishing guidelines for critical infrastructure protection that they used to inform owners and operators of their responsibilities. Further, they developed a set of auditing procedures for members of the unit to attempt to ensure that critical infrastructure sites were meeting their responsibilities. When undertaking audits, members of the CTCU liaised with the nominated contact person at each site and provided a functional overview of the location, reviewed security arrangements, and reviewed business continuity plans for critical infrastructure within their respective portfolio. The results of the audit were recorded for regulatory and review purposes (Anderson, 2005). However, it is important to note that while members of CTCU performed the reviews, the purpose of their involvement in these policing networks is as a facilitator, rather than simply a regulator, and this remained the case in late 2012. They therefore acted as sources of expert knowledge for owners and operators of critical infrastructure to access as often as needed. Thus, the practice of the CTCU neatly draws together the use of audit, risk management, and responsibilization to govern the security of key sites.

These processes have evolved under a broader emergency management framework but a similar logic underpins them. Since the Victorian government released its critical infrastructure protection strategy in 2007, there have been three major reviews of critical infrastructure arrangements (Public Accounts and Estimates Committee, 2011; VAGO, 2009, 2010). While the details are considerable, the simple point to draw from these inquiries is that the problems with networked security identified, in particular issues concerning coordination and governance, remain highly problematic, so much so that considerable hope is being placed in the review of the Terrorism (Community Protection) Act 2003 that is to take place in 2013.

Police–Private Security Partnerships: POLSEC

The protection of critical infrastructure necessarily involves private security companies in the provision of security products and personnel. A related, although more general, development was an experiment taking place in the state of Victoria. This involved formalized partnerships between police and private security referred to as POLSEC committees. Membership of POLSEC consisted of state police managers and a range of selected representatives deemed to have information relevant to private security operatives (for instance, police engaged in the collation and dissemination of criminal intelligence) and volunteers from the private security industry. Integrating police and private security into these new committees was aimed at "enhancing their understanding and respect of one another," enabling them to "work together to create a safer Victoria" (Cowan, 2004, p. 34). What began as a locally based experiment occurring almost simultaneously in two locations (one a regional center, the other in metropolitan Melbourne) quickly formalized into a new policing network, with a "state" POLSEC committee and regional subcommittees (a second regional committee was established in 2005).

One of us was a voluntary and founding member of a regional POLSEC committee. In this case, the committee emerged from another committee following a private security industry presentation on an emerging partnership between police and private security in metropolitan Melbourne. A local district inspector canvassed the level of interest in establishing such a partnership at the local level. The district inspector was well alert to the tendency of police to assume control or responsibility for such developments, often to the detriment of a more fully participatory partnership. He offered any person present the opportunity to chair the committee. The ensuing discussion resulted in police chairing the POLSEC committee, at least in the interim, in an attempt to ensure organizational support and legitimacy for POLSEC. There was no guidance on the purpose of the committee, its membership, or the nature of its relationship to other POLSEC committees. Indeed, at the time there were no other committees in operation; however, once the metropolitan Melbourne POLSEC committee was established, together with key members from the Victorian Security Institute (the key state-level industry partner), it assumed responsibility as a state-level committee, with regional committees assigned the role of subcommittees. The metropolitan committee established its central role by attending regional committee meetings, exhorting local private security members to become involved, and instituting a state-level award for police and private security members. This occurred after only a few months of having more than one regional POLSEC committee.

While POLSEC was a "bottom-up" initiative concerned with cooperation to enhance safety generally at the local level, it was left to the Victoria Security Institute to make the direct connection between POLSEC and terrorism following the July 7, 2005, bombings on the London transport system:

> In light of recent overseas terrorist events, governments at all levels are under increasing pressure to identify and mitigate acts of violence and terrorism in our communities. The private security industry is now being recognized for its enormous contribution toward public safety and is being engaged at many levels to assist in this process. (Victoria Security Institute 2005)

Although opportunistic in emphasizing "its enormous contribution," such claims point to the potency of negotiations within the "extended policing family" (Johnston, 2003) and the changing relations among different forms of policing. POLSEC focused more on "low policing" related to street crime than the "high policing" of national security (Brodeur 1983). More important, it was an attempt to create a formal policing network that integrates state and nonstate policing, to develop the means of sharing information and other resources, and to plan policing needs cooperatively. As in the case of critical infrastructure, private police are not coerced into partnership with the public sector but participate freely and with the encouragement of industry bodies. Indeed, the Victorian Security Institute actively pursued the development of POLSEC and its central role in its development as a means of enhancing the legitimacy of private policing, indicating how the "participatory spaces" opened by the state can be enthusiastically embraced by nonstate actors.

However, the POLSEC development was specific to a time and place: The rewriting of legislation and regulations governing private security (2004) at a time of increasing political awareness of the reach of nonstate policing (Department of Justice, 2000); the divestiture of state ownership of security or, in Garland's (2001) terms, the "end of sovereign crime control"; and the advent of responsibilization approaches all helped to create the political space for such a committee. However, such developments do not proceed down an evolutionary, unidirectional path but are always already failing and subject to the possibility of considerable changes that can only be understood via detailed empirical examination and analysis. In the case of POLSEC, the changing nature of a broader, all-hazards emergency management approach and changes to personnel saw POLSEC quickly fall in relevance, and it quietly fell into disuse, replaced by other committees that continue to seek to foster engagement and collaboration and address the ongoing concerns, such as information sharing. This continues to raise concerns about privacy and the potential for private police to use the relationship as one of enhanced legitimacy through "marketing" the relationship, an issue that remains a matter of local analysis.

Conclusion

Networks are increasingly developing in the fields of policing and security (Whelan, 2012). The POLSEC model was simply one of a number of initiatives in Australia (and elsewhere) where efforts have been made, often substantial, to have state police and private security work together in a number of ways. The extent that any of these developments develop into "habits of the heart" (Bellah, Madsen, Sullivan, and Tipton, 1985) in which trust, reciprocity, cooperation, common interests, and common good are fully developed (Delhey and Newton 2002, p. 6) remains a matter for ongoing empirical analysis (Palmer, 2009). While the nature of collaboration, cooperation, and partnerships such as POLSEC, TISN, and airport security needs to be assessed or evaluated in terms of practices, one concern, as Rhodes (1997) suggests, is a danger that networks become "self-steering interorganizational policy networks" stripped of democratic accountability. To enhance democratic outcomes, we need processes that provide far more clarity on the precise nature of vertical accountability, for instance, through parliamentary authorities such as the policing boards discussed in the Patten Commission in Northern Ireland (see Johnston and Shearing, 2003).

Alternatively, Considine argues that in the era of networks, partnerships, and joined-up governance, accountability moves away from vertical relationships or "lines of accountability" (Thynne and Goldring, 1987, p. 6) toward a "culture of responsibility" (Considine, 2002, p. 23) involving "navigational competence," which is "the proper use of authority to range freely across a multirelationship terrain in search of the most advantageous path to success" (Considine, 2002, p. 22). However, the metrics of "success" in networked counterterrorism policing needs to take account of not only the absence of terrorist incidents and the prevention of terrorist attempts and plans but also factors such as the impact on civil and political rights; the transparency of decision making; individual and agency responsibilities; and the effect of the feelings of insecurity of the population. The injunction to "be alert" to, but "not alarmed" by, the threats to "our way of life" needs to avoid the exclusionary bias of many of the securitization measures, which is a trend emerging across Western countries and beyond (Young, 1999).

Counterterrorism is reshaping policing and security arrangements in Australia in specific ways. Researching these changes demands close attention to what occurs in specific locations as much as it might relate to international comparisons along the lines of changes to the legal powers of policing authorities. Undoubtedly, such work is crucial. Yet, how the more global aspects of change are played out in any one location is variable, subject to their own historical and contemporary institutions and political relations (Palmer, 2009).

Central to the policing of counterterrorism in Australia has been the responsibilization and risk management strategies that pervade the criminal justice system generally. However, in relation to counterterrorism, such strategies take on specific features. The responsibilization of the citizenry generally needs to temper the potential for fear to develop into a debilitating constraint on "normal" activities; thus, the various exhortations to continue to work, shop, and travel in the manner of being alert but not alarmed. With critical infrastructure and essential services, governmental ambitions are concerned with shaping the choices of the "private sector" to ensure fully rationalized risk management to protect against threats to our way of life in a way that does not encroach, or at least only minimally does so, on the "freedoms" of the market. Thus, both the individual and the corporation are free to govern themselves while being alerted to the risks and the means to manage such risks. Finally, how multilateralized and networked policing and security are made accountable remains an underdeveloped area of policy development deserving of significantly more analysis.

Notes

1. An earlier version of this chapter was published as "Policing Across the Counter-Terrorism Continuum," *Police Practice and Research: An International Journal* (2006, 6(5), pp. 449–465). However, we have conducted additional empirical

research to test the veracity of our original analysis and our judgments on the directions of change, an approach we believe to be far too uncommon in social science research.

2. This did indeed occur subsequently when the then-chief minister of the Australian Capital Territory, John Stanhope, opposed key elements of the new draft legislation in September 2005 (cf. Stanhope, 2005) and subsequently made public draft legislation that other premiers, chief ministers, and the prime minister had agreed would remain confidential. Stanhope argued in the ACT Legislative Assembly that he did not make such an undertaking and believed it to be irresponsible to hand such authority to the commonwealth without broader public consultation (ACT Legislative Assembly, Hansard, 18 October, 2005, pp. 3744–3747). Stanhope attracted severe criticism for his stance. For instance, the then-Prime Minister John Howard argued that Stanhope was part of the "distortion" and "exaggeration" of the content of the legislation; that he was "not about informing the public" but rather "balancing his own political position" by "trying to pretend that in some way he [was] exposing draconian laws" when, according to the former prime minister, the laws were "unusual but we live in unusual circumstances" (Howard, 2005).

References

Anderson, M. (2005, July 25). *Management of Critical Infrastructure: A Victoria Approach.* Paper presented at Partners in Policing and Community Security convened by the Victoria Security Institute, Melbourne.

Australian Federal Police. (2012). *Annual Report 2011–2012.* Canberra: Commonwealth of Australia.

Australian Government. (2012, July). Attorney-General's Department submission, inquiry into the gathering and use of criminal intelligence, Parliamentary Joint Committee on Law Enforcement.

Australian Government's Critical Infrastructure Resilience Strategy. (2010). Retrieved from http://www.tisn.gov.au/Pages/default.aspx (accessed December 22, 2012).

Australian Productivity Commission. (2012). *Report on Government Services.* Canberra: Australian Government.

Bartels, L. (2010). *The Status of Laws on Outlaw Motorcycle Gangs in Australia.* Canberra: Research in Practice, Australian Institute of Criminology.

Bayley, D., and Shearing, C. (2001). *The New Structure of Policing: Description, Contextualization, and Research Agenda.* Washington, DC: National Institute of Justice.

Bellah, R. N., Madsen, R., Sullivan, W. M., Swindler, A., and Tipton, S. M. (1985). *Habits of the Heart.* Berkeley: University of California Press.

Brodeur, J.-P. (1983). High policing and low policing: Remarks about the policing of political activities. *Social Problems, 30*(5), 507–520.

Brodeur, J. P., and Dupont, B. (2006). Knowledge workers of "knowledge" workers? *Policing and Society, 16*(1), 7–26.

Clarke, J. (2008). *Inquiry into the Case of Dr. Mohamed Haneef,* Canberra: Attorney General's Office.

Commonwealth Government. (2002). *Let's Look Out for Australia*. Canberra: Government Printer.

Commonwealth Government. (2003, January 5). Advertisement. *The Age*, p. 5.

Commonwealth Government. (2004a). *Critical Infrastructure Protection National Strategy*, Version 2.1. Canberra: Government Printer.

Commonwealth Government. (2004b). *Protecting Australia Against Terrorism*. Canberra: Department of Prime Minister and Cabinet.

Considine, M. (2002). End of the line? Accountable governance in the age of networks, partnerships, and joined-up services. *Governance: An International Journal of Policy, Administration, and Institutions, 15*(1), 21–40.

Cooley, D. (Ed.). (2005). *Re-imagining Policing in Canada*. Toronto: University of Toronto Press.

Council of Australian Governments (COAG). (2005). Special meeting on counter-terrorism, 27 September communiqué. Retrieved from http://www.coag.gov.au/meetings/270905 (accessed May 2, 2006).

Cowan, R. (2004, September/October). The conundrum of police and security, *Security Insider*, 32–6.

Critical Infrastructure Protection Program. (2006). *What Is CIP?* Retrieved from http://cipp.gmu.edu/cip/ (accessed May 5, 2006).

Delhey, J., and Newton, K. (2002). *Who Trusts? The Origins of Societal Trust in Seven Nations*. Berlin: Social Science Research Center.

Department of Justice. (2000). *Victoria's Private Agents Act 1966: Discussion Paper*. Melbourne: Department of Justice.

Dupont, B. (2004). Security in the age of networks. *Policing and Society, 14*(1), 76–91.

Garland, D. (2001). *The Culture of Control: Crime and Social Order in Contemporary Society*. Oxford, UK: Oxford University Press.

Gill, P. (2006). Not just joining the dots but crossing the borders and bridging the voids: Constructing security networks after 11 September 2001. *Policing and Society, 16*(1), 27–49.

Golder, B., and Williams, G. (2004). What is "terrorism"? Problems of legal definition. *UNSW Law Journal, 27*(2), 270–295.

Hermer, J., Kempa, M., Shearing, C., Stenning, P., and Wood, J. (2005). Policing in Canada in the twenty-first century: Directions for law reform. In D. Cooley (Ed.), *Re-imagining Policing in Canada* (pp. 22–91). Toronto: University of Toronto Press.

Hocking, J. (2004). *Terror Laws: ASIO, Counter-terrorism and the Threat to Democracy*. Sydney: University of New South Wales Press.

Howard, J. (2005, October 16). *Prime Minister of Australia, New Room*. Media releases. Retrieved from http://www.pm.gov.au/news/interviews (accessed May 2, 2006).

Hutchinson, S., and O'Connor, D. (2005). Policing the new commons: Corporate security governance on a mass private property in Canada. *Policing and Society, 15*(2), 125–144.

James, S. (2005) New policing for a new millennium? In D. Chappell and P. Wilson (Eds.), *Issues in Australian Crime and Criminal Justice*. Chatswood, NSW: LexisNexis: Butterworths, 77–100.

Johnston, L. (2003). From "pluralisation" to "the police extended family": Discourses on the governance of community policing in Britain. *International Journal of the Sociology of Law, 31*(3), 185–204.

Johnston, L., and Shearing, C. (2003). *Governing Security: Explorations in Policing and Justice*. London: Routledge.

Jones, T., and Newburn, T. (1998). *Private Security and Public Policing*. Oxford, UK: Clarendon Press.

Jones, T., and Newburn, T. (1999). Urban change and policing: Mass private property reconsidered. *European Journal on Criminal Policy and Research*, 7(2), 225–244.

Jones, T., and Newburn, T. (2002). The transformation of policing? Understanding current trends in policing systems. *British Journal of Criminology*, 42(1), 129–146.

Loader, I. (2000). Plural policing and democratic governance. *Social and Legal Studies*, 9(3), 323–345.

Loader, I. (2002). Policing, securitization and democratization in Europe. *Criminal Justice*, 2(2), 125–153.

McCulloch, J. (2001). *Blue army: paramilitary policing in Australia*. Melbourne: Melbourne University Press.

Michaelsen, C. (2005). Antiterrorism legislation in Australia: A proportionate response to the terrorist threat? *Studies in Conflict and Terrorism*, 28(4), 321–339.

National Commission on Terrorist Attacks upon the United States. (2004). *The 9/11 Commission Report*. Washington, DC: U.S. Government.

National Counter-Terrorism Committee. (2012). *National Counter-Terrorism Plan* (3rd ed.). Canberra.

National Infrastructure Security Co-ordination Centre. (2006). Welcome to the National Infrastructure Security Co-ordination Centre. Retrieved from http://www.niscc.gov.uk/niscc/index-en.html (accessed May 1, 2006).

O'Malley, P. (2004). *Risk, Uncertainty and Government*. Coogee, NSW: GlassHouse Press.

O'Malley, P., and Palmer, D. (1996). Post-Keynesian policing. *Economy and Society*, 25(2), 137–155.

O'Neill, N., Rice, S., and Douglas, R. (2004). *Retreat From Injustice: Human Rights Laws in Australia* (2nd ed.). Sydney: Federation Press.

Palmer, D. (2009). *State Police in a State of Change: Re-making the Entrepreneurial Officer*. Staarbruken, Germany: VDM Verlag.

Palmer, D., and Whelan, C. (2007). Policing in the "communal spaces" of major event venues. *Police Practice and Research*, 8(5), 401–414.

Parliamentary Joint Committee on Law Enforcement. (2011). *Inquiry into the Adequacy of Aviation and Maritime Security Measures to Combat Serious and Organised Crime*. Canberra: Commonwealth of Australia.

Pickering, S., and McCulloch, J. (2010) The Haneef case and counter-terrorism policing in Australia. *Policing and Society*, 20(1), 21–38.

Public Accounts and Estimates Committee. (2011). *Review of the Auditor-General's Report on Preparedness to Respond to Terrorism Incidents: Essential Services and Critical Infrastructure*. 105th Report to the Parliament, No. 67, Session 2010–11, Parliament of Victoria. Melbourne: Government Printer.

Raab, J., and Kenis, P. (2009). Heading toward a society of networks: Empirical developments and theoretical challenges. *Journal of Management Inquiry*, 18(3), 198–210.

Rhodes, R. A. W. (1997). *Understanding Governance: Policy Networks, Governance and Accountability*. Buckingham, UK: Open University Press.

Rigakos, G. S. (2005). Beyond public-private: Towards a new typology of policing. In D. Cooley (Ed.), *Re-Imagining Policing in Canada* (pp. 260–319). Toronto: University of Toronto Press.

Rix, M. (2009). The case of Dr. Mohamed Haneef: An Australian "terrorism drama" with British connections. *Plymouth Law Review, 2*, 26–47.

Rothery, M. (2005). Critical infrastructure protection and the role of emergency services. *The Australian Journal of Emergency Management, 20*(2), 45–50.

Rudd, K. (2008, December 4). *The First National Security Statement to the Australian Parliament*. Address by the prime minister of Australia, the Hon. Kevin Rudd. MP.

Senate Legal and Constitutional Committee. (2002). *Consideration of Legislation Referred to the Committee: Security Legislation Amendment (Terrorism) Bill [No.2] and Other Bills*. Canberra: Parliament of Australia.

Senate Legal and Constitutional References Committee. (2002). *Inquiry into the Australian Security Intelligence Organisation Legislation Amendment (Terrorism) Bill 2002 and Related Matters*. Canberra: Parliament of Australia.

Shanahan, D. (2003, June 28–29). Feral federalism. *The Weekend Australian,* p. 20.

Stanhope, J. (2005, September 23). Security "solutions" cause for concern. *Canberra Times*.

Tham, J. K. (2004). Casualties of the domestic "war on terror": A review of recent counter-terrorism laws. *Melbourne University Law Review, 28*(2), 512–531.

Thynne, I., and Goldring, J. (1987). *Accountability and Control: Government Officials and the Exercise of Power*. Sydney: Law Book.

Valverde, M., and Cirak, M. (2003). Governing bodies, creating gay spaces: Policing and security issues in "gay" downtown Toronto. *British Journal of Criminology, 43*(1), 102–121.

Victoria Auditor General Office. (2009). *Preparedness to Respond to Terrorism Incidents: Essential Services and Critical Infrastructure*. Melbourne: Government Printer.

Victoria Auditor General. (2010). *Security of Infrastructure Control Systems for Water and Transport*. Melbourne: Government Printer.

Victoria Security Institute. (2005, July 25). *Partners in Policing and Community Security*. Media release.

Whelan, C. (2011). Network dynamics and network effectiveness: A methodological framework for public sector networks in the field of national security. *Australian Journal of Public Administration, 70*(3), 275–286.

Whelan, C. (2012). *Networks and National Security: Dynamics, Effectiveness and Organisation*, Surrey, UK: Ashgate.

Wheeler, J. (2002). *Airport Security—Report by the Rt. Hon. Sir John Wheeler, JP, DL, 2002*. Home Office Security. London: U.K. government. Retrieved from http://security.homeoffice.gov.uk/news-and-publications1/publication-search/general/airport-security.pdf?view=Standard&pubID=293371 (accessed May 3, 2006).

Wheeler, J. (2005). *An independent review of airport security and policing for the Government of Australia* Canberra: Australian Government

Yates, A. (2005). Who should pay for security? *National Security Practice Notes* retrieved July 8, 2005 from HYPERLINK http://www.homlandsecurity.org.au www.homlandsecurity.org.au

Young, J. (1999). *The exclusive society*. London: Macmillan.

Policing Terrorism
A Threat to Community Policing or Just a Shift in Priorities?

9

JOHN MURRAY

Contents

Introduction

The introduction of community policing has been heralded as the most significant and progressive change in policing philosophy, and there are good reasons for this claim. Having a distinctly proactive emphasis, community policing has proven to be a dramatic improvement to the traditional model of policing, which is essentially reactive. Characteristically, traditional policing almost invariably depends on a paramilitary structure that tends to distance police from the rest of the community. Community policing, on the other hand, relies on a cooperative community arrangement that, when working effectively, reduces not only the incidence of crime but also the fear of crime.

It has been frequently said that the terrorist events of September 11, 2001, have changed the world forever. To some observers, so has the public profile of policing. In many countries now, there have been signs of police reverting to (or in some cases simply reaffirming) paramilitarism, which is more in line with the traditional model of policing and clearly at odds with community policing. The threat of terrorism that exists today will test the resolve of police commissioners who choose to retain community policing as a dominant policing philosophy. In this new environment, there is no doubt the effectiveness of community policing will be challenged, and some will rationalize it away as being too soft to match the so-called war against terror. While some police forces/services will continue to rely on the community policing model, others will be tempted to return to a traditional model and varying degrees of paramilitarism. Williams (2003, p. 119) notes already in the United States that the "effort to incorporate the community policing model into traditional policing operations is faltering."

Another pressure on community policing is governmental influence: In the context of the drive for effectiveness and efficiency and the election value of law and order, some governments will promote the view that police should concentrate on core business, which will be interpreted as requiring police to focus on crime fighting. In this chapter, I examine, then contrast, traditional policing with community policing and in particular critique the paramilitarism of the former to challenge its relevance to policing generally.

Another major consideration in the maintenance of community policing as a dominant philosophy is the prevailing police culture. I comment on the cultural change that was needed in the transition to community policing, and while many police forces/services have ostensibly managed the cultural change to accommodate community policing, I warn of the underlying tension that probably still exists in police culture, which is likely to prefer the traditional model of policing. Put another way, operational police are likely to consider community policing inappropriate for policing terrorism. Consequently, for those police commissioners who would seek to retain community policing, this presents a real challenge, especially in a climate that tends to demand a more visible and aggressive force against terrorism.

Although trite, it has been frequently pointed out that police alone cannot successfully achieve crime control, and that the support of the community is critical—the same principles clearly apply to the prevention of terrorist acts (and prevention should surely be the emphasis). While threats against national security have justifiably shifted the focus of policing priorities to meet this critical demand, I argue that any shift in policing strategies overall should be in emphasis only and not an abandonment of community policing and a total return to the paramilitarism of the traditional model. The shift in focus to counter terrorism will quite rightly involve placing more resources in paramilitary units and providing frontline officers with the necessary skills. However, to do so by abandoning community policing as an overall philosophy will be counterproductive since it takes away the critical facility of prevention and community cooperation that are inherent in community policing. The two policing philosophies of paramilitarism and community policing can (and in this current environment should) coexist, but under the umbrella of community policing.

Transition from Traditional/Paramilitarism to Community Policing

For much of the developed world, the origins of the modern police service can be traced to the creation of the Metropolitan Police in London in 1829 (Reith, 1975). Introduced by Sir Robert Peel, the bill to proclaim the Metropolitan Police Act in England was accompanied by a set of principles for policing that I consider to have equal relevance today. The organizational structure and managerial philosophy that accompanied the establishment of this earliest police organization were consistent with the literal definition of paramilitarism (Auten, 1981; Reith, 1975). The paramilitary stamp was firmly put in Peel's police, evidenced by the fact that (a) Peel ensured the police must be stable, efficient, and organized along military lines (Waters & McGrath, 1974, referred to by Auten, 1981); (b) there was virtually no organizational model other than the military to emulate; and (c) there was a conscious decision that the inaugural leader of the Metropolitan Police should be a military person (Auten, 1981). In fact, the authors of the first manual of instruction adapted their text from the 1803 military manual of the Irish Constabulary Police, *Military Training and Moral Training* (Reith, 1975).

The move from a traditionally reactive, action-oriented style of policing to a service-oriented community policing model, which occurred since the 1980s, has arguably been the most significant positive change in policing philosophy. To Bayley (1994, p. 104), for example, "community policing represents the most serious and sustained attempt to formulate the purpose and practices of policing since the development of the 'professional' model in the early twentieth century." The introduction of community policing followed what were seen as the limitations of traditional policing and the need for change. Moore (1994, p. 285) neatly summarizes this (referring to the community policing movement):

> It is not hard to understand the attraction of the new ideas about policing. They seem to recognize and respond to what have come to be seen as the limitations of the "reform model" of policing: its predominantly reactive stance toward crime control; its nearly exclusive reliance on arrests as a means of reducing crime and controlling disorder; its inability to develop and sustain close working relationships with the community in controlling crime; and its stifling and ultimately unsuccessful methods of bureaucratic control (Sparrow, Moore, & Kennedy, 1990). In contrast the new ideas point to a new set of possibilities: the potential for crime prevention as well as crime control; creative problem solving as an alternative to arrest; the importance

of customer service and community responsiveness as devices for building stronger relations with local communities; and "commissioning" street-level officers to initiate community problem-solving efforts. (Sparrow et al., 1990)

Researchers and commentators have found police services that have embraced community policing refer to its cornerstone as the collaborative partnership between the community and the police, engaged in a process that identifies and solves problems of crime and disorder (Bayley, 1994; Goldstein, 1990; Rosenbaum, 1988; Sherman et al., 1998). While there appears to be no single definition of community policing, Oliver and Bartgis (1988, p. 491) note there is a constant theme in the literature:

> The majority of definitions focus on an increase in police and community interaction, a concentration on "quality of life issues," the decentralization of the police, strategic methods for making police practices more efficient and effective, a concentration on neighbourhood patrols, and problem-oriented or problem-solving policing.

Public attitudes to the police will also be a determinant in the success of community policing. A hostile or fearful community, for example, will be disinclined to cooperate with police (Reisig & Giacomazzi, 1998). Police, as Roberg (1994, pp. 251–252) notes, may not be unduly concerned about that since many line officers have been "recruited, trained and socialized in a traditional law enforcement orientation and may have a stake in preserving the status quo." Oliver and Bartgis (1988) found line officers had the capability to ignore, circumvent, or sabotage the desires and expectations of the community.

Since the transition from traditional policing required a substantial change in police culture, it is appropriate to examine what the cultural traits of traditional policing are, and how, or to what extent, they contrast with those of community policing.

Police Occupational Subculture: A Bias toward Traditional/Paramilitary Policing?

There is no doubt that given the extensive authority and discretion held by police that they have the potential to have a dramatic impact on the lives and liberties of citizens. Reflecting on the importance of maintaining a keen interest in policing, Van Maanen (1978, p. 311) thought policing to be "possibly the most vital of our human service agencies ... too important to be taken-for-granted, or worse, to be ignored." It certainly follows, therefore, that the ideology, values, principles, and preconceptions that are generally held by police and that consequently determine police culture are of critical consideration. Unlike most other vocations, discretion in policing is strongest at the lowest level of the organization and while decisions to arrest are open to scrutiny, *most* police decisions involve actions other than arrest and are therefore largely without scrutiny or control.

Occupational police culture has been the subject of regular examination by many theorists, the most prominent of them being Manning (1977) and Skolnick (1966, 1985) in the United States; Cain (1973) and Reiner (1992) in Britain; and Chan (1996, 1997, 1999) and Prenzler (1997) in Australia. Many definitions and descriptions of police culture have followed, including "developed recognizable and distinct rules, customs, perceptions and interpretations of what they see, along with consequent moral judgements" (Skolnick & Fyfe, 1993, p. 90); and "an identifiable complex of common culture, values, communication symbols, techniques, and appropriate behaviour patterns" (McBride, 1995, p. 214). Reiner (1992, p. 21) equates it with the "values, norms perspectives and craft rules" that inform police conduct.

Skolnick (1966) refers to the "working personality" of police, which is associated with the police task and is characterized by suspiciousness, internal solidarity, social isolation, and conservatism. Reiner's (1992) subsequent work resulted in similar conclusions. He found that a "central feature of cop culture is a sense of mission [and that to police themselves] policing is not just a job but a way of life with a worthwhile purpose" (Reiner, 1992, p. 111). He also notes that the "core of the police outlook is this subtle and complex intermingling of the themes of mission, hedonistic love of action and pessimistic cynicism" (p. 114). Pertinent to this chapter, he found that "most policemen are well aware that their job has bred them an attitude of constant suspiciousness which cannot be readily switched off [accompanied by a] marked internal solidarity, coupled with social isolation" (pp. 114, 115). These findings have been supported to varying degrees by Fitzgerald (1989), Goldstein (1976, 1990), Skolnick and Fyfe (1993), and Wood (1997).

The most interesting aspect of the general findings about operational police culture as outlined is that when summarized they are almost diametrically opposite to what I (Murray, 2002) have identified as the appropriate/ ideal characteristics of a community police officer, which include a genuine belief in community consultation and problem solving; commitment to the notion of equal partnership with the community; creativity and innovation; freedom to exercise discretion at the lowest level of policing; and excellent communication skills to be able to develop a rapport with the community and, in turn, win trust and respect. Table 9.1 contrasts these "ideal" characteristics for a community police officer with the cultural traits identified in research.

I suspect, however, the research findings are not as stark as they appear since they tend to ignore the positive aspects of police culture. Chan (1997), in making this point, believes police culture has become a convenient label

Table 9.1   Competing Police Profiles

"Ideal" Profile for Community Police Officer	Research Profile for Operational Police
Commitment to community consultation and problem solving	A sense of mission about police work but a distancing from the rest of the community
Open and accessible in the provision of a service	Suspiciousness
Creative and innovative in promoting solutions to problems and crime prevention	A pragmatic view of police work which discourages innovation and experimentation
Freedom to exercise discretion at the lowest level of policing so as to incorporate a problem-solving mentality as an alternative to arrest	A preference for action orientation and arrest
Excellent communication skills so as to be able to develop a rapport with the community	An isolated life coupled with a strong code of solidarity with other police officers
	A cynical or pessimistic perspective about their social environment

for a range of negative values, attitudes, and practice norms among police officers; Prenzler (1997) notes that judicial and scholarly references to police culture have been almost universally pejorative. James and Warren (1995, p. 4) suggest this to some extent can be explained by the fact that

> the origins of cultural explanations for police behaviour can be traced to attempts by sociologists in the 1960's to explain an enduring anomaly in policing: the breaking of rules by the people whose primary occupation and sole purpose is to enforce rules.

Despite studies repeatedly showing that most police work involves situations where no crime has occurred, there is a preference by police for action orientation rather than service provision (Feltes, 1994; Reiner, 1992, 1994; Scott, 1998; Skolnick, 1985; Waddington, 1999). At the same time, some governments place a heavy reliance on response-based performance measures, such as the number of arrests, as indicators of police effectiveness since quantitative targets are easy to define and present a more convenient solution to political demands (Redshaw & Sanders, 1995).

Subculture and Its Alignment to Models of Policing

Traditional policing, which places a heavy emphasis on paramilitarism, and community policing, which is founded on a more democratic model, give rise to quite different cultures. Many police services have successfully managed the cultural transition from action to service orientation that accompanied the shift from the traditional to the community policing model, while others have experienced resistance arising from the preference within police culture for crime fighting rather than problem solving. This tension becomes pertinent in the light of outside pressures today, such as the imperative to address terrorism and national security. Some services have preferred to retain the traditional model of policing, albeit in modified form. As police services around the world address national security, an examination of the differences in police culture that tend to be aligned to traditional versus community policing is appropriate.

Craft or Professional Culture?

Proponents of traditional policing tend to regard policing as a craft or trade, which is best learned "on the job." It is assumed in this model that it is best to have the majority of training/mentoring undertaken by experienced officers in a master/apprentice arrangement. Certainly, in former times, "outside" help was neither requested nor respected. For community policing, an open approach is adopted for recruitment, training, and development, interpreted by some as a move toward policing being a "profession." What *profession* means is, of course, open to different interpretations but has generally been thought within policing circles to include the development of a body of knowledge, a strict code of ethics, and working to values rather than rules. In cultural terms, with traditional policing there is a strong preference for the status quo, by which seasoned officers perpetuate existing culture, resulting in insularity and an "us" (police) and "them" (community) mentality. With community policing, a culture develops that places a great deal of reliance on community expectations and a willingness to join with, and learn from, experts outside policing.

Paramilitarism or Democratic Managerial Culture?

Traditional policing, as Auten (1981, p. 68) notes, promotes a paramilitaristic managerial style that will exhibit at least some of the following characteristics:

- a centralized command structure with a rigidly adhered-to chain of command;
- a rigid superior–subordinate relationship defined by prerogatives of rank;
- control exerted through the issuance of commands, directives, or general orders;
- communications being primarily vertical—from top to bottom;

- initiative being neither sought nor encouraged;
- an authoritarian style of leadership;
- an us–them division between senior officers and the rest; and
- discipline being rule based and punitive.

Traditional policing relies heavily on these characteristics not only to ensure effectiveness and efficiency through command and control but also to maintain discipline. Proponents of community policing have never denied the need for command and control but point out that occasions when it is required are relatively few, and that its emphasis in the traditional model is disproportionate and counterproductive. With community policing, there is a more democratic style of management that relies on personal credibility rather than rank-based authority.

With the traditional model, the culture typically manifests an expectation of unquestioned acceptance of direction from a senior officer and one-way communication. This culture assumes that subordinate ranks need to be told what to do, that rank decides the "right" decision, and those down the ladder will have little to offer. The more democratic style in community policing allows empowerment to be devolved to the lowest possible level to allow greater decision making at the operational level. This gives rise to a culture that allows initiative and problem solving. The culture inherent in community policing also recognizes the need for command and control for those occasions when it is required and will adapt for the occasion.

Authoritarian or Problem-Solving Culture?

With traditional policing, there is an emphasis on arrests and the strict enforcement of laws, little consideration of prosecutorial discretion, limited interest about the causes of crime, less emphasis on crime prevention, and a general assumption that police will know what is best for the community at large. Community policing, on the other hand, is founded on the primacy of crime prevention and a conscious commitment to joining with the community in problem solving. The cultural expectations for these two models are dramatically different. Skolnick (1966) and Reiner (1992), previously mentioned in this chapter, found with traditional policing that police culture demonstrates a tendency for action orientation and a general distancing from the community. With community policing, the culture will show a tendency for openness, innovation, community interest, service orientation, and a spirit of problem solving.

Compliant or Adaptive Culture?

The traditional model of policing tends to have

1. A centralized structure with headquarters as the source of orders, rules, and regulations;
2. Standardization and uniformity;
3. Measurement of performance based on quantitative criteria such as the number of arrests;
4. Excessive specialization; and
5. A narrow definition of the duties of a patrol officer as limited to attending complaints and working to predetermined rules and practices.

This relatively compliant model meets with problems when confronted with situations not readily covered by existing directives, general orders, or policy and procedure.

Community policing adopts a more adaptive approach through

1. A decentralized structure with the aim to bring the police closer to the community, with headquarters the source of support direction, norms, and values;
2. Encouragement and support for flexibility;
3. Measurement of performance based not only on quantitative but also on qualitative criteria, such as the achievement of community goals or solving problems;
4. A move from specialization to a balance between versatility and specialization; and
5. The patrol officer as a generalist responsible for attending complaints, solving problems, activating the community, preventing crime, and undertaking preliminary crime investigations, with the discretionary powers of the patrol officer recognized and developed.

With traditional policing, officers are trained to work to established rules and regulations. The culture therefore tends to be regimented to act on direct orders with the assumption that the rank-based authority ensures not only compliance but also efficiency and effectiveness. With community policing, there is a more flexible structure, and a culture develops that is more conducive to recognizing that there is usually no single solution to problems/issues, and that by recognizing the valuable contribution from those in the field, a more practical resolution is likely. At an operational level, officers will have more confidence to deal with community issues.

Recognizing the Appropriate Model

A shift from traditional to community policing needs a major transition in both managerial and cultural terms. Plainly, the characteristics of traditional policing are not suited to community policing. Table 9.2 highlights differences between the two models. As the "world changed" after September 11, 2001, the question that now has to be asked is whether we are seeing a reversion to the paramilitarism of the traditional policing model or merely a shift in priorities.

The Threat of Terrorism and Impact on Community Policing

Prior to September 11, 2001, many countries in the developed world had lapsed into a laissez-faire approach to national security. The terrorist attacks in the United States on domestic soil would bring that complacency to a dramatic end, and priority for "homeland security" would become a catchcry, not only in the United States but also in many countries. This required strategic consideration about how military and civil services would reconfigure to address this fresh challenge. While defense forces would obviously feature in the reassessment, policing would also have increased responsibilities. In many countries, the changes have been dramatic and have plainly been much more than tightening existing practices. De Guzman (2002, p. 8), for example, describes the reaction in the United States as the "fortification" of the country. Policing across the world, to the average observer, became visibly different. It was not only the fact there were more police about, but also police had assumed a more aggressive style of dress and manner.

Prior to September 11, some writers had already expressed concern about the shift in policing toward paramilitarism. Weber (1999, p. 2), referring to the United States, for example, expressed alarm at the "spawning of a culture of paramilitarism in American law enforcement [with] local police officers ... increasingly emulating the war-fighting tactics of soldiers." McCulloch (2001b), also prior to September 11, considered that the threat of terrorism in Australia had been used to justify significant changes in the role of the police and its shift toward paramilitarism. To these writers, the civil–military separation was breaking down, and the lines that traditionally separated the military mission from the police were becoming distinctly blurred. Moreover, as Weber (1999, p. 5) contends,

> Over the last century police departments have evolved into increasingly centralized, authoritarian, autonomous, and militarized bureaucracies, which has led to their isolation from the citizenry.

Table 9.2 Transitions between Traditional and Community Policing

Traditional Policing and Links to Paramilitarism	Community Policing and Democratic Management	Culture – Contrasting and Comparing
Policing as a Craft Traditionally, policing was regarded as a craft that was best learned "on the job."	Policing as a Profession There has been a conscious drive for policing to be accepted as a "profession."	Culture Developed on the Job With traditional policing, there is a strong reliance on the status quo and learning from experienced officers. With community policing, a more "open" culture developed that places a great deal of reliance on community expectations.
Paramilitary Management Style Traditional policing incorporates a managerial style that is either based entirely on military lines or at least draws on their principles.	Democratic Management Style While command and control is necessary, these situations are relatively few, and management allows contributions from all ranks regarding how the job is done.	Empowerment or Disempowered Culture A paramilitary culture assumes that authority is linked to rank. With a democratic style of management, the culture is one that empowers all officers.
Authoritarian Approach to Policing Traditional policing promotes strict enforcement of laws, little concern about the causes of crime, limited prosecutorial discretion, and there is less emphasis on preventing crime.	Problem-Solving Approach to Policing Here, there is an understanding of what causes crime, and there is a conscious commitment to joining with the community to prevent crime.	Linking Culture to the Philosophy In traditional policing, there is a tendency for authoritarianism defensiveness, cynicism, and action orientation, which together result in a general distancing from the community. In community policing, the culture is open, consultative, and geared to solving problems.
Inflexible Structure In the traditional model, there tends to be a rigid, centralized bureaucracy with officers working to practices.	Flexible Structure Community policing devolves authority and culture decision making, which encourages initiative.	From Compliant to Adaptive Culture With traditional policing, this tends to be regimented and compliant. Community policing is adaptive, recognizing predetermined rules, and officers work to values and standards that there is usually no single solution to problems/issues.

(Continued)

Table 9.2 Transitions between Traditional and Community Policing (Continued)

Traditional Policing and Links to Paramilitarism	Community Policing and Democratic Management	Culture – Contrasting and Comparing
		From Institutional to Personal Discipline
Blame Culture	Learning Culture	
The paramilitary model of policing assumes that police officers will inevitably do something wrong, and when they do they should be punished.	A learning culture recognizes the failure of the punitive model and educates/corrects minor and understandable breaches rather than punishing them.	The punitive model creates apprehension, anxiety, defensiveness, and denial. An "us–them (management)" culture results. In a learning culture, officers work to values, and minor breaches are regarded as curable mistakes, moving from threat to incentive.
Insularity and Defensiveness	Openness and Consultation	Move toward Transparency
In traditional policing, there is a tendency toward the notion that police are the only ones who knew anything about policing. Academics or other commentators are not appreciated.	In community policing, other expert advice is invited, and individual police contributions are considered.	With traditional police, there was a defensive culture—a tendency toward craft secrecy. Inherent in community policing is that police are part of the community, and a desired culture is one that recognizes and works to a model that allows the public to know how and why the police operate the way they do.

[a] In listing the characteristics of traditional policing and the link to paramilitarism, I have drawn largely from those identified by Auten, J. H. (1981). *Police Studies*, 4(2), 67–78.

If Weber is correct, what she is describing is either a shift from community policing back to the traditional model or that police have not made the transition at all. It should be remembered she made this comment prior to September 11. I am concerned that after September 11 there seems to be a move that would see community policing and all its fine principles undermined by a reversion to the traditional model of policing, rationalized by the need to counter terrorism.

McCulloch (2001a, p. 4), referring to Australia, is more cynical as she describes "community policing [as] the 'velvet glove' covering the 'iron fist' of more military styles of policing." This is certainly not my observation. While McCulloch and I both accept that paramilitary policing and community policing are actually complementary (McCulloch, 2001a, p. 4), we do so for different reasons. She considers references by police to community policing are "rhetoric [and] well published strategies designed to counter the negative image and public antipathy arising from the use of coercive paramilitary tactics." I, on the other hand, believe the complement between paramilitary policing and community policing in Australia to mean the maintenance of a capability to counter extreme acts of violence but within a genuine community policing model.

As we face the "war on terror," rather than moving away from community policing, police commissioners should look to its qualities and specifically note how this policing philosophy can be used to their advantage. To abandon or diminish it would be counterproductive and would undo the conscious drive over the decades that has taken policing to the high level of societal acceptance it now enjoys. It follows, therefore, that I cannot accept comments like those of de Guzman (2002, p. 11), who believes that, "[In] the context of war against terror, some tenets of community policing appear to be inconsistent with the implementation of these new police roles." He continues, "The events of *September 11* threaten the utility as well as the continued existence of some community policing ideals on several grounds" (see the following discussion). While he concedes community policing should "probably not be abandoned," it is appropriate to examine the four points he suggests support the fact that community policing in its present form would be unable to meet the demands introduced by the threat of terrorism.

First, de Guzman (2002, p. 11) states the philosophical ideal in community policing of winning the hearts and minds of the community will not be effective against terror since one cannot reason with terrorists. It is futile, he continues, for police to try, and patrols should be made aware that they should not deter but detect and prevent violent terrorist acts. I consider this an extremely narrow point of view. Community–police partnerships work best when they are structured to encourage information sharing from all parts of the community. This *especially* includes groups that tend to be unwilling to assist the police. For de Guzman to refer to this fundamental aspect of community policing as "futile" in the context of prospective terrorism is unproductive. To exclude or isolate any subgroup from a community policing service amounts to more than failing in a civic duty—it also ignores a most important source of information for police to gauge what they are up against (Bayley & Bittner, 1984). Today, a more thoughtful initiative would be to rebuild trust with specific ethnic/cultural communities through a genuine commitment by police to protect them and their neighborhoods, workplaces, and places of worship (Lyons, 2002). Community policing, when working well, will deflect rumors and reduce misinformation and distortion.

Second, de Guzman (2002, p. 11) believes the introduction of strategies against terrorism will negate assumptions of community cooperation and trust that are implicit in community policing. Terrorists are constantly employing deceit; therefore, he argues, police should be reluctant to invest their trust on such unidentifiable forces. I take a contrary view. Successful detection and prevention of terrorism depend on information. From experience, we know terrorists can successfully occupy a position within a conventional community. A community–police relationship that is based on mutual trust is more likely to uncover matters that are helpful in identifying prospective terrorists. A more formal or authoritarian police–community relationship would distance police from the rest of the community, and only actual law breaking is likely to be reported. However, a good community–police relationship would encourage general dialogue and is more likely to uncover valuable suspicious information; this can only be brought about by trust and mutual respect. Enlisting the community in its own defense encourages it to take control of its own destiny.

Third, de Guzman (2002, p. 11) points out that the partnership of community policing in which both parties have to reach a consensus about strategies of crime prevention and police operations will fail in today's environment since police will not be able to reveal their strategies to the community. He considers that if, in their preparation of counterterrorism strategies, the police decide to hold back, the community will sense this, and consequently trust will be breached and such partnerships will inevitably wither away. Again, I take a distinctly different view on this point. In existing community policing partnerships, the community has never expected that police confide confidential information about investigations or give specific information about operational tactics. So, there is nothing essentially different when dealing with terrorism. Further, to take a position that police will decide what is best for the community could be interpreted as arrogant and in breach of a fundamental tenet of public accountability. The community has a right to certain information and, in the context of terrorism, for example, should be made aware of the level of threat so that individuals can make decisions about their own disposition. Basic assumptions of community policing are that police are part of the community (as civilians) and that collaboration should exist in how crime, terrorism, and other community problems are addressed. The contribution community policing can make in this area is extremely positive. In terms of prevention, it can allow the community to focus on the importance of notifying early warnings/signs, consistent with the spirit that it is in everybody's interest. The community should feel comfortable about coming forward with information no matter how slight they believe its connection to terrorism.

De Guzman's (2002, p. 12) fourth point is that parochial policing is promoted in community policing, but the war on terror necessitates broader collaborative policing. The level of collaboration, he contends, not only should be within the department but also should include other local departments and federal or state agencies since in the war on terror the planning space may be distant from the target phase. Thus, efforts to make communications and collaborations among and between police departments should be a constant undertaking. In my view, community policing, when working effectively, is not parochial and in fact is multidisciplinary on the basis that police by themselves seldom have the answer for all community problems. Community policing, therefore, uses a broad rather than a narrow (parochial) approach. Police regularly work with specialists at local and national levels, and in the context of the threat of terrorism they also work at an international level.

Conclusion

The traditional model of policing relies on paramilitarism characterized by rank-based authority and command and control. In this model, the organizational structure is hierarchical and inflexible, making it difficult to meet the challenges of a rapidly changing environment. Policing here is predominantly reactive and unable to develop and sustain close working relationships with the community in controlling crime. Community policing is eminently sensible since it concentrates on crime prevention.

The transition to community policing has not been easy for most police services since the prevailing culture of operational police has shown a distinct preference for action orientation and a lack of interest in "soft" policing with which community policing has been identified. Even for those services that have successfully made the transition, it is likely that the tension within the culture still exists, and that moves or even suggestions to revert to the traditional paramilitary style would meet with a great deal of support from the rank and file.

The world has certainly changed after September 11, 2001, but there is no need to move away from community policing as the prevailing philosophy. Clearly, there has to be a shift of priorities that allows policing strategies to focus on national security. To assume, however, that paramilitarism as an overarching model is best suited to do this is a serious miscalculation. A reversion to a traditional model of policing will undo the decades of great work that has placed modern community policing as an exemplar of public service in a civil and democratic society.

Using the principles of community policing is a much more sensible and effective way of dealing with terrorism. It has been accepted that police cannot fight crime alone and must rely on the community. The same principle applies to terrorism. A community–police relationship that is built on trust and mutual respect is much more likely to give early warnings about terrorist acts. Rather than move policing away from community policing, it should be reinforced, especially in light of the cultural traits in operational police that tend to indicate a preference for action. The commitment of police commissioners over the years to make the necessary transition to achieve this cultural change must not be forgotten. Moreover, as they reconfigure policing strategies to meet the threat of terrorism (as they must), they should be alert to the likelihood that operational police might prefer to move to an action-oriented style of policing characterized by paramilitarism. In their eagerness to give public reassurance, politicians also might prefer this model. The road ahead will be demanding for police leaders. What must be resisted is the temptation to fall back to the methods of policing that ignore the profound and ethically based principles of community policing.

References

Auten, J. H. (1981). The paramilitary model of police and police professionalism. *Police Studies, 4*(2), 67–78.

Bayley, D. H. (1994). *Police for the future.* New York: Oxford University Press.

Bayley, D. H., & Bittner, E. (1984). Learning the skills of policing. *Law and Contemporary Problems, 47*(4), 35–39.

Cain, M. (1973). *Society and the policeman's role.* London: Routledge & Kegan Paul.

Chan, J. (1996). Changing police culture. *British Journal of Criminology, 36*(1), 109–134.

Chan, J. (1997). *Changing police culture: Policing in a multi-cultural society.* Cambridge, UK: Cambridge University Press.

Chan, J. (1999). Police culture. In D. Dixon (Ed.), *A culture of corruption.* Sydney: Hawkins Press.

de Guzman, M. C. (2002, September/October). The changing roles and strategies of the police in time of terror. *ACJS Today,* pp. 8–13.

Feltes, T. (1994). New philosophies in policing. *Police Studies, 17*(2), 29–48.

Fitzgerald, G. E. (1989). *Report of a Commission of Inquiry Pursuant to Orders in Council,* Brisbane Commission of Inquiry into Possible Illegal Activities and Associated Police Misconduct. Queensland: Government Printer.

Goldstein, H. (1976). Improving the police: A problem-oriented approach. *Crime and Delinquency, 25,* 236–258.

Goldstein, H. (1990). *Problem oriented policing.* New York: McGraw-Hill.

James, S., & Warren, I. (1995). Police culture. In K. Bessant, K. Carrington, & S. Cook (Eds.), *Cultures of crime and violence: The Australian experience.* Bundoora, Victoria, Australia: La Trobe University Press.

Lyons, W. (2002). Partnerships, information and public safety: Community policing in a time of terror. *Policing: An International Journal of Police Strategies and Management, 25*(3), 530–542.

Manning, P. (1977). *Police Work.* Cambridge, MA: MIT Press.

McBride, R. B. (1995). Discrimination. In W. Bailey (Ed.), *The encyclopaedia of police science* (2nd ed.). New York: Garland.

McCulloch, J. (2001a). *Blue army*. Melbourne: Melbourne University Press.

McCulloch, J. (2001b). Paramilitary surveillance: S11, globalisation, terrorists and counter-terrorists. *Current Issues in Criminal Justice, 13*(1), 23–35.

Moore, M. H. (1994). Research synthesis and policy implications. In D. Rosenbaum (Ed.), *The challenge of community policing*. London: Sage.

Murray, J. (2002). Police culture: A critical component of community policing. *The Australian Journal of Forensic Sciences, 34*(2), 57–71.

Oliver, W. M., & Bartgis, E. (1988). Community policing: A conceptual framework. *Policing: An International Journal of Police Strategies and Management, 21*(3), 490–509.

Prenzler, T. (1997). Is there a police culture? *Australian Journal of Public Administration, 56*(4), 47–65.

Redshaw, J., & Sanders, F. (1995, January 11). What does the public want? *Policing,* pp. 56–60.

Reiner, R. (1992). *The politics of the police* (2nd ed.). Brighton, UK: Harvester.

Reiner, R. (1994, March 10). What should the police be doing? *Policing,* pp. 151–157.

Reisig, M. D., & Giacomazzi, A. L. (1998). Citizen perceptions of community policing: Are attitudes toward police important? *Policing: An International Journal of Police Strategies and Management, 21*(3), 547–561.

Reith, C. (1975). *The blind eye of history: A study of the origins of the present police era*. Montclair, NJ: Paterson Smith.

Roberg, R. R. (1994). Can today's police organizations effectively implement community policing? In D. P. Rosenbaum (Ed.), *The challenge of community policing: Testing the promises*. Thousand Oaks, CA: Sage.

Rosenbaum, D. (1988). Community crime prevention: A review of the literature. *Justice Quarterly, 5,* 323–395.

Scott, J. (1998). Performance culture: The return of reactive policing. *Police and Society, 8,* 269–288.

Sherman, L. W., Gottfredson, D., Mackenzie, D. L., Eck, J., Reuter, P., & Bushway, S. D. (1998, July). *Preventing crime: What works, what doesn't, what's promising* (Research in Brief). Washington, DC: National Institute of Justice.

Skolnick, J. H. (1966). *Justice without trial: Law enforcement in democratic society*. New York: Wiley.

Skolnick, J. H. (1985). Suspicion, danger and isolation. In W. Terry (Ed.), *Policing society: An occupational view*. New York: Wiley.

Skolnick, J. H., & Fyfe, J. (1993). *Above the law: Police and the excessive use of force*. London: Free Press.

Sparrow, M. K., Moore, M. H., & Kennedy, D. M. (1990). *Beyond 911: A new era for policing*. New York: Basic Books.

Van Maanen, J. (1978). On watching the watchers. In P. K. Manning & J. Van Maanen (Eds.), *Policing: A view from the street*. Santa Monica, CA: Goodyear.

Waddington, P. A. J. (1999). Police (canteen) sub-culture. *British Journal of Criminology, 39*(4), 765–797.

Weber, D. C. (1999). *Warrior cops: The ominous growth of paramilitarism in American police departments*. Retrieved from http://www.cato.org/pubs/briefs/bp50.pdf

Williams, E. J. (2003). Structuring in community policing: Institutionalising innovative change. *Police Practice and Research, 4*(2), 119–129.

Wood, J. (1997). *Royal Commission into the New South Wales Police Services: Final report* (Vols. 1–3). Sydney: Government of the State of New South Wales.

Community Policing in Post–September 11 America

10

A Comment on the Concept of Community-Oriented Counterterrorism

BEN BROWN

Contents

Introduction

More than a century has elapsed since the first police departments were formed in the United States, and in that time policing has advanced a great deal. Whereas police officers of the late 1800s and early 1900s were notorious for their brutality, disorganization, and inefficacy, over the past century the police in the United States have evolved into a reasonably well-organized army of trained public servants. In addition, toward the end of the 20th century, there was a nationwide movement among police officials to develop strategies and tactics that enhance public safety by means of encouraging public support and cooperation with law enforcement officers, a movement known as *community policing* (Pelfrey, 1998; Uchida, 1997; Wadman & Allison, 2004). Although there is no universally agreed-on definition of what constitutes a community policing or community-oriented policing program, the two key elements are

1. Quality relations between law enforcement and the citizenry, and
2. Concerted problem-solving efforts among law enforcement officers and local residents that focus on identifying and eliminating the causes of crime in the community (Community Policing Consortium, 1994).

The roots of community policing date back to the efforts of police reformers in the 1970s, such as New York Police Commissioner Patrick Murphy, who emphasized the need for quality police–community relations (Wadman & Allison, 2004, pp. 136–137), and scholars such as Professor Herman Goldstein (1979), who argued that police officials needed to break away from reactive tactics and address the underlying causes of social disorder. During the 1980s and early 1990s, community policing achieved greater acceptance and was endorsed by President William J. Clinton when he signed into effect the 1994 Violent Crime Control and Law Enforcement Act, which included funding for a hundred thousand new officers, with the stipulation that the newly hired officers be engaged in community policing efforts (Bayley, 1994; Community Policing Consortium, 1994; Cordner, 1997; Moore, 1994; U.S. Department of Justice, 1994; Wadman & Allison, 2004). Community policing continued to increase throughout the 1990s as police officials across the United States instituted a diversity of community-oriented methods, such as setting up police ministations in dilapidated neighborhoods, organizing neighborhood watch groups, holding meetings with community residents to discuss local problems, and organizing public cleanup projects. By the year 2000, more than two thirds of all local police agencies were engaged in some form of community policing effort (Cordner, 1997; Hickman & Reaves, 2003; Moore, 1994; Roth, Roehl, & Johnson, 2004). Although President George W. Bush never displayed the same enthusiasm for community policing as his predecessor, by the time President Bush was sworn into office in January 2001, the community policing movement appeared to have enough momentum to continue rolling forward on its own merits.

Then, on the morning of September 11, 2001, nineteen men hijacked four commercial jets and piloted two of them into the World Trade Center and one into the Pentagon, with the fourth jet crashing in the Pennsylvania countryside while the passengers and crew attempted to regain command of the craft. It was the most destructive terrorist incident in history, resulting in the deaths of roughly 3,000 innocent people and a financial loss estimated to be in excess of a trillion dollars. In response, law enforcement agencies at all levels sought to fortify the United States. The police in New York City scrambled to contain the aftermath of the collapse of the World Trade Center, the Federal

Aviation Administration (FAA) grounded all domestic flights and diverted all incoming international flights, U.S. Customs and INS (Immigration and Naturalization Service) officials stopped the flow of traffic across international points of entry, the FBI (Federal Bureau of Investigation) launched a massive investigation, and local law enforcement agencies throughout the nation were put on heightened alert (National Commission on Terrorist Attacks upon the United States, 2004).

In the nation's capital, there was a bipartisan effort among lawmakers to draft counterterrorism legislation. Consequently, the USA PATRIOT Act (Uniting and Strengthening America by Providing Appropriate Tools Required to Intercept and Obstruct Terrorism Act of 2001) was penned, passed, and signed into law at breakneck speed, and law enforcement agencies were granted sweeping new powers, such as the authority to use roving wiretaps (a proposal that had been rejected by Congress during the debates over the 1996 Anti-Terrorism and Effective Death Penalty Act), the authority to use "sneak-and-peek" search warrants, and the authority to collaborate and share information with intelligence agencies (Bulzomi, 2003; Doyle, 2002; White, 2004; Whitehead & Aden, 2002; Wong, 2006a, 2006b). There was also a reorganization of federal law enforcement agencies, inclusive of the creation of the Department of Homeland Security, the creation of the Transportation Security Administration, and the restructuring of priorities among several federal agencies, such as the FBI and DEA (Drug Enforcement Agency), with each agency receiving an increase in funding to enhance counterterrorism measures (Donohue, 2002; Stuntz, 2002; White, 2004). Moreover, without seeking the approval of Congress, the Bush administration surreptitiously authorized a number of tactics inclusive of the warrantless wiretapping of suspected terrorists and the torture of suspected terrorists and "enemy combatants" by U.S. intelligence, law enforcement, and military personnel ("Controversy Continues," 2005; Isikoff, 2008, 2009; Pious, 2006; Savage, 2009; Sinnar, 2003; Taylor & Thomas, 2009; U.S. Office of Legal Counsel, 2001, 2002a, 2002b, 2003, 2005).

There is no question that the events of September 11 required an immediate response, inclusive of an enhancement of national security measures. However, the declaration of a "war on terrorism," the use of aggressive counterterrorism tactics, and the new powers granted to law enforcement officials generated concern among civil libertarians, racial/ethnic minorities, and immigrants. Moreover, many of the counterterrorism tactics violate the basic principles of community policing. Tapping phones, monitoring Internet activity, surveilling religious gatherings, surreptitiously searching homes, and detaining people for extended periods of time without filing charges or granting them access to legal counsel are a lousy means of winning the hearts and minds of the citizenry. In essence, the U.S. response to the events of September 11 sparked an ideological rift in the law enforcement arena.

The Rift of September 11

In contrast to community policing strategies that emphasize cooperation and quality relations between law enforcement and the public, many of the counterterrorism strategies and tactics implemented in the aftermath of the attacks of September 11 were highly aggressive and involved little concern about basic human rights or fostering positive interaction between law enforcement and the public. Consider, for example, the treatment of immigrants. When the FBI launched the investigation into the September 11 attacks, federal agents targeted young Muslim males who had recently immigrated to the United States and immediately began making arrests based on little or no credible evidence. Within a couple of months, roughly a thousand people had been arrested (Fine, 2003).

In addition, the USA PATRIOT Act enhanced the power of federal law enforcement agents to detain noncitizens, and Attorney General Ashcroft sought to have local law enforcement officials authorized to enforce federal immigration law. As a result, over the next few years dozens of local and state law enforcement agencies made arrangements with federal immigration authorities that allowed the local and state agencies to aid in the enforcement of federal immigration laws, and officers began utilizing such tactics as questioning stopped drivers about their nationality or immigration status and screening arrestees to ascertain whether they were legal residents of the United States (Axtman, 2002; Constable, 2008; Dorell & Welch, 2007; Garza, 2006; Ortiz, Hendricks, & Sugie, 2007; U.S. Immigration and Customs Enforcement, 2008; Wade, 2002). Given that immigrants are often hesitant to interact with criminal justice officials (Davis & Erez, 1998), the targeting of immigrants by federal agents and the practice of having local and state police officers enforce federal immigration laws undoubtedly generated an increase in fear of the police within immigrant communities and reduced many immigrants' willingness to report crimes or otherwise cooperate with law enforcement, thereby reducing the potential for effective community policing programs in areas with large immigrant populations.

The targeting of immigrants was by no means the only aggressive homeland security tactic implemented following the September 11 attacks. To provide examples of assertive tactics that affected the general populace, public access to national landmarks such as the Statue of Liberty and the Washington Monument was restricted, and local police agencies in a number of cities (e.g., Boston, Chicago, New York) tightened transit security by means such as using bomb-sniffing dogs to randomly search passengers' bags. It is also important to note that federal officials such as Ashcroft were not the only people advocating assertive homeland security tactics in the wake of the events of September 11. Professor De Guzman (2002), for instance, argued that to combat terrorism police departments need to curtail community policing efforts and increase the use of intrusive patrolling and investigative methods. Then, there were the legislators, criminal justice officials, and technology developers and suppliers who envisioned and sought to devise Orwellian new surveillance technologies such as facial recognition software and computer programs capable of scanning millions of e-mail messages (Stephens, 2003). Concisely stated, the September 11 terrorist attacks against the United States fortified the ideological divide between community policing advocates and counterterrorism hawks. Whereas the advocates of community policing favor methods that involve cooperative efforts between the police and the public, counterterrorism hawks maintain that aggressive and invasive investigative tactics are the best means of enhancing public security. If this divide were of a purely philosophic nature, it would be possible to simply debate the issue in classrooms and conference centers, but that is not the case. Ideologies shape policies, which in turn dictate the allocation of financial resources. And, in the years following the events of September 11, federal funding for counterterrorism ballooned, while federal funding for community policing was decimated.

Throughout the late 1990s, the Office of Community Oriented Policing Services (COPS) provided roughly a billion dollars a year in grants to local agencies for the purpose of hiring new officers, but in fiscal year 2003, the COPS office provided less than $200 million for this purpose; by 2006, the federal government had ceased funding the COPS hiring grants (DeSimone, 2003; Geraghty, 2003; U.S. Office of Management and Budget, 2007; Wade, 2002). At the same time federal authorities were cutting funds for local law enforcement agencies, they began requiring that local agencies comply with new homeland security measures, such as increased patrols of potential terrorist targets (e.g., public water supplies) and developing first-response capabilities for terrorist attacks, requirements that forced police agencies to shift funds from community-oriented programs into homeland security measures (Geraghty, 2003; Haberman, 2001; White, 2004).

In sum, the war on terrorism took a toll on the community policing movement. There was an increase in aggressive security measures, such as proactive patrols around national landmarks, enhanced enforcement of federal immigration law, an increase in technologically enhanced investigative tactics such as bugging homes, and a decrease in federal funding for community policing efforts. However, there is scant evidence to suggest that the decrease in support for community policing and the increased use of aggressive tactics and invasive technology are effective means of reducing the threat of terrorism or controlling crime and disorder.

The Limits of Aggressive Tactics

There is no question that there are situations that require aggressive police tactics, such as saturation patrols and dynamic "no-knock" entries of residences by SWAT (special weapons and tactics) teams. That does not mean, however, that combative tactics are an effective means of curbing crime. Although there are studies that suggest that aggressive policing contributes to a reduction in violence, such studies have focused on areas plagued by high rates of street-level violence. For instance, studies conducted in Dallas and Kansas City indicated that aggressive policing tactics contributed to reductions in certain types of violence (e.g., gang-associated violence) in high-crime neighborhoods. However, the studies also showed that the tactics had no impact on the overall rate of violent crimes, property crimes, social disorder crimes, or calls for police service (Fritsch, Caeti, & Taylor, 1999; Sherman, Shaw, & Rogan, 1995).

Moreover, several scholars, such as Tyler (1990), Sherman (1993), and Stuntz (2002), concluded that forceful policing methods encourage public hostility toward the police, especially in impoverished urban areas with large racial/ethnic minority populations. In fact, almost every major urban riot over the past half century has been precipitated by combative policing tactics and the concomitant public hostility toward the police among racial/ethnic minorities (Uchida, 1997; Wadman & Allison, 2004). It is not only racial/ethnic minorities who resent aggressive policing. Decades of empirical research has consistently shown that negative police–citizen contact and even witnessing or otherwise having knowledge of negative police–citizen contact contributes to unfavorable attitudes toward the police (Brown & Benedict, 2002).

The problems associated with forceful tactics are not confined to municipal police agencies. There are numerous incidents involving federal agencies, such as the shootings at Ruby Ridge, the raid on the Branch Davidian compound in Waco, and the malicious prosecution of Dr. Wen Ho Lee, which indicate that once criminal justice officials adopt a combative attitude in carrying out their duties, it becomes all too easy to destroy the lives of innocent people. And, as demonstrated by Timothy McVeigh's 1995 bombing of the Alfred P. Murrah Federal Building in Oklahoma City, an action that McVeigh took as a means of revenge for the federal assault on the Branch Davidian compound (Michel & Herbeck, 2002), the use of combative tactics by federal agents can generate hostility toward the government and retaliatory actions. In sum, there is little proof that aggressive law enforcement tactics reduce crime, but there is ample evidence that assertive law enforcement tactics contribute to the hostile defiance of legal authorities.

Similarly, there is scant evidence to suggest that aggressive law enforcement tactics are effective against terrorists, but there are numerous incidents that show that combative counterterrorism measures generate hostility toward the government and foster public support for terrorists. For example, in the 1970s the British government forcefully arrested, interrogated, and incarcerated suspected members of the Irish Republican Army (IRA). The tactics led to the arrests of many IRA leaders and reduced the violence in Northern Ireland and England, but the end result was wrongful convictions of innocent people, the torture of Irish prisoners, intense hostility toward the British government, and greater cohesion among members of the IRA. And, while there was a reduction in violence, the violence did not stop. The use of violence by the IRA and other paramilitary groups continued throughout the 1970s and 1980s, resulting in the deaths of more than 2,000 people. The violence subsided only when British authorities negotiated a cease-fire with the Provisional IRA and other paramilitary groups in 1994 (Conroy, 2000; Donohue, 2002; Simonsen & Spindlove, 2004; White, 1991).

To provide another example, consider the investigation of the bombing at Centennial Olympic Park in Atlanta on July 27, 1996. In their haste to identify a suspect, the FBI targeted Richard Jewell, the security guard who found the bomb. Federal agents interviewed Jewell, searched his apartment and a mountain cabin he had used, and leaked information to the press, thus making life a nightmare for Jewell and his mother, but failed to arrest him—a form of psychologically manipulating (i.e., "sweating") a suspect. Yet, the FBI never produced any substantive information to indicate why Jewell was a suspect. Moreover, despite the lack of evidence to implicate Jewell in the bombing and despite desperate pleas from both Jewell and his mother to clear his name (one of which was broadcast on the CBS news program *60 Minutes*), the U.S. Department of Justice refused to acknowledge that Jewell was no longer a suspect until October 26, almost a full 3 months after Jewell was identified as the focus of the investigation (Thomas & McAllister, 1996; Yoder, 1996).

The FBI later identified Eric Robert Rudolph as a suspect in the 1996 Olympics bombing, as well as a suspect in several other bombings. Federal authorities then stormed forward and launched a massive search for Rudolph. Once again, the aggressive tactics failed. Despite one of the largest manhunts in U.S. history, Rudolph disappeared into the mountains of North Carolina. He was inadvertently apprehended 7 years later by a rookie patrol officer who thought Rudolph was a vagrant. Rudolph denied that he had help in the wilderness, but given that he was arrested while scavenging for food near a grocery store dumpster, it is doubtful he survived by feasting on tree bark and wild game (Isikoff, 2003; Skipp & Campo-Flores, 2003). Moreover, it is questionable regarding whether any human could withstand 7 years of social isolation and not become clinically insane. A more plausible scenario is that

Rudolph received assistance from local residents who were more willing to aid a suspected bomber than they were willing to help the federal authorities who forcefully descended on the quiet North Carolina countryside.

In sum, combative tactics have shown to be of limited use against both criminals and terrorists. Moreover, in numerous cases such as the beating of Rodney King and the assault on the Branch Davidian compound, the use of aggressive tactics has produced disastrous backlash. While the intense public outrage surrounding excessive force by law enforcement may be short lived, the subsequent silent distrust of law enforcement can last for generations.

The Incompatibility of Combative Ideologies and Human Rights

Another issue to consider is that once policy makers embrace a combative ideology (e.g., the war on terrorism), procedural safeguards are often disregarded, and human rights are violated. As demonstrated by the internment of Japanese Americans during World War II and the post–September 11 detentions of Middle Eastern immigrants, the adoption of a combative ideology often leads to the violation of human rights by increasing racial/ethnic profiling and the mistreatment of racial/ethnic minorities. Hence, policy makers must be cautious about embracing a combative ideology that may legitimize the abuse of human beings. Not only do such measures violate the Fourteenth Amendment, the use of tactics that target racial/ethnic minorities may hamper the gathering of counterterrorist intelligence.

In the event that counterterrorist strategies target and segregate persons of Arab descent from mainstream Americans—for example, invasive airport security procedures that discourage Middle Eastern immigrants from flying, invasive background checks of persons of Arab descent who apply for government jobs, mass rejections of visa applications submitted by persons in Middle Eastern nations, or the surveillance of mosques and Islamic activities—the end result will be an increase in hostility toward the United States among those demographic groups, both in the United States and abroad. Moreover, the use of policies and practices that discourage Islamic immigrants from participating in social and political activities means that the views of such immigrants will not be articulated in public discourse, which may prevent the disclosure of information about anti-American activities, including terrorist activities (Carey, 2002; Lyons, 2002).

To provide another example of the manner in which a combative ideology can foster violations of human rights, consider the research of Conroy. In a detailed and disturbing analysis of torture, Conroy (2000) demonstrated that once an agenda of aggressive counterterrorism has been set in place as happened in Northern Ireland in the 1970s and Israel in the 1980s and 1990s, government officials become all too willing to use torture. Unfortunately, an examination of post–September 11 events shows that Conroy's conclusions are in no way exaggerated. Following the events of September 11, the Bush administration surreptitiously authorized the torture of suspected terrorists and "unlawful combatants" held in captivity outside the United States (U.S. Office of Legal Counsel, 2002b, 2003, 2005), and many of the people imprisoned by U.S. authorities in the facilities in Guantanamo Bay, Cuba, and the Abu Ghraib facilities in Iraq were physically and psychologically abused (Barry, Hosenball, & Dehghanpisheh, 2004; Higham, 2004). While there is no substantive evidence that U.S. law enforcement officials used torturous interrogation techniques on the hundreds of people initially swept up in the investigation of September 11, a review of the treatment afforded to the September 11 detainees conducted by the inspector general of the U.S. Department of Justice showed that many of the detainees were abused by correctional officers (Fine, 2003). The problem is not only that the war on terrorism ideology fostered the unconscionable treatment of human beings, but also that the abuse of suspected terrorists and insurgents blemished the ideals of humane democracy for which the United States stands and compromised the ability of U.S. leaders to advocate humanitarian reform. Case in point, in an attempt to justify the invasion of Iraq and the removal of Saddam Hussein, the Bush administration claimed that Hussein was involved with the September 11 attacks, that Hussein possessed weapons of mass destruction, and that Hussein was a savage despot. The first two allegations proved false, but there is no dispute that Hussein was a vicious tyrant (Bowden, 2002; Pincus & Milbank, 2004; Pollack, 2004). Hence, the Bush administration had one reason for removing Hussein from power, which may ultimately be judged as morally justified.

However, in response to the events of September 11, the Bush administration authorized a diversity of despotic measures inclusive of mass arrests of Middle Eastern immigrants, the indefinite detention of suspected terrorists, the use of torture during interrogations of suspected terrorists, and the transfer of suspected terrorists to the custody of foreign nations to be interrogated and tortured: tactics that have failed to be proven as effective counterterrorism measures and violate a number of basic human rights as guaranteed by the 1948 U.N. Universal Declaration of Human Rights. Although such tactics were not equivalent to the atrocities carried out by Hussein's minions, the behaviors of U.S. officials were impossible to justify in the court of world opinion, tarnished the reputation of the United States as a bastion of civil liberties, and imbued President Bush's criticisms of Saddam Hussein with a tinge of hypocrisy. Moreover, the combative U.S. response to the events of September 11 set the stage for a global increase in the abuse of human rights.

In an essay written in reaction to September 11, Kennedy (2001, p. 75) predicted that the U.S. response to terrorism would place new strains on U.S. officials who must deal with "unsavory regimes," and that aggressive U.S. counterterrorism strategies might force U.S. officials to overlook the actions taken by Russia against Chechnya or the actions taken by China against Tibet. Unfortunately, Kennedy's predictions proved accurate. For instance, when Chechen rebels seized a group of hostages in a Moscow theater in October 2002, Russian officials responded by pumping a noxious gas into the theater to render the rebels unconscious, stormed the theater, and shot the rebels. The tactic terminated the standoff between the Chechen rebels and Russian authorities, but more than 100 of the hostages died as a result of inhaling the gas. Observers from around the world commented on the similarity between Russian and U.S. antiterrorist rhetoric and on the kind words of support Russian President Vladimir Putin received from President Bush, support that President Putin would likely not have received if the deadly raid had taken place before U.S. officials began utilizing aggressive counterterrorist tactics (Besserglik, 2002; Dixon, 2002; McGrory & Shepherd, 2002). In short, the war on terrorism ideology embraced by the Bush administration contributed to the commission of heinous behaviors by U.S. law enforcement, intelligence, and military personnel; curtailed the ability of U.S. authorities to criticize foreign governments for human rights violations; and contributed to a global increase in state-sanctioned brutality.

Community-Oriented Counterterrorism

In contrast to common criminals such as burglars, drug addicts, and domestic violence offenders who engage in crimes with little planning and no motivation other than a quick dollar or the inability to control their most basic instincts, the devotees of terrorists such as Aum Shinrikyo and Osama bin Laden are disciplined, organized, and motivated by strong religious and political beliefs (Albini, 2001; White, 2004). And, as demonstrated by the 1983 bombing of the U.S. Embassy in Beirut, the 1995 dispersion of nerve gas in the Tokyo subway system, and the 1993 and 2001 attacks on the World Trade Center, terrorist groups spend considerable time and energy planning an attack. Thus, whereas it would be foolish to think that law enforcement officials could gather enough information to preemptively intervene in a burglary or spousal assault, there is reason to believe that law enforcement agents can gather sufficient intelligence to intervene in terrorist activities before the operatives go tactical. This is not to suggest it is possible to eliminate terrorist attacks, but simply that an essential component of any counterterrorism program is intelligence gathering (Bracken, 2001; Sloan, 2002).

Regardless of whether the scenario involves municipal detectives investigating a murder or federal investigators gathering intelligence about terrorist activity, a supportive public is the best tool a law enforcement agency can have. As pointed out by the distinguished FBI criminal profiler, John Douglas, the public is the most effective partner a law enforcement agency has in identifying and apprehending unknown subjects, and it is Douglas's position that "the more you share with the public, the more they're going to be able to help you" (Douglas & Olshaker, 1998, p. 11). Consider, for instance, the sniper attacks in the Washington, D.C., area in the fall of 2002. Despite aggressive measures such as police roadblocks and the use of advanced technology like the surveillance conducted with military aircraft, John Allen Muhammad and John Lee Malvo terrorized D.C. and avoided capture for weeks. The key to their arrest was cooperation between law enforcement and the citizenry. Specifically, police officials informed reporters that Muhammad and Malvo were suspects in the sniper investigation. Although the officials withheld a description of the 1990 Chevrolet Caprice the suspects were driving, reporters culled the information from police scanners and broadcast it. Consequently, two cooperative citizens heard the information on the radio, spotted the vehicle at a rest stop, and called 911 (Thomas, 2002).

To provide another example, there was the search for Angel Maturino Resendez, the serial killer best known as the "railway killer." A national manhunt involving federal, state, county, and municipal law enforcement agencies failed to prevent Resendez from venturing back and forth across the U.S.–Mexico border. At one point, Resendez was detained by Border Patrol agents, who deported him to Mexico because their computer systems were incompatible with the computer systems of the FBI, and the Border Patrol agents were unaware that Resendez was a fugitive suspect. Fortunately, not everyone involved in the hunt was dependent on technology. Rather than relying on computer software, Sergeant Drew Carter of the Texas Rangers took the time to develop a working relationship with Resendez's sister and was able to convince her to plead with her brother to turn himself in. As a result, Resendez voluntarily returned from Mexico and surrendered to Sergeant Carter (Howlett, 1999; Sandberg & Castillo, 1999).

The bottom line is that technologically advanced investigative and intelligence-gathering techniques are no substitute for a cooperative public. This point was perhaps best illustrated by the case of the mail bomb terrorist known as the Unabomber. Despite an 18-year investigation, federal agents were unable to identify the serial bomber until several influential newspapers (e.g., the *Washington Post*) published the anonymous bomber's countercultural manifesto, at which point David Kaczynski recognized the work and stepped forward to indicate that his brother, Theodore Kaczynski, was a likely suspect (Beck, 1995; Klaidman & King, 1998). Although science and technology continue to advance at a rapid pace, even the latest and most advanced technology has not yet proven to be a quality means of gathering counterterrorist intelligence in a timely fashion.

As a case in point, as part of its post–September 11 efforts to enhance the surveillance of terrorist suspects and collection of intelligence, the FBI installed a large (but undisclosed) number of wiretaps and electronic bugs that recorded hundreds of hours of conversation each day, yet there was a sizable delay between the time the conversations were recorded and the time that intelligence analysts received the information. The problem was that the FBI had few interpreters who could speak languages such as Arabic and Farsi. In addition, the FBI had difficulties recruiting Middle Eastern immigrants to serve as translators. For example, many Israelis who applied for positions with the FBI were unwilling to submit to the strict requirements of working for the FBI, such as renouncing their Israeli citizenship (Klaidman & Isikoff, 2003). Concisely stated, it is only by means of neighborly involvement with the populace that law enforcement officials can earn the trust of the people who they must depend on to provide information on criminal activities, and the same holds true in the case of gathering intelligence on terrorist activities.

Granted, the use of community policing efforts such as having officers participate in neighborhood groups to (overtly or covertly) obtain information on possible terrorist activities has serious ramifications. As noted by White (2004, p. 12), the dilemma surrounding the use of local police officers to gather counterterrorist intelligence is that such operations would require the collection of political intelligence. This, in turn, alters the role of the police and raises questions about invasions of privacy, trampling constitutional rights, and the abuse of power. Moreover, the distrust between local and federal law enforcement agents, the virtual absence of intelligence analysts within local law enforcement agencies, and the lack of an adequate infrastructure for sharing intelligence between local and federal law enforcement agencies pose enormous hurdles (Sloan, 2002; White, 2004).

Since the events of September 11 and the overhaul of the nation's federal law enforcement and intelligence apparatuses, efforts have been made to correct such problems, the most significant effort being the development of fusion centers. Between 2003 and 2012, hundreds of millions of tax dollars were spent on the creation of more than 70 such centers located across the United States. In theory, fusion centers function as information and intelligence hubs linking local, state, tribal, and federal law enforcement agencies (and private security agencies as well), the goal being the empowerment of law enforcement and homeland security professionals to better protect society. In practice, the process is far from flawless. An investigation of fusion centers conducted by the U.S. Senate Permanent Subcommittee on Investigations (2012), a subcommittee of the Committee on Homeland Security and Governmental Affairs, showed that "fusion centers often produced irrelevant, useless or inappropriate intelligence reporting" and that "many produced no intelligence reporting whatsoever" (U.S. Senate Permanent Subcommittee on Investigations, 2012, p. 2). Concisely stated, many of the issues that plagued local, state, and federal law enforcement agencies prior to the events of September 11—in particular, issues centering on the lack of quality information and intelligence gathering and the lack of effective cooperation and communication between law enforcement agencies—have yet to be resolved.

Although the use of community policing methods to gather intelligence raises significant ethical and constitutional questions and although an effective method of analyzing and sharing counterterrorist intelligence has yet to be devised, at the very least the use of community-oriented tactics designed to create positive relationships between law enforcement officials and the citizenry should be considered as a means of gathering counterterrorist intelligence. In comparison to the use of highly intrusive counterterrorism measures favored by homeland security hard-liners, it is possible that community-oriented methods of gathering intelligence would not only yield quality intelligence but also reduce the abuse of government power. Based on a comparison of policing tactics in Indianapolis, Indiana, and St. Petersburg, Florida—where the police in Indianapolis utilized a "broken windows" model that emphasized the suppression of public disorder, while the police in St. Petersburg adopted a "community partnership" model that emphasized cooperative efforts between officers and residents—Terrill and Mastrofski (2004) found that police officers in Indianapolis used more coercion than officers in St. Petersburg. Similarly, Worrall's (1998) analysis of civil liability lawsuits filed against municipal police departments showed that a commitment to community policing programs was correlated with a low incidence of lawsuits. In short, whereas aggressive counterterrorist police tactics suggested by scholars such as De Guzman (2002) would increase the potential for the abuse of power, cooperative partnerships between law enforcement and the citizenry would discourage officers from dehumanizing or using coercive force on people, which in turn could prove beneficial in gaining public cooperation and gathering counterterrorist intelligence.

Summary Remarks and Prospects for the Future

In an article researched and written prior to the September 11 attacks, Albini (2001) described the increase in the capacities of terrorist organizations and warned that terrorist attacks were a problem that will continue to plague advanced nations, including the United States. Unfortunately, even before that article was published in *Criminal Justice Policy Review* in December 2001, Albini's forecast proved accurate. Albini (2001, p. 274) also accurately predicted that: "If the U.S. government responds in its traditional manner, it will react by giving the government more equipment and laws to fight the terrorists; this will include an increase in its use of wiretapping to monitor telephone calls." Albini concluded that the traditional U.S. response to terrorism (i.e., granting law enforcement the authority to use invasive and repressive tactics) will fail and argued that U.S. officials must develop new approaches to the problem of terrorism.

In response to Albini's call for new approaches to the problem of terrorism, it is herein suggested that U.S. policy makers, homeland defense officials, and law enforcement officials incorporate the basic principles of community policing into counterterrorist policies and tactics. Obviously, as this approach has not been thoroughly tried or tested, there is no substantive evidence to indicate it will work. There are, however, numerous studies that have documented the value of good relations between the police and the community (e.g., Glensor & Peak, 1998; Mazerolle, Ready, Terrill, & Waring, 2000). In addition, as discussed, there is an abundance of evidence that suggests that combative law enforcement tactics often do more harm than good, that aggressive counterterrorism tactics have failed to reduce terrorist activities, and that combative ideologies encourage the unconscionable treatment of human beings. Thus, the conceptualization and development of community-oriented counterterrorist strategies is worth consideration.

While there are numerous issues that must be resolved before a community-oriented counterterrorism strategy could be implemented on a national scale—issues that, as evidenced by the heretofore discussed failure of fusion centers (U.S. Senate Permanent Subcommittee on Investigations, 2012), have yet to be resolved—many police departments already have an organizational infrastructure capable of supporting community-oriented methods of gathering counterterrorist intelligence. Moreover, although the tasks of federal law enforcement agencies are of a different nature than those of local police departments, that does not mean federal agencies are incapable of incorporating an emphasis on quality public relations and cooperative interaction with the citizenry into their operational philosophies. Hence, when it comes to the prospect of forging a network of law enforcement officials who are capable of both handling disorder at the local level and gathering counterterrorist intelligence, integrating intelligence gathering techniques into local community policing programs and integrating the principles of community policing into federal law enforcement policies are more practical, prudent, and promising than increasing police patrols around national landmarks, using advanced technology to arbitrarily eavesdrop into private conversations, and interrogating Arab Americans at random. This is not to suggest that there is no place for aggressive tactics and advanced technology in law enforcement and counterterrorism operations, but simply that the abundant use of such methods is unwise.

Fortunately, there are a number of indicators that the groundwork for a national community-oriented counterterrorism strategy is being laid. In contrast to the mass arrests and invasive investigative tactics used in the immediate aftermath of the events of September 11, in the following months and years a number of policy makers and criminal justice officials recognized the shortcomings of combative investigative and counterterrorist intelligence-gathering tactics and began adopting a more nuanced approach (Ortiz et al., 2007). For instance, during the investigation into the events of September 11 when federal investigators focused considerable resources on Michigan (home to one of the greatest concentrations of Arabs in the United States), many public officials, ranging from administrators at the University of Michigan to members of the Dearborn Police Department, discouraged federal investigators from utilizing harsh investigative tactics. U.S. attorneys in Michigan also recognized the potential hazards associated with alienating the state's Arab population, and during the investigation into the events of September 11, the U.S. Attorney's Office in Michigan sent politely worded letters to the Middle Eastern immigrants identified as interviewees inviting them to contact the office and arrange a convenient time and location to be interviewed. It was believed that such an approach was preferable to sending federal agents to the homes of the immigrants without warning, a method that had been used in some areas (Brill, 2002; Lengel, 2001; Peterson, 2001; Thacher, 2005; Wilgoren, 2001). To provide another example, FBI officials in New Jersey brought in a local lawyer who was active in Muslim communities to conduct a seminar on cultural awareness for FBI agents and police officers and provide suggestions on abiding by Islamic etiquette when interacting with Muslims, such as removing one's shoes on entering a Muslim household (Brill, 2002).

In the years that have elapsed since the events of September 11 and the Bush administration's declaration of a war on terrorism, a number of FBI officials have voiced opposition to the targeting of immigrants as terrorist suspects, have opposed the surveillance of facilities where Muslims meet such as mosques, have argued against the use of torture to obtain information, and have launched programs designed to improve relations with the public and encourage public assistance with the gathering of counterterrorist intelligence (Brill, 2002; Dyer, McCoy, Rodriguez, & Van Dyun, 2007; Gaylord, 2008; Hosenball & Klaidman, 2002; Isikoff, 2009; Vest, 2005). In addition, shortly after taking the oath of office in 2009, President Barack Obama issued a number of executive orders and memorandums that reversed a number of the Bush administration's counterterrorism policies, such as the use of torture to obtain counterterrorist intelligence (Lewis, 2009; Shane, Mazzetti, & Cooper, 2009; Spetalnick, 2009; Stolberg, 2009; U.S. Department of Justice, 2009). Of special significance, after President Obama was sworn into office, the U.S. Office of Legal Counsel (2009, p. 1) issued a memorandum that made it clear that "several opinions issued by the Office of Legal Counsel in 2001–2003 respecting the allocation of authorities between the President and Congress in matters of war and national security do not reflect the current views of this Office."

Moreover, although (as of this writing) President Obama has not proven able to fulfill his 2008 campaign pledge to close the detention facility at Guantanamo Bay—one of the most controversial remnants of the Bush administration's war-on-terrorism ideology and practice—President Obama did issue an executive order in an effort to close the facility and has not abandoned efforts to shutter the facility, having overseen the elimination of new detainee transfers to the facility and a significant decrease in the number of detainees held there. Whereas the military detention facility at Guantanamo Bay once housed hundreds of detainees (the detainee population peaked at approximately 680 in 2003) and had achieved international notoriety for brutal interrogations and living conditions, in recent years there have been no notable reports that the detainees have been treated in a manner inconsistent with the Geneva Convention; as of the fall of 2012, the number of detainees held in the military detention facility in Guantanamo Bay had dwindled to 166 (U.S. Government Accountability Office, 2012). Having been elected to a second term in office, there are no indicators that President Obama intends to reverse any of his executive orders pertinent to constitutionally cognizant counterterrorism strategies or his measured approach to homeland security and containing the threat of international terrorism. Concisely stated, although no overarching national strategy of community-oriented counterterrorism has been formulated, there are scattered indicators that the nation's law enforcement apparatus is moving away from the combative approach adopted in the wake of the September 11 attacks and back toward a community-oriented model of law enforcement.

In light of the previous failures and unintended consequences of combative counterterrorism strategies and tactics, the development of counterterrorism policies that place an emphasis on good public relations and cooperative problem solving represent a step in the right direction. What is needed is a national strategy of community-oriented counterterrorism. Such a strategy would reduce the potential for violations of human dignity (in both the United States and abroad), increase public support and cooperation with law enforcement, help generate quality counterterrorism intelligence, help restore the international status of U.S. authorities as protectors of basic human rights, and provide U.S. officials with an opportunity to set an example of humane governance. Although the development and implementation of a national community-oriented counterterrorism strategy will not be easy, the evolution of community-oriented counterterrorism holds promise not only for enhancing homeland security but also for protecting the civil liberties that are essential to the progress of a free nation such as the United States and for spreading the ideals of democracy throughout the world. And, a global increase in democracy may help reduce problems such as the extreme poverty and rampant political corruption in developing nations—the problems that foster widespread disenchantment and disenfranchisement among the populace, which in turn fuel the development of terrorist organizations such as Al Qaeda and the Shining Path (Albini, 2001; Amanat, 2001; Bibes, 2001)—and thus prove to be the single best means of ridding the planet of violent terrorist organizations.

References

Albini, J. L. (2001). Dealing with the modern terrorist: The need for changes in strategies and tactics in the new war on terrorism. *Criminal Justice Policy Review, 12*(4), 255–281.

Amanat, A. (2001). Empowered through violence: The reinventing of Islamic extremism. In S. Talbott and N. Chanda (Eds.), *The age of terror: America and the world after September 11* (pp. 25–52). New York: Basic Books.

Axtman, K. (2002, August 19). Police can now be drafted to enforce immigration law. *Christian Science Monitor, 94*(186), p. 2.

Barry, J., Hosenball, M., & Dehghanpisheh, B. (2004, May 14). Abu Ghraib and beyond. *Newsweek, 143*(20), 32–38.

Bayley, D. H. (1994). International differences in community policing. In D. P. Rosenbaum (Ed.), *The challenge of community policing: Testing the promises* (pp. 278–281). Thousand Oaks, CA: Sage.

Beck, M. (1995, July 10). Flummoxing the feds. *Newsweek, 136*(2), pp. 44–45.

Besserglik, B. (2002, October 28). Putin defends pre-dawn raid. *Herald Sun (Melbourne, Australia)*, p. 12.

Bibes, P. (2001). Transnational organized crime and terrorism: Columbia, a case study. *Journal of Contemporary Criminal Justice, 17*(3), 243–258.

Bowden, M. (2002, May). Tales of the tyrant. *Atlantic Monthly, 289*(5), 35–53.

Bracken, P. (2001). Rethinking the unthinkable: New priorities for national security. In S. Talbott and N. Chanda (Eds.), *The age of terror: America and the world after September 11* (pp. 173–191). New York: Basic Books.

Brill, S. (2002, January 28). The FBI gets religion. *Newsweek, 139*(4), 32–33

Brown, B., & Benedict, W. R. 2002. Perceptions of the police: Past findings, methodological issues, conceptual issues, and policy implications. *Policing: An International Journal of Police Strategies and Management, 25*(3), 543–580.

Bulzomi, M. J. (2003, June). Foreign Intelligence Surveillance Act before and after the USA PATRIOT Act. *FBI Law Enforcement Bulletin, 72*(6), 25–31.

Carey, H. F. (2002). Immigrants, terrorism and counter-terrorism. *Peace Review, 14*(4), 395–402.

Community Policing Consortium. (1994, August). *Understanding community policing: A framework for action* (NCJ 148457). Washington, DC: U.S. Department of Justice, Office of Justice Programs, Bureau of Justice Assistance.

Conroy, J. (2000). *Unspeakable acts, ordinary people: The dynamics of torture*. Berkeley: University of California Press.

Constable, P. (2008, August 23). Many officials reluctant to help arrest immigrants. *Washington Post*, p. B1.

Controversy continues regarding detainees held by the CIA, renditions to other countries. (2005, July). *American Journal of International Law, 99*(3), 706–707.

Cordner, G. W. (1997). Community policing: Elements and effects. In R. G. Dunham and G. P. Alpert (Eds.), *Critical issues in policing: Contemporary readings* (3rd ed., pp. 451–468). Prospect Heights, IL: Waveland Press.

Davis, R. C., & Erez, E. (1998, May). *Immigrant populations as victims: Toward a multicultural criminal justice system* (NCJ 167571). Washington, DC: U.S. Department of Justice, Office of Justice Programs, National Institute of Justice.

De Guzman, M. C. (2002, September/October). The changing roles and strategies of the police in a time of terror. *ACJS Today, 22*(3), 8–13.

DeSimone, D. C. (2003, April). Federal budget a mixed bag for state and local governments. *Government Finance Review, 19*(2), 66–69.

Dixon, R. (2002, October 29). Putin vows to strike terrorists - anywhere: Words echo those of Bush after Sept. 11. *The Gazette (Montreal, Quebec)*, p. A1.

Donohue, L. K. (2002). Bias, national security, and military tribunals. *Criminology and Public Policy, 1*(3), 339–344.

Dorell, O., & Welch, W. M. (2007, March 30). Local police confront illegal immigrants. *USA Today*, p. 1A.

Douglas, J., & Olshaker, M. (1998). *Obsession*. New York: Pocket Books.

Doyle, C. (2002, April 18). *The USA PATRIOT Act: A sketch (RS21203)*. Washington, DC: Library of Congress, Congressional Research Service.

Dyer, C., McCoy, R. E., Rodriguez, J., & Van Dyun, D. N. (2007, December). Countering violent Islamic extremism: A community responsibility. *FBI Law Enforcement Bulletin, 76*(12), 3–9.

Fine, G. (2003, June). *The September 11 detainees: A review of the treatment of aliens held on immigration charges in connection with the investigation of the September 11 attacks*. Washington, DC: U.S. Department of Justice, Office of the Inspector General.

Fritsch, E. J., Caeti, T. J., & Taylor, R. W. (1999). Gang suppression through saturation patrol, aggressive curfew, and truancy enforcement: A quasi-experimental test of the Dallas anti-gang initiative. *Crime and Delinquency, 45*(1), 122–139.

Garza, C. L. (2006, October 23). HPD procedure shift draws concern among immigrants; officers now must ask anyone arrested for proof of citizenship. *Houston Chronicle*, p. B1.

Gaylord, A. A. (2008, April). Community involvement: The ultimate force multiplier. *FBI Law Enforcement Bulletin, 77*(4), 16–17.

Geraghty, J. (2003, April 9). Democratic study indicates police strain under homeland securities duties. *States News Service*, p. 1008099u1552.

Glensor, R. W., & Peak, K. (1998). Lasting impact: Maintaining neighborhood order. *FBI Law Enforcement Bulletin, 67*(3), 1–7.

Goldstein, H. (1979). Improving policing: A problem-oriented approach. *Crime and Delinquency, 25*(2), 236–258.

Haberman, C. (2001, October 27). Visions of a long struggle, strains on police and help for victims. *New York Times*, p. 1B.

Hickman, M. J., & Reaves, B. A. (2003, January). *Local police departments, 2000* (NCJ 196002). Washington, DC: U.S. Department of Justice, Office of Justice Programs, Bureau of Justice Statistics.

Higham, S. (2004, June 13). A look behind the "wire" at Guantanamo. *Washington Post*, p. A1.

Hosenball, M., & Klaidman, D. (2002, June 17). A leap of faith. *Newsweek, 139*(24), p. 32.

Howlett, D. (1999, July 14). Handshake ends hunt in railway killings. *USA Today*, p. 1A.

Isikoff, M. (2003, June 9). Flushed from the woods: A lucky break ends a seven-year manhunt. *Newsweek, 141*(23), 35.

Isikoff, M. (2008, December 22). The fed who blew the whistle. *Newsweek, 152*(25), 40–48.

Isikoff, M. (2009, May 4). "We could have done this the right way": How Ali Soufan, an FBI agent, got Abu Zubaydah to talk without torture. *Newsweek, 153*(18), 18–21.

Kennedy, P. (2001). Maintaining American power: From injury to recovery. In S. Talbott and N. Chanda (Eds.), *The age of terror: America and the world after September 11* (pp. 55–79). New York: Basic Books.

Klaidman, D., & Isikoff, M. (2003, October 27). Lost in translation. *Newsweek, 142*(17), 26–30.

Klaidman, D., & King, P. (1998, January 19). Suicide mission. *Newsweek, 131* (3), 22–25.

Lengel, A. (2001, November 27). Arab men in Detroit to be asked to see U.S. attorney. *Washington Post*, p. A5.

Lewis, N. (2009, February 2). Justice department under Obama is preparing for doctrinal shift in policies of Bush years. *New York Times*, p. A14.

Lyons, W. (2002). Partnerships, information, and public safety: Community policing in a time of terror. *Policing: An International Journal of Police Strategies and Management, 25*(3), 530–542.

Mazerolle, L. G., Ready, J., Terrill, W., & Waring, E. (2000). Problem-oriented policing: The Jersey City evaluation. *Justice Quarterly, 17*(1), 129–158.

McGrory, D., & Shepherd, R. (2002, October 28). Mystery gas kills 115 hostages. *The Times (London)*, p. 1.

Michel, L., & Herbeck, D. (2002). *American terrorist: Timothy McVeigh and the tragedy at Oklahoma City*. New York: Avon Books.

Moore, M. H. (1994). Research synthesis and policy implications. In D. P. Rosenbaum (Ed.), *The challenge of community policing: Testing the promises* (pp. 285–297). Thousand Oaks, CA: Sage.

National Commission on Terrorist Attacks Upon the United States. (2004). *The 9/11 Commission report: Final report of the National Commission on Terrorist Attacks Upon the United States*. New York: Norton.

Ortiz, C. W., Hendricks, N. J., & Sugie, N. F. (2007). Policing terrorism: The response of local police agencies to homeland security concerns. *Criminal Justice Studies, 20*(2), 91–109.

Pelfrey, W. V. (1998). Precipitating factors of paradigmatic shift in policing: The origin of the community policing era. In G. P. Alpert and A. Piquero (Eds.) *Community policing: Contemporary readings* (pp. 79–92). Prospect Heights, IL: Waveland Press.

Peterson, J. (2001, December 3). *U to support students in investigation* (statement from University of Michigan Office of Communications). Retrieved January 17, 2009, from http://www.ur.umich.edu/0102/Dec03_01/6.htm

Pincus, W., & Milbank, D. (2004, June 17). Al Qaeda-Hussein Link is dismissed. *Washington Post*, p. A1.

Pious, R. M. (2006). *The war on terrorism and the rule of law*. Los Angeles: Roxbury.

Pollack, K. M. (2004, January/February). Spies, lies, and weapons: What went wrong. *The Atlantic Monthly, 293*(1), 78–92.

Roth, J. A., Roehl, J., & Johnson, C. C. (2004). Trends in the adoption of community policing. In W. G. Skogan (Ed.), *Community policing: Can it work?* (pp. 3–29). Belmont, CA: Wadsworth/Thomson.

Sandberg, L., & Castillo, J. (1999, July 14). Resendez-Ramirez gives up. *San Antonio Express News*, pp. 1A, 6A.

Savage, D. G. (2009, January 16). Court calls warrantless wiretaps legal; the ruling allows eavesdropping on international calls, even when Americans may be involved. *Los Angeles Times*, p. A14.

Shane, S., Mazzetti, M., & Cooper, H. (2009, January 23). Obama reverses key Bush policy but questions on detainees remain. *New York Times*, p. A16.

Sherman, L. W. (1993). Defiance, deterrence, and irrelevance: A theory of the criminal sanction. *Journal of Research in Crime and Delinquency, 30*(4), 445–473.

Sherman, L. W., Shaw, J. W., & Rogan, D. P. (1995, January). *The Kansas City gun experiment* (NIJ 150855). Washington, DC: U.S. Department of Justice, Office of Justice Programs, National Institute of Justice.

Simonsen, C. E., & Spindlove, J. R. (2004). *Terrorism today: The past, the players, the future* (2nd ed.). Upper Saddle River, NJ: Pearson Prentice Hall.

Sinnar, S. (2003, April). Patriotic or unconstitutional? The mandatory detention of aliens under the USA PATRIOT Act. *Stanford Law Review, 55*, 1419–1456.

Skipp, C., & Campo-Flores, A. (2003, June 23). Still probing. *Newsweek, 141*(25), 10.

Sloan, S. (2002). Meeting the terrorist threat: The localization of counter terrorism intelligence. *Police Practice and Research, 3*(4), 337–345.

Spetalnick, M. (2009, January 23). Obama acts to burnish U.S. image abroad: President moves quickly to roll back several Bush policies, names troubleshooters. *Toronto Sun*, p. AA1.

Stephens, G. (2003, January). Can we be safe and free? The dilemma terrorism creates. *USA Today Magazine, 131*(2692), 16–18.

Stolberg, S. G. (2009, January 22). On first day Obama quickly sets a new tone. *New York Times*, p. A1.

Stuntz, W. J. (2002). Local policing after the terror. *Yale Law Review, 111*, 2137–2194.

Taylor, S., & Thomas, E. (2009, January 19). Obama's Cheney dilemma. *Newsweek, 153*(3), 20–26.

Terrill, W., & Mastrofski, S. D. (2004). Working the street: Does community policing matter? In W. G. Skogan (Ed.), *Community policing: Can it work?* (pp. 109–135). Belmont, CA: Wadsworth.

Thacher, D. (2005). The local role in homeland security. *Law & Society Review, 39*(3), 635–676.

Thomas, E. (2002, November 4). Descent into evil. *Newsweek, 140*(19), 21–38.

Thomas, P., & McAllister, B. (1996, October 27). Guard no longer a suspect in Olympic Park bombing; Justice Department serves formal notice. *Washington Post*, p. A1.

Tyler, T. R. (1990). *Why people obey the law*. New Haven, CT: Yale University Press.

Uchida, C. (1997). The development of the American police: An overview. In R. G. Dunham and G. P. Alpert (Eds.), *Critical issues in policing: Contemporary readings* (3rd ed., pp. 18–35). Prospect Heights, IL: Waveland Press.

U.S. Department of Justice. (1994). *Violent crime control and Law Enforcement Act of 1994: Briefing book*. Washington, DC: Author.

U.S. Department of Justice. (2009, April 16). *Department of Justice releases four Office of Legal Counsel opinions* (Press Release 09–356). Washington, DC: Author.

U.S. Government Accountability Office. (2012, November). *Guantanamo Bay detainees: Facilities and factors for consideration if detainees were brought to the United States* (GAO-13-31). Washington, DC: Author. Retrieved December 1, 2012, from http://www.gao.gov/assets/660/650032.pdf

U.S. Immigration and Customs Enforcement. (2008, August 18). *Delegation of immigration authority section 287(g) Immigration and Nationality Act*. Washington, DC: Author. Retrieved May 19, 2009, from http://www.ice.gov/partners/287g/Section287_g.htm

U.S. Office of Legal Counsel. (2001, October 23). *Memorandum for Alberto R. Gonzales, counsel to the president, William J. Haynes, II, general counsel, Department of Defense re: authority for use of military force to combat terrorist activities within the United States*. Washington, DC: U.S. Department of Justice. Retrieved August 17, 2009, from http://www.usdoj.gov/opa/documents/memo-militaryforcecombat us10232001.pdf

U.S. Office of Legal Counsel. (2002a, June 27). *Memorandum for Daniel J. Bryant, assistant attorney general, Office of Legislative Affairs re: applicability of 18 U.S.C § 4001(a) to military detention of United States citizens*. Washington, DC: U.S. Department of Justice. Retrieved August 17, 2009, from http://www.usdoj.gov/opa/documents/memodetentionuscitizens06272002.pdf

U.S. Office of Legal Counsel. (2002b, March 13). *Memorandum for William J. Haynes, II, general counsel, Department of Defense re: the president's power as commander in chief to transfer captured terrorists to the control and custody of foreign nations*. Washington, DC: U.S. Department of Justice. Retrieved August 17, 2009, from http://www.usdoj.gov/opa/documents/memorandum03132002.pdf

U.S. Office of Legal Counsel. (2003, March 14). *Memorandum for William J. Haynes, II, general counsel of the Department of Defense re: military interrogation of alien unlawful combatants held outside the United States*. Washington, DC: U.S. Department of Justice. Retrieved August 17, 2009 from: http://www.aclu.org/pdfs/safefree/yoo_army_torture_memo.pdf

U.S. Office of Legal Counsel. (2005, May 10). *Memorandum for John A. Rizzo, senior deputy general counsel, Central Intelligence Agency Re: Application of 18 U.S.C. §§ 2340-2340A to the combined use of certain techniques in the interrogation of high value al Qaeda detainees*. Washington, DC: U.S. Department of Justice. Retrieved August 17, 2009, from http://www.aclu.org/safefree/general/olc_memos.html

U.S. Office of Legal Counsel. (2009, January 15). *Memorandum for the files re: status of certain OLC opinions issued in the aftermath of the terrorist attacks of September 11, 2001*. Washington, DC: U.S. Department of Justice. Retrieved August 17, 2009, from http://www.usdoj.gov/opa/documents/memostatusolcopinions01152009.pdf

U.S. Office of Management and Budget. (2007). *Budget of the United States government, fiscal year 2007*. Washington, DC: Author.

U.S. Senate Permanent Subcommittee on Investigations. (2012, October 3). *Federal support for and involvement in state and local fusion centers*. Washington, DC: Author. Retrieved October 20, 2012, from http://www.hsgac.senate.gov/subcommittees/investigations/media/investigative-report-criticizes-counterterrorism-reporting-waste-at-state-and-local-intelligence-fusion-centers

Vest, J. (2005, July). Pray and tell. *The American Prospect, 16*(7), 47–50.

Wade, B. (2002, June 1). Local law enforcement is getting robbed. *American City and County*, p. 1.

Wadman, R. C., & Allison, W. T. (2004). *To protect and to serve: A history of police in America*. Upper Saddle River, NJ: Pearson Prentice Hall.

White, J. R. (2004). *Defending the homeland: Domestic intelligence, law enforcement, and security*. Belmont, CA: Wadsworth.

White, J. R. (1991). *Terrorism: An introduction*. Pacific Grove, CA: Brooks/Cole.

Whitehead, J. W., & Aden, S. H. (2002). Forfeiting "enduring freedom" for "homeland security": A constitutional analysis of the USA PATRIOT Act and the Justice Department's anti-terrorism initiatives. *American University Law Review, 51,* 1081–1133.

Wilgoren, J. (2001, December 1). A nation challenged: The interviews; University of Michigan won't cooperate in federal canvas. *New York Times*, p. B6.

Wong, K. C. (2006a). The making of the USA Patriot Act I: The legislative process and dynamics. *International Journal of the Sociology of Law, 34*(3), 179–219.

Wong, K. C. (2006b). The making of the USA PATRIOT Act II: Public sentiments, legislative climate, political gamesmanship, media patriotism. *International Journal of the Sociology of Law, 34*(2), 105–140.

Worrall, J. L. (1998). Administrative determinants of civil liability lawsuits against municipal police departments: An exploratory analysis. *Crime and Delinquency, 44*(2), 295–313.

Yoder, E. (1996, August 2). FBI casually hurts man it can't arrest. *Denver Post*, p. B7.

Terrorism Old and New Counterterrorism in Canada[1,2]

STÉPHANE LEMAN-LANGLOIS
JEAN-PAUL BRODEUR

Contents

Introduction

When the Hon. Paul Martin succeeded Jean Chrétien as Canada's new prime minister in December 2003, his most conspicuous move was to appoint a cabinet that included a new Department of Public Safety and Emergency Preparedness (PSEP, now Public Safety Canada), clearly patterned on the U.S. Department of Homeland Security. The first minister to be appointed to the Public Safety portfolio was the Hon. Anne McLennan, who also served as vice prime minister of Canada, a telling expression of the importance of the new ministry. The creation of PSEP was not a response to a direct attack—Canada, although explicitly mentioned by Al Qaeda spokesmen as among targeted countries, had not been the object of recent terrorist attacks. Instead, its creation testifies to the global character of the new counterterrorism (CT), whereby countries are accountable to each other and must show diligence and dedication to the war on terror. It also bears witness to the enduring worldwide defensive stance that followed the tragedy of September 2001 and the perception that political violence was evolving toward what was referred to as a "new" terrorism (Hoffman, 1997; Laqueur, 1997, 1999, 2003; Pape, 2003). In our view, the label *new terrorism* is misleading as some of its characteristics have always been central to terrorism; it is too heavily colonized by religious language, often using the justifications offered by the terrorists as *explanations* of their actions; it is too close to an idealized version of Al Qaeda central that has ceased to be applicable; and finally it has been applied too soon and too liberally. In short, it should be replaced. Yet, it is undeniable that terrorism is a constantly fluctuating, dynamic category, and it is inevitable that new forms of terrorism—new tactics, new structures, new objectives, new targets, new discourses, and new audiences—will emerge, new, in an atheoretical sense. It then follows that equally new forms of CT should be adopted.

Our analysis rests on three assumptions: (a) Efficient CT necessitates knowledge of the kind of organization that is being fought; (b) the knowledge that is needed must support action—that is, it must be knowledge that can efficiently match core features of terrorist organizations with police responses; (c) persistent terrorism is not caused by structural problems in CT agencies and therefore does not necessitate organizational reform, although other, very good reasons may exist for such reform. In particular, it does not imply that CT agencies should imitate terrorist group structure (even if every terror group shared structural characteristics, which they in fact do not). Although some structural isomorphism may naturally occur between criminal and countercriminal groups, it is a *result* of prevention or repression activities and not a condition of their success (Manning, 1980). For instance, no credible demonstration has been made that "it takes a network to fight a network" or even that terror groups are more "network-like" than classic policing organizations.

In line with these assumptions, this chapter is divided into four parts, followed by a brief conclusion. First, we propose a broad typology of terrorism based on our current research. Second, we present typical instances of terrorism in Canada and compare the features of various kinds of terrorism. Third, we review the most threatening kind of terrorism that plagued Canada in the 1970s to highlight one of the most important factors of a successful police response: parallelism between police and terrorist strategies. Our final section identifies a few potentially successful CT strategies against what we refer to as "restoration" terrorism.

Terrorism in Canada, 1973–2003: An Operational Typology

Attempting to produce a typology of events that are both rare and extremely diverse in nature can be a perilous undertaking. At worst, it can distort the events that are being considered by imposing forms dictated by the researcher's needs rather than the particular characteristics of the events under consideration. In an attempt to avoid this, the typology we offer in this section is at once minimal in its determining variables and maximal in its scope. Various typologies of terrorism already exist and have been based on tactics, the nature of the objectives, the extents of the damage inflicted, the causes, or the size, type, or organization of the groups (see Schmid, 2011, for an overview). We found these to be extremely helpful in building our dataset but not so much in terms of direct consequence for policing.

At the outset, we built a *qualitative* database of all incidents that took place in Canada between 1973 and 2003, using a number of existing sources. One major source was the work of Kellett, Beanlands, Deacon, James, and Lapalme (1991), who have produced a monumental reference on terrorism and political violence in Canada up to 1989, itself based in part on work by Ross (1988). Starting from this, we have completed the chronology through the 1990s and 2000s (in part with the help of Mickolus, 1980, 1993; Mickolus, Sandler, Todd, and Murdock, 1989; Mickolus and Simmons, 1997; and Vareilles, 2001). We also added much contextual information on the incidents and increased the amount of cross-incident linking in an effort to escape the conventional database approach, which has produced solid research to date but tends to homogenize theoretical approaches to political violence and terrorism. We have instead adopted what one might call a "narrative" database, in which incidents are considered together rather than being extracted as discrete events. We also manage and data mine it with qualitative research packages rather than typical database software.

From the outset, we decided to move away from set, prestructured classifications and the obligation to think of terrorism as a list of separate incidents. Incidents are deceptive both in their apparent internal unity (often constructed by the media and by stakeholder entities) and in their artificially enhanced discreteness. The stories of terrorism we are working with are complex and intermeshing and vary greatly in the degree in which they result from planned action. We would also like to avoid some of the problems that Kellett et al. (1991) had with classification, especially when filing *incidents* and ignoring relationships between them, even the most obvious, such as the identity of the perpetrators. This approach led to their categorizing one attack by the Direct Action/"Squamish Five" members, the Litton Industries bomb of 1982, as "left wing," while another, the firebombing of the "Red Hot Video" premises a few months later, is categorized as "single-issue" terrorism, opposition to pornography apparently not considered to be "left wing." Even if "left" and "right" wing were helpful categories, which is doubtful, this incident-based classification clearly does not fit the reality it is meant to describe. This problem is not particular to the work of Kellet et al. and is present in all traditional databases.

Finally, our database is deliberately built with an extremely wide interpretation of the phrase "terrorism in Canada" not only with respect to the "terrorism" element, which we take to include hoaxes, threats, individual attacks, support activities such as fund-raising, and failed or foiled plots, but also with regard to the "Canadian content" of the situations being considered. To us, any link to Canada is considered of interest, even if it is only that an airplane hijacked in the United States had to refuel in Gander on its way to a third country. Any plotting, preparation, or fund-raising activity in Canada, even if the actual attacks are to take place elsewhere, is of course included (one may explore the data with infinitely varied definitions of terrorism; see Leman-Langlois and Ouellet, 2009).

Still, for the more quantitatively inclined, we can produce an approximate count of terrorist events in Canada drawn from 400 entries during the 1973–2003 period: 6 hijackings; 2 airplane bombings; 73 disruptive hoaxes; 9 hostage takings or kidnappings; 4 letter bombs; 170 bombs, firebombs, and arson; 59 threats; 35 attacks on individuals; 45 acts of vandalism; 14 plots and foiled attacks; and 32 instances of support (we are now in the process of updating to 2013).

For the purposes of this chapter, it is not necessary to devise a universal and definitive typology. The one we propose simply attempts to differentiate between the broad variants of terrorism in Canada in a way that might be helpful in identifying potential responses. Note that we do not expect this typology to be useful outside Canada or in reasonably comparable liberal democracies where terrorism is exceptional. However, it has proven helpful in sorting out the contents of our database. In most cases, these contents are *situations*, rather than events or actors, meaning that events that are linked together through their perpetrators or through practical consequences (for instance, murder following a kidnapping) are considered as a unit.

These units were then analyzed to extract the rationale behind the chain of events or the set of actions committed by a group. Excluding cases for which no rationale could be identified, we then ran a thematic analysis of these rationales and found that they could be sorted according to two qualitative variables. The first variable is the *scope* of the desired impact (however unrealistic from the observers' point of view). That scope can be very narrow,

Table 11.1 Matrix of Terrorist Rationales

	Scope of Desired[a] Impact	
Justification of Action[b]	Narrow	Wide
Forward looking	Demand-based threats	Revolutionary threats
Backward looking	"Private-justice" threats	"Restoration" threats

[a] Likelihood of success or reasonableness of expectations and desires is not considered.

[b] This is an internal moral justification, regardless of whether it would be considered legitimate by others.

such as putting an end to the release of sour gas around the perpetrator's ranch, or extremely wide if it involves fundamental changes in society, such as abandoning the capitalist-liberal system. The second variable is the *time frame* of the point of reference that is held as a justification for the act. When terrorist acts are a response to a perceived (real or otherwise) slight or injustice that happened in the past, we consider them to be "backward looking"; if, on the contrary, the act is meant to achieve a goal at a later time (e.g., to force an entity to fulfill a demand), we categorize it as "forward looking." This gives us four broad threat categories based on the underlying rationale of the perpetrators, as presented in Table 11.1.

Note that this rationale-based typology can also be applied to what is often referred to as "state terrorism," in both its international "state-sponsored" and its domestic or repressive guises. We do not consider Canada to be engaged in state terrorism on any noticeable scale, but it has been known to give refuge to individuals who have engaged in such terrorism in their respective countries. Private enterprises whose actions support repressive regimes might also be considered as involved in state terrorism.

Demand-Based Threats

Demand-based threats have always been the most common type of terrorism in Canada. Typically, they involve small groups, often ad hoc formations, focused on a specific object that is perceived as a problem. They are forward looking in the sense that the action taken is aimed at correcting a problem. Here, despite the frequent conviction that the authorities who might or should be responsible are incompetent, corrupt, or actually at the source of the problem, the main goal is not to *punish* them but to ameliorate a situation. It is interesting to note that these demands are often not addressed to the state, as has traditionally been understood to be the case with conventional terrorism. In many cases, the acts amount to violent intimidation of private persons, groups, or enterprises. It should also be noted that the category does not quite fit the conventional "single-issue" type used in the literature since that category spans both our backward-looking and forward-looking categories.

In Canada, demand-based threats consist mainly of acts of vandalism by animal rights and ecology groups. Their targets include mink farms, university departments and private laboratories that use animals for tests, as well as meat-packing plants. Ecoterrorism is rare, but Canadians are sometimes involved in acts of sabotage abroad, such as the Sea Shepherd Conservation Society's attack on whaling equipment in Iceland in November 1986. Alberta farmer and commune leader Weibo Ludwig was involved in over 150 incidents of vandalism against oil installations around his property in 1997 and 1998. He was trying to stop oil companies from polluting the area with sour gas.

Another important area of demand-based threats is the targeting of abortion clinics and their staff. Actions have included stealing and destroying medical equipment, vandalizing premises with acid, destroying and attempting to destroy premises by arson or bombing, threatening staff (one repeated target has been Dr. Henry Morgentaler, who was the leading advocate of free abortion), and three cases in which obstetricians who performed abortions were shot.

Demand-based threats also include local, temporary states of unrest, limited to a micro level, such as one in 1979 when parents of children in Langley, British Columbia, set fire to five school officials' homes in a dispute over the admission of their children to school.

"Private Justice" Threats

"Private justice" involves a response to an event, situation, or conflict that is intended to obtain retribution, as defined by the attacker. In its various guises, it may attempt to obtain reparation and redress, but more often than not its main goal is punishment. It can be a sophisticated response or straightforward revenge, but it is always characterized by a claim of previous victimization. This is what Black (1983) refers to as "self-help" justice, deployed when existing, institutionalized mechanisms for justice are assumed to be inefficient or corrupt—or, in the case of terrorism, as part of the problem.

Examples of private justice threats include the many acts of arson and other forms of destruction committed in British Columbia by members of the Doukhobor religious community. The fundamentalist, radical "Sons of Freedom" (SOF), or "Freedomites," a subset of the wider group, typically reacted against the presence of installations or buildings that were deemed to be offensive in some way to the religious purity of the physical context in which they lived. Most of these attacks were intended to destroy unholy or sacrilegious buildings, monuments, and the like. Others were essentially punitive, targeting the property of individuals who were perceived to be Doukhobor victimizers. Repeated regulatory and legal attacks on the Doukhobor lifestyle by the provincial and federal governments contributed to chronic escalations of the conflict. The SOF burned homes, schools, a post office, municipal buildings, and Canadian Pacific rail tracks. SOF arsonists have been far less active during the period under study than in the first half of the 20th century, when they burned hundreds of homes and other buildings. Active mainly between 1980 and 1986, when they committed some 40 cases of arson and bombings, the SOF are no longer active and are a good example of attrition through the aging of its core members and the failure to recruit new supporters. There are a few exceptions, such as the burning of a computer lab in 2001, causing some $150,000 (Canadian dollars) worth of damage. The arsonist, an 81-year-old woman, was trying to commemorate an important Doukhobor religious anniversary.

This category also includes acts of political violence carried out by xenophobic groups such as skinheads, the KKK, and various other groups, some of which have ties to U.S. groups. In many cases, xenophobic attacks have been carried out by ad hoc groups who have used the "KKK" symbol to threaten their victims but have no confirmed relation with the KKK. East Indian immigrants in British Columbia have been targeted, suffering beatings, murders, arson, bombings, and cross burnings. In April 1981, three Canadian extremist right-wingers were embroiled in a plot to overthrow the government of Dominica and set up a white supremacist utopia on the island, which might have pushed their private justice, xenophobic threats into revolutionary threats. In 1986, a bomb was placed in a Canadian Immigration Center in Vancouver, with a note blaming Canadian immigration policy for "dumping" "third-world persons" in Canada. In 1988, five skinheads were caught on tape bragging about their murder of Nirmal Singh Gill, 65, on the grounds of the temple where he worked. In 1992, Austrian police arrested a group of neo-Nazis who were plotting violent attacks in Vienna and found they were financed in part by Canadian-based Holocaust denier Ernst Zundel.

In 1986, Québecair was sold to CP Air, leading to a series of threats against Québecair and CP Air flights and planes. The sale of the airline, seen as a symbol of Quebec entrepreneurship, was interpreted by some as a theft of an important Quebecois asset by Western, anglophone Canada. The disruption of operations could have been a knee-jerk reaction but may have been intended to cause financial losses.

In the same province, the perennial language/nationalist debate has provoked a great number of small incidents clustered around political events perceived as attacks against the French or English language in Quebec, as interpreted by citizens with opposing political positions. One of these events was the 1980 referendum on the independence of Quebec, when multiple cases of threats, against both the "Yes" and "No" camps, were recorded. Tempers flared again in 1982 around the constitutional debate and a new language law. Actions included leaving unarmed dynamite in various politically meaningful sites, especially Parti Quebecois (perceived as anti-English) offices, the destruction of billboards, attempted arson, and various forms of vandalism against shops and other commercial enterprises displaying English-only signs. In December 1986, a court ruling allowing bilingual signs provoked a new wave of bomb threats, Molotov cocktail attacks, and other forms of vandalism against enterprises without a sufficiently French appearance. Another ruling in December 1988 triggered attacks, one of which caused $200,000 worth of damage to the Montreal offices of Alliance Quebec (an "English rights" organization). In 2000, ex-FLQ (Front de libération du Québec or Quebec Liberation Front) member Rhéal Mathieu was arrested for attempted arson against companies with English names (especially Second Cup cafes) and against a church where an English rights group was to meet. Finally, and more recently, the debate around the fusion of municipalities within metropolitan Montreal became polarized over the language issue and, in late 2003, served as the focus point for militant threats and acts of vandalism against a former municipality's town hall.

In this category should be included three types of state terrorism. First, there are repressive states abroad that attempt to control their dissidents who have sought refuge in Canada. Such was the case of Libya, which was in 1988 in the middle of an FBI investigation into travel agencies used as fronts for Libyan agents. One such agency, the Manara Travel Agency in Ottawa, which was closely tied to xenophobic groups in Canada and the United States, was dismantled when the FBI arrested some of its operators for plotting to kill Iran–Contra conspirator Oliver North. During the end of the 1970s, Yugoslavia attempted to silence its dissidents in Canada, and some of them reacted by attacking Yugoslavian government targets in Canada, as well as other institutions that were seen as friendly to the Tito regime. After the publication of *The Satanic Verses* in 1988, Iran pronounced a fatwa against its author, Salman Rushdie. In Canada, this translated into threats and arson attacks on bookstores that carried the book as well as counterthreats against Iranians in Canada. When the government of Canada refused to designate the book as hate literature, Revenue Minister Otto Jelinek and Foreign Affairs Minister Joe Clark were also threatened. Iran has also sent agents to Canada, for instance, Mansour Ahani, who was arrested in Italy in 1992 for plotting the assassination of a prominent Iranian dissident, and Djafar Seyfi, who was caught attempting to intimidate Iranians in Canada. Second, a few Canadian-based transnational enterprises have been supporting repressive regimes abroad, which may or may not count directly as terrorism but could eventually provoke retaliation here. Third, there are former agents of repressive states who migrate to Canada. For instance, Léon Mugesera, instigator of the Rwandan genocide, arrived in Canada in 1993 and was only expelled in 2012.

Revolutionary Threats

Revolutionary threats aim at fundamental changes at the state level. In Canada, they are usually aimed at another country, with Canada serving as a base for action elsewhere (e.g., India). One exception would be the FLQ, as already explained.

The Armenian Secret Army for the Liberation of Armenia (ASALA) conducted a series of attacks on various targets in the beginning of the 1980s. Its overall goal was the independence of Armenia from Turkey, and it targeted Turkish diplomats in Canada, newspapers felt to be unsympathetic to its cause, and other Armenians who questioned its approach or refused to fund it when asked. In May 1982, a bomb placed in an Air Canada freight terminal in Los Angeles was defused 15 minutes before it was timed to explode. It was meant as retaliation for the arrest of Armenian extremists in Canada some weeks earlier. The Justice Commandos for the Armenian Genocide (JCAG) assassinated a Turkish diplomat in Canada in August 1982. In 1985, three ASALA gunmen invaded the Turkish embassy in Ottawa, killing a security guard and holding the building for 4 hours. Two weeks after their arrest, ASALA sent a letter to the Royal Canadian Mounted Police (RCMP) threatening to blow up the Toronto subway if the trio was not released from custody. The Montreal RCMP office received the same threat against the Montreal Metro.

The IRA is also the source of some events concerning Canadians. In a few cases, Canadian citizens were arrested at the U.S. border while trying to smuggle IRA members across. In 1994, a Canadian was arrested in Spain for attempting to deliver weapons to the group. As well, while we have not inventoried the fund-raising activities of the IRA in Canada, we think it likely that they were quite extensive.

Sikh extremists were particularly active between 1984 and 1990. The Indian government attack on separatists who had barricaded themselves in the Golden Temple of Amritsar, Sikhism's most important shrine, occurred in 1984. The attack left the temple severely damaged and hundreds dead or wounded. Some terrorist attacks were direct responses to the outcome (whether it was a victory, defeat, or massacre is part of the definition of the problem) at Amritsar and, to the extent that this was their motivation, could thus be considered private justice. For instance, shortly after the attack, a group of Sikhs assaulted the Indian high commissioner, and another stormed the Indian consulate in Toronto. However, the entire situation exists only because of the preexisting claims and demands for an independent Sikh homeland (*Khalistan*, "land of the pure") in India.

Sikh extremism in Canada ranges from raising funds for violent attacks to intimidation and assassinations. While the overall goal is the creation of an independent homeland, much violence in Canada occurs around the more immediate power struggles between groups and the intimidation (and murder) of vocal dissidents (most notably newspaper editor Tara Singh Hayer, who survived a shooting in 1988 but was finally killed in 1998, while wheelchair bound). However, with the Air India/Tokyo airport bombings of June 1985 (another Air India plane was scheduled to be bombed in May 1986, but the plot was foiled by police in Montreal), Sikh extremism produced the most severe act of terrorism in Canadian history as well as one of the deadliest worldwide. The attack, targeted toward an Indian airplane, in fact killed passengers who were in majority Canadian. Months before the attacks, extremist Sikh leaders had publicly wished that thousands of Indians be killed to avenge the attack on the temple.

Tamil terrorism in Canada is limited to fund-raising activities, mostly in Toronto; there are a handful of exceptions, most directed against intragroup dissidence, with damage to property and violent attacks against individuals who failed to conform to the demands of the group. Tamil terrorist financing organizations are particularly adept at disguising their activities, even fooling then-ministers Paul Martin and Maria Minna into participating in a fund-raising dinner in May 2000.

Direct Action, a small group named after a French extremist group, targeted capitalism in general as well as certain of its aspects that it felt to be particularly hateful, such as pollution (by blowing up a power relay station) and war (by blowing up cruise missile subcontractor Litton). In 1982, its members were arrested in Squamish, British Columbia, and were subsequently referred to as the "Squamish Five."

When a state of emergency was declared in South Africa in 1986, there were a few incidents in Canada (as well as elsewhere) to protest against the apartheid government. Some of these, credit for which was claimed by the Azanian People's Liberation Front (APLF), an essentially unknown organization, while ultimately revealed as hoaxes, caused heavy financial losses. In one instance, the APLF claimed to have poisoned South African fruit, which then had to be destroyed; 3,000 bottles of wine were also destroyed when another group using the name Direct Action claimed to have poisoned them.

Canadians Christine Lamont and David Spencer were arrested and tried for the kidnapping of a supermarket chain owner in Brazil in an attempt to finance various leftist revolutionary groups in South America. In 1993, when a cache of weapons and false papers was discovered by accident in Nicaragua, letters by Lamont and Spencer were found with passports in the name of one of the World Trade Center (WTC) bombers.

"Restoration" Threats

As we shall see, "restoration" is the category that is closest to common definitions of *new terrorism*. Restoration represents a category of rationales that aim to reestablish, re-create, and restore what is described as an ideal moment in history. This idealized world may have existed at any time in the past but is more likely to come from a very distant, usually mythical, past. Religious or eschatological aspects may be present but are not required. The distinctive feature here is that the idealized world has been *lost* and therefore has proven that it can in fact exist and that human actions can bring it back. Contrary to idealized revolutionary worlds, there are available narratives of past glory, complete with actors, institutions, tragedies, and ultimately, an unjust outcome. These narratives can be called on to understand the present, to recruit members and supporters, and ultimately to justify actions taken toward restoration. We believe that this system of justification, or reinterpretation, is the most powerful motivator toward extreme acts of mass violence. Such deeds, separately or combined, can be described as epic, desperate, or self-sacrificial in a grandiose, wide-scale perception of a Manichean historical narrative. Though individually held insignificant, agents are not devalued because they understand their actions as part of a collective movement.

One powerful illustration is Osama bin Laden's references to the Muslim debacle in Spain in the 15th century as a slight that must be remedied. His hortatory discourse over the need for a regained Muslim international dominance is at least in part meant to recruit followers and justify more down-to-earth power struggles; bin Laden had much more immediate demands as well, the top three being the evacuation of Western forces from holy lands; the end to exterior assistance to corrupt, repressive regimes (especially in Saudi Arabia and Egypt); and the end to support for Israel (bin Laden, 2005; for a discussion, see Ould Mohamedou, 2007).

This message finds a much broader audience than Al Qaeda supporters per se and has appealed to individuals living in Canada with no link to the central network. Perhaps the most important event in this category is the "millennium bomber" incident, Ahmed Ressam's attempt to set off a bomb at the Los Angeles airport in 1999 or 2000. The plot failed, but the story speaks volumes about the workings of Islamic restoration threats in Canada. Trained in Afghanistan and given "seed money" to devise an attack on the United States, Ressam was arrested by chance—and because he could not stay calm under pressure (he was also feverous with malaria at the time). His connections to terrorists in France, the United States, Afghanistan, Algeria, and Canada reveals a group of individuals that falls somewhat short of being a network but was animated by a powerful overarching mission to strike for the greater glory of Islam.

Visions of historic struggles within millenarian or other eschatological worldviews also fit this category and share an absolutist morality that leaves no room for compromise or negotiation. The Muslim extremists' desire to restore the golden age of the Caliphate or their battle against the "apostates" who rule Islam-dominated countries today is one example. Egypt and its "pharaohs," as Islamic fundamentalists refer to Egyptian secular leaders, have been prominent targets. In 1995, the Egyptian embassy in Pakistan was bombed with the financial help of Canadian citizen Ahmad Kahdr (whose sons Abdulrahman and later Omar were released from Guantanamo by the U.S. military; Kahdr senior was killed in a firefight with the Pakistani army).

Revolutionary and Restoration Terrorism: A Contrast

Canada has been largely—and happily—ignored by history: it has generally been spared from violence, although thousands of Canadians fought and lost their lives in European wars. However, when leftist terrorism was rampant in Europe, with groups such as the Red Brigades, the Baader-Meinhof gang, and several others motivated less by Marxism than by nationalism (the Basque separatist terror group Euskadi ta Askatasuna and the Irish IRA), Canada also had a revolutionary terrorism episode.

The FLQ as a Canadian Prototype of Revolutionary Terrorism

A Canadian prototype of revolutionary terrorism, this terrorist episode took place mainly in the province of Quebec, where a group that called itself the Front de libération du Québec (FLQ or Quebec Liberation Front) was active between 1963 and 1973. In October 1970, it generated the greatest political crisis in Canadian history.

The history of the FLQ falls into two periods. The first spans 1963 to 1968, when the FLQ's political platform was based on traditional right-wing nationalism, and its main demand was the independence of Quebec, justified by a discourse of religious, language, and ethnic differences between the French Quebecois population and the rest of Anglo-British Canada (Fournier, 1998, p. 35). It made no social or economic demands, and its political focus was limited to jurisdictional matters. It can thus be described as demand-based terrorism during the first part of its history. During that time the FLQ perpetrated numerous bomb attacks to obtain media attention, but it was generally careful not to target people and was in fact responsible for only a few accidental casualties.

By 1968, the police had arrested many members of this first FLQ wave, and the group started to reorganize itself under the leadership of intellectuals who were pursuing a new set of goals: The traditional goal of Quebec's independence was coupled with the goal of emancipating the working class, and both objectives were pursued at the same level of militancy. This evolution toward revolutionary terrorism was accompanied by increased violence. This is to be expected since revolutionary goals have higher stakes than limited demands. The tradition of not endangering peoples' lives was generally upheld, but FLQ attacks gradually became more and more vicious. In January 1969, a bomb exploded near the home of the Montreal police chief; in February of the same year, another bomb at the Montreal Stock Exchange wounded 20 people, 2 seriously. On June 14, 1970—the National Day of French-Canadians—a bomb exploded at the Department of Defense in Ottawa, killing one person.

The policy of not targeting individuals changed drastically in October 1970. On October 5, 1970, the FLQ's "Libération" cell abducted James Richard Cross, a British diplomat appointed to the U.K. consulate in Montreal. The FLQ made several demands, one of which was the public reading, on state television, of its manifesto. The Canadian government gave in to this demand, and the manifesto was read on state television by a news anchor on October 8 (it had been read the day before by a private radio station). Unexpectedly, the manifesto, which denounced the exploitation of Quebec's working class by both the English- and French-speaking "bourgeoisie," had a profound impact on Quebec public opinion. Its positive reception transformed what had been perceived as a simple kidnapping into a national issue. This issue became a full-fledged crisis with the dramatic abduction of the vice premier of Quebec, Pierre Laporte, by another FLQ cell, the "Chénier" cell (it was later learned that the cells were not acting according to a coordinated plan—they in fact were not cells at all).

The police forces in Quebec seemed to be overwhelmed, and on October 15 the federal government used forgotten World War I legislation (the War Measures Act) and enacted a set of emergency regulations that abrogated civil liberties in Quebec (Brodeur et al., 1971). The Canadian Forces were activated in Quebec, and on October 16 some 500 citizens were arrested and put in preventive custody[3] (all were later released without criminal charges). On October 17, the body of the abducted minister was found in the trunk of a car, and the "October crisis" reached its climax. One of his abductors, Bernard Lortie, was arrested in Montreal on November 6. At the end of November, the RCMP finally discovered where Cross was being held hostage. His release was negotiated in exchange for safe conduct to Cuba for his five captors, and he was freed, unharmed, on December 3, 1970. The three remaining members of the Chénier cell who had abducted Laporte were arrested on December 28, bringing the crisis to an end. As we shall see in the third part of this chapter, the FLQ continued its armed struggle from 1970 to 1973 but was ultimately defeated by the police. It was no longer a threat after 1973.

Contrasting Demand-Based, Revolutionary, and Restoration Terrorism

Although not as violent as other terrorist organizations that operated at the same time in other parts of the world, the FLQ can serve as a basis for the formulation of hypotheses about the various features that define different paradigms of terrorism. One of these features may be the differential historical context in which they take place, as demand-based terrorism was mostly present in the 1970s and 1980s, while restoration terrorism, for instance, appeared in the 1990s. Yet, one cannot predict that the context conducive to demand-based threats will not return; for instance, activities on the extreme right in Europe and North America may bring about a new era of classic terrorism soon. Furthermore, historical context usually fails to predict or to account for exceptions, which is particularly disconcerting when such exceptions are historical events in themselves. For instance, large-scale massacres such as the 1985 bombing of an Air India flight out of Vancouver, which killed 320 people, and the explosion of a Pan Am flight over Lockerbie in December 1988 (270 casualties) were anomalies with respect to the conventional type of terrorism that had occurred in the 1960s and 1970s (Baader-Meinhof in Germany, Red Brigades in Italy, ETA in Spain, IRA in Ulster and the United Kingdom, and various groups of Palestinian terrorists, the Palestinian groups having never fit clearly in the paradigm from the beginning).

Thus, we set aside, for the moment, accounts of terrorism that rely on comparing historical contexts, as they are not sufficiently reliable. Our categories of terrorism should not be interpreted as eras or waves (Rapoport, 2002) or stages in a global evolution, even though they can be analyzed that way as well (see Leman-Langlois and Ouellet, 2009). Some of the features that we discuss may seem obvious, but they are important to understanding distinct types of terrorism in Canada.

Territoriality

Most demand-based and revolutionary threats operate within one country, their main goal being to change specific aspects of society or its political regime or to provoke the secession of a part of its territory inhabited by a minority group (ethnic, linguistic, or religious). The Palestinians, who operated both inside and outside Israel, were a partial exception to this model. IRA terrorists bombing British targets in London were acting internationally according to their worldview but not according to that of their targets. Yet, exceptions aside, we should accept a minimum level of loss of detail to permit useful generalizations. With that in mind, we can safely claim that restoration terrorism is, contrary to demands-based or revolutionary terrorism, more likely to operate across borders, internationally or transnationally.

Terrorism as Communication

There are two leitmotifs in the literature on terrorism. The first is that terrorism is the weapon of the weak (Laqueur, 1987, and his numerous followers); the second that it is a form of communication (Crelinsten, 1997; Gressang, 2001; Schmid and de Graaf, 1982; Wieviorka, 1988; Wieviorka and Wolton, 1987). That terrorism thrives on media coverage is true of all its forms. This truism should not, however, blind us to important differences between types of terrorism.

- *Signature.* Demand-based terrorism devoted considerable effort to claiming responsibility and to justifying, or at least explaining, its deeds. The issue of signature plays a lesser role in restoration and revolution terrorism. For instance, the attacks against the Air India (1985) and the Pan Am (1988) flights were never claimed by any organization or any state or protostate. Libya has belatedly accepted responsibility for the Lockerbie incident. After the longest investigation in Canadian history, charges were finally brought in 2003 against suspects of the Air India bombing (unsuccessfully), and the motives have finally become explicit. As has been the case with more recent attacks, it would seem that the medium has become the message, that implicit signatures may deliberately be used to maximize the insecurity they seek to provoke.
- *Dominant feature.* Terrorism is a mixture of physical violence and informational content, and terrorist organizations could be categorized according to the balance they strike between violence and information. The FLQ would then be at the least-violent end of the spectrum as its general strategy was to derive maximum effect from minimal violence, accompanied by explicit communiqués that spelled out the *meaning* of the violence (in many cases, sending a threatening communiqué was the only violence). This balance has been reversed in restoration terrorism, where maximum violence is not accompanied by discursive explanation.
- *Words and images.* Demand-based and revolutionary terrorism communicated mostly through the written word, in a national language understood by a limited audience generally considered to be capable of grasping the arguments being made. Restoration terrorism communicates through images of devastation, intended for an international audience that does not share one language or whose particular situation may not fit an overly specific or overly generalized political argument. For the great German sociologist Jürgen Habermas, the collapse of the WTC twin towers was a unique event in the history of terrorism because its enfolding could be watched on television, in

real time, throughout the world (Habermas, Derrida, and Borradori, 2003, pp. 53–78).

- *Privileged channels.* The creation of all-news channels such as CNN, Fox News, and Al-Jazeera has brought about a new level of conflict, sometimes referred to as *infowar,* as these news organizations often openly take part in the conflict by adopting an explicitly biased approach or by openly or secretly cooperating with powerful stakeholders. One way media are easily manipulated is in creating mediagenic images: striking, spectacular, sensational images that industrial news outlets cannot resist. Transnational forms of terrorism are present on more media outlets and become omnipresent, at least for a time.

- *Radicalization.* This feature is partly a result of the preceding ones, which it blends together. We think of radicalization as the intensification of a conflict at all levels, including infowar. More important, it also refers to a simplification, often a dichotomization, coupled with what might be thought of as a *medicalization* of the conflict, usually on the part of the authorities. Both sides of the conflict start to ignore the issues at stake and to refer to each other as morally or mentally defective. Demand-based terrorism blends physical aggression with an explicit intention to convey its meaning and its implications. It is reflexive violence: It reflects purpose, in some instances with a certain level of complexity (e.g., political independence and social reform), and repeatedly tries to communicate this purpose (Brodeur, 1991). In several cases, terrorists claim to be the "military wing" of a legitimate political movement concurrently attempting to achieve the same goals, but through persuasion instead of violence. Restoration terrorism, on the other hand, is uninterested in conveying an articulate message. Instead, it produces a form of expressive violence that signifies little beyond anger, frustration, and a desire to expose what it perceives as the weaknesses of its enemy. This is why some observers have concluded that the content of expressive violence is so thin that it can regress into nihilism (Glucksman, 2002; Ignatieff, 2004; Wieviorka, 1988).

Interestingly, Canadian law (among others) explicitly defines terrorism as violent action in pursuit of goals, be they political, religious, or "ideological." Yet, one important aspect of restoration extremism today is precisely the absence of logical connection between tactical means and strategic ends. The adopted means are so catastrophic that they do not allow for a distinction between means and goals: They are either all instrumentality or all finality, without external purpose—the destruction becomes a goal in itself.

Motivation

Although most conventional definitions of terrorism require political motivation, the importance of religion as an alternate motivating factor in terrorism is a complex, and much studied, matter (Leman-Langlois, 2008). Even
though religious concepts and rationales are far from new in terrorism, the
multiplication of religious rationalizations in what Schmid (2011) calls "terrorist theories of terrorism" is a current trend that has redefined the question for many observers, often in explicitly xenophobic terms. Transnational
forms of terrorism today seem to share a few characteristics that drive these
perceptions: First, it is (erroneously, when one considers the statistics) considered as the foremost threat to security in Western democracies; second, it
is also understood as coming from third-world countries, and more precisely
from Arabic or Muslim regions, which has appeared to some as the manifestation of an ongoing clash of civilizations. This is also contradicted by the
data. The terrorist groups we have followed are by no means representative or
artifacts or by-products of one civilization or another (the problem of defining *civilization* notwithstanding).

Furthermore, the distinction between politics and religion is often problematic, especially with all forms of fundamentalism. Islam, for instance,
may be easy to narrow down to a religion for people who are not part of it,
but for its more enthusiastic adepts, the separation of politics and religion is
a sin since the only truly moral politics follows the revealed truths of religion.
This is by no means unique to Islam.

The best way to model the relationship between politics and religion in
trying to understand terrorism is probably to use the notion of "dominant
feature" that we used previously to depict the balance between violence and
communication. In terms of its dominant feature, fundamentalist terrorism,
whether Islamic, Sikh, or Hindu, could be said to be *mainly* motivated by
religion, which we would characterize briefly as beliefs organized around
revealed truths and supernatural authority. This would account for two additional features. First, demand-based and revolutionary terrorism rest on a
political program that is to be realized in time, this time being determined
in identical units, such as years. The time frame of religious terrorism that
is embodied in notions of holy struggle is much less defined and tends ultimately to blend with timelessness or eternity, as conceived by religion.

The second element in modeling the contrast between politics and religion is much more problematic, and for want of a better term, we shall use
the word *irrationality* to designate it. Some caution is warranted here since
irrationality is a notorious conceit often used to deny an alternative logic
of thought to an action that we fail to understand or that we mean to condemn—or medicalize. Thus, the introduction of an element of irrationality
in our understanding of religiously motivated terrorism can also serve as a

reminder that there is much that escapes us in considering worldviews that we feel foreign to our own and that we should be cautious in our conclusions on them. The danger is to assume that since religious doctrine tends to be irrational in the classic sense, those who espouse it must be irrational beings.

Individualization

This last feature, individualization, can also be seen as forming a spectrum between two extremes. At one end, both terrorists and their victims are individuals with a precise identity. For instance, in 1975 the terrorist known as Carlos attacked an Organisation of Petroleum Exporting Countries (OPEC) conference held in Vienna, taking some 70 hostages and killing 3. In this case, the victims were targeted for their symbolic value, and the terrorist had an elaborate escape plan that finally worked. Although many forms of terrorism have slipped into violence for its own sake (Wieviorka, 1988), individuals who engage in them have not renounced their own identity and plan to enjoy the fruits of victory. And, as we just saw, they generally target individuals who are directly linked to the object they are opposing (heads of state, diplomats, bankers, and so forth).

The reason some have referred to new terrorism as "bit-by-bit genocide" is that some history-making terror attacks, although statistically rare, struck without discrimination and caused mass, anonymous murder. Random men, women, and children are indiscriminately killed because they are perceived to belong to a broadly defined enemy group, or even if they simply happen to share the same space as the symbolic targets. Importantly, in the case of suicide attacks, this depersonification is also reflected on the side of the perpetrators, who are used as expendable bomb delivery systems and who only regain their name, for propaganda purposes, after their death.

Correspondence between Features of Demand-Based Terrorism and Successful Counterterrorism

One purpose of our comparison between types of terrorism is to lead us into a discussion of police strategy, building on our assumption that police CT tactics must be woven on the distinctive warp of their targets. As we have seen, Canadian police agencies did not expect the October Crisis of 1970, and the Canadian Forces were activated in Quebec in an effort to regain control over what was understood to be a highly unstable situation. However, it is unquestionable that the battle against the FLQ was won by the police, and only after military intervention had made matters worse. The instrument of this success was infiltration, which produced invaluable intelligence information and allowed manipulation of the membership.

The FLQ tried to reorganize after the October Crisis, but it was infiltrated by a key police informant (among others) from November 4, 1970, until its dissolution in 1973 (Quebec, 1981a, 1981b).[4] This informant, Carole de Vault, held the key position of courier between the various remaining FLQ cells and was thus able to brief her police handlers extensively on the activities of the cells.[5] Even more crucially, she was entrusted with the task of issuing the FLQ communiqués, which she eventually wrote herself, under the supervision of her police handler. In November 1971, the Montreal police department CT unit succeeded in recruiting yet another informant, who operated at the top of the organization. The FLQ had become so much of a police colony that when it tried to disband in December 1971, at the call of one of its main ideologues (Pierre Vallières), the RCMP issued a fake FLQ communiqué in the name of a fictitious cell denouncing Vallières as a turncoat and urging the FLQ terrorists to continue to pursue the armed struggle (Quebec, 1981a, p. 91). The FLQ increasingly became an object of derision in Quebec, and after 1973 it was replaced, as the clandestine group to be reckoned with, by the Maoist organization En Lutte, which was not a terrorist organization. One of the two main police informants active in the FLQ pursued his activities within the Maoist group, which dissolved after learning that it had been infiltrated.

Keeping the FLQ as a case study of demand-based and revolutionary "conventional" terrorism, we now look at how the four aspects of terrorism (territoriality, communication, motivation, and individualization) might affect the probability of success of CT strategies.

Territoriality. Demand-based and revolutionary terrorism are domestic activities. Thus, terrorists and counterterrorists usually share the same nationality and a common physical appearance, language, and culture. As shown by the police struggle against the FLQ, this ethnic homogeneity greatly facilitates infiltration and, more generally, the collection of human intelligence. Differences in physical appearance, language, customs, and other conspicuous features help insulate terrorist organizations from police and intelligence agencies.

Communication. In the case of the demise of the FLQ, this was the critical feature. The major strength of this group was not violence but communication; the public approval of the FLQ manifesto generated the October crisis. With unerring instinct, the police succeeded in infiltrating the FLQ where it mattered most: in the writing of its communiqués. Restoration terrorists offer a much decreased grip for manipulation, as their communications are minimal.

The 21st century communications have evolved to a point where no direct correspondence exists between today's terrorist or criminal organizations and their 20th century counterparts. Some commonalities will continue to be observable, to be sure, but in many ways, the deck has been thoroughly reshuffled, and police organizations must invent entirely new ways of doing business, at least as far as communications are concerned. This does not mean that terrorists are more elusive than ever; indeed, in many ways they leave deeper, more frequent, and more durable traces of their activities and identity.

Motivation. The motivation of the FLQ was directly related to its actions, meaning that a clear, direct connection existed between its actions and its goals. This linkage allows two things: First, likely targets can be identified and protected (target hardening). Second, negotiation is possible and with the FLQ helped resolve at least one of the issues (the liberation of one hostage). In the case of more ambitious revolutionary or restoration terrorism, however, for which targets tend to be larger and the attacks less discriminate, the number of potential targets increases exponentially and cannot realistically be "hardened." However, the resources needed to attack them tend to become more sizable or more difficult to obtain, as is the case with controlled substances (poisons, explosives, CBRN materials). One additional police strategy in these cases is to intensify surveillance of the means by which these substances can be obtained. However, since many sufficiently powerful explosives can be made at home with ordinary ingredients, this is not likely to yield results.

Individualization. Target individualization was a prominent feature of the FLQ—it abducted a British diplomat and a Quebec government minister who was reputed to be corrupt. Again, this feature permits target protection—all cabinet ministers and British diplomats were put under protection during the October Crisis. Individualization was also a feature of the FLQ's members. Although the various cells of the organizations were insulated from one another, a cell was not infrequently comprised of members of the same family. This facilitated the work of investigators, who only needed to identify one member of a cell to discover the identity of others.

We have summed these conclusions in Table 11.2. The table also includes private justice terrorism, which on the whole shares many characteristics with demand-based threats, with the added feature that those who engage in it tend to self-identify, in the sense that their grievances about specific injustices, by their very nature, tend to point to their author. This greatly simplifies surveillance and investigation activities.

Table 11.2 Strategic Parallelism between Types of Terrorism and Policing Strategies

Type	"Actionable" Characteristics	Possible Responses
Demand based	1. Emphasis on message 2. Proximate goals 3. No ethnocultural disparity	1. Interference with delivery 2. Target hardening, strategic negotiation 3. Infiltration
Private justice	1. High predictability, proximate goals, identifiable targets 2. Self-identification 3. No ethnocultural disparity	1. Target hardening 2. Surveillance/arrest 3. Infiltration
Revolutionary	1. Emphasis on message 2. More restricted resources needed 3. Communication network needed 4. Proximate goals 5. No ethnocultural disparity	1. Interference with delivery 2. Surveillance of procurement 3. Surveillance of communications 4. Strategic negotiation 5. Infiltration

Finding Correlations between Features of Restoration Terrorism and Successful Counterterrorism

It is useful to further clarify the nature of restoration threats since, as is the case with revolutionary threats, their scope places them closer to the boundary where police responses may be replaced by military responses. We have already seen how the Canadian Forces were brought in to deal with what was presented at the time as an insurrection led by the FLQ. In this case, faulty intelligence and political maneuvering were at the heart of the disproportionate response. However at the international level, both revolutionary and restoration terrorism often acquire an insurgent facet and, as such, may be claimed as military targets. We believe that to the extent that the response is deployed within the boundaries of generally peaceful democracies, the police are best equipped to play a leading, if not an exclusive, CT role.

Since this category includes transnational threats, it may be helpful to distinguish between what we would call "primary" and "secondary" areas of activity. Primary activity areas are those where terrorists and terrorist groups conduct their principal operations (from our target point of view) (i.e., violent attacks). Secondary activity areas serve as bases for support activities, such as recruitment, planning, sheltering fugitives, and funding. Secondary areas tend to have low levels of violence, in part because of the nature of the activities and in part to minimize political and police attention. Our data show that Canada, by this measure, is for the most part a secondary activity area and has suffered little from transnational political violence. Let us consider the same four aspects to see if we can match them to police strategies that might be more successful for Canadian and U.S. policing and intelligence agencies in their struggle against restoration threats.

Territoriality. Terrorist activities in Canada, a secondary activity area, generally involve fund-raising, organizing, recruiting, intimidating, and other support activities. These are, for the most part, conducted by foreign nationals or Canadians who are part of minority ethnic groups, which complicates infiltration efforts. Not that infiltration is impossible—witness "American Taliban" John Walker Lindh and, on a less anecdotal note, the fact that most ethnic Canadians are not terrorists, are not controlled by terrorists, and that many have joined various counterterrorist agencies, thus being in a position to play a part in infiltration. Yet, in our opinion, in these cases infiltration remains especially difficult and probably not the best way to spend limited counterterrorist resources. More important, this has led from time to time to the broad infiltration and close surveillance of whole communities on the sole basis that they are mainly comprised of immigrants from a particular part of the world—say, the Middle East. This is tantamount to practicing racial or ethnic profiling on a grand scale, when this practice has already been shown to flaunt human rights when applied on a limited, individual scale. The problem with infiltration is that it seems trapped in a vicious circle: One needs to infiltrate to identify terrorists, but when these are very few or nonexistent, infiltration only generates feelings of harassment and dread that may be conducive to retaliation terrorism in unfairly targeted communities.

Communication. We have described the absence of an articulated communication strategy with defined audiences that characterizes restoration terrorism: Its actions, the spectacular destruction that they wreak, are its means of communication. However, international terrorists must communicate with one another to operate. These communications can be intercepted, as can traces of money transfers and other needs in manpower and logistics. Any possible success in this endeavor, as has been repeated in many other places, depends less on the quantity of intercepted information than on the ability to analyze it in a timely fashion. With that said, however, we do not think that international terrorism represents an important fraction of the overall terrorism pie, and to devote too many resources to this is going to be counterproductive.

Motivation. We have seen that the motives and rationales produced by restoration terrorism are too broad and too far removed from actions to help in devising preventive tactics. One may reasonably expect attacks against populated infrastructures (in particular, public transportation), which maximize mediagenic destruction and loss of life. This is, however, not descriptive enough to be of any practical use. To the extent that controlled substances may be needed for maximum damage, rigorous monitoring of all means of procuring these substances, as was suggested for revolutionary terrorism, might be of help—but it is unlikely to be very effective. Thus, realistically, we believe that resources would be better spent on emergency response and disaster mitigation.

To the extent that Canada is a secondary activity zone, it is not violence, but support activities that must be countered. We do not believe that monitoring and countering money flows, in the hope of cutting off terrorism from its funding, will noticeably affect terrorist groups or their plans. Terrorist attacks are not expensive; furthermore, the expenses are not proportional to the damage done, with the Air India attack costing a little over $3,000. Direct Action started its crime and terrorism spree in part *because* of lack of money. The only other common support activity in Canada is recruitment. For example, since the mid-2000s young Canadians of Somali descent have joined or attempted to join the ranks of al-Shabaab in Somalia. The fact that many have *attempted* to join is a testimony to the difficulty that such recruitment represents. In most cases, the families of the new recruits, perfectly aware that a departure for perennially war-torn Somalia meant almost certain death, alerted the authorities.

Individualization. As explained, restoration terrorism deindividualizes both its victims and its agents, with the rare exception of emblematic figures, as was bin Laden or, already to a much lesser extent, Ayman al-Zawahiri within the Al Qaeda mythology. The exception also extends to the more local level, for regional leaders such as Abdel Wadoud or Belmokhtar in Al Qaeda in the Islamic Maghreb or al-Zarqawi in Iraq, for instance, but the ordinary member has no name. However, because these organizations promote, in addition to a worldview, a *lifestyle,* complete with the authoritarian imposition of rituals, they may unwittingly provide CT agencies with a certain level of self-identification: Potential terrorists may act differently than others and thus reveal their affiliation. We see this in the case of Ahmed Ressam, who joined a group of political extremists already under surveillance by the Canadian Security Intelligence Service but who were considered to be relatively harmless—just a "bunch of guys" (BOG; see Sageman, 2004, p. 101). A stronger analytic capacity might have made it possible to identify this BOG or some of its members, such as Ressam, as constituting a real threat. The difficulty lies in identifying the line between talkers holding meetings to rant against Israel and call for jihad and potential terrorists who

Table 11.3   Strategic Parallelism between Restoration Terrorism and Policing Strategies

Type	"Actionable" Characteristics	Possible Responses
Restoration	1. More/restricted access resources needed 2. Communication network needed 3. Self-identification more likely	1. Surveillance of procurement 2. Surveillance of communications 3. Surveillance/arrest 4. Improved analysis of surveillance products

are likely to take action. To make this distinction between the two groups, one needs background knowledge about terrorism and, as noted, a strong analytic capability to apply this general background to particular cases.

That said, it bears repeating that future restoration-inspired terrorists will self-recruit, self-train, and conduct low-intensity attacks against symbolic targets. To focus too much attention on worldwide networks is likely to produce few results, as data show greatly diminished activity in that sector. At the same time, it will ignore the threats coming from unconnected, informal, and ad hoc groups. Yet, these groups usually coalesce around extremists who have self-identified in the past through militant activities. This was the case of the Toronto 18, a rare CT success, with the group appearing on the radar first through the political extremism of one of its members.

Table 11.3 completes the categories set up in Table 11.2. It should be immediately obvious that CT strategies that parallel restoration threats reside at the boundary set by civil rights, and the risk of abuse is high. This is problematic for not only the obvious reason but also because it is counterproductive since global narratives of restoration terrorism routinely count disproportionate security responses as "wins" that undermine the confidence of Westerners in their own governments or expose their hypocrisy (bin Laden, 2005). Increased interception and surveillance of mere suspicion based on apparent affiliation are extremely dangerous to our civil liberties and should be considered only where there are strict accountability and overview/review structures, which are sorely lacking in many police agencies in Canada.

Conclusion

One last feature of the Ressam affair allows insight into the nature of terrorism prevention. CT agencies are often criticized for failing to prevent terrorist attacks that kill hundreds, if not thousands. Yet, there is a crucial difference between an actual attack and one that has been prevented. We know in all its painful detail what we failed to prevent since the event unfolded completely, with all its tragic consequences. In fact, at times even the terrorists themselves did not foresee some of these consequences, such as the collapse of the twin towers of the WTC. In contrast, when an event is prevented, we have only very limited knowledge of what might have occurred. For instance, we know exactly what we failed to prevent on September 11, 2001; we can count the dead and assess the damage. We are in no such position with the failed attack of the millennium bomber, who was intercepted with a trunkload of explosives. We can try to imagine what might have happened if he had been able to set off his bomb at the Los Angeles airport, but we cannot know, among the many possible scenarios, what might have happened. For instance, the truck might have been blown up near an underground fuel tank, which would also have exploded, setting off a chain of catastrophic events. It might also have failed to detonate altogether. All we can know for sure is that Ressam was prevented from setting off his homemade bomb at the Los Angeles airport. The cost in lives, property, social trauma, and economic health of his having succeeded remains pure conjecture. The bottom line is that when considering prevention, it is probable that blame for failure will always be greater than praise for success. This should be remembered when the performance of security services, police organizations, and their individual members is being assessed.

Notes

1. This is a revised version of a paper first published in *Police Practice and Research*, 6(2), 121–140.
2. We wish to thank the Canadian Social Sciences and Humanities Research Council (SSHRC) for its financial assistance.
3. Fournier (1998, pp. 507–512) gives a list of 355 names, explicitly designated as incomplete.
4. Quebec (1981b) (the Duchaîne Commission) and (1981a) (the Keable Commission) are two reports bearing respectively on the FLQ and on CT in Quebec that were commissioned by the provincial government of Quebec. One of us (Brodeur) was director of research for the Keable Commission, drafting its report, and was a consultant for the Duchaîne report.
5. De Vault became a public figure after her testimony before the Keable Commission and coauthored a book on her activities as a police informant (de Vault and Johnson, 1981).

References

bin Laden, Osama. (2005). *Messages to the World: The Statements of Osama bin Laden*, edited by B. Lawrence. London: Verso.

Black, Donald. (1983). Crime as social control. *American Sociological Review, 48*, 34–45.

Brodeur, Jean-Paul. (1991). Countering terrorism in Canada. In Stuart Farson, David Stafford, and Wesley K. Wark (Eds.), *Security and Intelligence in a Changing World: New Perspectives for the 1990s* (pp. 182–200). London: Cass.

Brodeur, Jean-Paul, et al. (Eds.). (1971). *Québec occupé*. Montreal: Parti-Pris.

Crelinsten, Ronald D. (1997). Television and terrorism: Implications for crisis management and policy-making. *Terrorism and Political Violence, 9*(4), 8–32.

de Vault, Carole, and Johnson, William. (1981). *Toute ma vérité: les confessions de l'agent S.A.T.* [Section antiterroriste] 945–171. Montreal: Stanké.

Fournier, Louis. (1998). *FLQ: histoire d'un mouvement clandestin*. Outremont, Quebec: Lanctôt Éditeur.

Glucksman, André. (2002). *Dostoïevski à Manhattan*. Paris: Laffont.

Gressang, Daniel. (2001). Audience and message: Assessing terrorist WMD potential. *Terrorism and Political Violence, 13*(3), 83–106.

Habermas, Jurgen, Derrida, Jacques, and Borradori, Giovanna. (2003). *Philosophy in a Time of Terror* (pp. 53–78). Chicago: University of Chicago Press.

Hoffman, Bruce. (1997). The confluence of international and domestic trends in terrorism. *Terrorism and Political Violence, 9*(2), 1–15.

Ignatieff, Michael. (2004). *The Lesser Evil: Politics in an Age of Terror*. Princeton, NJ: Princeton University Press.

Kellett, Anthony, Beanlands, Bruce, Deacon, James, Jeffrey, Heather, and Lapalme, Chantal. (1991), *Terrorism in Canada, 1960–1989*. Ottawa: Ministry of the Solicitor General of Canada, National Security Coordination Centre, Police and Security Branch.

Laqueur, Walter. (1987). *The Age of Terrorism*. London: Weidenfeld and Nicolson.

Laqueur, Walter. (1997). *Postmodern Terrorism*. United States International Information Program. Retrieved from http://usinfo.state.gov/journals/itgic/0297/ijge/gj-3.htm

Laqueur, Walter. (1999). *The New Terrorism: Fanaticism and the Arms of Mass Destruction*. New York: Oxford University Press.

Laqueur, Walter. (2003). *No End to War: Terrorism in the Twenty-First Century*. New York: Continuum.

Leman-Langlois, Stéphane. (2008). Le terrorisme à motif religieux au Canada, caractéristiques et évolution entre 1973 et 2006. *Criminologie, 41*(2), 9–30.

Leman-Langlois, Stéphane, and Ouellet, Geneviève. (2009). Évolution du terrorisme au Canada, 1973–2006. In S. Leman-Langlois and J.P. Brodeur (Eds.), *Terrorisme et antiterrorisme au Canada* (pp. 58–72). Montreal: Montreal University Press.

Manning, Peter K. (1980). *The Narc's Game: Organizational and Informational Constraints on Drug Law Enforcement*. Cambridge, MA: MIT Press.

Mickolus, Edward F. (1980). *Transnational Terrorism: A Chronology of Events, 1968–1979*. Westport, CT: Greenwood Press.

Mickolus, Edward F. (1993). *Terrorism, 1988–1991: A Chronology of Events and a Selectively Annotated Bibliography*. Westport, CT: Greenwood Press.

Mickolus, Edward F., Sandler, Todd, and Murdock, Jean M. (1989). *International Terrorism in the 1980s: A Chronology of Events. Volume 1: 1980–1983; Volume 2: 1984–1987*. Ames: Iowa State University Press.

Mickolus, Edward F., and Simmons, Susan L. (1997). *Terrorism, 1992–1995: A Chronology of Events and a Selectively Annotated Bibliography*. Westport, CT: Greenwood Press.

Ould Mohamedou, Mohammad-Mahmoud. (2007). *Understanding al Qaeda: The Transformation of War*. London: Pluto Press.

Pape, Robert. (2003). The strategic logic of suicide terrorism. *American Political Science Review*, 97(3), 1–19.

Quebec. (1981a). *Rapport de la Commission d'enquête sur les opérations policières sur le territoire québécois (Keable Commission)*. Quebec: Ministry of Justice.

Quebec. (1981b). *Rapport sur les événements d'octobre 1970 (Duchaîne Commission)*. Quebec: Ministry of Justice.

Rapoport, David. (2002). Four waves of modern terrorism. *Anthropoetics*, 8(1), 46–73.

Ross, Jeffrey Ian. (1988). Attributes of domestic political terrorism in Canada. *Terrorism*, 11, 213–233.

Sageman, Marc. (2004). *Understanding Terror Networks*. Philadelphia: University of Pennsylvania Press.

Schmid, Alex. (2011). *The Routledge Handbook on Terrorism Research*. London: Routledge.

Schmid, Alex, and de Graaf, Janny. (1982). *Violence as Communication*. London: Sage.

Simon, Jonathan. (1997). Governing through crime. In George Fisher and Lawrence Friedman (Eds.), *The Crime Conundrum: Essays on Criminal Justice* (pp. 171–190). Boulder, CO: Westview Press. Retrieved from http://personal.law.miami.edu/~jsimon/

Vareilles, Thierry. (2001). *Encyclopédie du terrorisme international*. Paris: L'Harmattan.

Wieviorka, Michel. (1988). *Sociétés et terrorisme*. Paris: Fayard.

Wieviorka, Michel. (1995). *Face au Terrorisme*. Paris: Liana Lévy.

Wieviorka, Michel, and Wolton, Dominique. (1987). *Terrorisme à la une*. Paris: Gallimard.

Policing Revolutionary and Secessionist Violence   III

The Use of Informants in Counterterrorism Operations

12

Lessons from Northern Ireland

KIRAN SARMA

Contents

Introduction

This chapter examines the use of informers in the battle against the Provisional Irish Republican Army (IRA) and its political wing Sinn Fein in Northern Ireland and makes some observations regarding the effectiveness of this technique as a counterterrorism strategy.* At the time of writing, the IRA had "laid down its arms," ending more than three decades of "struggle," and it is an opportune time to consider the role the informer has played in this struggle.

The chapter is based on a review of material published by the republican movement (the IRA and Sinn Fein), the security services, autobiographical accounts of intelligence personnel and former informers, and interviews

* An earlier version of this chapter was published in 2005. Sarma, K. (2005). Informers and the battle against republican terrorism: A review of 30 years of conflict. *Police Practice and Research: An International Journal*, 6(2), 165–180. doi:10.1080/15614260500121161.

with actors from both republican and security groups. The chapter focuses on the period from 1971 to 2000, a period during which the intelligence and law enforcement services in the United Kingdom and the Republic of Ireland used informers in the battle against republican terrorism.

In 1993, Stella Remington, then head of MI5, said:

> Counter-terrorism is not an exact science. In an open and democratic society, initial advantage will always be with the terrorists. We will never be able to obtain 100 percent advance information of terrorist plans and intentions. (Remington, 1993b)

Remington's comments are based on the understanding that terrorists are presented with a huge variety of possible targets that exhibit qualities varying in military, symbolic, economic, and propagandistic value. Few are chosen for attack, but protection for all must be maintained by law enforcement agencies. This places the security services on a continuously defensive and disadvantaged footing and hands the attackers the luxury of deciding when and where "the action" will take place (Sarma, 2009).

A second feature of terrorism renders it particularly difficult to counter. Driven by the need to survive, such groups tend to be small, cohesive, and secretive. The circle of those aware of impending attacks is kept to a minimum to ensure operational security and personnel anonymity. Given this level of cohesion, there is little opportunity to infiltrate their ranks using undercover operatives (Segaller, 1987). Similarly, awareness of electronic surveillance systems (bugging, tracking, and artificial intelligence [AI] software), personal surveillance strategies, and interrogation methods is high, the result being that contemporary organizations school their activists in countersurveillance and counterinterrogation methods (Clutterbuck, 1994; Harnden, 1999; Holland and Phoenix, 1996; Remington, 1993a; Smith, 1997). As a result of the emphasis placed on internal security within such groups, little information relating to impending attacks leaks unintentionally from within.

A second feature of terrorism renders it particularly difficult to counter. Driven by the need to survive, such groups tend to be small, cohesive, and secretive. The circle of those aware of impending attacks is kept to a minimum to ensure operational security and personnel anonymity. Given this level of cohesion, there is little opportunity to infiltrate their ranks using undercover operatives (Segaller, 1987). Similarly, awareness of electronic surveillance systems (bugging, tracking, and artificial intelligence [AI] software), personal surveillance strategies, and interrogation methods is high, the result being that contemporary organizations school their activists in countersurveillance and counterinterrogation methods (Clutterbuck, 1994; Harnden, 1999; Holland and Phoenix, 1996; Remington, 1993a; Smith, 1997). As a result of the emphasis placed on internal security within such groups, little information relating to impending attacks leaks unintentionally from within.

Robin Evelegh (1978) notes that "the only weapon that can destroy a subversive organization in the end is information given to the government from within the terrorist ranks" (p. 133). Their membership of, or association with, a terrorist organization grants access to high-grade intelligence on impending attacks, attackers, terrorist personalities, command structures, and strategic policy. Such intelligence permits law enforcement and security agencies to take steps to prevent the attack, facilitates prosecution of active terrorists, and enables strategists to develop counterterrorism policies required for the future.

Informers in Ireland

Kevin Tollis (1995) notes that:

> In republican communities an atavistic hatred of informers runs back to the Dublin Castle spies who betrayed the 1798 United Irishmen Rising and were deemed responsible for sending the father of Irish Republicanism, Theobald Wolfe Tone, on the road to the gallows. On the bloody stage of Irish history, the informer is the villain. A cultural bogeyman who has played his part in the downfall of endless fine and noble patriots. The informer is the Judas within, the betrayer, the fountainhead of all Irish misery and a convenient scapegoat for centuries of glorious failure. (p. 194)

Successive republican revolutionary organizations have faced enemy forces operating on informer-led intelligence. Since 1641, when an informer, Owen O'Connolly, supplied the information that led to the arrest, conviction, and execution of leaders of the Great Rebellion in return for financial security, revolutionaries have recognized the threat posed by intelligence leaked from within their own communities and have adopted an uncompromising stance to deter such actions becoming commonplace (Boyd, 1984).

In the period 1971 to 2000, the IRA murdered 71 men and women who, they claim, were guilty of providing information to the security services. What information is available on their careers working for the state makes for chilling reading and is perhaps indicative of the actions of informers in the conflict and their treatment by both the security services and the IRA.

Between January 1976 and August 1977, six alleged informers (Seamus O'Brien, Kieran McCann, Brian Palmer, Vincent Heatherington, Myles McGrogan, and William Martin) were executed in circumstances outlined in some detail in Martin Dillon's (1991) *The Dirty War.* Vincent Heatherington, a Catholic civilian from Belfast, was executed on July 7, 1976. Heatherington and another Catholic, Myles McGrogan, had been held on remand in the republican-controlled "A" wing of Crumlin Road Prison awaiting trial for murder. During the IRA's debriefing of Hetherington and McGrogan, the former confessed to working for Special Branch and offered the names of a number of other informers. His statement implicated McGrogan and Seamus O'Brien from Andersonstown in West Belfast, James Green from Falls Road, and Gregory Brown, a loyalist informer. All were later killed—McGrogan, O'Brien, and Green by the IRA and Brown by the loyalist paramilitary group the Ulster Defence Association (UDA) (Dillon, 1991).

The damage informers working within the republican movement could cause the organization was highlighted following the execution of IRA volunteers Maurice Gilvarry, Anthony Braniff, and James Young. According to the republican movement, all three not only worked for the Special Branch, passing information relating to weapons dumps, volunteer movements, safe houses, and operations, but also acted as saboteurs, foiling attacks by altering bombs and firearms (see *An Phoblacht/Republican News* [*AP/RN*], 1981a, 1981b, 1984). Christopher Harte, executed in February 1993, was accused of passing information to the security forces that led to the death of another member, Pearse Jordan, and the seizure of weapons and explosives. Joseph Mulhern was executed for supplying information that led to the arrest of six IRA activists (*AP/RN*, 1993a).

Martin Brown and Caroline Moreland were more recent victims of the IRA's campaign against informers. Both were killed in 1994. Brown, according to the republican movement, was recruited in 1990 following a hit-and-run incident. According to the republican movement's statement, Brown, on the orders of his Special Branch "handlers," approached IRA members and offered his house as a weapons dump. His activities included an attempt to infiltrate the organization and passing of information that led to the seizure of weapons. Moreland, according to Martin McGartland (1997), was a "stalwart IRA sympathizer" who helped orchestrate a failed bomb attack on the Royal Courts of Justice in the center of Belfast in late 1990 (p. 173). The IRA executed Moreland 4 years later for allegedly luring two volunteers to the city center to be photographed by Special Branch operatives. Apparently, she had been recruited in 1992 after her fingerprints were found on bomb components. A statement released by the republican movement after her death claimed that she had been taught anti-interrogation methods by her handlers, and a local priest noted that her face was "mutilated beyond recognition and her head completely disfigured" (cited in McGartland, 1997, p. 173).

Undoubtedly, the most controversial elements of informer employment in Northern Ireland have surrounded the use of agent provocateurs and supergrasses. Since the 1980s, a succession of revelations surrounding the Brian Nelson affair has highlighted the use of the agent provocateur as a weapon of assassination for the security services. Nelson alleges that not only did his handlers allow him gather intelligence for the UDA for attacks against republicans, but that they actively assisted in these endeavors (Kearney, 1999). It is increasingly accepted that the British Army's' Force Research Unit (FRU) supplied much of the intelligence that Nelson passed on to UDA terrorists for use in assassination attempts. Generally, these were montages from FRU files on republicans, but details of the target environment were also provided. Nelson cited one particular case, the planned assassination of Sinn Fein councillor Harry Fitsimmons, in which the FRU provided unobstructed access to the target, who was subsequently assassinated by a UDA hit squad (Davis, 1999).

Holroyd and Burbidge (1989) note that MI5 and the British Army policy

> was basic and shortsighted—use whatever means, legal or illegal, to blackmail the source into acting out of fear for his or her safety, then force them to carry out operations which cannot be traced back to the handler, unless the former is prepared to risk his or her life by confessing what he or she had done. (p. 40)

According to their account of handler practices in Northern Ireland, some agencies were in fact directing terrorism in the sanctioning and orchestration of attacks through agent provocateurs. This raises a number of serious ethical and moral issues regarding the running of informers within paramilitary organizations. Under Home Office guidelines relating to "Informants who take part in a crime," Section 1.92 (b) clearly states that

> Where an informant gives the police information about the intention of others to commit a crime in which they intend that he shall play a part, his participation should be allowed to continue only where:
>
> I. he does not actively engage in planning and committing the crime;
> II. he is intended to play a minor role; and,
> III. His participation is essential to enable the police to frustrate the principle criminals and to arrest them (albeit for lesser offences such as attempt or conspiracy to commit the crime, or carrying offensive weapons) before injury is done to any person or serious damage to property. The informant should always be instructed that he must on no account act as *agent provocateur*, whether by suggesting to others that they should commit offences or encouraging them to do so, and that if he is found to have done so he will himself be liable to prosecution. (Document published in Taylor, 1987, p. 359)

Mark Urban (1992) notes that neither the then- Royal Ulster Constabulary (RUC) nor British Military Intelligence is bound by Home Office guidelines, and Martin Dillon (1991) confirms suspicions that RUC Special Branch was involved in the running of agent provocateurs. On February 3, 1980, for example, Patrick Mackin and his wife, Velvet, were gunned down in the living room of their home in North Belfast by an IRA unit. Mackin had been a prison officer but was retired. According to Martin Dillon (1991), the "triggerman" was Maurice Gilvarry, who was at the time an informer for the RUC Special Branch. In fact, Special Branch approached the Criminal Investigative Division (CID) and gave them the names of three republicans who they claimed had been the culprits. Apparently, inconsistencies in Special Branch accounts raised suspicion among senior CID officers, and it later transpired that although two of those named by the Special Branch were indeed involved, prosecuted, and convicted of the murders, the third was freed amid suspicion that he was being framed for the murder. Gilvarry was never arrested. Dillon raises the question: "Were Special Branch prepared to allow him commit murder on behalf of the IRA, to keep him in place as an agent?" (p. 396).

Even greater concern surrounded the use of supergrasses. *Supergrasses* were informants offered leniency in return for divulging information about, and testifying against, a number of alleged terrorists. The system led to the large-scale imprisonment of alleged paramilitaries in the 1980s. Greer (1995), in the most authoritative study of the use of supergrasses in Northern Ireland, notes that the system emerged as a small step beyond "deliberately recruiting highly paid informers to developing a system for their appearance as witnesses in court" (p. 49). The first successful supergrass trial leading to terrorist convictions occurred in March 1980. Stephen McWilliams, an IRA member and informer, was rescued by British soldiers as he was being interrogated by an IRA internal security team. He provided testimony during the trails of seven IRA members party to his abduction, detention, and interrogation. Six of the accused, including veteran republican Martin Meehan, were convicted (Coogan, 1995; Greer, 1995).

By June 1981, when James Kennedy testified at the trails of 10 alleged members of the IRA, 8 of whom were subsequently convicted on charges of "membership of an illegal organisation," the supergrass system had reportedly brought the IRA leadership "close to panic" (Urban, 1992, p. 135). Patrick Bishop and Eamonn Mallie (1994) note that the "IRA worked out a two handed approach to winning the supergrasses back" (p. 408). The supergrass system was dependent on the testimony of the informer and once retracted would destroy the basis of the prosecution's case. Tactics were employed to encourage the supergrasses to retract their statements. In 1982, an amnesty was announced for all those who retracted, and families and solicitors were used as mediators in conveying promises of safe passage from Northern Ireland (Bishop and Mallie, 1994). Between August 1982 and October 1983, Robert Brown, Sean Mallon, Jackie Goodman, Patrica Hughes, Robert Lean, and William Skelly ended their services as supergrasses by retracting their statements (Coogan, 1995; Greer, 1995). Eamon Collins (1998) reports being told by a family member that the republican movement had guaranteed his safety from reprisal if he retracted his statements. Collins did so, and those held on remand on the basis of his testimony were released. For those who refused to retract, more invasive measures were adopted. The wife of Robert Brown, for example, was kidnapped and held until he retracted (Bishop and Mallie, 1994).

Simultaneously, the supergrass system was increasingly coming under pressure over the unreliability of uncorroborated testimony, the enormous incentives being offered to the informers, and moral and legal acceptability of the system as a whole. A report by a former member of the judiciary accepted that the RUC had regularly programmed supergrasses to "concoct and rehearse statements" (see Coogan, 1995, p. 520). Eamonn Collins (1998) reports being offered £100,000, a new identity, and life abroad in return for his services. Given that all but one of Northern Ireland's supergrasses were motivated by self-preservation, the exception being Kevin Grady, who testified in accordance with the guidelines of his Christian sect, the reliability of the source of information was increasingly being questioned (Bishop and Mallie, 1994). With the large numbers of retractions and inherent unreliability of the supergrass system, it gradually fell into disuse in the mid- to late 1980s.

The IRA's Response to Informers

The IRA's response to informers was twofold. On one level, the IRA took defensive steps to ensure that information leaking from within the organization was of limited value to the security services and educated the community and their own membership regarding the tactics that the recruiters employ. On a second level, the organization took a number of offensive steps that included identifying, torturing, and eliminating informers and gathering intelligence through surveillance and other means.

Organizational Restructuring

In the 1970s, the IRA was structured along the brigade/battalion/company structure of earlier organizations that trusted operational and personnel security to a large number of activists. The security services needed only to "turn" one member of each battalion or company to compromise all pending attacks by that section of the organization and obtain the identity of each activist. Thus, in 1976 senior members of the organization implemented a change to a cellular system modeled loosely on that of the Red Brigades and Baader-Meinhof organizations to "emphasise a return to secrecy and strict discipline" (Coogan, 1995; Taylor, 1987). In a puritanical employment, the cell system dissects an organization into active service units (ASUs) manned by approximately four activists known to each other by aliases. The unit is in turn directed, and its activities sanctioned, by a higher unit of anonymous supervisory members who communicate with the ASUs through a courier—this cell format being maintained to the highest level (Bishop and Mallie, 1994). The effect of the structure is that operational and personnel information is strictly curtailed, and the organization is almost impregnable to infiltration at any meaningful level. It also slim-lined the organization into a war machine that could be maintained by a disproportionately small number of activists over a long period of time (Glover, 1978).

It is clear that the IRA never intended to implement this structure in whole. An internal document discovered in 1977 stated:

> Ideally a cell should consist of four people. Rural areas, we decided, should be treated as separate cases to that of city and town Brigade/Command areas.
> For this reason our proposals will affect mainly city and town areas. ...
> CELLS; as we have already said, as from now, all recruits are to be passed into a cell structure.
> Existing Battalion and Company Staff must be dissolved over a period of months with present Brigades then deciding who passes into the (reorganised) cell structure and who goes into the Brigade controlled and departmentalised Civil Administration. ... Cells must be specialised into IO cells, sniping cells, executions, bombings, robberies, etc. (IRA, 1976)

In fact, apart from the dissection of companies into ASUs, the structure of the organization today is very much the same as it was in the early 1970s. In Belfast, for instance, the brigade and battalion structures remain unchanged. The supreme decision-making and coordination authority remains the Belfast Brigade led by an officer in command (O/C). Of the 10 senior IRA members sitting on the brigade, 3 are officers commanding the three battalion areas of the city. The remaining members are junior O/Cs, formerly company O/Cs, within these battalion areas and are tasked with overseeing ASUs within their communities. Thus, the brigade/battalion structure has survived, and the only meaningful restructuring occurred at the lowest "active" level of the organization.

What the reorganization did change was the number of hard-core activists and the nature of peripheral support. The organization was streamlined into a couple of hundred (most estimations are between 200 and 300) members (Keeley, 1982). This central structure was in turn supported by the "Auxiliaries," not only in charge of community policing, which was becoming an escalating occupation of the republican movement, but also tasked with providing operational support to ASUs; Cumman na mBan, for women who work in support of the IRA (see Ward, 1993); and Na Fianna Eireann, the youth wing of the republican movement.

Clearly, this is well short of the ideal cell structures adopted by some of the left-wing organizations active on the continent in the 1970s and 1980s, a format that would have been unworkable in the incestuous nature the IRA (Bishop and Mallie, 1994). As one IRA member of the time noted:

> *Republican:* Well you see the big mistake ... is that they tend to think the IRA as a mass mobilization of people. The IRA at its very best was 200 people. At its absolute maximum it was 200 people. On the periphery of that you had safe houses ... places where you could put dumps ... especially in the city you needed a house to put a dump or in the country to put yourself down. Here you needed another place to put your ammunition in and another place to put your personnel in. On the periphery you had a lot of people. But the core of the IRA was about 200 maximum. There was a time in about 1985/1986 I could have named virtually every IRA volunteer in Ireland. That's how tight it is. It's not any bigger than that.
>
> *Author:* So the cell structure was not working as a security measure at all?
>
> *Republican:* The thing about the cell structure was that ... it started about 1977/78 and that was about the time I joined the Republican Movement ... and the cell structure had just been put into place. If you take a place like Monoghan where you had as many as 16 active IRA members who drank together, who slept in the same house. ... These boys had no ties to family ... so they put the movement before their family ... so you had the same 16 men drinking in the Clara Inn as it was called at that time. You had them sleeping in the same safe houses ... you get them arrested at the same time ... when they disappear you knew that a job was going to happen. ... I would never have called the IRA a secret army. I call them a fairly secret army because I could have gone into Armagh and I knew the IRA operatives in it and I was no high-ranking person in it. I was just an ordinary volunteer. I could go into Tyrone and I would know every volunteer in it ... except for the new recruits 16, 17, 18, 19 years of age ... but you would know the core because the core were consistently getting arrested. British Intelligence and the Special Branch knew exactly who they were. They were constantly getting arrested. ... They were constantly imprisoned. So if you made any visit to prison at all you knew exactly who they were ... because for example when I was in Crumlin Jail in the 1980s there was something like 160/170 republican prisoners. So I knew 160/170 Republicans and then when I get back onto the street those Republicans eventually went back into there areas and therefore you knew who they were. It is as simple as that. It is a fairly secret army. It's a small core ... 200 volunteers ... within that you know that you have got technical experts, finance men, intelligence people, strategists,

> propagandists all those people ... but in reality its not hard to know
> who they are. (Interview with private republican source, Belfast,
> 1998

What the cell system did provide was operational security. Knowledge of impending operations were kept between the ASU and the area O/C, and although specialist bomb makers and the area quartermaster would be aware of an impending attack, the target or target time would generally not be provided. The only non-ASU members with prior knowledge would be a scout team and an intelligence officer if he or she had set up the operation. This was much more secure than the company structure, for which up to 20 activists would have prior knowledge of a planned attack and be in the position to disseminate this intelligence by either loose talk or directly to handlers.

In fact, the only operational environment where the cell structure ensured both operational and personnel security, was within the so-called England Department. ASUs were kept to four members, and identities of operatives were kept secret. Couriers were used to transport directives and finances, and activists managed their own arms dumps. ASUs were unaware of the identities of others active within the England Department. Perhaps of greatest contrast to the structure in Belfast was that members of the England Department lived outside republican areas, shunned republican clubs and commemorations, and did not espouse their republican ideals. At its best, the England Department was an example of the effectiveness of the ASU format and the internal security it provided (Dillon, 1994; McKee and Franey, 1988).

But, central to this chapter, restructuring also minimized the level of infiltration that could be attained by informers. While the operations of one ASU may be compromised, to effectively compromise all activities would require a large number of informers. In assessing the impact of the introduction of the new structure, Smith (1995) noted that arrests for paramilitary offenses dropped by 465 within 1 year. The security forces in turn attempted to circumvent this limitation by encouraging informers to attain positions such as "intelligence officer" and quartermaster, with access to multiple ASUs. The advantage of attaining such positions was outlined in the autobiographical account of Martin McGartland. McGartland notes that his position as intelligence officer

> brought me into contact with numerous IRA men from different cells. ... I
> had fallen into a most privileged position of trust which provided me with an
> extraordinary range of contacts. ... They would often speak in my presence of
> planned targets, murders, bombings and future operations before final deci-
> sions had been made. More importantly, it provided the Special Branch with a
> remarkable early-warning system. (1997, p. 173)

The cell structure was almost insurmountable for the counterterrorism forces charged with domestic security in England. Little information from informers run in Northern Ireland, relating to impending operations on the mainland, was obtainable, and the situation was compounded by inter-agency rivalry (Dorril, 1993). Thus, organizations such as Scotland Yard and MI5 placed increasing importance in the interception of communications, various other forms of electronic surveillance and personal surveillance in preempting attacks (Cusack, 1999).

Anti-interrogation Education

Of central relevance to the IRA's battle against informers was the creation of an activist base capable of withstanding long hours of interrogation, incorporating physical and psychological torture, at the hands of the security services. The reorganization document cited noted:

> The three-day and seven-day detention orders are breaking volunteers and it is the Republican Army's fault for not indoctrinating volunteers with the psychological strength to resist interrogation. (IRA, 1976, n.p.)

Members breaking under interrogation had led to the gathering of large amounts of intelligence on IRA structure, personnel, arms, and operations. One precaution adopted by the IRA, and discussed previously, was the implementation of the cell structure that limited the information that any one volunteer could divulge. A second was the education of activists in anti-interrogation methods.

Prior to becoming a fully fledged member of the IRA, the recruit attends a series of lectures based on the contents of the organization's training manual, the *Green Book*. The recruit is also told to expect "shock" tactics, such as being "dragged along the road ... kicked, punched and the insults start." A section, "What a Volunteer Should Do When Arrested," states:

1. The most important thing to bear in mind when arrested is that you are a volunteer of a revolutionary army ... that your cause is a just one ... that as a soldier you have taken the chance expected of a soldier and that there is nothing to be ashamed of in being captured.
2. You must bear in mind that the treatment meted out to you is designed to break you and so bleed you of all the information you may have with regard to the organization to which you belong.
3. They will attempt to intimidate you by sheer numbers and by brutality. ... Volunteers must condition themselves to the obvious fact that they can be arrested and if and when arrested they should expect the worst and be prepared for it. (IRA, n.d.)

The main body of the anti-interrogation chapter is devoted to the interrogation tactics employed by the RUC.

> After the prisoner has been placed in a cell ... "The Interrogators," will crowd
> around the outside of the cell door from time to time, shouting threats and
> insults, telling the prisoner what they will do to him when they go into the
> cell.
>
> After some time the interrogators will enter the cell and ask the prisoner
> to make a confession. During this period he may be subjected to assaults and
> abusive language. ... At this stage he will be fingerprinted and other questions
> will be put to him, related to the specific charge or other charges. ... If the
> evidence does not indicate a degree of guilt on the specific charge, he will be
> accused of all kinds of vague activity. ... Pressure will take the form of physi-
> cal and psychological torture, most probably he will be punched and kicked
> around the cell while they scream at him to make a confession. ...
>
> Another set of interrogators will enter the cell, possibly carrying a file with
> the prisoner's name on it. They will act quite friendly and sympathetic towards
> him, telling him that they do not condone the activity of the previous inter-
> rogators, that they were mad, crazy and possibly they may kill him when they
> come in later. ... The interrogators will then open up the file and pretend to
> read extracts from it, related to the prisoner's past life and activities, even the
> most intimate and private aspects of his life and will be read to him. ...
>
> After a period of time another set of interrogators will enter the cell, again
> these interrogators will be particularly brutal and nasty towards him. ... The
> torture used will now take on a three-fold purpose:
>
> 1. Physical Torture.
> 2. Subtle Psychological Torture.
> 3. Humiliation. (IRA, n.d)

The "Physical Torture" is defined as "beatings, kicking, punching
and twisting of limbs, it may even be burning from cigarette ends." The
"Psychological Torture" that can be expected during the interrogation may
involve threats and intimidation directed against family, friends and self.
"Humiliation" "takes the form of stripping the prisoner of his clothes and
remarks passed about his sexual organs." In defending against these practices, the recruit is informed that

> the best anti-interrogation is to SAY NOTHING. ... Ask to see your doctor and
> keep on doing so. ... DO NOT INDULGE IN CONVERSATION WITH THE
> POLICE. Most volunteers speak from a sense of fear thinking mistakenly
> that if they speak, torture or ill treatment will not be used. ... Therefore the
> best defense is to remain COOL, COLLECTED, CALM and SAY NOTHING.
> (IRA, n.d.)

McGartland (1997) reports being told that the RUC would attempt to break his will using sleep deprivation, refusal to allow access to bathroom facilities and inadequate food and water. The aim of the interrogation was to "break" the activist's "spirit" so the need to keep mentally alert and physically strong was stressed (p. 136). The possibility of the use of physical violence and the importance of requesting a private general practitioner was also conveyed. For fear of making incriminating statements, McGartland reports being instructed to respond to any question with the following statement:

> When interviewed I will refuse to co-operate but this does not mean I am guilty. I want Madden and Finucane to represent me. (McGartland, 1997, p. 136)

Eamon Collins, recounting one interrogation, notes:

> They said the mortar attack was a dastardly deed; someone would have to be brought to justice. I kept silent, although I had already started to break one of the key anti-interrogation strictures: I was listening to what they were saying. I tried to block their words from entering my mind. I tried to concentrate on a rousing song, a person, an event, a flickering flame, a spot on the wall, but I still found myself listening to them. I listened—and communicated through my body language that I was listening—in order to get them to ease off the pressure. They knew I was listening and they did ease off, engaging in long-winded and fairly innocuous speeches. I felt temporarily in control, but I had already made the cardinal error of allowing the interrogators to enter my mind. (1998, p. 260)

All activists released after the 7-day detention session were debriefed by a special team of IRA members not only so that the movement was kept abreast of developments in interrogation techniques but also to determine what information, if any, was passed to the security services (Collins, 1998). Similarly, those who were held on remand or incarcerated for offenses were subjected to a lengthy debrief by fellow inmates, as was illustrated in the Heatherington and McGrogan cases outlined previously. New interrogation techniques, presumably, were conveyed in anti-interrogation lectures.

It is difficult to estimate the importance of these developments, but it certainly minimized the surprise element that interrogators may utilize and thus placed activists in a more confident and secure footing. In any case, the interrogation powers of the police, and the forms of physical and psychological abuse they could use, were curtailed following the implementation of the Bennet report recommending CCTV in interrogation cells, rotation of detectives, access to a medical practitioner every 24 hours, and presence of a supervisor (Bennett, 1979; Bishop and Mallie, 1994).

Educating the People

Defensive measures adopted to counter informer recruitment among sympathetic communities center around the dissemination of information relating to methods of recruitment, the damaging effects of loose talk, and the importance of coming forward if approached. The primary method of disseminating such information is through *An Phoblacht/Republican News* and the organizing of press conferences where recruitment attempts are exposed.

These articles, primarily coverage of reported recruitment attempts, tend to follow a consistent format. Sensational and emotive headings—"RUC Trawling for Informers" (*AP/RN*, 1989e, p. 11); "Ballymurphy Man Living in Fear" (*AP/RN*, 1989a, p. 11); "RUC Hound Lenadoon Man" (*AP/RN*, 1989d, p. 10); "Branch Bribery Attempt" (*AP/RN*, 1989b, p. 10); and "Youth's Terror of RUC" (*AP/RN*, 1989f, p. 10), for example—are employed in which the RUC, MI5, or British Army is undermined using euphemistic language. "MI5," we are told, "spreads web to Paris" (*AP/RN*, 1992, p. 2). The use of "web" conveys the use of spider-like qualities of "stealth," "entrapment',"and "creepyness" by MI5 in the recruitment attempt.

Articles generally begin by outlining name, age, occupation, and place of residence of the individual reporting the approach. Sometimes, the audience is informed that the individual has been advised to hold a press conference to publicize his or her ordeal as a method of deterring future RUC approaches. Details of the circumstances leading up to the recruitment attempt and the recruitment attempt itself are provided in the main section of the article and conclude with a plea to those experiencing harassment to approach Sinn Fein. This format is adequately illustrated in the alleged attempted recruitment of Joe Doherty in 1989.

In an article, 'RUC Force Derryman to Flee' (*AP/RN*, 1989c, p. 5), the reader is introduced to Joe Doherty, "a 29-year-old Derryman and father of two, who fled to the 26 counties ... following an RUC attempt to intimidate him into becoming an informer." Doherty "appeared with his solicitor at a Sinn Fein press conference in Derry on Monday, April 3rd, and revealed details of the RUC manipulation." A former detainee on the word of supergrass Raymond Gilmore, he was released after 2 years on remand. He was arrested at an Easter Sunday parade in Derry and interrogated by four sets of detectives. During questioning, he "made verbal admissions to four robberies of which he [was] completely innocent." He was then questioned by two plainclothes detectives 'from the Government' who asked him to supply information on republicans "who they could then set up." Doherty agreed "so he could get out of custody" but on release went to Sinn Fein and a solicitor. Then, Sinn Fein councillor Hugh Brady organized a press conference and "advised anyone who finds themselves in a similar position to immediately contact a solicitor or Sinn Fein" (p. 5).

Themes present in this article, and indicative of those common across almost all similar stories, include the scrupulousness of the RUC, their ruthless interrogation methods, the innocence of the victim, and the salvation found in publicizing the recruitment attempt. The suggestion that the RUC required the information to "set up" republicans is also clever as it plays on alleged "shoot-to-kill" activities of the security services in the north.

Articles aimed at directly and unambiguously explaining the methods of recruitment employed by the security services are also presented in the pages of *An Phoblacht/Republican News*. In July 1992, an article, "RUC Refines Its Informers Strategy," announced:

> Recently it has come to light that the RUC has once again redesigned its strategy for the recruitment of agents and spies because of its lack of success against the IRA. The sinister and cynical nature of the changes proves that the RUC are prepared to use any means available to pressurise people and to force people to work as informers. (*AP/RN*, 1992c, pp. 8–9)

The article contrasts early attempts by "Britain's counter-insurgency" teams to recruit informers who compromise themselves under interrogation with the following:

> The RUC's new strategy ... [of making] a definite decision to target a person and wear him or her down until there is "agreement" to provide information or until the victim publicises what is being done. (*AP/RN*, 1992c, pp. 8–9)

A number of examples of this new strategy are outlined, and the reader is told:

> People in nationalist districts should, for their own safety, be wary of the consequences of these dirty tricks because everyone and anyone is a potential target in the RUC strategy of recruiting informers.
>
> Regardless of the circumstances of an informer's recruitment, there are a number of salient facts about the process that exposes the RUC's cynicism and cruel exploitation of the informer. The facts are that those who end up working for the RUC do so because they have been compromised and forced to work as informers—they don't necessarily do so out of any sense of anti-republicanism.
>
> Another fact is that when someone has been broken and agrees to work for the RUC the person then ends up being no better than a puppet. The RUC promise they will do whatever is necessary to protect the informer but at all times they are using the informer to suit their needs, and if this means sacrificing him or her then this will be done. ...

But there is in fact a way out. Making your case public, going to a solicitor or coming forward to "confess" are all ways out; doing so breaks the silent fear and intimidation that the RUC needs for playing its game. The glare of publicity exposes the manipulation simply because the person, whether they have informed or are coming under pressure to do so, have the guarantee of safety when they come forward. (*AP/RN*, 1992c, pp. 8–9)

The victimology of the informer is an important theme that recurs in much of the informer material. Its purpose is to highlight that recruitment attempts are generally made against people who are compromised or in some way vulnerable to the approaches of the RUC. Again, the "way out" is identified as a move to publicize the injustice of the approach through a Sinn Fein press conference.

The Execution of Informers and Offering of Amnesties

That the IRA has executed 71 informers in the Irish Republic, Northern Ireland, and England since 1971 is in itself an effective deterrent to those who may find themselves compromised by the security services and tempted to "turn" informer to escape prosecution.

The IRA's first informer execution was of John Joseph Kavanagh on January 27, 1971. Two weeks later, the body of Edward Bell was found outside Belfast City. In October of the same year, they killed Robert McFarland and Thomas Kells. All four were Protestants. Kavanagh and Bell were IRA members, and the former had been arrested for possession of firearm cartridges. McFarland and Kells had also been arrested prior to their executions but for non-terrorism-related offenses. Dillon and Lehane (1973) suggest that the republican movement may have been operating from some form of prisoner release list, believing that a number of individuals within the nationalist community had been compromised by the RUC.

Execution, while widely employed, was just one of a variety of punishments used against suspected informers. Some suffered less-extreme retribution. In 1991, for example, the Belfast Brigade of the IRA released a statement admitting responsibility for the punishment shooting of a 25-year-old man from North Belfast after he admitted working for the "crown forces." The original sentence had been "life in exile," but the victim had returned to the province and allegedly reestablished contact with former handlers (*AP/RN*, 1992b, p. 2).

"Tarring and feathering," generally reserved for females, was another popular punishment for alleged informing, and its symbolic function was illustrated in an article published in *The Volunteer*, a republican publication in Derry, on November 10, 1972.

During the last war, the German Army succeeded in occupying the Channel Islands which are under British rule. ... Many of the local females openly kept company with German officers and soldiers. Some men acted as quislings for the Germans and helped to compile dossiers on those Islanders most opposed to German rule.

The "loyal" islanders had ways of dealing with these fraternisers. The females had their heads shaved, tarred and feathered. ... The men suffered the same fate as the women. ...

The occupying army [the British] needs the help of fraternisers and quislings. The methods they employ to secure this form of assistance is variable. Inviting girls out for a drink or to attend sponsored dances is one way of meeting the female population. In most cases the "average soldier" is usually a professional intelligence officer in the British Army and even during the course of the conversation they extract a lot of information from innocent girls. ... We make this appeal to anyone who needs our help to escape. If you must fraternise with soldiers, then fraternise with the soldiers of the Irish Republic [IRA], the Guardians and Defenders of the Irish People. ...

Like the Channel Islanders we deplore fraternisation. Unlike the Channel Islanders we have taken no action against the unfortunates caught in the British Web. (*The Volunteer*, 1972, p. 3)

Five days later, on November 15, an article published in the nationalist *Irish News* outlined the IRA's beating of 39-year-old Belfast mother Agnes Griffith:

Mrs. Griffiths was first taken from her home ... and after her hair had been cut off and she had been beaten up, she was tied to a lamp post and had tar poured over her. A statement by the O.C. of "A" Company, 3rd. Battalion IRA., last night said Mrs. Griffiths had been "observed entering and leaving British Army posts for the past two months. She was dealt with leniently on Saturday because she is the mother of four children and was ordered to leave the country within 48 hours. Let this incident be a warning to anyone passing information to the British." (*Irish News*, 1972, p. 4)

Republican sources report that tarring and feathering became less frequently used during the 1980s as a result of community backlash. What became increasingly used, however, was exiling of suspected informers. In November 1993, the Tyrone Brigade of the IRA ordered 18-year-old Francis Whitehouse to leave the country or face execution. Two years previously, according the organization's statement, the youth had been recruited by the RUC Special Branch while being questioned in relation to petty crime offenses. The youth admitted to IRA interrogators that he had supplied information on republicans in Coalisland in return for payments of between £20 and £30 and £200 for information that led to the seizure of two AK47 assault rifles (AP/RN, 1993b). Similarly, when Gerard McGivern approached members of the Belfast Brigade and admitted to supplying information to RUC Special Branch, he was ordered to leave the "six counties" (*AP/RN*, 1992d).

Exiling had an important function in that, along with the issuing of amnesties, it offered an avenue of escape for the informer who, for whatever reason, wished to terminate his associations with the security services. However, it is the complementary measures of physical punishment (executions and beatings) and passive compassion (exiling and total amnesties) that render IRA policy on informers such an effective double-edged sword countering informer intelligence. There is no better illustration of this strategy than the carefully choreographed announcements of amnesty. In January 1982, a week after the IRA's execution of alleged informer John Torbitt, the republican movement announced

> a two-week-long amnesty to anybody who is working, or has worked, as an informer for the British Army or RUC. The only condition of the amnesty, and of its guarantee of immunity from punishment or execution for those who take up the IRA's offer, is that informers must contact the Republican Movement within the two-week period and detail fully the information that they have given to the enemy. The amnesty offer applies equally to civilians and to any members of the Republican Movement who have agreed to act as informers, and will be honoured however serious the nature of the information which has been given. Once the two week offer has expired though, the IRA have warned, they are in a strong position to take stern and immediate action against a number of Brit and RUC informers known to them, if these people have not already come forward. (*AP/RN*, 1982, p. 2)

Similarly, in August 1990, 2 weeks after the killing of alleged IRA informer Patrick Flood, the IRA announced:

> We have decided to declare an amnesty for one week commencing midnight on Sunday, August 11th, at midnight. We urge all those involved in passing any information to the crown forces to come forward during these seven days before it's too late. Remember, history shows that you will inevitably be caught, with most regrettable but necessary consequences.
>
> We guarantee and publicly state that anyone coming forward to us between these dates will not be harmed in any way. This opportunity may never arise again. (*AP/RN*, 1990, p. 2)

Undoubtedly, active informers would have felt under considerable pressure following the execution of Torbitt and Flood, and the amnesty was cleverly timed to offer a painless way out of a potentially fatal situation. On February 18, 1982, on conclusion of the amnesty, the IRA announced the following:

The Irish Republican Army's offer of an amnesty for informers, which commenced on January 30th for a two week period and which ended last weekend, has proved to be a great success, with a significant number of persons coming forward. (*AP/RN*, 1992e, p. 2)

In conclusion, retribution has formed an import element of the IRA's battle against informer generation. Their policy of treating leniently those who come forward voluntarily to provide a full statement to the organization and the intermittent offering of amnesties provide an effective escape avenue for already-active informers who fear execution at the hands of republicans and are working under high levels of duress and anxiety. But, perhaps of greatest relevance here is that the symbolism of crime and punishment reinforces perceptions of the informer as being guilty of crimes against the republican community and thus plays an important part in contemporary demonization.

The Interrogation of Suspected Informers and Allegations of Torture

Interrogating suspected or known informers was an important element of intelligence gathering available to the IRA. Perhaps the most detailed first-hand account of interrogation at the hands of an IRA internal security team was provided during the trial of Sinn Fein "Director of Publicity" at that time, Danny Morrisson, and five other republicans, charged with the attempted murder of Sandy Lynch. During the trial, Lynch, who had worked as an RUC Special Branch informer within the Belfast Brigade, reported that he was lured to a house in West Belfast on what he believed was a target surveillance operation. On entering the premises, he was blindfolded with crepe bandages and searched from head to foot by a number of men, who checked his hair, nose, and ears and between his toes. A metal detector was run over his body, and an antibugging device was activated in the room where he was to be held (*Daily Telegraph*, 1991).

They said they had done their home-work on me, that they had been watching me for weeks and they were quite sure I was the man they were after. They were saying that I was a tout and a bastard. ... One told me he was from the Northern Command [of the IRA], that he had been trained in Lybia and enjoyed his work and that he would break me. He told me I wouldn't get any sleep or be able to go to the toilet or do anything. They would be talking to me in teams and while one team was talking the other would rest. He said I would get very tired and thirsty and hungry, that I would become disorientated. ... He said he might give me an amnesty if he thought I was working under duress for the police. He said he would give me an hour, and after the hour the amnesty would be withdrawn and he couldn't help me. (McKittrick, 1990, p. 6)

According to Lynch's testimony, within 5 minutes of the amnesty expiring, he made a statement to the interrogators outlining his activities as a RUC informer. He then repeated the statement on paper and for an oral recording. Luckily for Lynch, British Army and RUC personnel raided the building.

The use of torture in the interrogation of informers is also alleged but is strongly denied by the IRA. According to family members, Patrick Lynch was bound and gagged, had nails driven through his fingertips, and had burns inflicted by his IRA interrogators (McKittrick, 1990). Allegations of torture also surround the deaths of John McAnulty, Eamonn McGuire, Brian McNally, Anthony Braniff, and Caroline Moreland, to name but a few. The families of many of the victims state that under interrogation and torture, anybody would admit to informing if they were offered an amnesty. The suggestion is that some were offered an amnesty during interrogation and torture but were subsequently executed.

Discussion and Conclusion

The reality is that across geopolitical landscapes, informers are at the coal face in the battle against terrorism in its many guises, are necessary to protect members of society, and as an intelligence-gathering strategy, are here to stay. Indeed, one of the key themes emerging from this research is that the informer is a particularly effective mechanism for addressing terrorist violence. Certainly, at times during the Northern Irish conflict, informers have literally crippled the IRA. Their information has led to the arrest of hundreds of members of the organization, some of whom were subsequently induced to become informers themselves. Operations were prevented, activists arrested or killed, and arms seized. On another level, knowledge of the potential damage informers could cause, and the fact that almost anyone could be coerced into working for the state, led to a certain level of paranoia within the republican movement and damaged morale.

The use of informers has been a controversial strategy for the security services. Allegations that members of the British Army's agent handler unit, the FRU, allowed loyalist and republican informers to participate in murders to protect their position in their respective organizations have been widely accepted. Chief Constable Sir John Stephens, who was given the task of investigating informer practices in Northern Ireland, has publicly supported the veracity of such allegations, and one would suspect that more damaging revelations are yet to emerge.

Clearly, the best way for intelligence agencies to avoid similar debacles is through the adoption of responsible codes of conduct and good governance and oversight. While on a surface level it may restrict the autonomy of the security services, in the longer term it will ensure public confidence in their actions and minimize the possibility that the kinds of scandals that have emerged in Northern Ireland in recent years will occur again.

Ironically, the republican movement has turned these scandals to their advantage, incorporating the propaganda messages as part of a more elaborate propaganda effort that strives to further alienate the republican community from the British State. Moreover, they have successfully used the Nelson affair as a fulcrum in raising international awareness of the less-than-commendable actions of the then-RUC, MI5, and British Army.

Also of interest is the way that terrorist groups deal with the threat of informers. The republican movement's response has been multifaceted, energetic, and effective. They put in place a system of punishments with varying degrees of severity that range from simple verbal warnings, to curfews, punishment beatings, and executions. They attempted to educate members of the public regarding the methods used by the security services in recruiting informers and have issued amnesties when informers came forward voluntarily.

One of the core impediments to recruitment is the ingrained prejudice against informers that runs throughout Irish society. The damage they have caused to the struggle for independence has been immortalized in Irish song, storytelling, and poetry, and when combined with contemporary experiences and energetic propaganda campaigns waged by the republican movement, a robust demonology emerges (Sarma, 2007).

The picture that emerges is that terrorists evolve and develop in response to the actions of those that seek to undermine them. As this evolution proceeds, awareness of informers increases and leads to increased alienation from the police and potentially promotes the relationship between the community and the terrorists. Moreover, it becomes increasingly difficult to recruit informers, leading to the security services adopting more coercive methods in their attempts to do so and consequentially may contribute to the community alienation cycle.

Reaching an understanding of the extent to which these issues apply to other low-intensity conflicts requires more research. Certainly, the lesson from Northern Ireland is that the successes for the security services have been tainted with the reality that informers and human tragedy appear to go hand in hand. There were 71 IRA informants murdered by the organization, many of whom suffered brutal torture before being executed. Many were simply victims themselves, coerced into working for the security services. Despite the demonology surrounding the informer, being dumped on a back road in Armagh with a bullet in the back of the head is a very inhumane end. If this is sometimes lost on members of the security services, it is not on members of the community or group they seek to infiltrate. Moreover, if recent revelations are accurate, informers were complicit in the murder of innocent civilians and, rather than a strategy for protecting communities, were sometimes a tool for their victimization.

The conclusion is that while informers are effective in combating terrorism, it is not a risk-free strategy. Perhaps the best way to ensure that policing practices are in keeping with societies' expectations is to look to the mistakes of the past and put safeguards in place for the future.

References

An Phoblacht/Republican News (AP/RN). (1981a, January 24). Extremely reluctant. AP/RN, p. 3.

An Phoblacht/Republican News (AP/RN). (1981b, October 3). Ardoyne informer executed. AP/RN, p. 3.

An Phoblacht/Republican News (AP/RN). (1982, January 28). IRA offer informers' amnesty. AP/RN, pp. 1–2.

An Phoblacht/Republican News (AP/RN). (1984, February 16). RUC agent executed. AP/RN, p. 3.

An Phoblacht/Republican News (AP/RN). (1989e, March 2). RUC trawling for informers. AP/RN, p. 11.

An Phoblacht/Republican News (AP/RN). (1989a, March 2). Ballymurphy man living in fear. AP/RN, p. 11.

An Phoblacht/Republican News (AP/RN). (1989d, January 1). RUC hound Lenadoon man. AP/RN, p. 10.

An Phoblacht/Republican News (AP/RN). (1989b, January 19). Branch bribery attempt. AP/RN, p. 10.

An Phoblacht/Republican News (AP/RN). (1989f, November 9). Youth's terror of RUC. AP/RN, p. 6.

An Phoblacht/Republican News (AP/RN). (1989c, April 6). RUC force Derryman to flee. AP/RN, p. 5.

An Phoblacht/Republican News (AP/RN). (1990, August 9). IRA announces amnesty. AP/RN, War News, p. 2.

An Phoblacht/Republican News (AP/RN). (1991, June 27). Belfast statement. AP/RN, War News, p. 2.

An Phoblacht/Republican News (AP/RN). (1992a, August 13). MI5 spreads web to Paris. AP/RN, p. 2.

An Phoblacht/Republican News (AP/RN). (1992b, March 16). By the summer you'll be dead. AP/RN, p. 3.

An Phoblacht/Republican News (AP/RN). (1992c, July 2). RUC refines its informers strategy. AP/RN, pp. 8–9.

An Phoblacht/Republican News (AP/RN). (1992d, July 4). Informer comes forward. AP/RN, War News, p. 3.

An Phoblacht/Republican News (AP/RN). (1992e, February 18). Come forward say IRA. AP/RN, p. 2.

An Phoblacht/Republican News (AP/RN). (1993a, July 1). Informer worked for RUC for three years. *AP/RN*, p. 2.

An Phoblacht/Republican News (AP/RN). (1993b, November 11). Informer ordered out. *AP/RN*, War News, p.3.

Bennett, H. G. (1979). *The Bennett Report into Charges of Brutality against the RUC.* CMND 7497.

Bishop, Patrick, and Mallie, Bishop. (1994). *The Provisional IRA.* Ealing, UK: Corgi.

Boyd, Andrew. (1984). *The Informers: A Chilling Account of the Supergrasses in Northern Ireland.* Dublin: Mercier Press.

Clutterbuck, Richard. (1994). *Terrorism in an Unstable World.* London: Routledge.

Collins, Eamon. (1998). *Killing Rage.* London: Granta Books.

Coogan, Tim Pat. (1995). *The IRA (rev. ed.).* London: Harper Collins.

Cusack, Jim. (1999, May 31). Much of the truth about British Army's "dirty war" in the north in the 1970s is likely to remain buried. *Irish Times*, p. 4.

Daily Telegraph. (1991, May 9). Police informer's weekend of terror brought downfall of IRA godfather Danny Morrison. *Daily Telegraph* (Belfast), p. 7.

Davis, Nicholas. (1999). *Then-Thirty-Three: The Inside Story of Britons Secret Killing Machine in Northern Ireland.* London: Mainstream.

Dillon, Martin. (1991). *The Dirty War.* London: Arrow Books.

Dillon, Martin. (1994). *25 Years of Terror: The IRA's War against the British.* London: Bantam Books.

Dillon, Martin, and Lehane, Denis. (1973). *Political Murder in Northern Ireland.* Northern Ireland: Penguin Books.

Dorril, Stephen. (1993). *The Silent Conspiracy: Inside the Intelligence Services in the 1990s.* London: Heinemann.

Evelegh, Robin. (1978). *Peace in a Democratic Society: The Lessons of Northern Ireland.* London: Hurst.

Glover, J. M. (1978). *Northern Ireland: Future Terrorist Trends.* London: MOD Intelligence Staff.

Greer, Stephen. (1995). *Supergrasses: A Study in Anti-Terrorism Law Enforcement in Northern Ireland.* Oxford, UK: Clarendon Press.

Harnden, Toby. (1999). *Bandit Country: The IRA and South Armagh.* London: Hodder and Stoughton.

Holland, Jack, and Phoenix, Susan. (1996). *Phoenix: Policing the Shadows: The Secret War against Terrorism in Northern Ireland.* London: Hodder and Stoughton.

Holroyd, Fred, and Brubridge, Nick. (1989). *War without Honour: Military Intelligence in Northern Ireland.* Great Britain: Medium.

IRA. (1976). Staff Report. Unpublished internal document of the Republican Movement.

IRA. (n.d.). The Green Book. Unpublished internal document of the Republican Movement.

Irish News. (1972, November 15). Beaten-up mother was spy, say IRA. *Irish News*, p. 4.

Kearney, Vincent. (1999, November 7). Army in collusion probe. *Sunday Times* (Dublin).

Keeley, Kevin. (1982). *The Longest War: Northern Ireland and the IRA.* Dingle, Ireland: Brandon.

McGartland, Martin. (1997). *Fifty Dead Men Walking: The Heroic True Story of a British Agent Inside the IRA*. London: Blake.

McKee, Grant, and Franey, Ros. (1988). *Time Bomb: Irish Bombers, English Justice and the Guildford Four*. London: Bloomsbury.

McKittrick, David. (1990, October 31). Police informer tells of interrogation by IRA. *The Independent* (London), p. 6.

Remington, Stella. (1993b). *MI5: The Security Service*. London: HMSO.Remington, Stella. (1993). The Richard Dimbley Lectures. BBC Video Library.

Sarma, K. (2007). Defensive propaganda and IRA political control in republican communities. *Studies in Conflict and Terrorism*, 30(12), 1073–1094. doi: 10.1080/10576100701670888.

Sarma, K. (2009). Informers and the battle against the IRA: The plight of the informer in Northern Ireland. In S. Dam and J. Hall (Eds.), *Inside and Outside the Law* (pp. 213–219). Oxford, UK: Inter-Disciplinary Press. Retrieved from http://www.inter-disciplinary.net/wp-content/uploads/2009/09/iol16revc.pdf.

Segaller, Stephen. (1987). *Invisible Armies: Terrorism into the 1990s*. London: Sphere Books.

Smith, M. L. R. (1995). *Fighting for Ireland: The Military Strategy of the Irish Republican Movement*. Oxford, UK: Routledge.

Smith, Michael. (1997). *New Cloak, Old Dagger: How Britain's Spies Came in from the Cold*. London: Victor Gollancz.

Taylor, Peter. (1987). *Stalker: The Search for the Truth*. London: Faber and Faber.

The Volunteer. (1972, November 10). Fraternisation the British way. *The Volunteer* (Derry), p. 3.

Tollis, Kevin. (1995). *Rebel Hearts: Journeys within the IRA's soul*. London: Picador.

Urban, Mark. (1992). *Big Boys' Rules: The Secret Struggle against the IRA*. London: Faber and Faber.

Ward, Margaret. (1993). *Unmanageable Revolutionaries: Women and Irish Nationalism*. London: Pluto Press.

Defeating Terrorism
A Study of Operational Strategy and Tactics of Police Forces in Jammu and Kashmir (India)

13

YATEENDRA SINGH JAFA

Contents

Introduction

The most lethal form of terrorism that India has ever witnessed has risen in the state of Jammu and Kashmir. More than 30,000 people, including civilians, terrorists, police, and army soldiers, have died there since the terrorist campaign began in 1989 (Yahoo!Groups, 2001). After 13 years of stern police and military action, this movement remained alive and dangerous and still attracts a number of Muslim youth of the state. Terrorists frequently strike with lethal effect, occasionally at well-defended targets.

It is thus clear that an armed response alone cannot defeat terrorism. There is need for a multiprong approach: redress of the people's economic and political grievances, efficient use of intelligence for ferreting out terrorists, vigorous criminal prosecution of those charged with terrorist acts, and curbing the police excesses. In this context, this chapter examines the factors responsible for the growth of terrorism in Jammu and Kashmir. It details the nature and magnitude of the terrorist movement, its foreign connections, the training that the terrorists receive, and the weapons, equipment, and tactics they employ. Analyzing the nature of counterterrorism policing, this chapter attempts to establish that the police forces can substantially debilitate the terrorist movement by isolating its activists from the masses and winning over the people. Therefore, appropriate changes in the strategy, tactics, and behavior of the police forces are suggested. The opinions expressed in this chapter are solely those of the author.

Genesis and Growth of Terrorism

Why did the pacific and secular people of Kashmir embrace Islamist terrorism after living as part of India for 42 years? There is no theory that can explain all types of insurgencies in the world. Walter Laqueur says:

> National oppression and social inequalities are frequently mentioned as the root causes of terrorism and it is true that happy, contented groups of people do not, if ever, throw bombs. But this does not explain why the struggle for political freedom, for national liberation or for secession, has only occasionally led to terrorism, and why certain national minorities have opted for terrorism and others have not. (Laqueur, 1999, p. 36)

Supporting this view, a student of the Naxalite movement in India says:

> Any generalization on the subject is not possible. In our own country, we have seen people taking up arms against the government in different areas for

altogether different reasons. What is significant is that the same reasons existing in other regions did not produce a similar violent outburst. (Singh, 1995)

Terrorist movements in different parts of the world or in different parts of the same country have broadly similar features, but not common causes. Each of such movements is unique in nature as it is born out of singular local conditions, although it also may be affected by external influences, as happened in Jammu and Kashmir. The basic cause of the Kashmir revolt was the total alienation of Kashmiri Muslims from India due to erosion of their cultural identity, suppression of their political rights, and unemployment among educated Muslim youth. Pakistan indeed fomented terrorism in Kashmir after it failed to grab this territory by military action in 1947 and 1965. It also provided armed support and religious inspiration by training, arming, and indoctrinating Kashmiri rebels. But, Pakistan could successfully do so only because the internal conditions in Kashmir had already prepared the ground for the advent and growth of this violent movement.

While granting independence to India and creating Pakistan as a Muslim state in August 1947, the British rulers gave to the princely states in the subcontinent the option to join India or Pakistan or negotiate their status and relationship with each of the two new nations. Pakistan coveted the Muslim-majority Kashmir region of the state of Jammu and Kashmir. In October 1947, it assisted an invasion of Kashmir by Pakistani Muslim tribesmen, and the Pakistani army reinforced it. To save his kingdom, the state's ruler signed an Instrument of Accession with India. Jammu and Kashmir joined the Indian Union with a large measure of autonomy: Under its special status, India's jurisdiction over it extended only to external affairs, defense, and communications. This also legitimized the Indian military presence in the state. Having driven back the Pakistani raiders from most areas of Kashmir, India referred the Kashmir dispute to the United Nations in December 1948. The ceasefire imposed by the Security Council on January 1, 1949, left almost two thirds of the territory of Kashmir with India and one third with Pakistan, established the U.N. presence on both sides of Kashmir, and provided for a plebiscite in the future. On January 26, 1950, India promulgated its written constitution, which confirmed the special status and autonomy of Jammu and Kashmir within the Indian Union.

A pro-Pakistan Muslim minority existing in Kashmir at the time of the partition of the subcontinent desired its merger with Pakistan. But, the overwhelming yearning of the Muslims there was for *azadi* ("independence") because they regarded themselves as culturally different from the rest of the Indian subcontinent. However, their coreligionist tribespeople's aggression changed the situation. They now willingly accepted the state's merger with India as they believed that their interests would be safe in a secular country. Azadi for most of them now meant autonomy within the Indian Union and noninterference in their culture, administration, and politics. Subsequent political developments, however, caused discontent among them. Reminding people that the status of Kashmir was still undecided in the United Nations, disgruntled Kashmiri leaders revived the demand for a plebiscite. The *mirwaiz* ("chief priest") of the Hazratbal mosque in Srinagar (summer capital of the state) who had earlier migrated to Pakistan-controlled Kashmir returned to Kashmir and became the rallying point for pro-Pakistan elements. A separatist sentiment thus began to grow in Kashmir, which Pakistan sedulously fostered.

India responded to Pakistan's seditious and secessionist activity in Kashmir by tightening its political and administrative control over the state and vastly enlarging its military and police presence there. However, Muslims resented the consequent dilution of their special status, and Sheikh Abdullah, their most influential leader, who had supported the state's accession to India and was at that time prime minister of the state, raised the issue of Kashmir's right of self-determination. During a meeting (January 1948) with Warren Austin, the U.S. representative at the United Nations, he pointed out "that there is a third alternative, namely, independence. ... He did not want his people torn by dissensions between India and Pakistan" (Bhattacharjea, 1994, p. 181). On July 13, 1953, he openly declared that it was not necessary for Jammu and Kashmir to become an appendage of either India or Pakistan (Verma, 1994, p. 46). He was dismissed and arrested on August 8, 1953, for his antinational activities.

The autocratic regime (1953–62) of the next prime minister of Jammu and Kashmir, Bakshi Ghulam Mohammed, further eroded the state's autonomy and suppressed political dissent. In 1955, Mirza Afzal Beg, Sheikh Abdullah's lieutenant, launched a political party, the All India Jammu and Kashmir Plebiscite Front, to struggle for a plebiscite for determining the future of Kashmir. Bakshi rigged the elections to the legislative assembly in 1957 to keep pro-plebiscite elements out of the legislature. On his release from prison in 1958, Sheikh Abdullah promptly issued a statement demanding plebiscite and the right of self-determination. He was again arrested. From now on, influential Kashmiri political and religious leaders constantly drilled into the public mind the ideas of separation and independence of Kashmir or its merger with Pakistan.

These ideas gained strength from several other circumstances. The supercilious attitude and conduct of non-Kashmiri officials of the federal police and military forces, who served in large numbers in Kashmir, hurt the Kashmiri pride: The Muslims regarded these forces as an army of occupation. They also felt that they were suspects being watched by the Indian intelligence agencies. They saw establishment (January 1965) of a state unit of the Congress party that controlled the federal government as an Indian imposition on the state politics and organized widespread protests in Kashmir. Recognizing the growing resentment among the people, Jai Prakash Narain, an eminent national leader, wrote to the Indian prime minister in 1966: "We profess democracy, but rule by force in Kashmir. ... The problem exists not because Pakistan wants to grab Kashmir, but because there is deep political discontent among the people" (Verma, 1994, p. 53).

Pakistan's severe defeat in the 1971 war with India presented an opportunity for settling the Kashmir problem. The people of Kashmir realized that Pakistan could not acquire Kashmir by force, and a plebiscite was no longer possible. Sheikh Abdullah made the Kashmir accord with India in 1975, under which he abandoned the title of prime minister and the demand for self-determination, changed the name of his party from the Plebiscite Front to National Conference, and accepted the post of chief minister of the state. As he was immensely popular on account of his struggle for preserving Kashmir's cultural and political identity (he was known as the Lion of Kashmir), the vast majority of the people supported him, and there was considerable peace in Kashmir. He died in 1982, and his son, Farooq Abdullah, became the state chief minister.

However, subsequent political developments reversed the process of normalization and created conditions for an armed revolt. The State Unit of the Congress party encouraged a revolt in Farooq Abdullah's National Conference party. Reduced to a minority, his government fell in 1984, and G. M. Shah, leader of the defectors, became chief minister with the support of the Congress legislators in the state and blessings of the Indian government. There was a wave of protest against this "political skullduggery," in which India got directly involved (Marwah, 1995, p. 55). G. M. Shah was sacked in March 1986, and the governor's rule was promulgated, followed by an arrangement between the government of India and Farooq Abdullah to reinstate the latter as chief minister and restore the Congress party to power. This aroused so much resentment that anti-India Islamic groups in September 1986 formed the Muslim United Front (MUF) to challenge Farooq Abdullah and the Congress in elections. Cessation of political interference by the Indian government was one of the demands in their election manifesto.

Installed as chief minister in November 1986 and heading a coalition government, in which the Congress was a partner, Farooq Abdullah was generally perceived to have rigged the state assembly election in 1987 and won an unexpectedly huge majority. Even the Congress, having little following in Kashmir, won five of the six seats it contested. The MUF was deprived of several seats, which it was confident of winning. The participation of the MUF in the state legislature would have diverted its leaders' rebellious tendencies into democratic channels to India's ultimate advantage. Denied this opportunity, they chose the terrorist path and became the nucleus of violent militancy in Kashmir. Several of the Muslim political parties, which had been components of the MUF, formed militant wings.

Many of the militants were the disappointed political workers and traditional opponents of the National Conference in the 1987 elections. Young
men, aged sixteen and twenty-five, they came from the towns of Srinagar,
Anantnag, Pulwama, Kupwara and Baramulla. Unlike their forbears who had
campaigned for education and political rights in the 1930s, the majority were
well-educated—doctors, engineers, teachers, policemen—who had become
alienated by Indian government policies in New Delhi and lack of job opportunities. Their grievances were as much economic as political. (Schofield,
1997, p. 240)

Nearly 10,000 graduates were unemployed when the terrorist upsurge began
in Kashmir in 1989. Among those with school-leaving qualifications, unemployment was around 40,000–50,000 (Schofield, 1997, p. 239).

Terrorist incidents began in May 1987 with an assault on Farooq
Abdullah's motorcade in Srinagar. Sniper attacks were common throughout the year. The victory of the mujahideens against the Soviet Union in
Afghanistan in 1988 encouraged the Kashmiri militants, who went in large
numbers to Pakistan-controlled Kashmir for training and weapons for waging an armed struggle. Pakistan's Inter-Services Intelligence Directorate (ISI)
trained them and equipped them with weapons released from the Afghan
war. Violent protests grew in 1988. There were anti-India demonstrations and
police firings. The flash point came in December 1989, when the Indian government conceded the militants' demands and released five of them in return
for freeing their hostage, Rubaiya Sayeed, daughter of India's home minister.
This triggered an outburst of the Muslims' accumulated disaffection. The
Muslims believed that if militants could humble India, then independence
was achievable. They rejoiced and danced in the streets. Henceforth, the terrorist movement rapidly grew with popular support.

To stem the unrest, India promulgated (January 19, 1990) the governor's rule in the state. The same night, there were house-to-house searches,
and 300 arrests were made in Srinagar that evoked huge protests the next
day (January 20l 1990). In this inflamed atmosphere, security forces shot
and killed many protestors at Gawakadal Bridge in Srinagar, causing an
upsurge of public anger in major towns of Kashmir. Thousands would
gather in the streets, chanting "Indian dogs, go back," "we want freedom."
"With this incident, militancy entered a new phase. It was no longer a
fight between the militants and the security forces. It gradually assumed
the form of a total insurgency of the entire population" (Puri, 1993, p.
60). During February, March, and April 1990, there were daily protest
marches. The revolt spread when the Indian army shot dead (March 1,
1990) 17 unarmed protestors in Srinagar, and a federal police force killed
(May 21, 1990) many unarmed mourners accompanying the dead body of

a Muslim leader, Mirwaiz Maulvi Farooq, in Srinagar. As a security expert has stated:

> Few acts of a government inflame anti-government sentiments more than police firings on unarmed mobs, resulting in a large number of casualties. The management and dispersal of these mobs could not have been worse, even if allowance is made for the very difficult situation prevailing then. Without this upsurge in the hostility of the people against the government, militancy and terrorism might not have engulfed the state so completely. The maximum recruitment to terrorist groups took place in December 1989 and during the first few months of 1990. (Marwah, 1995, p. 89)

Dimensions of the Terrorist Movement

Terrorism Defined

The U.S. Code of Federal Regulations defines *terrorism* as "unlawful use of force and violence against persons or property to intimidate or coerce a government, the civilian population, or any segment thereof, in furtherance of political or social objectives." All these elements are manifest in the terrorist movement in Jammu and Kashmir. Its objectives are to wage a holy war against what they perceive as an oppressive non-Muslim regime; separate Kashmir from India and merge it with Pakistan; drive out Hindu and Sikh minorities; and turn the land into a region of Islamic fundamentalism. The methods of the terrorists include attacks on the police and other security forces; disruption of administrative, social, and political activity; and terrorizing the civilian population by large-scale killings and destruction of public and private property.

Terrorist Organizations and Their Foreign Links

The terrorist movement was initially led by Kashmiri youth, who were trained and armed in Pakistan-controlled Kashmir. During 1989–1991, they formed militant groups and conducted a ferocious campaign of terror. They killed civilians and public servants, kidnapped individuals for ransom or release of their accomplices, and forced the mass exodus of Hindus from Kashmir. However, the indigenous movement weakened when the army and police forces gained the upper hand in 1992–1993, and most of these groups became defunct. The movement has since been controlled by foreign jihadis (Islamist warriors). In December 1993, during a state visit to Pakistan, Maulana Araslan Rahmani, the deputy prime minister of Afghanistan, acknowledged that Afghanistan had played a major role in uniting Islamist organizations, Harkat ul-Jehad al-Islami (HUJI) and Harkat ul-Mujahideen (HUM), into the potent Harkat ul-Ansar group for fighting in Kashmir. According to Rahmani, this merger was part of the active support given by Afghanistan to the Islamist fighters in Kashmir, Tajikistan, Bosnia, Palestine, and elsewhere (McCollum, 1994).

According to a report of Peter Chalk, an expert on terrorism at the Rand Corporation, Washington, D.C., Pakistan provides training and logistical, financial, and doctrinal support to Kashmiri insurgents. Numerous training camps have been identified in Pakistan-controlled Kashmir. Basic courses are run on weapons handling, demolition, and urban sabotage. Selected militants are trained in special skills, such as use of heavy arms, reconnaissance, and sniper assaults. Most of the camps are located near major Pakistani military establishments, which, according to Indian intelligence, provide the bulk of the military resources, including weapons, ammunition, explosives, binoculars, night vision devices, communications, and uniforms. The report says that the annual ISI expenditure on sustaining militancy in Jammu and Kashmir is between US$125 and US$250 million. Pakistan remains a center of ideological indoctrination for the Kashmir struggle, which is largely coordinated through its numerous madrassas, the theological schools. Trainers in these schools equate the concept of jihad—holy war or striving for justice—with guerrilla warfare. Jihadi warriors are trained to fight for capturing Kashmir for Pakistan and the Islamic cause. The ISI "has sought to specifically replicate and transplant the success of the anti-Soviet Afghan campaign in Kashmir, exhorting foreign militants to participate in the conflict as part of the wider moral duty owed to the jehad" (Chalk, 2001).

In recent years, four major groups have been active in Jammu and Kashmir: HUM, Jaish-e-Mohammed (JEM), Lashkar-e-Taiba (LET), and Hizb ul-Mujahidin (HM). With the exception of HM, these are nonindigenous organizations, and their leaders and activists are mostly foreigners. Formerly known as the Harkat ul-Ansar (HUA), the HUM is an Islamic militant group based in Muzaffarabad and Rawalpindi. It trained its cadres in Pakistan and Afghanistan, and its members were mostly Pakistanis and Kashmiris and included Afghans and Arab veterans of the Afghan war. It conducted many operations in Kashmir in the 1990s. It was linked to the Kashmiri militant group Al-Faran that kidnapped five Western tourists in Kashmir in July 1995. It collects donations from Saudi Arabia and other Gulf and Islamic states and from Pakistanis and Kashmiris. Its head (amir) was Fazlur Rehman Khalil, who was linked to Osama Bin Laden and signed his fatwa in February 1998, calling for attacks on U.S. and Western interests. He turned over the command of the HUM to Farooq Kashmiri in February 2000. In 2000, the HUA was reported to be operating in Kashmir under the name of HUM, having several thousand armed members in Pakistan-controlled Kashmir, Pakistan, and Indian Kashmir (U.S. Department of State, 2000).

The JEM (Army of Mohammed) was formed in 2000 by Maulana Masood Azhar, an HUA leader, after his release from captivity in India. It is aligned with the pro-Taliban political party in Pakistan, Jamiat-e-Ulema-e-Islam, Fazlur Rehman faction (JUI-F). It is based in Peshawar and Muzaffarabad, but its members have conducted terrorist activities primarily in Kashmir. The JEM maintained training camps in Afghanistan until the fall of 2001. Most of its cadres and material resources have been drawn from two militant groups, HUJI and HUM. It has close ties with Afghan Arabs and the Taliban, and Bin Laden was suspected of funding it. It collects funds by seeking donations in magazines and pamphlets. It has several hundred armed members located in Pakistan-controlled Kashmir, Pakistan, and Jammu and Kashmir (Terrorist Group Profiles, 2003).

The LET (Army of the Pure) is the armed wing of the Pakistani religious organization Markaz ud-Dawa-wal-Irshad (MDI), which recruited volunteers to fight alongside the Taliban in Afghanistan (Council on Foreign Relations, 2004). The LET is led by Abdul Wahid Kashmiri and is one of the largest and best-trained groups fighting in Kashmir, and almost all its cadres are foreigners—mostly Pakistanis from madrassas and Afghan veterans of the Afghan war. Its camps are in Muzaffarabad and Muridke. It collects donations from the Pakistan community in the Persian Gulf and United Kingdom, Islamic nongovernment organizations, and Pakistani and Kashmiri businesspeople. It also maintains a website (under the name of its parent organization, ud-Dawa), through which it solicits funds and provides information on the group's activities (Federation of American Scientists, 2003a).

The HM group was founded in 1989. It officially supports the liberation of Kashmir and its accession to Pakistan. Led by Syed Salahuddin, it mostly consists of ethnic Kashmiris. It also has Pakistani links, as it is the militant wing of the Pakistan-based Islamic organization Jamaat-e-Islami. It reportedly operated in Afghanistan through the mid-1990s and trained alongside the Afghan Hizb-i-Islami Gulbuddin (HIG) in Afghanistan until the Taliban takeover (Federation of American Scientists, 2003b). It is estimated to have several hundred members in Jammu and Kashmir and Pakistan. Occasionally, inactive or unknown terrorist outfits also come to notice for violent activities. Al Mansoorian, believed to be a new name of the LET, claimed responsibility for attacking the residence of the chief minister of the state on October 18, 2003. The same day, a district court in Delhi sentenced three members of HUJI to 10 years of imprisonment for hatching a conspiracy to kill the president of India and abduct two prominent Indian sportsmen (*The Hindu*, 2003j). The HUA resurfaced in Kashmir when one of its battalion commanders was killed in an encounter on September 7, 2003 (*Hindustan Times*, 2003i).

Coordination and Conflict between Terrorist Groups

Reports indicate an operational nexus between the JEM and LET and their common links with other fundamentalist organizations in Pakistan. A major militant group, Sipah-e-Sahaba, is a loose alliance of Islamic groups that includes the JEM and LET (World News, 2002). Since Pakistan outlawed these groups, attacks in Kashmir and Pakistan have often been carried out under other guises. One group calling itself al-Qanoon or Lashkar-e-Omar is thought to be a coalition of members of JEM, LET, and other Pakistan-based Islamist groups, including the anti-Shiite Lashkar-e-Jhangvi organization (Council on Foreign Relations, 2004). The Indian government also publicly implicated the JEM along with the LET for the attack on the Indian parliament on December 13, 2001. Differences arose between the HM's Pakistan-based leaders and its several commanders in Jammu and Kashmir (Federation of American Scientists, 2003b). A dominant faction of the HM was merged with the Hizb-i-Islami after it broke away from the HM leader, Syed Salahuddin (*The Hindu*, 2003h). The JEM also split in June 2003 after its chief, Masood Azhar, expelled 12 leaders (*Hindustan Times*, 2003g). Maulana Umar Farooq is the head of this faction, known as Jamat-e-Furqan, and he directs its militant activities in Kashmir. No credible reports are available on the impact of these internal differences on the terrorist movement.

Number of Terrorists

The exact number of terrorists present in Jammu and Kashmir is not known as they adopt elusive tactics and move stealthily. No one on the Indian side knows how many come from, or go to, Pakistan-controlled Kashmir, where they receive training, weapons, and money. However, they have a large and strong presence in the state. A senior army officer stated in 2003: "From a purely military assessment, infiltration has not stopped. It continues to be at the same rate as last year. They (terrorists) are all over" (*Hindustan Times*, 2003f, p. 1). Nearly 3,000 terrorists are estimated to be currently present in the state. Local Muslim youth continue to join their ranks.

When the local terrorist movement flagged in Kashmir in the early 1990s, the ISI increasingly inducted foreign fighters to bolster it. The governor of Jammu and Kashmir estimated in 2002 that foreign militants constituted 50% of the terrorists in the state (*The Hindu*, 2002a). Although this assessment is not corroborated, the number of foreign militants killed since 1993 had definitely grown, as shown in Table 13.1.

Table 13.1   Table Title?

Year	Total Terrorists Killed by Security Services	Foreign Terrorists Killed by Security Services	Foreign Terrorists % of Total Terrorists Killed
Up to August 31, 2003	919	483	69.60
2002	1,707	1,063	62.3
2001	2,020	1,198	58.8
2000	1,520	870	53.9
1999	1,082	548	50.6
1998	999	406	40.6
1997	1,075	260	24.2
1996	1,209	213	17.6
1995	1,332	77	5.7
1994	1,596	77	4.8
1993	1,310	79	6.0
1992	819	6	0.73
1991	844	2	0.2
1990	550	0	0.0
Total	16,982	5,282	—

Source: Indian Army. (2003). http://www.armyinkashmir.org/militant.html

Weaponry

Terrorism began as an urban struggle in the narrow streets and lanes of cities and towns of Kashmir, for which the main weapons used were AK-47 Kalashnikovs, AKs-56 (Chinese version of AK-47), and hand grenades. In 1991–1992, the police forces deployed overwhelming manpower, conducted intensive patrolling, and manned sandbagged bunkers and pickets round the clock at crossroads, bridges, and other strategic points. These measures blunted the enemy assaults during close encounters. From 1993 onward, the police forces also started using AK-47s, which were more effective for close-quarter combat than their standard weapons, the 9-mm automatic carbines and the semiautomatic 7.62 self-loading rifles (SLRs). Meanwhile, terror had spread to rural mountainous areas, and the ISI supplied sniper rifles, machine guns, and rocket-propelled grenades, mostly of Russian and Chinese make, for attacking the security forces at long range. Among the weapons used by terrorists are 107-mm rockets, 60-mm mortars, and 40-mm automatic grenade launchers (Soviet and Chinese models). In April 1998, police forces seized a 127-mm antiaircraft gun in Kupwara district of Kashmir (*The Times of India*, 1998). According to the police, militants possess surface-to-surface missiles and Pakistan-made plastic-tube improvised explosive devices marked "Shaheen," which can blow up vehicles by remote control (*The*

Hindu, 1999). On December 13, 2002, a shoulder-fired Anza Mark-I SAM (surface-to-air missile) was discovered in Kupwara (*Hindustan Times*, 2002h). Anza is a heat-seeking missile of the Stinger type, having a range of 4.2 kilometers and usable against aircraft. Table 13.2, showing the weapons and ammunition seized by the security forces during 1990–2001, indicates the terrorists' firepower.

Operational Tactics and Skills

Terrorists employ guerilla and military tactics, including hit-and-run strikes, raids, ambush, and use of mines and remote-controlled explosives for destroying troops and vehicles. Their expert use of weapons, timing of attacks, and selection of targets and terrain indicate a high level of professionalism. They use the narrow and winding lanes and by-lanes of urban areas to strike by surprise and melt away in crowded areas. They use the hills, forests, and gullies of the mountainous terrain for their hideouts and ambushes. They undertake dangerous suicidal (fidayeen) missions. The deadliest fidayeen assault so far has been the bombing of the Jammu and Kashmir legislature on October 1, 2001, when a suicide bomber rammed a car full of explosives into the main gate of the building, killing 29 persons, including 5 policemen (*CNN*, 2001). They also engage the Indian army and police forces in regular encounters and exhibit a high degree of tactical skill and grit in such situations. For instance, on November 4, 2001, three LET fighters attacked an army camp at village Batapora in Anantnag district, Kashmir. They killed four soldiers and injured six during a long gun-fight with the army. The army shot one terrorist, but the other two escaped after inflicting more casualties on the army (*Hindustan Times*, 2001b). On May 14, 2002, three terrorists shot their way into an army camp at Kaluchak near Jammu. The encounter with soldiers lasted 4 hours, until the army used rocket launchers to finish them off (*Hindustan Times*, 2002b). On July 18, 2002, three terrorists hiding in Banihal town on the Jammu-Srinagar highway engaged army and police units for 10 hours. They injured two army officers, seven soldiers, and three policemen before they were shot (*Hindustan Times*, 2002c).

Areas of Operation

Organized terror was largely an urban movement in the Kashmir valley during the first 2 years of militancy (1989–1990). It reached Doda district in 1992 and soon spread to other districts in the Jammu region. The aim of launching militancy in the Jammu region is to expel Hindus from its largely Muslim areas, such as Doda, Poonch, and Rajouri, and to ease the pressure on terrorists in Kashmir by engaging Indian troops elsewhere (*India Today*,

Table 13.2 Equipment Seized by Indian Policing Agencies 1990–2003

Type of Arms	1990	1991	1992	1993	1994	1995	1996	1997	1998	1999	2000	2001	2002	Up to Sept. 15, 2003	Total
Assault rifle	1,240	2,320	3,504	2,209	2,196	2,055	2,150	1,725	1,520	1,244	1,405	1,646	1,571	974	25,759
Machine gun	77	151	165	154	152	76	102	81	81	59	51	43	22	27	1,240
Rocket launcher	173	112	159	78	115	80	91	119	244	186	112	192	108	103	1,873
Sniper rifle	—	—	9	54	41	38	49	60	34	13	16	12	7	6	339
Mortar	—	—	—	4	3	3	1	6	7	17	2	76	34	30	184
Pistol	751	849	756	921	940	965	1,052	1,024	584	385	482	370	308	244	9,631
Radio set	—	—	29	132	211	246	413	444	583	409	460	462	503	488	4,340
Grenade	2,502	1,784	2,391	4,363	2,603	2,870	3,949	5,124	5,883	6,000	7,955	5,956	3,477	3,063	58,381
Ammunition (million rounds)	0.188	0.272	0.321	0.313	0.456	0.343	0.356	0.294	0.321	0.220	0.309	2.941	0.147	0.122	6.603
Mines (antipersonnel and tank)	750	136	226	592	1,006	634	552	408	541	305	386	264	111	160	6,071
Antiaircraft guns	—	—	—	—	—	—	—	—	1	—	—	—	—	—	1
Missile launchers	—	—	—	—	—	—	—	1	1	2	1	1	—	—	5
Flamethrowers	—	—	—	—	—	—	—	—	21	6	52	—	—	7	86
Explosives (kg)	231	274	285	2,950	1,342	1,489	2,487	6,790	3,691	3,233	3,469	3,714	1,765	1,913	33,681
Improvised explosive devices	—	18	86	136	126	811	245	1,020	514	466	718	11	—	—	4,151
Assorted weapons	—	—	—	—	—	—	—	—	—	16	24	—	—	—	1,128

Source: Indian Army. (2003). http:/www.armyinkashmir.org/militant.html

2001). Terrorists now operate in urban and rural areas all over the state and have extended their activity to other states of India. They attacked the Indian parliament at New Delhi on December 13, 2001, and killed six police personnel and two civilians before they were shot down (*The Times of India*, 2001). They hit the U.S. Center in Kolkata on January 22, 2002, killing four policemen. On September 24, 2002, they attacked a Hindu temple in Gandhinagar, capital of Gujarat, killing 32 persons and injuring 70 (*The Hindu*, 2002e).

Targets

The main targets of the terrorists are personnel of the police forces and army, their headquarters, army camps, and residential areas. On January 24, 1992, they planted a bomb in the office of the director general of Jammu and Kashmir State Police, which gravely injured him and three other senior police officers. On July 31, 2002, they entered a high-security residential complex of senior police and civil officers in Rajouri, Jammu region. They lobbed grenades at the policemen on duty and later engaged an army column in a gun battle. An Indian army captain and four terrorists died in this encounter (*SifyNews*, 2002a). Six major attacks on army camps have so far occurred: November 1999, Badami Bagh cantonment, Srinagar (10 soldiers killed); January 12, 2000, Anantnag camp (12 soldiers killed); September 12, 2000, Beerwah camp (12 soldiers killed); May 13, 2002, Kaluchak cantonment (24 persons, including 10 children, 8 women, and 5 soldiers killed); June 28, 2003, Sunjwan camp (12 soldiers killed); and July 22, 2003, Tanda camp (9 soldiers killed) (*Hindustan Times*, 2003h). The most audacious of these strikes was at Tanda, in which a brigadier died and two lieutenant generals, two major generals, and a brigadier of the Indian army received injuries (*The Hindu*, 2003i).

Terrorists hit symbols of government authority, such as storming the state legislature at Srinagar on October 1, 2001, and the Indian parliament at New Delhi on December 13, 2001. They also attack political leaders and try to sabotage political activity. They tried to disrupt the state assembly election during September–October 2002 because Pakistan wanted the people to boycott the election. On September 11, 2002, they killed Mushtaq Ahmed Lone, the state law minister, and seven others, including three security men, at an election meeting in Kupwara district. The same day, 10 personnel of the police forces and 2 civilians were killed near an election rally in Surankote town, Poonch district (*Hindustan Times*, 2002e). The third phase of the election was particularly gruesome, with about 30 lethal strikes on a single day (*Hindustan Times*, 2002g). These included an attack on a bus in Kathua district in the Jammu region in which eight civilians died and an ambush on a vehicle in Pulwama, Kashmir, in which six soldiers of a federal police force were killed (*Hindustan Times*, 2002g).

The Hindu and Sikh minorities have been targeted for ethnic cleansing. On March 20, 2000, terrorists massacred 35 Sikhs at the village of Chattisinghpura in Kashmir (*The Hindu*, 2002b). On August 5, 2002, they attacked Hindu pilgrims on their way to the Amarnath cave, the holiest Hindu shrine in Kashmir, killing 9 and injuring 33 (*Hindustan Times*, 2002d). Hafiz Saeed, Pakistan-based chief of LET, has declared that killing Hindus was a part of their jihad against India (*The Hindu*, 2003d). Therefore, they also attacked non-Kashmiri Hindus working or travelling in the state. The largest such killing was of 38 Hindu migrant laborers on July 13, 2002, at a shantytown near Jammu city ("Kashmir—12 Women, Child Killed," 2002). Muslim government employees, public functionaries, suspected police informants, or those who deny shelter and food to terrorists also become their victims. On August 28, 2001, five members of a Muslim family, including two women and two infants, were shot in Poonch district (*Hindustan Times*, 2001a). On April 10, 2002, terrorists killed five members of a Muslim family and injured four in Doda district (*Hindustan Times*, 2002a). On August 24, 2002, they gunned down 12 Muslims, including three women, in three separate strikes in Rajouri and Doda districts (*The Hindu*, 2002c).

The Indian army has collected evidence of the attempts of the terrorists to turn Kashmir into a fundamentalist Islamic society. In 2001, the LET directed that women should wear full-bodied veils (burkas) and has tried to enforce the dress code with singular cruelty. On July 23, 2001, they abducted and gang raped a 16-year-old girl of Batpora Sallar, Anantnag district. On August 2, 2001, they killed a young woman in the same village. On August 3, 2001, they shot and critically injured a Muslim girl in the village of Bulbul, Nowgam, Kupwara district. On August 7, 2001, they threw acid on the faces of two young women teachers at a school in Srinagar (Indian Army, 2001). All these victims had violated the LET's dress code.

Recent Terrorist Activity and Future Trends

The pattern of terrorist strikes indicates that the terrorist groups lower or intensify their activity according to the policy of Pakistan. The number of terrorist strikes declined after the assembly election held in the fall of 2002, as it was a watch-and-wait situation for Pakistan. However, violence grew after Pakistan declared Kashmir as the "cornerstone" of its foreign policy on March 12, 2003 (*The Hindu*, 2003b). On March 14, 2003, terrorists killed a deputy superintendent of police and a police head constable in Poonch town (*The Hindu*, 2003c). On March 15, 2003, they attacked a police post in Udhampur district in the Jammu region, killing 11 policemen (*Hindustan Times*, 2003b). They shot dead 30 Hindus on March 24, 2003, at Shopian town in Kashmir (*Hindustan Times*, 2003c). On April 26, 2003, they stormed the state-owned Srinagar radio station and blew up an explosive-laden car at its gate. Three terrorists, two soldiers, and a civilian official died in the ensuing gun battle (*The Hindu*, 2003e). On April 29, 2003, they engaged the army in Doda district. Thirteen terrorists and six soldiers died in this encounter (*Hindustan Times*, 2003d).

At present, the terrorist violence is low, apparently because of a thaw in India's relations with Pakistan. However, terrorists still murder people and hit security forces and government establishments to show their striking capability and keep the Kashmir issue alive. On October 18, 2003, they attacked the official residence of the state chief minister, killing two security personnel and injuring three (*Hindustan Times*, 2003l). On February 27, 2004, the chief minister escaped an assassination bid at a public meeting. A girl died and eight persons were injured in this assault (*The Hindu*, 2004a). On March 3, 2004, the LET attacked the Jammu district jail in an attempt to free some under-trial prisoners, mostly Pakistani nationals, killing six persons, including four policemen (*The Hindu*, 2004b). On January 1, 2005, a deputy inspector general of the state police and five other police officials were wounded in a powerful explosion caused by an improvised explosive device (*The Hindu*, 2005). On January 7, 2005, the Al-ansoorian claimed responsibility for a fidayeen raid on the income tax office in Srinagar, in which three persons, including an officer and a soldier of federal police forces, were killed, and six soldiers of these forces were wounded (*Hindustan Times*, 2005). Pakistan has not closed the jihadi training-cum-staging camps. Although it banned the JEM and LET in January 2002 under pressure from the United States, it subsequently released from custody prominent figures in both organizations (*The Wall Street Journal*, 2003). Syed Salahuddin, Rawalpindi-based chief of HM, stated on May 18, 2003, that his organization would continue the jihad in Kashmir (*The Hindu*, 2003f). Major indicators show that terrorism would continue in Kashmir, and deterioration in the relations between India and Pakistan would in all likelihood intensify terrorist violence.

Counterterrorist Strategy and Tactics

The counterterrorism strategy is simply to hunt down the terrorists. L. K. Advani, India's home minister, spelled it out on Independence Day, 1998: "We are satisfied with the progress we are making. Daily eight to ten militants are being eliminated. The process of attrition is on. ... There is no other solution but just to eliminate the terrorists" (Amnesty International, 1999). The tactics consist of area domination through massive deployment of force on the ground, quick reaction to terrorist attacks for engaging the adversary, and preventive raids on hideouts and caches of arms after developing intelligence obtained from arrested terrorists or their associates. The entire focus is on curbing terrorism by decimating the terrorists and preventing terrorist attacks.

Deployment of the Police Forces

Clear territorial jurisdictions and operational tasks have been allocated to the Jammu and Kashmir police and the federal police forces. There was considerable subversion of personnel of the state police in Kashmir in 1989–1992. It was also an ill-trained and ill-equipped force unequal to the terrorist onslaught and was mostly deployed for routine police work. It now has some commando companies, which conduct joint operations along with other forces. It also provides intelligence to facilitate counterterrorist action. However, the main responsibility of combating terrorists has been with the Indian military and police forces. The army guards the line of control between Jammu and Kashmir and Pakistan-controlled Kashmir. Its counterinsurgency force, Raashtriya Rifles, conducts operations in the hinterland for short periods on specific information. Two federal police forces, Border Security Force (BSF) and Central Reserve Police Force (CRPF), are stationed in large strength on a long-term basis in cities and towns that are the hub of terrorist activity. They deploy their men in pickets or in bunkers in section or half-section strength every 200–300 yards. Each battalion has its tactical headquarters and the company/platoon headquarters within its area of deployment. These forces also conduct operations in the rural areas falling within their respective jurisdictions. Operational coordination has developed between the different police forces and between the police and military, and joint operations are frequently organized.

Tasks and Tactics

The police forces use defensive and offensive tactics. They guard vulnerable places and vital installations, such as the residences of the governor and chief minister, power plants, telecommunication centers, radio/TV stations, major bridges, and the vital Jawahar tunnel, providing the only all-weather road link from India to Kashmir. They deploy road-opening parties (RoPs) to secure roads used by VIPs and police and military convoys. Foot patrols are sent out daily from the company/platoon headquarters into streets, lanes, by-lanes, marketplaces, and residential areas to show police presence and encourage civilian activity. The offensive action is in the form of quick retaliation in the event of a terrorist attack. Reinforcements are called, the area surrounding the scene is cordoned, and a search for the culprits starts. Suspects are detained, causing fear among their relations that they would be tortured in interrogation centers. Meanwhile, there would be another terrorist strike, causing fatalities among civilians, civil servants, or security personnel, and the same pattern of counteraction would be repeated. During the early phase of militancy (1990–1993), there were almost daily terrorist attacks, armed encounters with terrorists, and cordoning and searching of entire localities. The frequency of such counteraction has now declined with fewer militant hits.

Conduct and Behavior of the Police Forces

While the people take advantage of the substantial peace and security brought about by the federal police forces in Kashmir to conduct their daily activity, they abhor these forces for their excesses committed against the civilian population. The police abuses have occurred for various reasons.

Most personnel of these police forces do not belong to Jammu and Kashmir. They do not understand the Kashmiri language, the depth of fear of terrorists and of the police forces existing among the masses, or the people's anger over the police excesses. They mistake the sullen aloofness of Kashmiris as unwillingness to cooperate or a sign of complicity with terrorists. If a soldier were shot by a terrorist in a crowded area, they usually suspected that Muslim residents were concealing the terrorist's presence. The prejudice, which such suspicion aroused among them, has often triggered abuse of force against Muslims. On January 6, 1993, fifty persons were killed in Sopore town, allegedly after the BSF used excess lethal force in retaliation against a grenade attack in which two BSF soldiers were injured. On October 22, 1993, thirty-one civilian demonstrators were killed and 73 injured when the BSF retaliated against alleged shooting by militants in Bijbehara town, Kashmir. A BSF court of inquiry held several of its personnel responsible for excessive use of force.

Sometimes, the use of lethal force by the police forces appears to be wanton. In 1990, a BSF party raided a house in Mashali Mohalla in Srinagar and killed nine members of a family in a senseless shooting. The charge sheet given to the concerned officials accused them of murder. Following the killing of 35 Sikhs in the village of Chattisinghpura in Kashmir on March 20, 2000, a police and paramilitary joint team lodged a report with the police on May 25, 2000, that they had encountered and killed five foreign terrorists responsible for the massacre of Sikhs. When local citizens organized a protest alleging that these were fake encounters, CRPF and local police shot and killed nine of them. The chief minister later declared that the forensic test of the DNA samples of the deceased had established that the five killed on May 25, 2000, were civilians and not foreign terrorists (*The Hindu*, 2002b). On January 13, 2003, people of Bandipora town in Kashmir organized a protest march alleging wanton shooting of a youth by a security force (*The Hindu*, 2003a).

Unrestrained shooting also occurs due to command-and-control failures. A local commander would lose his nerve or temper and order shooting. The shooting at an unarmed crowd at Gawakadal Bridge in Srinagar on January 20, 1990, mentioned previously was one such incident. Another occurred on May 21, 1990, when hundreds of agitated mourners carrying the dead body of their slain leader to the burial ground in Srinagar became unruly, and a curfew was announced in the area without any preparation for enforcing it.

> It was left to a CRPF picket comprising a head constable and eight constables at Hawal near Islamia College to disperse the frenzied mourners. The CRPF picket panicked when they saw the huge procession menacingly advancing towards them. Sensing danger they fired indiscriminately, killing many of the mourners. (Marwah, 1995, p. 101)

Indeed, the use of excessive force due to panic reaction under danger has been the standard response of the security forces. Each time a patrol on foot or vehicle came under attack, troops would mechanically fire weapons at hand, and innocent civilians were frequently hit in retaliatory fire. *Time* magazine carried the photograph of a 22-year-old girl killed by Indian troops, "who shot wildly when a candidate's convoy struck a land mine" during the legislature election in the state (*Time*, 2002, p. 25).

There are also numerous complaints against the police and armed forces about custodial violence and disappearance of Muslims. The government acknowledges some of these. Mufti Mohammed Sayeed admitted in May 2003 that there had been four custodial deaths since he took over as chief minister of Jammu and Kashmir in October 2002 (*The Hindu*, 2003g). His daughter, Mehbooba Mufti, president of the ruling party in the state, observed on May 10, 2003, that "state terrorism" had not ceased, and that "for the past one month complaints of human rights violations by security forces are galore" (*Hindustan Times*, 2003e, p. 11). Even ordinary situations are handled in an unprofessional manner. On August 1, 2002, the army raided and searched late at night the Srinagar office of the BBC, which caused adverse publicity that was totally avoidable (*SifyNews*, 2002b). On September 1, 2002, Muhammed Jaleel, Srinagar bureau chief of a national daily, was beaten by the police when he went to inquire about an incident near his house (*The Hindu*, 2002d). Personnel of these forces have developed disregard for human life and human dignity in an area where death and destruction are a common occurrence.

Suggested Changes in Operational Strategy and Tactics

A fresh approach to policing in Jammu and Kashmir should be developed on three basic considerations. First, the terrorist movement is a long-term challenge for the police forces. Although the majority of the people are disgusted with the violence and bloodshed that has blighted their lives, Muslim youth continue to join the terrorist movement due to their deep frustrations and police excesses. Second, as the armed response to terrorism has not been employed carefully, it has led to civilian complaints. Custodial violence and unrestrained retaliation against terrorist strikes harm the counterterrorism effort more than the terrorists. A populace that feels harassed and humiliated will not cooperate with the security forces and would not readily give information about the terrorists. Third, the abuse of force, at least in professional terms, is a symptom of unskilled policing. On these bases, specific suggestions for refining the counterterrorism strategy and tactics are made in the subsequent paragraphs.

Attitudinal Change

The foremost requirement is to help the rank and file of the federal police forces to overcome their irrational dislike and distrust of the Muslims of Kashmir, who are primarily victims of the terrorist movement rather than its participants. "They have had their fill of war, which began 13 years ago as an indigenous rebellion against Indian rule and is sustained now by imported militants, who often indulge in sheer terrorism" (*The Economist*, 2002, pp. 26–27). The people also realize that Pakistan has failed in its attempt to wrest Kashmir through terrorism. The MORI (Market and Opinion Research International) poll conducted in April–May 2002 revealed that about 61% of the people of Jammu and Kashmir felt that they would be better off politically and economically as Indian citizens (*The Guardian*, 2002). Even some separatist leaders such as Mirwaiz Umar Farooq seem inclined to settle for autonomy of the state within the Indian Union (*The Economist*, 2002). These facts are hardly known to the troops. Better awareness of the situation would help the police personnel avoid harsh behavior toward the civilian population. This will in turn reduce the hostility of the people against the police forces.

Better Intelligence for Planning Operations

Reliable intelligence facilitates successful counterterrorist action and helps in minimizing harassment of innocent citizens. Unsuccessful operations have often been mounted on half-baked information, resulting in a waste of resources. Such operations also annoy the people of the locality where they are conducted and cause harassment to the persons targeted. An instance is the arrest and prosecution of a Kashmiri youth and journalist, Iftikhar Gilani, under the Official Secrets Act for having downloaded an article to his computer from the Internet, which showed movements of the Indian army in Jammu and Kashmir. The Ministry of Home Affairs, the nodal authority for counterterrorism in India, dropped the prosecution after the director general of military operations informed the court that the document in question, contrary to the claim of Delhi Police, was not secret or sensitive (*Hindustan Times*, 2003a). It is advisable to strike only when precise information is available, unless the quarry is so important that one cannot wait for confirmed intelligence.

Tactical Changes

Security Precautions for Minimizing Troop Casualties

Unrelenting pressure of work and performing the same operational duty every day generates fatigue, monotony, and laxity among troops. A temporary lull in the terrorist activity also makes them complacent and slack. Terrorists wait for such moments, catching soldiers off guard, for inflicting heavy casualties. Such situations, although not entirely preventable, can be substantially minimized if security is strengthened at police stations and military and police camps, which have been the targets of successful lethal attacks. The supervisory officers can ensure adequate alertness by regular, and sometimes by surprise, checking of the sentries and guards. Precautions are also necessary against attacks during movements of troops on foot or in vehicles. In 1991–1992, about 10 BSF soldiers were dying each month as they failed to take basic precautions while moving in the interior areas of cities. Various successful measures were then taken, such as parking vehicles away from crowded areas to evade grenade attacks, vigilance against enemy fire while shopping for the daily provisions for the troops, and mounting camouflage nets on trucks and bunkers to prevent injury from grenade assaults. In particular, cautious patrolling was practiced so that troops did not bunch up, but moved forward, two at a time, while the other members of the patrol would look out for danger and slowly follow them.

Cordon-and-Search Operations

A major reason for operational overreaction is the anxiety of junior officers to control the damage caused by terrorists. Sometimes they take hasty action because if they do not act promptly, then their superiors would brand them as lax or cowardly. They rush to the scene of a terrorist attack with their soldiers, cordon the area, call out reinforcements, fan out in the neighborhood, and launch searches for the elusive terrorists in lanes, by-lanes, and houses, causing considerable inconvenience to the residents. This was the usual pattern of counterterrorist operations during the early 1990s. Old men and women would sit out in the cold or drizzle, young men were isolated, and suspects among them would be taken to interrogation centers. The terrorist would slip away in all such cases, but the entire neighborhood became a captive herd. It is correct to send forces to the scene in the event of a terrorist attack to control the situation, reassure the people, and help victims of the terrorist strike. But, the decision to organize a cordon-and-search operation ought to be taken at a sufficiently high level of command, after due deliberation and assessing its utility. Similarly, troops often rush madly on hearing of a terrorist strike without appropriate planning and are ambushed. A professional response should be calculated. The sensible course of action is to think the way a terrorist thinks when the terrorist plans an attack and anticipate the terrorist's tactics to avoid casualties among the troops.

Management of Processions of Unarmed Protesters

The BSF and CRPF have often handled protests by unarmed agitators in Kashmir for which they lack suitable weaponry, training, tactics, and temperament. Being armed with semiautomatic and automatic weapons like carbines, AK-47s, and 7.62 SLRs, they have used excessive force for quelling protest marches and mourning processions. A security expert recalls, regarding the shooting of unarmed mourners in Srinagar on May 21, 1990, that the CRPF units had no tear gas and were not equipped with any other crowd control equipment, like ropes, mobile barricades, and batons. They only carried rifles (Marwah, 1995, p. 55). In 1991–1992, as inspector general of the BSF in Kashmir, I experienced a serious dilemma. Agitated women shouting slogans in a frenzy would advance menacingly and come threateningly close to the BSF troops. Shooting of unarmed persons was out of the question. As BSF troops carried only automatic and semiautomatic weapons, the idea of issuing batons to them for handling such situations was mooted. It was not accepted on the ground that the BSF, whose primarily role was guarding the international border against an external enemy, should not have nonlethal weapons. However, a sensitive environment like Kashmir calls for greater flexibility and improvisation for handling protest marches and unlawful assemblies. Forces like the BSF and CRPF that are deployed on long-term internal security duty in Jammu and Kashmir should be trained to handle crowds and protest marches with the help of nonlethal weapons, such as tear gas, batons, shields, stun grenades, dogs, and plastic bullets. Men with automatic weapons should be kept close by and can be brought into operation if unavoidable. Local commanders of these forces need intensive training in the skill of using calibrated force, increasing the quantum of force according to the level of the threat.

Avoiding Complaints of Misbehavior with Women

There are numerous complaints that police personnel have misbehaved with local women during their operations. There have often been molestation and rape of local women. The people understandably detest the police forces for such misconduct as much as for the killing of innocent persons. A practical solution is to carry along a section of the women police who can search women and their belongings. In 1991–1992, there was only a company of CRPF women soldiers in Kashmir, which was monopolized by the army for its operations. I proposed to the BSF headquarters to raise a battalion of women soldiers. The proposal was rejected on the ground that women had no place in a force meant to perform the hard duty of guarding the frontiers of the country. However, women soldiers in the BSF would be useful as more than half of this force is deployed on an internal security role on a long-term basis in civilian areas.

Denial of Funds to Terrorist Groups

Terrorist groups raise funds to buy arms, organize logistics, and aid the families of slain militants. It is believed that they rely heavily on hawala transactions to obtain money from abroad. Earlier, the police and intelligence agencies had not focused on this aspect. However, after September 11, 2001, they saw the United States freezing the finances of such outfits and have since activated their intelligence in this direction:

> The recovery of Rupees 50 lacs (equivalent to about one hundred thousand dollars) from a vehicle in Srinagar in Jammu and Kashmir in November 2001 and Rupees 35 lacs from Delhi in January 2002 are one result of the intensification of this drive. (Marwah, 2003, p. 336)

On September 11, 2003, the police arrested Nayeem Khan, a member of the general council of the Hurriyat Conference, a pro-Pakistan political group in Kashmir, on the charge of receiving Rs.9 lacs (approximately $20,000) through hawala transactions from the Pakistan-based militant outfit Jammu and Kashmir Islamic Front (*Hindustan Times*, 2003j). On September 16, 2003, Delhi police arrested a hawala trader on the charge of supplying Rs.200,000 (approximately $4,320) to Noor Mohammad Tantray, a JEM terrorist. Tantray and his two associates were also caught with a truck laden with weapons and ammunition (*Hindustan Times*, 2003k). Such operations should be intensified as they hurt the terrorists and enhance the counterterrorist effort.

Public Service

The police forces in Jammu and Kashmir are perceived as instruments of repression. This image can be changed through humanitarian service to the people. The army provides medical and other help to the people in the forward areas of Jammu and Kashmir, and these people in turn assist the army in many ways. The army's example can be followed by police forces in urban and rural areas for winning over the people. When the BSF troops were deployed for counterterrorism duty in the cities of Srinagar, Sopore, and Baramulla during autumn 1991, the people hated and avoided them completely. After pacifying these areas, the BSF established medical centers in two neighborhoods in Srinagar. After initial hesitation, many ailing people, especially women with gynecological complaints, started visiting these clinics. They received medical care and free medicines from the BSF doctors, and the BSF gained considerable goodwill of the people. Another area of public service is the recruitment of local educated youth in the federal police forces. The government started recruitment and training centers for the BSF and CRPF in Kashmir, and local youth began joining these forces. This generated employment for many educated youths of Kashmir, who received a salary during their training and could send money to their poor parents. Vigorous and systematic recruitment of Kashmiri youth in Indian security forces would provide an extraordinary opportunity for helping and fraternizing many local families.

Leadership Role

As the police are a hierarchical and militaristic organization, only senior officers can develop a more professional approach to counterterrorism. They alone can change the attitudes of their juniors and impart to them appropriate operational tactics and skills. However, there is no serious effort in these organizations to minimize the abuse of force. The police leaders either regard such aberration as isolated individual incidents or feel that their troops are fighting a grim battle and disciplinary action would demoralize them. Hence, they ignore police excesses unless their own command comes under scrutiny. Training is a tried method for achieving reform in police practices. It is also a major responsibility of the police leadership. Generally, a battalion coming from outside Jammu and Kashmir is deployed for counterterrorist operations after about 2 weeks of orientation training. The preinduction training of at least a month would be appropriate, which should simulate the real-life situations, including the terrain, hazards, and threats. Such training should also inculcate genuine concern among the troops for human rights.

Conclusion

Terrorists commit acts of extreme cruelty, some of which are calculated to provoke a brutal response from the police forces. Terrorists and their supporters highlight it as indiscriminate repression. It also alienates the people and creates popular sympathy for the terrorists' cause. The state government, aware of the adverse effect of the behavior of the police forces, has declared that there is need to provide a healing touch to the people. It has released a number of youths that were detained on minor charges of pursuing militant activities. It has also disbanded the Special Operations Group (SOG) of the state police, which had acquired notoriety for excesses. However, as the real fight against terrorism is being waged not by the state police but by the federal police forces, initiatives for improving the operational strategy and tactics have to be developed by these forces. The right approach would be to deal firmly with terrorists, which these forces are already doing, but to spare the innocent common man who is the victim of terrorism as much as of the zeal and overreaction of the police forces. The assembly elections held in 2002 amidst an environment of terror and fear recorded an impressive 44% voting. This was the people's vote against unrest and bloodshed as they were disgusted with the terrorist atrocities. This was a setback for the terrorists, and it presents an opportunity for the police forces to defeat terrorism by harnessing the people's yearning for peace. Therefore, while keeping the pressure on the terrorists, these forces can heal the wounds of a tormented and terrorized people by thoughtful policing. Skills and practices, such as exercising restraint in using lethal force, minimizing civilian casualties by eschewing a trigger-happy or recklessly authoritarian approach, avoiding needless house searches and detentions of Muslim youth, and taking proactive welfare measures to help the masses, can significantly help in weaning the people away from terrorism. Otherwise, the security forces would go on killing terrorists endlessly without any hope of killing terrorism.

References

Amnesty International. (1999). "Disappearances" in Jammu and Kashmir. Retrieved from http://web.amnesty.org/libraray/Index/eng20002199

Bhattacharjea, A. (1994). *Kashmir: The wounded valley* (p. 181). New Delhi, India: UBS.

Chalk, P. (2001). *Pakistan's role in the Kashmir insurgency.* Washington, DC: Rand. Retrieved from http://www23.brinkster.com/pakterror/pakistan-terrorism-kashmir.htm

CNN. (2001, October 1). Bombing at Kashmir assembly kills at least 29. Retrieved from http://cnn.com/2001/WORLD/asiapcf/south/10/01/india.kashmr/

Council on Foreign Relations. (2004). *Terrorism: Questions and answers. Kashmir militant extremists.* Retrieved from http://www.terrorismanswers.com/groups/harakat.html

The Economist. (2002, September 14). Kashmir's elections, a terrible beginning, pp. 26–27.

Federation of American Scientists. Intelligence Resource Program. (2003a, April 30). *Lashkar-e-Taiba/Lashkar-e-Tayyaba* (pp. 1–2). Retrieved from http://www.fas.org/irp/world/para/lashkar. htm

Federation of American Scientists. Intelligence Resource Program. (2003b, May 2). *Hizbul-Mujahidin* (p. 1). Retrieved from http://www.fas.org/irp/world/para/hm.htm

The Guardian. (2002, June 1). Majority would opt for Indian citizenship, says poll. Retrieved from http://www.guardian.co.uk/pakistan/Story/0,2763,725987,00

The Hindu, Indian national daily (1999, March 1). J&K militants equipped with hi-tech weapons, p. 5.

The Hindu. (2002a, April 22). External support sustaining militancy in J&K, p. 5.

The Hindu. (2002b, July 17). Security forces killed civilians, p. 5.

The Hindu. (2002c, August 25). 12 shot dead in Jammu, p. 1.

The Hindu. (2002d, September 2). Scribe beaten up in Srinagar, p. 5.

The Hindu. (2002e, September 26). Siege ends at temple, p. 1.

The Hindu. (2003a, January 14). Protest against killing of youth in J&K, p. 5.

The Hindu. (2003b, March 13). Kashmir cornerstone of Pak. foreign policy, p. 1.

The Hindu. (2003c, March 15). Fidayeen attack in Poonch: Two cops killed, p. 5.

The Hindu. (2003d, April 14). Killing Hindus is part of "jehad": Lashkar chief, p. 5.

The Hindu. (2003e, April 27). "Fidayeen" bid to storm Srinagar radio station, p. 1.

The Hindu. (2003f, May 21). No ban, only curbs on Hizb activities: Pak, p. 5.

The Hindu. (2003g, May 25). Talks with Pak. Good for J&K: Mufti, p. 7.

The Hindu. (2003h, July 11). Hizb splits, p. 1.

The Hindu. (2003i, July 23). Brigadier killed, 4 officers injured in "fidayeen" attack on army camp, p. 1.

The Hindu. (2003j, October 19). 10 years RI, p. 1.

The Hindu. (2004a, February 28). Mufti escapes bid on life, p. 1.

The Hindu. (2004b, March 4). Lashkar attack on Jammu jail, 7 killed, p. 1.

The Hindu. (2005, January 2). DIG among 11 injured in blast, p. 8.

Hindustan Times. (2001a, August 29). Two priests beheaded, 5 of family killed in J&K, p. 1.

Hindustan Times. (2001b, November 5). Lashkar kills four armymen in J&K, p. 1.

Hindustan Times. (2002a, April 11). Terrorists kill five Muslims in Doda, p. 1.

Hindustan Times. (2002b, May 15). 30 die in Jammu suicide strike, p. 1.

Hindustan Times. (2002c, July 19). 10-hr encounter on yatra eve, p. 1.

Hindustan Times. (2002d, August 7). Terrorists kill 9 pilgrims, p. 1.

Hindustan Times. (2002e, September 12). Law minister among 22 killed in J&K, p. 1.

Hindustan Times. (2002f, October 3). Blood-splattered third round in J&K elections, p. 1.

Hindustan Times. (2002g, December 15). Pak Army missile recovered in J&K, p. 11.

Hindustan Times. (2003a, January 14). Gilani released, may claim damages, p. 1.

Hindustan Times. (2003b, March 17). Militants storm police post in J&K, kill 11, p. 1.

Hindustan Times. (2003c, April 11). Lashkar militant arrested for Nadimarg killings, p. 11.

Hindustan Times. (2003d, April 30). Thirteen militants, six soldiers killed in Doda encounter, p. 1.

Hindustan Times. (2003e, May 11). Mehbooba targets father's Govt, p. 11.

Hindustan Times. (2003f, May 30). More troops sent to J&K to turn heat on ultras, p. 1.

Hindustan Times. (2003g, July 7). Blow to Azhar as Jaish splits, p. 7.

Hindustan Times. (2003h, August 3). Complacency making army vulnerable in J&K: Expert, p. 5.

Hindustan Times. (2003i, September 11). Pak cricketer Afridi's terrorist cousin killed in J&K encounter, p. 1.

Hindustan Times. (2003j, September 12). Hurriyat leader Nayeem held with hawala money, p. 5.

Hindustan Times. (2003k, September 17). Hawala trader held for Jaish links, p. 5.

Hindustan Times. (2003l, October 18). Fidayeen attack at Mufti's residence, p. 5.

Hindustan Times. (2005, January 8). Five killed in Srinagar fidayeen attack, p. 15.

India Today, Indian Newsweekly. (2001, August 27). Kashmir militancy, p. 18.

Indian Army. (2001). Talibanisation of Kashmir: Lashkar-e-Taiba's diktats to locals. Retrieved from http://www.armyin kashmir.org/articles/taliban kashmir.html

Indian Army. (2003). Terrorists killed in J&K. Retrieved from http://armyinkashmir.org/civilian html

Laqueur, W. (1999). *The new terrorism* (p. 36). London: Oxford University Press.

Marwah, V. (1995). *Uncivil wars: Pathology of terrorism in India* (p. 55). New Delhi, India: HarperCollins.

Marwah, V. (2003). India. In A. Yonah (Ed.), *Combating terrorism* (p. 336). New Delhi, India: Manas.

McCollum, B. (1994, June 22). *Speech in the House of Representatives, USA. Pakistan supports terrorist rebels in Kashmir.* Retrieved from http://www.kashmir-information.com/Miscellaneous/Pak_terrorism.html

Puri, B. (1993). *Kashmir: Towards insurgency* (p. 60). London.

Schofield, V. (1997). *Kashmir in the crossfire* (p. 240). New Delhi, India: Viva Books.

SifyNews. (2002a, August 1). Militants sneak into Rajouri VIP enclave, 5 killed. Retrieved from http://news.sify.com

SifyNews. (2002b, August 3). Army raids BBC office in Kashmir. Retrieved from http://news.sify.com

Singh, P. (1995). *The Naxalite Movement in India. Daryagang.* Delhi, India: Rupa.

Terrorist Group Profiles. (2003, May 2). *Jaish-e-Mohammed (JEM) (Army of Mohammed).* Dudley Knox Library, Naval Postgraduate School. Retrieved from http://libraray.nps.mil/home/tgp/jem.htm

The Times of India. (1998, April 25). Anti-aircraft gun seized in Kashmir, p. 5.

The Times of India. (2001, December 14). Suicide raid stuns nation, p. 1.

The Wall Street Journal. (2003, April 16). Now tackle Kashmir, p. 1. Retrieved from http://meaindia. nic.in/bestof the web/2003/04/16bow02.htm

Time. (2002, October 7), p. 25.

U.S. Department of State. (2000). *Patterns of global terrorism. (K) Appendix B: Background information on terrorist groups.* Retrieved from http://wwwe.state.gov/s/ct/rls/pgtrpt/2000/2450.htm

Verma, P. S. (1994). *Jammu and Kashmir at the political crossroads* (p. 46). New Delhi, India.

World News. (2002, January 4). Pakistani police round up over 100 Muslim militants. Retrieved from http://www.namibian.com.na/2002/January/world/023747B82E.html

Yahoo!Groups. (2001). Humanrightsnews: Message 2313 of 5919. Retrieved from http://groups.yahoo.com/group/humanrightsnews/message/2313?source=1

Sri Lankan Terrorism
Assessing and Responding to the Threat of the Liberation Tigers of Tamil Eelam (LTTE)

14

CÉCILE VAN DE VOORDE

Contents

Introduction

Few countries have suffered the consequences of ethnic separatism and cultural nationalism as severely as Sri Lanka in its postcolonial period. The Asian island has been besieged by an ethnic conflict between its Sinhalese majority and the Tamil minority for decades. One of the strongest militant nationalist groups in Sri Lanka is the Liberation Tigers of Tamil Eelam (LTTE), or Tamil Tigers, a fierce terrorist group fighting for an independent Tamil nation and famous for its aggressive use of suicide terrorism. Insofar as it has grown from an insurgent group into a transnational terror network, the LTTE poses a significant threat to Sri Lankan security that has been poorly assessed and inadequately addressed. The trademark use of suicide terrorism by the LTTE in the Sri Lankan ethnic war is examined. An analysis of the fight against LTTE terrorism, including important policy recommendations, follows.

Suicide Terrorism: The LTTE's Trademark

Suicide Terrorism and the Sri Lankan Ethnic Conflict

To comprehend the essence of Sri Lanka's enduring ethnic war and the impact of LTTE terrorism in Sri Lanka, one must understand both the phenomenon of suicide terrorism and the Tamil struggle since the 1980s.

Genesis and Main Characteristics of Suicide Terrorism

Suicide terrorism is characterized by the willingness of physically and psychologically war-trained individuals to die in the course of destroying or attempting to annihilate enemy targets in furtherance of certain political or social objectives (Schweitzer, 2002; Whittaker, 2002). Hence, a suicide terror operation is

> a politically motivated violent attack perpetrated by a self-aware individual
> (or individuals) who actively and purposely causes his own death through

blowing himself up along with his chosen target. The perpetrator's ensured death is a precondition for the success of his mission. (Schweitzer, 2002, p. 78)

Until recently, the phenomenon was witnessed in only a dozen countries, mainly Sri Lanka, Lebanon, and Israel. It has now spread across the world and even reached the United States.[1] The unprecedented proliferation of suicide terrorist attacks against Western interests since 1995 has, in effect, made governments and the public glaringly aware of how vulnerable they are to this extremely violent, adaptive form of terrorism.

Rather than a sui generis phenomenon, suicide terrorism is an integral feature of the historical development of oppositional terrorism. Suicide terrorism may appear to be innovative and unique, and it certainly "constitutes a significant escalation in terrorist activity" (Ganor, 2002a, p. 1). Nonetheless, suicide terrorism merely mirrors the development of general terrorist tactics, as well as the ability of terrorist groups to refine their methods of operation to wage the most efficient and cost-effective psychological warfare of all, which also coincides with the advancement of technology and the evolution of the socioeconomic forces inherent in today's society (Ganor, 2002a; Schweitzer, 2002).[2] Suicide terrorism is also a factor of the profound underlying animosity between terrorist organizations and their governmental foes. As such, it is also not a new phenomenon, but one rooted in the historical, social, and psychological dimensions of international terrorism, as a result of centuries of opposition between diverse terror groups and their actual or perceived enemies.

Suicide attacks have been a long-standing modus operandi for terrorist groups. In ancient times, attacks by legendary sects such as the Jewish Sicarii (Zealots) and the Islamic Hashishiyun (Assassins) were the precursors of today's suicide terrorism. From the mid-18th century to the mid-20th century, various Muslim communities in Asia also opted for terrorist suicide attacks in their fight against European colonialism (Crenshaw, 2002; Dale, 1988): Suicide operations were used to fight Western hegemony on the Malabar Coast of southwestern India, in Northern Sumatra in Atjeh, as well as in the southern Philippines in both Mindanao and Sulu. Since the 1980s, suicide terrorism has predominantly affected the Middle East and southern Asia. Finally, it is noteworthy that the unparalleled suicide terrorism campaign waged by the clearly non-Islamic separatists of the LTTE in Sri Lanka is a notable exception to the contemporary trend of suicide terrorism, which is primarily the result of the use and misuse of Islam as a political tool by Islamist, fundamentalist movements attempting to generate great ideological and religious zeal.[3]

Synopsis of the Sri Lankan Conflict

The ethnic separatism and nationalism that have fueled the LTTE are integral features of the conflict opposing Sri Lanka's Sinhalese majority and the Tamil minority. It is therefore important to fully understand the roots, characteristics, and consequences of the ethnic war that has torn the island of Sri Lanka apart for decades.

Historical Overview

The island of Sri Lanka, known as Ceylon until 1972, gained independence from the British colonial rule in 1948. Since then, Sri Lanka[4] has been a sovereign nation within the Commonwealth of Nations and has had a democratic multiparty governmental system. The population of Sri Lanka is about 20 million. Sinhalese and Tamils are the main ethnic groups represented on the island, and religious and ethnic divergences between them have endured for centuries (Laqueur, 1999; Mitra, 1995; Morrison, 2001; Roberts, 1979, 1992; Wilson, 1988). Today, the Sinhalese constitute about 70% of the population and are mainly concentrated in the southwestern portion of the island. They speak Sinhala and are traditionally Buddhist. The Tamils, on the other hand, make up approximately 18% of the total Sri Lankan population, mostly because of the massive exodus that followed the civil war of 1983 and bloody ethnic riots of 1987. Tamils speak Tamil and are traditionally Hindu, with a small percentage of Christians.

Sri Lanka has been rocked by terrorism since the early 1970s. Cultural nationalism has since driven tens of thousands of Tamil insurgents to violently protest the Sinhalese rule and attempt to dismantle a democratic regime they deem oppressive and inequitable (Laqueur, 1999; Mitra, 1995; Morrison, 2001; Rajasingham-Senanayake, 2000; Roberts, 1992; Wilson, 1988). In 1972, following the lead of a brutal and revolutionary military mastermind, Velupillai Prabhakaran, an antigovernment uprising of scores of educated and unemployed Tamil youth marked the beginning of a bloody war between the Sinhalese majority and the Tamils, Sri Lanka's largest minority group. Two years later, several Tamil militants created the Tamil New Tigers (TNT), a military youth movement that was rapidly turned into a new, powerful, and deadly terror apparatus at the hands of Prabhakaran and his closest associates.

Ethnic Separatism, Cultural Nationalism, and the Birth of the LTTE

On May 5, 1976, Velupillai Prabhakaran and members of the TNT officially founded the Liberation Tigers of Tamil Eelam, or LTTE. A direct offshoot of the Sri Lankan ethnic struggle, the LTTE perpetrated its first terrorist attack in September 1978 with the midair bombing of an Air Ceylon passenger jet. In July 1983, an upsurge of ethnic violence led Sinhalese mobs to murder over 300 Tamils. A civil war erupted between the Sinhalese-dominated government and the Tamil separatists, who demanded the creation of an independent Tamil nation, Tamil Eelam, in northern and eastern Sri Lanka. Tens of thousands of Tamils fled Sri Lanka and found refuge mainly in the southern Indian state of Tamil Nadu. The LTTE subsequently embarked on long-term guerrilla warfare against Sinhalese (or even Muslim) civilians and security forces in northern and eastern Sri Lanka. Government forces responded with extremely violent and indiscriminate reprisals. To this day, no definitive tactical or operational resolution of the ethnic conflict has been achieved. Cultural distinctiveness and ethnic identity have been of utmost importance for the Tamils for centuries and remain top priorities in their political agenda (Jeganathan, 1998; Joshi, 2001; Kapferer, 2001; Mitra, 1995; Rajasingham-Senanayake, 2000; *Tamil Eelam*, n.d.; Wilson, 1988).

The ethnic riots of 1987 not only strengthened the polarization of the Sinhala people and the Tamil minority but also resulted in an intensification of the Tamil struggle. The year 1987 marked the start of the LTTE's unrelenting suicide terrorism campaign with a series of "Tamil guerrilla attacks in the interests of ethnic autonomy [that] sparked violent anti-Tamil rioting, much of which received the support of agents of the state" (Kapferer, 1997, p. 174). Since then:

> Sri Lanka's terrorism has known no bounds. ... The loss of life that terrorists have caused since 1972 is reckoned to be some 58,000 civilians and military personnel, two-thirds of whom died in the years 1984–97. Seventeen prominent political leaders met their deaths. In the course of violent dissension within the LTTE's own ranks, thirty-two Tamil leaders have been killed. (Whittaker, 2001, p. 84)

Tamil Tigers and Suicide Terrorism: Group Profile and Activities

Any thorough investigation of the LTTE calls for an analysis of the ideological and structural profile of the group, as well as its activities.

Ideological and Structural Profile of the Tamil Tigers—LTTE Ideology and Goals

The Tamil Tigers argue they have suffered widespread discrimination at the hands of the Sinhalese majority, which is why they claim "armed resistance to this 'oppression' is lawful" (Whittaker, 2001, p. 77). Since 1987, the highly structured and militarized LTTE has established itself as the most powerful militant nationalist group in Sri Lanka. Indeed, "the LTTE is one of five groups, albeit the supreme one, that have achieved dominance over more than 35 Tamil guerrilla groups" (Hudson, 2000, pp. 135–136). A high-profile political and military group motivated by radical nationalist and separatist ideals, the LTTE has fought relentlessly for almost 30 years for the establishment of an independent and sovereign Tamil Eelam in northern and eastern Sri Lanka (Gunaratna, 1998, 2002; Hudson, 2000; Joshi, 1996; Kapferer, 2001; Laqueur, 1999; Morrison, 2001; Rajasingham-Senanayake, 2000; Roberts, 1992; Whittaker, 2002; Wilson, 1988).

The fundamental ideological beliefs and political actions of the LTTE cannot be defined in a one-dimensional way. Whereas a crude description would fit the LTTE strictly within a dichotomous revolutionary versus reactionary or left-wing versus right-wing framework, it is important to note that such reductionist labels do not apply to the Tamil Tigers. Instead, "the searing fundamentalism of aggression–hate–fanaticism" (Whittaker, 2001, p. 85) demonstrated by the LTTE illustrates the complexity of a group considered today to be the most dangerous and deadliest terrorist group in the world and certainly the most violent guerrilla organization of South Asia. Evidently, the LTTE is ever strengthened by a fanatical sense of unity within the group and the zealous personal devotion of its members who eagerly and in a "sense of shared fate ... compete for the honour of a glorious death" (Whittaker, 2002, p. 116).

LTTE Membership Profile

Members and Leadership

Headquartered in the Wanni region of Sri Lanka, the LTTE is composed primarily of Hindus, but a number of Christian Tamils have reportedly been joining the ranks for years. Current official statistics estimate the LTTE boasts between 8,000 and 10,000 armed members in Sri Lanka only, 3,000–6,000 of whom are believed to be trained fighters (Griset & Mahan, 2003). The LTTE recruits members within the Tamil community of the northern and eastern provinces. Cadres from other regions are merely "lower-rung 'troops' who do not hold any place of importance or rank" (Hudson, 2000, p. 137). Rank-and-file members are predominantly recruited from the lower-middle class, and virtually all LTTE cadres come from the lower castes. On the other hand, the LTTE's most hard-core members and its leaders typically come from the higher-status "fisher" or "warrior-fisherman" caste of Velvettihurai, and "many tend to be university-educated, English-speaking professionals with very close cultural and personal ties to the West" (Hudson, 2000, pp. 138–139).

The structure of the LTTE is twofold and consists of a highly organized, quasi-professional military branch and a secondary political branch. A Central Governing Committee administers both wings and is in charge of organizing and commanding the LTTE's subdivisions (Chalk, 2000).[5] The current supreme leader of the LTTE, Velupillai Prabhakaran, is described as a highly charismatic military genius and a brutal, manipulative, and megalomaniac revolutionary (Chalk, 2000; Gunaratna, 1998; Hudson, 2000). His uncompromising attitude, authoritarian decisions, and absolute power have never been disputed (not even by senior LTTE leaders). Thus, Prabhakaran has achieved a de facto God-like status within the group. Tens of thousands of Tamils have been galvanized by Prabhakaran and his illustrious greed for power. They eagerly sacrifice their lives for the independence of Tamil Eelam and strive to emulate "Asia's new Pol Pot" (Hudson, 2000, p. 142).[6]

Children

The LTTE is notorious for recruiting, training, and using children for its terrorist missions. Children actually occupy any positions within the group except leadership ones. In fact, of all the child combatants in the world, "children feature most prominently in the LTTE, whose fiercest fighting force, the Leopard Brigade (Sirasu puli), is made up of children" (Hudson, 2000, p. 138). Half of the Tamils recruited and trained by the LTTE between late 1995 and mid-1996 were between 12 and 16 years old. According to a Sri Lankan military intelligence report, 60% of all LTTE fighters in 1998 were 18 or younger, and almost 60% of LTTE members killed in combat since April 1995 were children (mainly boys and girls between the ages of 10 and 16). Official Sri Lankan statistics released recently show that the LTTE's fighting force has been reduced to 3,000 as a result of restrained recruitment efforts in the late 1990s. Consequently, the LTTE has had to rely heavily on its Baby Brigade of boys and girls aged 10–16 years old. In May 1999, the LTTE even tried to create a Universal People's Militia and imposed military training for anybody who was over the age of 15 and lived in LTTE-controlled areas (Hudson, 2000).

Women

The participation of women in suicide terrorist operations is an important idiosyncratic feature of the phenomenon that deserves much attention, especially when analyzing Sri Lanka's situation. Typically, group leaders will take advantage of the eagerness of the female recruits to demonstrate equality with the male followers, thus exploiting the need of some women to ascertain their position within the group as well as their absolute loyalty to the group and its leader (De Mel, 2002; Griset & Mahan, 2003; Mazurana, McKay, Carlson, & Kasper, 2002; Schweitzer, 2002). Recent statistics for female participation in suicide missions within the LTTE truly exemplify the significance of the role of women in suicide terrorism. Women compose a third of the LTTE membership and, in 2000, "they participated in about 30% to 40% of the group's overall suicide activities" (Schweitzer, 2002, p. 84).

The involvement of women in suicide terror attacks is not a new feature of suicide terrorism. Women have been used in suicide operations by several renowned terrorist groups, mostly nationalist ones.[7] The LTTE, much like Turkey's KONGRA-GEL (formerly PKK, then KADEK), is a nationalist terrorist group well known for frequently having recourse to female suicide bombers. Women are either strongly encouraged to volunteer for suicide missions or conned into partaking in the most dangerous missions and most devastating attacks. Although the rationale for employing female suicide terrorists varies from group to group, a common feature is the use of harmless-looking female members posing as pregnant women to circumvent extreme security measures and safely approach their targets.

Suicide Commandos

The elite brigade known as the Black Tigers is a subdivision of the LTTE's Central Governing Committee and a distinctive feature of the LTTE (Chalk, 2000; Hudson, 2000; Whittaker, 2001). This commando unit "operates a battlefield strategy known as 'Unceasing Wave'. ... The terrorist arsenal and methods are substantial and lead to horrendous damage and casualties" (Whittaker, 2001, p. 84). The suicide commandos of the Black Tigers brigade carry glass capsules containing sodium or potassium cyanide around their necks, which they must use to kill themselves and avoid capture should they fail to carry out their mission; otherwise, they will "face some more painful form of death at the hands of the LTTE" (Hudson, 2000, p. 139). The Black Tigers unit is composed of both men and women. Women actually play a vital and highly strategic role in the military force of the LTTE and, more specifically, within the elite suicide commando unit. One of the most publicized suicide attacks perpetrated by the LTTE, the 1991 assassination of Indian Prime Minister Rajiv Gandhi, was carried out by a female 18-year-old Sri Lankan Tamil Hindu.

"Destroy Everything that Destroys You": Modus Operandi and Target Selection

Since the first suicide attack of 1987, suicide terrorism has become the LTTE's foremost method of operation owing to its massive political impact and high potential for crippling the economy of the region (Chalk, 2000; Gunaratna, 2002; Joshi, 2001; Karmon, 2002; Schweitzer, 2002). Overall, as far as implementation, frequency, and total of attacks are concerned, the LTTE's highly effective and extremely brutal suicide terrorism campaign surpasses the more publicized ones waged by Hezbollah or Hamas. Today, the Tamil Tigers are the most thriving and fiercest terrorist group to have ever resorted to suicide terrorism. Since July 1987, the LTTE has carried out nearly 200 suicide terror attacks in both Sri Lanka and India, killing and wounding thousands of innocent people. In 2000, "[t]he LTTE's track record for suicide attacks [was] unrivaled" (Hudson, 2000, p. 50), and today, even though similar attacks have recently multiplied in other parts of the world (Iraq, Israel, Chechnya, etc.), the LTTE is still considered by terrorism analysts as the prime and most inexorable user of suicide terrorism.

Targets for LTTE attacks vary and can be civilian, military, political, economic, or cultural; stationary or mobile; human beings or infrastructures (Gunaratna, 2000; Hudson, 2000; Joshi, 2001). Over the years, the Tamil Tigers have "integrated a battlefield insurgent strategy with a terrorist program that targets key government and military personnel, the economy, and public infrastructure" (Simonsen & Spindlove, 2000, p. 221). The most spectacular suicide terrorist attack perpetrated by the LTTE to date may have been the October 1997 truck bombing of the freshly inaugurated World Trade Center in Colombo, Sri Lanka's capital, which injured over 100 civilians, killed 18 people, and resulted in considerable collateral damage to adjacent structures (Simonsen & Spindlove, 2000). However, the LTTE has favored strategic targets with high symbolic value, such as key political, military, and cultural figures in both Sri Lanka and India. In fact, the LTTE "is the only terrorist group to have assassinated three heads of government" (Hudson, 2000, p. 135): Indian Prime Minister Rajiv Gandhi in 1991, Sri Lankan President Ranasinghe Premadasa in 1993, and former Sri Lankan prime minister and presidential hopeful Gamini Dissanayake in 1994. The LTTE has also assassinated several prominent political and military figures, including Defense Minister Ranjan Wijeratne in 1991, commander of the Sri Lankan Navy Vice Admiral W. W. E. C. Fernando in 1992, Minister of Industries and Industrial Development C. V. Gooneratne, as well as hundreds of law enforcement officers, security personnel, monks, and innocent civilians. Sri Lanka's incumbent president, Mrs. Chandrika Bandaranaike Kumaratunga, was also wounded in a botched suicide terrorist attack that targeted her in December 1999.

The Spirit of Martyrdom

The religious ramifications of the Sri Lankan ethnic war are all the more significant as they impinge on both sides of the conflict. Whereas the Tamils are predominantly Hindu and abide by a strict caste system, the Sinhalese people are largely Buddhist (Kapferer, 1997; Whittaker, 2001). This religious and ethnic schism is deeply intensified by the fact that

> in the current context of intra-ethnic and inter-ethnic violence, officers of the state make intense appeals to the key Buddhist value of non-violence. Further, there is, in the current situation, an implication that the state as constituted in reference to the Buddha ideal of non-violence is the supreme agent of Buddhist morality, a morality which is even present in the exercise by the state of extreme violence. It is a violence in the interest of the order of a Buddhist state. (Kapferer, 1997, p. 175)

As a result, religious fanaticism has been a driving force for members of the LTTE, and the cult of martyrdom has been an enduring and central feature of LTTE terrorism (Joshi, 2001; Schweitzer, 2002; Whittaker, 2002). Where "the power of the bomb is linked to the power of martyrdom" (Crenshaw, 2002, p. 29), the LTTE's suicide commandos perceive their self-sacrifice as a way of legitimizing their cause, inspiring imitation, and promising individual glory. In their sacred fight for freedom, they view suicide and their own fanaticism as having "a positive value where martyrdom is a rational terminal decision demonstrating a worthy and invincible cause" (Whittaker, 2001, p. 85). This fervent cult of martyrdom has actually led some scholars and terrorism analysts to argue that the problem of terrorism in Sri Lanka will never completely disappear, especially since the blatant "remorseless zeal of Tamil fighters is never lessened by their savage losses" (Whittaker, 2002, p. 43).

Sri Lanka had the highest rate of suicide in the world for 2003 and also remained the world leader in suicide terrorist attacks. Suicide is a very important feature of Sri Lankan society and "[t]he indoctrination of the positive value of suicide has been especially intense in Sri Lanka where almost all the candidates among the Tamil Tigers are in their teens" (Laqueur, 1999, pp. 100–101). For the overzealous Tamil Tigers, especially the youngest and most impressionable ones, death or self-destruction becomes the only suitable substitute for capture and imprisonment. However, not unlike other suicide terrorists in the world, the suicide commandos of the LTTE are not primarily suicidal and usually do not suffer from any diagnosable psychological disorder or cognitive impairments impeding effective problem-solving skills (Perina, 2002). Rather, they are eager to sacrifice their lives for the Tamil cause and the accomplishment of a sacred mission in honor of their charismatic leader.[8] In contrast to the stereotypes conveyed by the media and pervading in the general public, these terrorists are not mentally ill or deranged fanatics. On the contrary, they "are often well educated and capable of sophisticated, albeit highly biased, rhetoric and political analysis" (Hudson, 2000, p. 49). These individuals are indoctrinated and conditioned to make sure they can meet the needs and satisfy the interests of the LTTE. The LTTE typically assigns some religious holiness to its commands and proscriptions to ensure the decisions will not be challenged, which encourages self-discipline and, in turn, entirely precludes critical and independent thinking.

Taming the Tigers: The Fight Against LTTE Terrorism

Official Attempts to Combat and Eliminate a Growing Threat

In a country riddled with violence and conflict, tepid strategies have been devised by Sri Lankan authorities to face up to LTTE terrorism. Although a cease-fire was agreed on and informal peace talks have been conducted since 2002, major obstacles have hindered the creation and implementation of effective and efficient policies.

Sri Lanka's Strategies to Counter and Eradicate LTTE Terrorism

Antiterrorism, Counterterrorism, and State Violence   Official steps taken by the Sri Lankan government against the LTTE have been hindered by the very activities of the terrorist group. Indeed, "[d]ue to the LTTE's intensive suicide campaign, Sri-Lankan politicians seem reluctant openly to confront or declare an all-out war against the group" (Schweitzer, 2002, p. 81). Nevertheless, Sri Lankan authorities have attempted to devise both antiterrorist (or preventive) and counterterrorist (or operational) measures to quell the Tamil Tigers. Thus far, repression by Sri Lanka's government forces has been particularly brutal and arbitrary, but no operational solution to the enduring LTTE problem has been proposed, and no efficient preventive measures have been implemented. The Tamil Tigers continue their struggle for the creation of an independent Tamil Eelam and recurrently voice their discontent with any effort made by the Sri Lankan authorities to compromise with them in favor of a political solution to the ethnic conflict.

Open dissatisfaction with the approach adopted by Sri Lanka and the violent repression used to quash the LTTE has actually extended far beyond the Tamil community. In fact, a widespread controversy arose after the Sri Lankan government "sought to contain and then eliminate anti-state terrorism by means of a mixture of political and diplomatic moves allied to the employment of force" (Whittaker, 2001, p. 86). Specifically, many scholars, nongovernmental organizations, and governments throughout the world have condemned the systematic use of torture by the Sri Lankan police against suspected LTTE members (often as the result of false accusations in unrelated minor cases). The Asian Human Rights Commission, among others, has vehemently denounced the endemic and systemic problem posed by this flagrant violation of Sri Lanka's Convention Against Torture and Other

Cruel, Inhuman or Degrading Treatment or Punishment Act, No. 22 of 1994. Sri Lanka's policing methods have been described as "a manifest threat to the rule of law," and the "culture of barbarity in policing at all levels throughout the entire country" ("Torture Committed," 2002, p. 2) has been the subject of several damning official reports on the severe Sri Lankan police crisis (Asian Legal Research Center, 2002; Fernando, 2002; "Torture Committed," 2002).

The excessive violence that has characterized the reprisals against the LTTE certainly has not contributed to the peaceful resolution of the raging ethnic conflict. Since police practice has been perceived as a clear manifestation of state terror not only by the LTTE and the Tamil population, but also by outside organizations and foreign governments, it is clear that a different approach to solving Sri Lanka's ethnic struggle must now be implemented. Change is desperately needed, all the more as the citizens of Sri Lanka now feel they have "no redress from the law," that "systems of justice have broken down," and that "bringing the culprits to book is politically too burdensome for [a] complicitous government" (De Mel, 2002, p. 101). Besides, unless efforts are made to radically alter the policies developed thus far to counter the Tamil insurgency and its complex ramifications, the use of terror to force terror out of Sri Lanka may very well backfire and result in a momentous increase in LTTE recruitment of ultramotivated and fanatical terrorists.

Peace Talks   At the other end of the political and diplomatic spectrum, several national organizations and foreign representatives have encouraged negotiations between the Tamil separatists and the Sri Lankan government. Following the 1987 ethnic riots, Indian Prime Minister Rajiv Gandhi initiated peace talks. The help of India was solicited by Sri Lanka in an effort to facilitate an objective and neutral mediation; India's Tamil-dominated southern states even provided bases and supplies for the Sri Lankan Tamil guerrillas. The promising Indo-Sri Lankan Peace Accord of 1987 stipulated some autonomy be given to the Tamils in northern and eastern Sri Lanka, but also established the Indian Peacekeeping Force (IPKF) to replace Sri Lankan troops in the Jaffna peninsula. The radical left Sinhalese youth movement *Janatha Vimukhti Peramuna* (JVP) denounced the peace accord as an attempt to destroy Sri Lankan territorial integrity and coordinated a guerrilla insurgency to undermine the government. Although the JVP insurgency was trampled, the peace process stalled and the involvement of India ultimately proved to be a political and military fiasco. The peacekeeping force withdrew from Sri Lanka in April 1990 and a number of significant violent confrontations between the Sri Lankan army and the LTTE ensued over the following years, claiming many lives on both sides.

In September 2002, the LTTE agreed to a cease-fire and informal peace talks with the government. Sri Lankan President Chandrika Bandaranaike Kumaratunga even consented to negotiations regarding a rebel plan for interim self-rule as long as they aimed at putting an end to the long-standing conflict, not creating a de facto state. The LTTE has vehemently rejected that approach, and the talks have been rather deadlocked for months now. Today, progress toward peace seems to have come to a standstill, and the end of the Sri Lankan ethnic war has yet to be reached.

Major Obstacles to the Eradication of the LTTE Threat

The dispersion of the Tamil community around the world, the internationalization of the LTTE, and the intrinsic inadequacies of Sri Lanka's counterinsurgency strategy have seriously impeded official efforts to reduce and ultimately eradicate the threat posed by the Tamil Tigers.

The Tamil "Diaspora" and the Establishment of an LTTE Global Network

In the late 1970s, a few Tamil political movements and militant groups tactically linked to the LTTE contributed to the expansion of the latter at the international level.[9] However, until the ethnic riots of July 1987, Tamil insurgents were unable to effectively raise money outside Sri Lanka in support of their war efforts. Following the 1987 riots, tens of thousands of Tamils left for Tamil Nadu or Western countries prone to welcoming them as political refugees. Overall, between 450,000 and 500,000 refugees took part in the Sri Lankan Tamil Diaspora that spread over 50 countries (Gunaratna, 1998; Hudson, 2000; Whittaker, 2001). Since then, highly efficient ways of exploiting the "growing togetherness" (Whittaker, 2001, p. 78) of the Tamil community worldwide have been devised for the LTTE to achieve its fund-raising goals. Tamil expatriates have become "the economic backbone of the terrorist campaign" (Hudson, 2000, p. 136), and it is now clear that the LTTE's "ruthless and barbaric attacks ... are nurtured by exorbitant foreign funds" (Sri Lanka Army, 2001). In effect:

> [t]he war effort of the LTTE is mainly paid for by expatriate Tamil communities in Canada, the United States, Australia, South Africa, and several European countries. Some of the money has come in voluntarily, but the LTTE has also enlisted enforcers, extracting contributions from those reluctant to pay. (Laqueur, 1999, p. 194)

Since 1985, the LTTE has therefore evolved from an insurgent group keen on suicide terrorism to a transnational and secretive network that is in fact as intricate as "the quasi-governmental structure built by the Tigers in Sri Lanka itself" (Whittaker, 2001, p. 79). Today, with bureaus and cells scattered across the globe, the LTTE has built a network that operates internationally in three major areas: publicity and political propaganda,[10] fund-raising,[11] and weapons acquisition. The military procurement abilities of the Tamil Tigers are the utmost illustration of the LTTE's international scope. Since the Indo-Sri Lankan Peace Accord of 1987, arms and ammunition procurement activities have stemmed from northeastern and southeastern Asia (especially China, North Korea, Cambodia, Thailand, Hong Kong, Vietnam, and Burma); southwestern Asia (Afghan pipeline); former Soviet republics (mainly Ukraine); southeastern Europe and the Middle Eastern region (Greece, Turkey, Bulgaria, Cyprus, and Lebanon); and Africa (usually Nigeria, Zimbabwe, and South Africa).

Sri Lankan authorities, foreign governments, as well as national and international law enforcement agencies have repeatedly expressed their concern regarding how the LTTE "derives much of its considerable funds from crime-related activities in many countries" (Whittaker, 2001, p. 80), most notably organized crime. Today, the LTTE is actively represented in about 40 countries. Throughout India and South Asia, the strength of the LTTE has intensified by way of ideological, economic, and technological ties to other insurgent groups. For instance, the LTTE has developed relationships with Sikh insurgents, Kashmiri Mujahideen, and over 20 Tamil Nadu separatist groups (including Tamil National Retrieval Force, People's War Group, Liberation Cuckoos, Peasants and People Party, MGR Anna Dravida Munethra Kalaham of Thirunavakarasu, Tamil National Movement of Nedumaran, Indian People's Party, Center for the Campaign of Tamil Education, Thaliai Nagar Tamil Society, Movement of the Educated Front, Tamil Nadu People's Movement, Thileepan Society, People's Education Center, Tamil Nadu Socialist Party, Republic Party of India, People's Democratic Youth Front, Liberation Organization of the Oppressed People, World People's Progressive Front, Human Rights Organization, Organization for Social History, Marxist Periyar Socialist Party). Moreover, the LTTE is now active across Southeast Asia and the Northern Pacific area (including Japan). In Europe, the United Kingdom has traditionally been the hub of LTTE political activism. After London and Paris, representatives and supporters of the LTTE have now multiplied in Eastern Europe and Scandinavia. In North America, the core of the LTTE endeavor is located in Toronto and New Jersey (Chalk, 2000; Gunaratna, 1998).

Inadequacies of Sri Lanka's Official Counterinsurgency Policy

Sri Lanka's maladaptive official response to the LTTE's guerrilla and terrorist campaign has contributed to the strengthening of the LTTE both on the island and overseas. In the absence of a methodical and strategic counterinsurgency policy, the Sri Lankan government, law enforcement agencies, and military forces have been unsuccessful in their fight against LTTE terrorism. The ultrasophisticated level of political propaganda employed by the Tamil Tigers has surpassed the abilities of Sri Lankan officials to counteract.

Although the government has tried since 1986 to produce a powerful counterpropaganda system to slow the fund-raising activities and arms procurement operations of the LTTE, no clear or effective operational or tactical measures have been implemented. Hence, the Sri Lankan government needs to reevaluate its foreign policy while focusing more on fighting LTTE propaganda and gaining official support for its cause from national representatives and other nations. Lessons need to be learned from past failures to finally make progress. This will require systematically assessing and fully acknowledging not only the complex ramifications of the military and nonmilitary activities of the Tamil Tigers in Sri Lanka, but also the extent and significance of the LTTE menace outside Sri Lanka. In addition, the success of any measures against the LTTE will depend heavily on the level and quality of the cooperation and communication between local, national, and international law enforcement agencies, military forces, and governmental organizations.

Important Policy Considerations
Sri Lankan authorities, with the help of foreign governments if necessary, need to establish and implement cohesive, integrated policies adapted to the LTTE's international dimension. Government representatives and law enforcement agencies must work together to adequately apply Sri Lanka's counterinsurgency approach to the unconventional threat they are targeting. Moreover, they should keep advocating for transnational cooperation against terrorism.

The Need for an Integrated Counterinsurgency Approach
The LTTE has jeopardized the domestic stability of both Sri Lanka and India for three decades. Inasmuch as "the combination of technological primitiveness together with sophisticated planning and effective implementation is the hallmark of virtually all suicide attacks" (Ganor, 2002b, p. 168), the persistence of the ultraviolent brand of LTTE suicide terrorism could have even more catastrophic outcomes for Sri Lanka and disastrous repercussions on the economy of the region. Innovative political and law enforcement measures need to be tailored to specifically fit the type of issues inherent in the Sri Lankan ethnic conflict and effectively meet the challenges posed by the LTTE. Adapting the response of the Sri Lankan government and the international community to the problem caused by the Tamil Tigers insurgency is the key element to help in the conceptualization and implementation of preventive and operational measures against the LTTE's global terror network. The expansion of the LTTE network overseas and the additional strength it has derived within Sri Lanka call for the creation of innovative political and law enforcement strategies specifically targeting Sri Lanka's vulnerabilities. It is only by thoroughly assessing and addressing the current threats and future challenges posed by the LTTE and its international terrorism network that progress can be made toward the implementation of efficient and effective

measures against the LTTE and, ultimately, the annihilation of this terrorist network.

The careful use of strategic and tactical terrorist profiles could prove a useful tool to combat and prevent LTTE terrorism. Although no operational answer to suicide terrorism has been found yet, the efficiency of both anti- and counterterrorist measures could potentially be optimized by applying principles of criminal profiling to the psychobehavioral profiling of the Tamil Tigers. Terrorism profiling consists of defining psychological, physical, and behavioral variables common to terrorists (groups or individuals). As a coordinated multidisciplinary effort to counter and thwart a global terrorist threat, it should help improve the ability of intelligence services and law enforcement agencies to fight transnational terrorism efficiently around the world. Ideally, effective and structured terrorism profiling would help identify and stop LTTE terrorists before attacks are carried out inside or outside Sri Lanka. The utility and reliability of the terrorism profiling tactics, however, would depend on the development of effective, productive, and targeted behavioral profiles assessing risks and vulnerabilities both in Sri Lanka and in foreign countries that have become an integral part of the LTTE global terror network since 1986.[12]

Sri Lanka's Role in the Global Fight Against Terrorism

Sri Lanka has been a forefront advocate of the fight against international terrorism. Since 1986, key Sri Lankan political figures have called for a joint effort to fight worldwide terrorism, and their country has become a major actor in the global war on terror.

The Need for Concerted International Action

President Kumaratunga has repeatedly urged the leaders of the commonwealth and other nations to form an international coalition against terrorism. For years now, she has called for intensive and collective action against international terrorism, declaring it was critical to pressure terrorist groups into rejecting aggression and abiding by purely democratic precepts. Admittedly, there has been an "optimistic trend in the international arena of the late 1990's ... [and] a growing readiness and interest on the part of more countries to cooperate in the fight against terrorism, on the local, regional and global arena" (Karmon, 2002, p. 43). President Kumaratunga called the Convention on the Suppression of Terrorist Bombings ratified by the United Nations in 1998 "a considerable moral victory for the international community in its fight against terrorism" (Liyanarachchi, 2001).

As the island republic has been torn apart by suicide terrorism and ethnic warfare for nearly two decades, the Sri Lankan government is well aware of the significant role it has to play in the global fight against terrorism. Today, Sri Lankan authorities want more than ever to make a positive example out of their country, however beleaguered it may be, and they have consistently singled themselves out as a heralding voice in the fight against international terrorism. Their role in the global war on terror is primordial and should certainly not be overlooked.

The LTTE and the Global War on Terror

In an effort to demonstrate concern for the enduring ethnic conflict raging in Sri Lanka and the potential threat posed at the national and international levels by the Tamil Tigers, the U.S. government designated the Tamil Tigers as a foreign terrorist organization pursuant to the Antiterrorism and Effective Death Penalty Act of 1996 and subsequently banned the LTTE in 1997 (Simonsen & Spindlove, 2000; Sri Lanka Army, 2001).[13] In June 2004, the United States officially declared it would not remove the LTTE from its list of terrorist organizations, despite the 2-year ceasefire and informal peace talks with the government. The position of the U.S. State Department shall remain so until the group categorically relinquishes the use of terrorism and rescinds such policies as the conscription of child soldiers.

Sinhalese and Tamils have expressed disparate feelings regarding a potential U.S. intervention in Sri Lanka, given the conflicting stakes they have in the outcome of the ethnic war. On the one hand, "Sinhala ultra nationalist sentiment yearns for the USA's war on terrorism to include the Liberation Tigers of Tamil Eelam within its purview and wreak destruction upon the Tigers, thereby eradicating forever the Tamil demand and struggle for equality" (Jeyaraj, 2001). On the other hand, the Tamil Tigers dread an inclusion of their nationalist group in the global "war on terror" launched by President George W. Bush following the September 2001 terrorist attacks on American soil.

Sri Lanka is one of the most dangerous places on earth; in fact, its seacoast, its military bases, and its airports and harbors are not secure today (Whittaker, 2002). Undeniably, one of the main issues to bear in mind is the security problem inherently posed by the long-lasting Sri Lankan conflict, which has turned the island of Sri Lanka into a high-risk war zone and could become a significant obstacle for any outside military intervention. Some may argue that a secessionist group like the LTTE, fighting to promote and achieve its national liberationist goals within its own country, does not represent a direct or serious threat against U.S. or other Western interests and should therefore not be heeded to. However, any official stance is most likely influenced by the fact that LTTE leader Velupillai Prabhakaran has publicly condemned Western nations for giving military support to Sri Lanka and periodically cautions them about putting their citizens at risk for terrorist attacks (Hudson, 2000).

According to the official stance of the United States, the resolution of the ethnic conflict must come not from war but from peaceful negotiations.

Insofar as the LTTE is "not involved in unbridled terror, has specific political demands, and is not averse to negotiations" (Jeyaraj, 2001), the U.S. government will unlikely use a fight against the LTTE as a pretext to go to war against the Tamils. Nonetheless, a shift in policy could be observed in the near future, depending on the redefinition by the United States of its ongoing global war on terror and how much attention is paid to both Prabhakaran's threats and the LTTE's sweeping international terror network. Ultimately, any improvement of the Sri Lankan situation may essentially be contingent on the nature of the LTTE's communication with Western nations in general and the United States in particular, as well as the readiness of the Tamil Tigers to reject any further use of terrorism and their permanent adherence to the peace process.

Conclusion

The Tamil Tigers have been engaged in an extremely violent secessionist war against the Sinhalese majority of Sri Lanka for three decades. Combined with a fervent cult of martyrdom and scores of high-profile suicide attacks against key political, military, and economic targets, the nationalist and separatist ideals of the Tamil Tigers have turned the LTTE into the world's most implacable and most brutal terrorist group. The Tamil Diaspora of the 1980s, the extensive use of political propaganda, and the involvement of the group in arms procurement and massive fund-raising activities have enabled the LTTE to increase its strength in Sri Lanka and its presence throughout the world. As a result, the Tamil Tigers have transformed their insurgent group into an international terror network that, much like their violent brand of suicide terrorism, seems to have no limits today. The globalization of the LTTE has become an influential phenomenon in an era when international security is more at stake than ever. Since the mid-1980s, the Sri Lankan government has attempted to combat and eradicate the LTTE using methods that have been highly criticized and mostly ineffective. The paradoxical measures adopted by Sri Lankan authorities, ranging from extremely violent reprisals to utterly unsuited policies, must change radically to adapt to the current issues and future challenges presented by the LTTE. International cooperation between governments, law enforcement agencies, and military forces is crucial to ensure that the transnational problem is adequately tackled. Sri Lanka has been permanently scarred by the unremitting violence of the ethnic conflict that has opposed Sinhalese and Tamils for decades. Nonetheless, despite the unyielding stance adopted by the Tamil Tigers regarding a peaceful political resolution of the ethnic issue, there is still hope that a political stratagem or tactical guidelines will bring about the truce Sri Lankans have been longing for. Major political and strategic adjustments must be made regarding the dealings of Sri Lanka and foreign nations with the LTTE before its tentacles reach too far and the grip of its international network becomes too strong.

Notes

1. Today, about 15 religious or secular terrorist groups are capable of using suicide terrorism against their own governments and foreign governments. Among them are the LTTE in Sri Lanka; Lebanon's Hezbollah (Party of God); Hamas (Harkat el Mukawma el Islamiya, or Islamic Resistance Movement) and the Palestinian Islamic Jihad (PIJ) of the Israeli occupied territories; the Kurdistan People's Congress (KONGRAGEL, f.k.a. Workers' Party of Kurdistan or PKK, then Kurdistan Freedom and Democracy Congress or KADEK) in Turkey; the Egyptian Islamic Jihad (EIJ) and the Gamaya Islamiya (Islamic Group, or IG) of Egypt; the Armed Islamic Group (GIA) of Algeria; India's Barbar Khalsa International (BKI); and Al Qaeda, Osama Bin Laden's Afghanistan-based network.
2. To this day, there is no exact, widely agreed-on definition of terrorism. Generally, terrorism is described as the unlawful, deliberate, and premeditated use of (or threat to use) force to further political or tactical goals; terrorism is typically used to intimidate or coerce governments, organizations, or civilian populations.
3. Modern-day forms of politicized Islam are derived from the Wahhabi reforms initiated in Arabia in the late 18th century. The Wahhabis formed an extremely conservative Islamic group that rejected any innovation that occurred after the 3rd century of Islam; they thrived predominantly in Arabia. Today, the extremist ideology developed by the Wahhabis is still promoted by their spiritual heirs in Saudi Arabia and the Al Qaeda network.
4. The island is known in full as the Democratic Socialist Republic of Sri Lanka. It became a republic in 1972 with the adoption of a new constitution that appointed a president to replace the British monarch as head of state. A revised constitution adopted in 1978 approved of the popular election of the president.
5. The LTTE's Central Governing Committee subdivisions include an International Secretariat (headed by Manoharan); an amphibious group (the Sea Tigers, headed by Soosai); an airborne group (the Air Tigers, headed by Shankar); an elite fighting wing (the Charles Anthony Regiment, headed by Balrajo); a suicide commando unit (the Black Tigers, headed by Pottu Amman); a highly secretive intelligence group; and a political office headed by Thamil Cheylam (political leader) and Anton Balasingham (political advisor and ideologue).
6. Velupillai Prabhakaran and LTTE's foremost intelligence officer and military chief, Pottu Amman, are the key LTTE figures formally accused of assassinating Indian Prime Minister Rajiv Gandhi. In addition, warrants have been issued for their arrest and that of several other LTTE leaders for the killing of 78 persons in the 1996 bombing of the Central Bank Building, as well as a series of criminal acts committed throughout the 1990s.
7. Fundamentalist Islamic terror groups seldom allow women to participate in terrorist activities, especially not suicide terrorism. Hezbollah, the Iran-backed militant Islamic group based in Lebanon, is a notable exception: The group

is notorious for having used female bombers during the Israeli occupation of southern Lebanon. Other groups, like Hamas and the Palestinian Islamic Jihad, occasionally resort to female suicide bombers as well.

8. This is very similar to the Islamic concept of *istishad*, that is, martyrdom and self-sacrifice in the name of Allah.

9. Following its creation in the mid-1970s, the LTTE had tactical links to the Tamil United Liberation Front (TULF), the Eelam Revolutionary Organizers (EROS), and the Tamil Liberation Front, later known as the Tamil Liberation Organization (TLO).

10. The LTTE's publicity/propaganda activities are centered around three crucial points or beliefs: The Tamils are innocent victims of the Sinhalese enemy government; the Tamils, as Sri Lanka's minority group, are incessantly discriminated against and militarily oppressed; and the peaceful coexistence of the Tamils with the Sinhalese in a single state is impossible.

11. Funds collected by the LTTE via international fund-raising are a vital module of the LTTE's National Defense Fund. Money is not obtained exclusively from the Tamil Diaspora; the LTTE frequently diverts funds raised as donations for humanitarian purposes. In addition, the LTTE has been involved in the lucrative international nexi of narcotics trafficking and arms procurement.

12. Despite the many possibilities it offers, terrorism profiling has several limitations. This complex methodological process is often impeded by a lack of communication and cooperation between international agencies. Its value may also be overestimated, and its misuse can be dangerous. Controversial issues may also become problematic (e.g., the use of ethnic/racial profiling instead of scientifically based psychological profiling or the balance between civil liberties and civil defense).

13. After being added to the U.S. State Department's list of international terrorist organizations in 1996, the LTTE launched a public campaign throughout the Jaffna peninsula using posters describing the U.S. reaction as appropriate considering the American government had collaborated with its Sri Lankan counterpart against the Tamil Tigers.

References

Asian Legal Research Center. (2002). Recommendations to address the use of torture by the police in Sri Lanka. *Article 2, 1*(4), 55–58.

Chalk, P. (2000). *Liberation Tigers of Tamil Eelam's (LTTE), international organization and operations: A preliminary analysis—A Canadian Security Intelligence Service publication*. Retrieved March 28, 2003, from http://www.fas.org

Crenshaw, M. (2002). "Suicide" terrorism in comparative perspective. In Anti-Defamation League (Ed.), *Countering suicide terrorism* (pp. 21–29). New York: Anti-Defamation League.

Dale, S. F. (1988). Religious suicide in Islamic Asia: Anticolonial terrorism in India, Indonesia, and the Philippines. *Journal of Conflict Resolution, 32*(1), 37–59.

De Mel, N. (2002). Fractured narratives: Notes on women in conflict in Sri Lanka and Pakistan. *Development, 45*(1), 99–104.

Fernando, B. (2002). Trying to understand the police crisis in Sri Lanka. *Article 2, 1*(4), 42–47.

Ganor, B. (2002a). Preface. In Anti-Defamation League (Ed.), *Countering suicide terrorism* (pp. 1–4). New York: Anti-Defamation League.

Ganor, B. (2002b). Suicide terrorism after September 11. In Anti-Defamation League (Ed.), *Countering suicide terrorism* (pp. 167–175). New York: Anti-Defamation League.

Griset, P. L., & Mahan, S. (2003). *Terrorism in perspective.* Thousand Oaks, CA: Sage.

Gunaratna, R. (1998). *International and regional security implications of the Sri Lankan Tamil insurgency.* Retrieved January 26, 2003, from http://www.ict.org.il

Gunaratna, R. (2000). Suicide terrorism: A global threat. *Jane's Intelligence Review, 12,* 52–55.

Gunaratna, R. (2002). Suicide terrorism in Sri Lanka and India. In Anti-Defamation League (Ed.), *Countering suicide terrorism* (pp. 101–108). New York: Anti-Defamation League.

Hudson, R. A. (2000). *Who becomes a terrorist and why: The 1999 government report on profiling terrorists.* Guilford, CT: Lyons Press.

Jeganathan, P. (1998). In the shadow of violence: "Tamilness" and the anthropology of identity in Southern Sri Lanka. In T. J. Bartholomeusz & C. R. de Silva (Eds.), *Buddhist fundamentalism and minority identities in Sri Lanka.* New York: New York State University Press.

Jeyaraj, D. B. S. (2001, September 30). USA policy towards LTTE. *The Sunday Leader.* Retrieved November 26, 2002, from http://xi.pair.com/isweb3/spot/sp0612/clip1.html

Joshi, C. L. (2001, June). Sri Lanka: Suicide bombers. *Far Eastern Economic Review,* 64–66.

Joshi, M. (1996). On the razor's edge: The Liberation Tigers of Tamil Eelam. *Studies in Conflict and Terrorism, 19,* 19–42.

Kapferer, B. (1997). Remythologizing discourses: State and insurrectionary violence in Sri Lanka. In D. Apter (Ed.), *The legitimization of violence.* New York: New York University Press.

Kapferer, B. (2001). Ethnic nationalism and the discourses of violence in Sri Lanka. *Communal/Plural, 9*(1), 33–67.

Karmon, E. (2002). Trends in contemporary international terrorism. In Anti-Defamation League (Ed.), *Countering suicide terrorism* (pp. 30–47). New York: Anti-Defamation League.

Laqueur, W. (1999). *The new terrorism: Fanaticism and the arms of mass destruction.* New York: Oxford University Press.

Liyanarachchi, W. (2001, November 2). *Sri Lanka role in combating global terror.* Sri Lanka Department of Information News. Retrieved June 24, 2003, from http://www.news.lk

Mazurana, D. E., McKay, S. A., Carlson, K. C., & Kasper, J. C. (2002). Girls in fighting forces and groups: Their recruitment, participation, demobilisation and reintegration. *Peace and Conflict: Journal of Peace Psychology, 8*(2), 97–123.

Mitra, S. K. (1995). The rational politics of cultural nationalism: Subnational movements of South Asia in comparative perspective. *British Journal of Political Science, 25*(1), 57–77.

Morrison, B. M. (2001). The transformation of Sri Lankan society, 1948–1999: The fragmentation of centralism. *African and Asian Studies, 36*(2), 181–202.

Perina, K. (2002). Suicide terrorism: Seeking motives beyond mental illness. *Psychology Today, 35,* 15–24.

Rajasingham-Senanayake, D. (2000). Democracy and the problem of representation: The making of bi-polar ethnic identity in post-colonial Sri Lanka. In A. Nandy, J. Pfaff-Czarnecka, E. T. Gomez, & D. Rajasingham-Senanayake (Eds.), *Ethnic futures: The state and identity politics in Asia* (pp. 99–134). Thousand Oaks, CA: Sage.

Roberts, M. (Ed.). (1979). *Collective identities, nationalism and protest in modern Sri Lanka.* Colombo, Sri Lanka: Marga Institute.

Roberts, M. (1992). Nationalism, the past and the present: The case of Sri Lanka. *Ethnic and Racial Studies, 16,* 133–166.

Schweitzer, Y. (2002). Suicide terrorism: Development and main characteristics. In Anti-Defamation League (Ed.), *Countering suicide terrorism* (pp. 77–88). New York: Anti-Defamation League.

Simonsen, C. E., & Spindlove, J. R. (2000). *Terrorism today: The past, the players, the future.* Upper Saddle River, NJ: Prentice-Hall.

Sri Lanka Army. (2001, September). *World's top suicide killers—Do they really have borders?* Retrieved February 9, 2003, from http://www.army.lk/News_Reports/September01

Tamil Eelam. (n.d.). Retrieved April 24, 2003, from http://eelam.com/tamil_eelam.html

Torture committed by the police in Sri Lanka. (2002). *Article 2, 1*(4), 2–3.

Whittaker, D. J. (Ed.). (2001). *The terrorism reader.* New York: Routledge.

Whittaker, D. J. (2002). *Terrorism: Understanding the global threat.* London: Longman/Pearson.

Wilson, J. (1988). *The break-up of Sri Lanka: The Sinhala Tamil conflict.* Honolulu: University of Hawaii Press.

Targeting Blue
Why We Should Study Terrorist Attacks on Police

15

JENNIFER C. GIBBS

Contents

Introduction

Terrorism is commonly thought of as attacks against the public (that is, unarmed, unsuspecting civilians), not against those who protect the public. Consequently, terrorist attacks targeting police officers have to date received little academic attention. However, the police have been victimized by terrorist attacks more so than one might expect. According to the Global Terrorism Database (GTD), police have been targeted by terrorist groups in 11,500 of the 98,112 recorded incidents between 1970 and 2010, comprising almost 12% of terrorism targets. For comparison, private citizens were attacked in only about twice as many incidents; private citizens are the most frequently attacked target (see Figure 15.1).[1] While police rank as the fifth most popular target type, they have been the focus of terrorists almost as much as the military, the government, and business entities. Given the relative popularity of targeting police, the lack of academic research to this unique target type is "surprising" (Freilich & Chermak, 2009, p. 145).

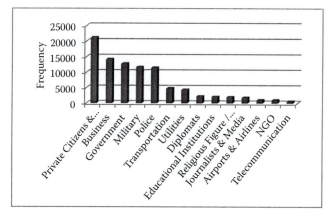

Figure 15.1 Distribution of terrorist attacks worldwide, 1970–2010, by target type. (Data source: National Consortium for the Study of Terrorism and Responses to Terrorism, 2011.)

Perhaps scholars have focused attention on other aspects of terrorism because attacks on police may not be considered "terrorism." Taking into account the police receive special training in weapons and tactics to defend themselves and others and considering they voluntarily put themselves in harm's way, the police may be considered "combatants," and therefore attacks on police may not be defined as terrorism. Indeed, violence—including terrorist violence—is considered part of the officer's job, as reflected in the concept of the "blue canary." Similar to the canary used by early miners to detect hazardous gases in the mine shafts, a blue canary is a responding officer who, unfortunately, falls victim to hazardous materials, signaling to other authorities to call a hazmat crew (Batista, 2005). Because violence seems to be inherent in policing, violence against the police is expected, and perhaps police are not viewed as "victims" of terrorist violence.

Another reason why scholars may prefer studying terrorism in general terms, instead of focusing on specific target types like the police, is to build a general theory of terrorism. A general theory explains terrorism within a broad scope (see, e.g., Braithwaite, 1989, for a discussion on theory). This provides for broad tests to promote empirical support for the theory. The practical purpose of a general theory is to direct policies (Akers & Sellers, 2004), which sometimes can be difficult to do when focusing narrowly on a topic.

With this in mind, the purpose of this chapter is twofold. First is the argument that attacks on police are, indeed, acts of terrorism. The second is that studying unique terrorism target types enhances theory and policy development. By exploring why police officers make attractive targets for terrorists, there is a discussion of whether attacks on police should be considered terrorism. The analysis examines the lessons learned about terrorism by disaggregating its study into a review of smaller categories of terrorism, concluding by encouraging scholars to devote attention to studying terrorist attacks targeting police to fill this gap in the literature.

Why Would Terrorists Target Police?

Terrorists choose certain targets for a variety of reasons. Among other incentives, terrorists attack for several reasons:

1. Symbolic reasons, as some targets are proxies for other desirable targets (like the government);
2. Practical reasons, because some targets may provide weapons or materials terrorists need or because targets may stand in the way of carrying out an attack;
3. Demonstrative reasons, to show terrorists' strength and commitment to their cause; and
4. Because targets are accessible, and they are low-hanging fruit or simply easy to attack.

As shown in Figure 15.2, these motives are not mutually exclusive. A target can be both symbolic and accessible. For example, civilians are practical targets because, in democracies at least, they can persuade the government to concede to terrorists' demands. Civilians also are easily accessible because they are ubiquitous. The police are a unique target for terrorists because the

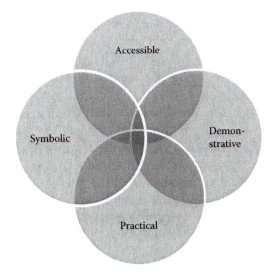

Figure 15.2 Reasons terrorists attack.

police fall into the intersection—that is, police can be targeted for all of these reasons—as explained in the following discussion.

Symbolic Targets

Bombing or otherwise attacking targets that are symbolic of an ideology—like the World Trade Center in New York City, one target of the September 11, 2001, attacks on the United States—is akin to attacking that ideology itself. Police make attractive targets for some terrorists because they are representatives of the government's coercive authority, making them *symbolic* targets. Some terrorist groups in the United States even have "hit lists" targeting police officers (Freilich & Chermak, 2009, p. 144) because police are in a "'brotherhood' [with] a tyrannical government" (Miller, 2010, p. 3). Indeed, this can be seen around the world. For example, both Pakistani and Afghani police are targeted by Taliban militants as symbolic attacks against foreign forces on the respective country's soil—in the former country because of U.S. drone strikes and in the latter country due to the long-standing U.S. military presence. Baker and Safi (2007, paragraph 5) reported in *Time* that Qari Yusuf Ahmadi, a spokesman for the Taliban, claimed that the Taliban will continue to target people—including the police—who work with foreigners. The Taliban also attack the police to disrupt the improving infrastructure, recently to recruit local police to join their forces (Salahuddin, 2012) and notably in Afghanistan because the Afghan National Police are part of counterinsurgency operations, suggesting terrorists also target the police for practical reasons—to which we now turn.

Practical Targets

Terrorists may select a target for its practicality. Considering that police have discretion whether to arrest/release members of terrorist organizations, they may be viewed as "roadblocks" that thwart terrorists' goals. Perhaps more important, as first responders to emergencies, police officers are strategic targets for terrorist groups (Alexander, 2007, p. 2). By overwhelming or incapacitating law enforcement, they become ineffective in resolving a terrorist attack, making the incident much bigger and with more fatalities as a terrorist attack on the police diminishes the capacity for police to respond to other incidents. Response systems are typically set up to deal with civilian incidents; when the responders are targeted, who responds to that incident is questionable. An attack on police—or even police response to a terrorist attack—can reduce police morale, increase stress on police, and increase costs to the public in terms of health care and missed time from work (see, e.g., Dowling, Moynihan, Genet, & Lewis, 2006; Drake, 1998, p. 73; Robbers & Jenkins, 2005). An attack on police may create more confusion and a weaker initial response to a terrorist incident, making the authorities seem ineffective (Drake, 1998, p. 73; see also Crenshaw, 1981, pp. 386–387, for the argument that terrorism, generally, may be to disrupt or weaken normal governmental operations). This casts doubt on the police's ability to protect the public (at least in some communities, where terrorist threats decrease police clearance of general crimes; see Weisburd, Hasisi, Jonathan, & Aviv, 2010), potentially decreasing the likelihood that the public will cooperate with them and thereby supporting the terrorists' cause (see Crenshaw, 1981, pp. 387–388). Similarly, attacks on police potentially reduce authorities' ability to detect and investigate terrorists, which enhances terrorists' ability to act in the future.

The Maoists in India targeted the police for practical reasons when the Indian government launched an offensive against Maoists' terrorism. In one 2010 incident, the group killed 75 police in an initial ambush, after which police reinforcements were attacked by Maoist guerillas when trying to collect the dead bodies of their colleagues (Kumar, 2010). As a result of the police failing to gather the fallen officers, the Indian Air Force was called in to remove the dead. The Reuters press agency reported the perception that Indian police officers are not competent to handle the Maoist terrorist threat (Kumar, 2010, pp. 3–9), implying they should no longer respond to such violence. In addition to its practicality, this attack also shows the group is capable of killing those who are trained in responding to violent offenders.

Demonstrative Target

With the police viewed as having a great deal of power and well prepared for violence, attacking the police demonstrates the terrorist group's capacity for violence and shows its strength (Alexander, 2007, p. 10). This is seen when terrorist groups defeat police practices, the terrorists consider themselves stronger. An example of this was seen in Pakistan on December 6, 2010, when Lashkar-e-Islami terrorists broke into the home of a Frontier Constabulary officer. Simply by seriously injuring his mother and brother and kidnapping the officer (National Consortium for the Study of Terrorism and Responses to Terrorism, 2011), this demonstrates to their followers and outsiders the power of the group.

Demonstrative attacks are also useful actions through which to gain publicity that helps with recruitment and garnering sympathy from "soft-liner" opponents and from "third parties" who might persuade opponents to concede to terrorists' demands (Pape, 2005, p. 9). Because of the heinous nature of attacking an agent of the state, attacks on police receive quite a bit of media attention, making police a target for terrorists interested in such attention.

316 | Examining Political Violence

Accessible Targets

Being ubiquitous, police officers are *accessible* targets. Due to the police routinely patrolling areas, they have police stations with minimal security available to the public, and people know the location of the stations. While active military units also may go on patrol, they are heavily armored—typically more so than the police. In addition, military bases are not accessible to anyone other than military personnel. A recent explosion at a police station in Turkey demonstrates the accessibility of the police to terrorist groups. A suspected militant associated with the PKK (Partiya Karkeran Kurdistan, which translates to the Kurdistan Workers Party) sped through a police checkpoint about 55 miles away before he rammed into a Turkish police station, where the bomb inside his vehicle exploded (BBC News, 2012). Several police officers were killed, and the bomb injured some children of officers, as police residences were nearby (BBC News, 2012).

While the police are targeted for all (symbolic, practical, demonstrative, or accessibility) of these reasons, other targets may or may not be. Other main targets of terrorist attacks—citizens, businesses, government personnel and installations, military, transportation and utilities, and religious institutions—may provide symbolic reasons for terrorists attacking them, especially citizens and transportation as they are easily accessible targets (Table 15.1). However, they do not serve a practical purpose as other targets do. Terrorists cannot demonstrate the symbolic potency of their group and their strength by attacking citizens as such targets do not demonstrate the capability of a terrorist group to threaten the security or political infrastructure of a state, thereby increasing the terror effect of that group. As most citizens do not have specialized training in defense, they are not perceived as "strong." One result of this is citizens are not practical targets because the risk structure for terrorists will not change with an attack on citizens. Also, citizens often are intended recipients of a message (with the exception of businesses, which may be practical targets for funding of terroristic enterprise).

Table 15.1 Reasons Terrorists May Attack Selected Targets

	Symbolic	Accessible	Practical	Demonstrative
Police	Yes	Yes	Yes	Yes
Business	Yes	Yes	Yes/no	Yes/no
Military	Yes	No	Yes	Yes
Government	Yes	No	Yes/no	Yes/no
Citizens	Yes/no	Yes	No	Yes/no
Transportation	No	Yes	Yes/no	No
Religious	Yes	Yes	No	No

Other targets are attacked for some, but not all, of these reasons. Businesses may be symbolic of capitalism, businesses are everywhere and easily accessible, and they can be practical targets for funding of terroristic enterprises. However, a terrorist attack on a business does not necessarily demonstrate a terrorist group's strength or commitment to the cause, but this may depend on the business. Government targets like diplomats, buildings, foreign embassies, and personnel are symbolic targets of the state. Some government targets, like one that houses money or caches of weapon, may be practical targets, and attacking some of the more heavily guarded government facilities or personnel can demonstrate a group's strength. But, many government buildings are not easily accessible because they are fenced off from the public or require identification to enter.

Similar to the police, the military, as representatives of the government's coercive force, is symbolic of the state, is a practical target to gain weapons or to weaken combatants who may impede a terrorist attack, and due to their weapons, training, tactics, and protection, is a target that establishes the strength of the terrorist group. Unlike the police, the military is not easily accessible as they are housed in heavily guarded bases and patrol in armored vehicles.

Transportation and utilities are not symbolic targets of the state and are not usually heavily guarded; while they are accessible targets, they may or may not be practical (unless they are attacked to provide some sort of cover for another attack). Finally, religious institutions are symbolic of a belief that may run counter to the terrorists' creed; given that many religions strive to help the populace, they are by nature accessible to everyone. But, religious institutions do not offer weapons or financing, and as a type of civilian target, they are weak relative to stronger targets like the military or police, blocking opportunity for a terrorist group to demonstrate its strength.

Attacking each of these targets is considered terrorism. Terrorists have more reasons to attack the police than any of these targets; in fact, police are the only target that definitely meets all four reasons for attack. Accordingly, attacks on the police also should be considered terrorism.

Indeed, terrorists have many reasons to target the police, yet we know little to inform policy or theory on terrorist attacks targeting police. Scholarly work on policing and terrorism typically focuses on other topics, like countering terrorism (e.g., Carter & Carter, 2009; Lum, Kennedy, & Sherley, 2006; Weisburd, Feucht, Hakimi, Mock, & Perry, 2009; Weisburd, Jonathan, & Perry, 2009); whether the police instead of the military should combat terrorism (Perliger et al., 2009); police preparedness and training (Chermak, Freilich, & Shemtob, 2009; Pelfrey, 2007); consequences of police responses to terrorism (Brodeur, 2007; Loader, 2006; Weisburd et al., 2010); organizational change (Nussbaum, 2007); police attitudes about terrorism (Freilich, Chermak, & Simone, 2009); or public attitudes toward the police (Jonathan, 2010). With few exceptions (Deflem, 2011; Deflem & Sutphin, 2006; Freilich

& Chermak, 2009), researchers rarely study police as victims of terrorism. This lack of attention to terrorist attacks targeting police is, as Freilich and Chermak point out, "surprising considering the large threat that terrorism poses, especially to law enforcement" (Freilich & Chermak, 2009, p. 145). Perhaps terrorist attacks on police are relatively absent from scholarly literature because some may not consider attacks on police "terrorism."

Are Attacks on Police Acts of "Terrorism"?

Terrorism is intentional violence on noncombatants by nonstate actors in the pursuit of an ideology, usually political. The GTD, for example, defines terrorism as an "intentional act of violence or threat of violence by a non-state actor" (National Consortium for the Study of Terrorism and Responses to Terrorism, n.d., paragraph 10). For a case to be included in the GTD, two of three additional criteria must be present:

1. The violent act was aimed at attaining a political, economic, religious, or social goal;
2. The violent act included evidence of an intention to coerce, intimidate, or convey some other message to a larger audience (or audiences) other than the immediate victims; and
3. The violent act was outside the precepts of International Humanitarian Law (National Consortium for the Study of Terrorism and Responses to Terrorism, n.d., p.11).

It is this third criterion that challenges whether attacks on police should be considered terrorism.

   At the heart of this debate is whether such attacks occur outside the precepts of international humanitarian law (IHL), which guides (usually interstate) armed conflicts. IHL suggests civilian casualties should be avoided during armed conflict, which should be directed toward combatants; a hallmark of terrorist activity is violating this rule, as civilians and noncombatants typically are targeted (Forst, 2009; Hoffman, 2006; Jenkins, 1980). The question arises whether police are considered civilians or combatants, and the answer determines whether an attack is considered terrorism—or something else (like assault or homicide). Attacks on the police *should* be considered terrorism where police are civilians and, as such, noncombatants. Western countries, like the United States and the United Kingdom, have police agencies that are separate and distinct from the military (Klockars, 1985). In these countries, attacks on police clearly are attacks on civilians and are in violation of IHL.

   Complicating the issue of determining whether police are a civilian body, many countries have multiple policing agencies. In Venezuela, for example, Dirección de los Servicios de Inteligencia y Prevención (Directorate of Intelligence and Prevention Services or DISIP) and Cuerpo Técnico de Policía Judicial (Judicial Technical Police, renamed the National Directorate of Criminal Investigation or CICPC) are the two main national investigative agencies, housed under the Ministry of Interior and Justice (Birkbeck, 2006; Policía Nacional Estará, n.d.). El Cuerpo de Policía Nacional Bolivariana (CPNB or National Police), responsible for transit systems, was established in 2009 (Policía Nacional Estará, n.d.). Venezuela also has state- and municipal-level police forces (Birkbeck, 2006). In addition to these civilian policing agencies, Fuerzas Armadas de Cooperación (FAC or National Guard or Armed Forces of Cooperation) is part of the military, housed under the Ministry of Defense (Birkbeck, 2006; Policía Nacional Estará, n.d.). With arrest powers, FAC is responsible for internal security, border protection, and Venezuela's highway system, functioning as a federal police force (Birkbeck, 2006; Policía Nacional Estará, n.d.). Similarly, the Turkish National Police, a civilian force, is responsible for policing urban areas, while the paramilitary Jandarma Genel Komutanlığı (the Gendarmerie) operates in conjunction with the military to secure rural areas, which comprise about 90% of Turkey (Library of Congress, 1995, 2008). While the Gendarmerie is part of the armed forces, it is housed under the Ministry of Interior during peacetime (Aydin, 2006). Supplementing the Gendarmerie, village guards were created in 1985 to serve as local militias, mainly in southeastern Turkey (Library of Congress, 2008). In addition, these agencies change over time, some becoming civilianized and others becoming paramilitary or part of the military. For example, the People's Police of Albania, created in 1945, initially was housed under the Ministry of Interior but became part of the Armed Forces in April 1991 (Shkembi, 2006). Since November 1999, the People's Police has been separate from the military (Shkembi, 2006). Following the IHL rule that terrorism is directed against noncombatant targets, determining whether particular police agencies are civilian bodies or part of the military is important.

Some may argue attacks on police should *not* be considered terrorism because police are *not* civilians: Police are part of the body of government, and in some (usually more autocratic) countries, police are part of the military. For example, the Royal Bahrain Police and the military "are one and the same" (Miller, 2006, p. 67). There, attacks on the police, who are part of the same body as the military, may be considered attacks against combatants and may not violate the precepts of IHL. However, military agencies are considered noncombatants during times of peace and when they are not on duty (Hull, 2001; National Counterterrorism Center, 2009)—in other words, when they are not actively involved in conflict; the same applies to police, even when they are part of a military body.

A further difficulty resolving the issue of police combatant status in terrorist incidents is that specific police agencies often are not reported. The GTD, perhaps the most comprehensive incident-level database on terrorism, does a remarkable job of separating cases where police were targeted; however, many of the news sources from which the data are drawn often only identify the "police" were victims, neglecting to specify the particular agency. This is true of another oft-used database to study terrorism, the RAND Database of Worldwide Terrorism Incidents. This challenge in determining combatant status can be compensated by defining police as civilian in countries where they are not part of the military forces and as noncombatants when they are part of the military forces, during times of peace.

While one criterion of IHL—noncombatant status—can be met, this may be a moot point because IHL may not even apply to terrorism. Again, IHL guides armed conflicts. Typically, armed conflict refers to war, and to invoke IHL, generally a state must be one of the parties (Bianchi, 2011). While terrorism is asymmetric armed conflict of an extremist group usually targeting the state, Bianchi observes, "Terrorism in and of itself is not inherently related to armed conflict and only comes under the regulation of IHL in certain particular situations" (2011, p. 3). Accordingly, terrorism, by definition, is not bound by IHL because terrorism itself refers to asymmetric conflict outside of war. Terrorism is a violation of IHL; indeed, violations of IHL may be called terrorism (International Committee of the Red Cross, 2010). Because terrorism violates IHL, terrorists are those who are not concerned with the driving principle of IHL—namely, the protection of civilians.

Regardless of the argument, attacks on police by terrorists are terrorism. However, we know relatively little about this particular target type. Beyond the debate over whether attacks on police are terrorism (they are), this target type may be neglected in scholarly literature for another reason. Some may argue that studying specific types of terrorism distracts from forming a broad, general theory of terrorism. The next section reviews this argument, assuming that attacks on police are indeed terrorism, and encourages the study of terrorist attacks targeting the police for both theory and policy development.

Studying Types of Terrorism

Disaggregating terrorism into types sometimes is frowned on. General theories are preferred because they offer universal causes of terrorism, attempting to explain many different types of terrorism across cultures (see, generally, Gottfredson & Hirschi, 1990, for arguments in favor of general theories over typological theories). Typologies, on the other hand, serve as classification systems, organizing "facts" of terrorism in meaningful ways to better understand it. Typologies of terrorism have focused on characteristics of terrorism offenses and on aspects of terrorists. For example, Smith (1994) differentiated between domestic and international terrorism. Combs (1997) pointed out types of terrorist tactics, including bombing, arson, hostage taking and kidnapping, assassinations and ambushes, aerial hijacking, and chemical–biological attacks, among others. Shifting focus from the offense to the offender, Hacker (1976) identified three types of terrorist offenders: criminals, crazies, and crusaders. Combs (1997) points out that identifying the commonalities among all types of terrorism can be useful (in her case, she used typologies to develop a definition of contemporary terrorism). However, typologies have been criticized on several grounds. First, there is no limit to the number of "types"—that is, the number of characteristics in a typology is arbitrary. Similarly, when to stop the typological breakdown is unclear. Categories should be mutually exclusive, but when they are, their explanatory scope may be limited. In addition, the boundaries between categories can be fuzzy, clouding conceptual clarity. For these reasons, many social scientists shy away from typological theories (see, e.g., Gottfredson & Hirschi, 1990; but see Gibbons, 1985). Indeed, the purpose of this chapter is not to argue in favor of typological theories. However, studying smaller aspects of terrorism can tell us a great deal, allowing scholars and policy makers to build on this information to develop theory and policy.

Pape (2003, 2005; Pape & Feldman, 2010), for example, focused his research on suicide terrorism campaigns—one type of terrorism. Contrary to popular opinion, Pape found that suicide terrorism is not driven by religion (used only as a recruiting tool), but rather a secular nationalist goal: "to compel modern democracies to withdraw military forces from territory that the terrorists consider to be their homeland" (Pape, 2005, p. 4). Pape (2005, p. 4) identified three main trends supporting this hypothesis:

1. Suicide terrorism attacks are not isolated but occur in organized campaigns;
2. Suicide attacks are more likely to target democracies, which are more easily persuaded by citizens to negotiate with the terrorist group; and
3. Groups sponsoring suicide terrorism campaigns aspire toward political self-determination, and a necessary first step is to remove a democratic power from a territory they want. This has implications for state governments.

Pape's (2005) hypothesis can be studied using other outcomes, like terrorism generally, broadening the scope of his findings. Braithwaite (1989) argues that the causal instances outlined in a general theory must account for most types of the behavior the theory claims to explain and must explain some variance in all of the cases. Indeed, one criterion used to evaluate theory is whether the theory is broad in scope. Accordingly, a good theory must account for a wide range of behaviors. Exploring theoretical predictors on specific types of terrorism—like terrorism directed at police—has the potential to demonstrate the broad scope of a theory or the limits of a theory.

In addition, target types matter. Terrorism is a struggle between those without power against those with power. Terrorist groups typically have limited resources and must focus their efforts wisely to have the biggest desired impact. Accordingly, they are selective in their targets (Sandler & Lapan, 1988, p. 259), and disaggregating target types allows for enriched theoretical development. For example, in their extensive review of newspaper reports of collective violence (e.g., riots, disorderly protests on college campuses), Martin, McCarthy, and McPhail (2009) found that organization type affected such violence against certain target types—namely, that state representatives like the police are more likely to be targets of violence in rallies than are civilians or bystanders, and larger collectivities increase the likelihood of violence against state representatives. Rorie (2008, p. 46) concludes that target type affected whether a terrorist group claimed an attack. Terrorists may attack the police for reasons both similar to and different from other targets. However, little is known about how target types compare because studies of terrorist attacks on police are scant (Freilich & Chermak, 2009).

One notable exception is the work of Freilich and Chermak (2009; see also Deflem, 2011; Deflem & Sutphin, 2006). Drawing from their Extremist Crime Database, focusing on attacks in the United States since 1990, these scholars critically examined two cases of right-wing extremist attacks on police in the context of situational crime prevention. They suggest a strategy to prevent such attacks on police can be found through hard and soft situational crime prevention techniques, which reduce the opportunity for "routine" encounters to escalate into violence. While their study was exploratory, they encourage additional research on extremist attacks on police—a recommendation echoed here.

Conclusion

This chapter has established that attacks on police should be considered terrorism. Police are attractive targets of terrorists for several reasons, and terrorist groups have more reasons to attack the police than most other targets. In many instances, police are noncombatants and are not actively engaged in warfare; accordingly, attacks on them are akin to attacks on civilians or military personnel during peacetime. Police are not actively involved in wartime conflict, so when they are attacked, they are victims of terrorists. In other instances, the line between the police and the military is blurred; in some countries—like Afghanistan—the police are specifically charged with fighting insurgents and terrorists. However, similar to military targets, attacks on police can be considered acts of terrorism when police are off duty or otherwise not engaged in active conflict. Any act of terrorism, though, is asymmetric conflict operating outside the boundaries of the IHL, so an attack on police by terrorists should be considered terrorism. In any event, little is known about terrorist attacks targeting the police.

Studying terrorist attacks on police is beneficial for both theoretical development and generating evidence-based policies that can protect both the police and the public. Terrorists have a lot to gain by attacking the police, and the public has much to lose when terrorists attack police—in terms of safety and morale. This chapter is a call to "academic arms" to study such attacks.

First, we need to know more about the nature and extent of this problem. Freilich and Chermak (2009) reported on extremist attacks on police in the United States. Deflem (2011) described terrorism against police in Afghanistan and, with Sutphin, reviewed attacks on police in Iraq (Deflem & Sutphin, 2006). These make a significant contribution to understanding such attacks, but more needs to be done. Further studies describing terrorist attacks on police are needed, outlining geographical areas high and low in attacks on police, which organizations are more likely to attack the police, whether police are primary or ancillary targets, and so on. These will help build theories about attacks on police, which likely will support theories of terrorism, generally.

Second, when we have more information describing terrorist attacks on police, researchers could compare attacks on police with attacks on other targets and explore the factors affecting terrorist attacks on police. Such studies would be beneficial, as researchers could find whether these factors are similar to or different from known correlates influencing terrorism against other targets, thereby strengthening the body of knowledge on terrorism. In addition, scholars can test theories of terrorism, which should apply to attacks on police if the theories are indeed broad in scope. For example, Pape's (2005; Pape & Feldman, 2010) theory that the presence of a foreign military—especially one of a different religion—on a country's soil spawns suicide attacks in that state may apply to attacks on police, especially when the police (paramilitary or otherwise) are helping that foreign military like the police helping the United States in Afghanistan. If support is found for this and other theories of terrorism using specific terrorist targets (like the police) as dependent variables, then the theory will be bolstered by having a broader scope. In short, focusing on terrorist attacks on police can contribute to moving the field forward.

Note

1. There are three target fields available in the GTD, allowing for more than one target type to be recorded per incident. Only the first target field was used to count the number of incidents involving each target type.

References

Akers, Ronald L., & Sellers, Christine Sharon. (2004). *Criminological theories: Introduction, evaluation, and application* (4th ed.). Los Angeles: Roxbury.

Alexander, Dean C. (2007). Terror attacks on law enforcement worldwide. *The Police Chief, 74*(2). Retrieved October 19, 2008, from http://policechiefmagazine.org/magazine/index.cfm?fuseaction=display_arch&article_id=1113&issue_id=22007

Aydin, A. H. (2006). Turkey. In Dilip K. Das (Ed.), *World police encyclopedia* (Vol. 2, pp. 855–861). New York: Routledge.

Baker, Aryn, & Safi, Ali. (2007, June 16). Terror target: the Afghan police. *Time.* Retrieved May 29, 2011, from http://www.time.com/time/world/article/0,8599,1634031,00.html

Batista, Ernie. (2005). No blue canaries: Implementing a PPE program protect the protectors. *Law Enforcement Technology, 32*(8), 94, 96–101.

BBC News. (2012, May 25). Deadly "suicide bomb" outside Turkish police station. *BBC News.* Retrieved June 4, 2012, from http://www.bbc.co.uk/news/world-europe-18204290

Bianchi, Andrea. (2011). Terrorism and armed conflict: Insights from a law and literature perspective. *Leiden Journal of International Law, 24*(1), 1–21.

Birkbeck, C. H. (2006). Venezuela. In Dilip K. Das (Ed.), *World police encyclopedia* (Vol. 2, pp. 903–911). New York: Routledge.

Braithwaite, John. (1989). *Crime, shame and reintegration.* New York: Cambridge University Press.

Brodeur, J.-P. (2007). High and low policing in post-9/11 times. *Policing, 1*(1), 25–37.

Carter, D. L., & Carter, J. G. (2009). The intelligence fusion process for state, local, and tribal law enforcement. *Criminal Justice and Behavior, 36*(12), 1323–1339.

Chermak, S. M., Freilich, J. D., & Shemtob, Z. (2009). Law enforcement training and the domestic far right. *Criminal Justice and Behavior, 36*(12), 1305–1322.

Combs, Cindy C. (1997). *Terrorism in the twenty-first century.* Upper Saddle River, NJ: Prentice-Hall.

Crenshaw, Martha. (1981). The causes of terrorism. *Comparative Politics, 13*(4), 379–399.

Deflem, M. (2011). Policing Afghanistan: Civilian police reform and the resurgence of the Taliban. In S. Carlton-Ford & M. G. Ender (Eds.), *The Routledge handbook of war and society: Iraq and Afghanistan* (pp. 114–124). London: Routledge.

Deflem, M., & Sutphin, S. (2006). Policing post-war Iraq: Insurgency, civilian police, and the reconstruction of society. *Sociological Focus, 39*(4), 265–283.

Dowling, Frank G., Moynihan, Gene, Genet, Bill, & Lewis, Jonathan. (2006). A peer-based assistance program for officers with the New York City Police Department: Report of the effects of Sept. 11, 2001. *American Journal of Psychiatry, 163*, 151–153.

Drake, C. J. M. (1998). The role of ideology in terrorists' target selection. *Terrorism and Political Violence, 10*(2), 53–85.

Forst, B. (2009). *Terrorism, crime, and public policy.* New York: Cambridge University Press.

Freilich, J. D., & Chermak, S. M. (2009). Preventing deadly encounters between law enforcement and American far-rightists. *Crime Prevention Studies, 25*, 141–172.

Freilich, J. D., Chermak, S. M., & Simone, J., Jr. (2009). Surveying American state police agencies about terrorism threats, terrorism sources, and terrorism definitions. *Terrorism and Political Violence, 21*, 450–475.

Gibbons, D. C. (1985). The assumption of the efficacy of middle-range explanation: Typologies. In Robert F. Meier (Ed.), *Theoretical methods in criminology.* Beverly Hills, CA: Sage, 151–174.

Gottfredson, M. R., & Hirschi, T. (1990). *A general theory of crime.* Stanford, CA: Stanford University Press.

Hacker, F. (1976). *Crusaders, criminals, crazies.* New York: Norton.

Hoffman, B. (2006). *Inside terrorism* (Rev. and expanded ed.). New York: Columbia University Press.

Hull, E. J. (2001, April 30). *Patterns of global terrorism, 2000.* Washington, DC: United States Department of State. Retrieved May 15, 2011, from http://www.state.gov/s/ct/rls/crt/2000/2419.htm

International Committee of the Red Cross (ICRC). (2010, October 29). Challenges for IHL—terrorism: overview. Retrieved June 4, 2012, from http://www.icrc.org/eng/war-and-law/contemporary-challenges-for-ihl/terrorism/overview-terrorism.htm

Jenkins, B. M. (1980). *The study of terrorism: definitional problems.* Santa Monica, CA: Rand. Retrieved May 15, 2011, from http://www.rand.org/content/dam/rand/pubs/papers/2006/P6563.pdf

Jonathan, T. (2010). Police involvement in counter-terrorism and public attitudes towards the police in Israel: 1998–2007. *British Journal of Criminology, 50*, 748–771.

Klockars, C. B. (1985). *The idea of police.* Beverly Hills, CA: Sage Publications.

Kumar, Sujeet. (2010, April 6). Maoists kill 75 police in central India attack. *Reuters.* Retrieved June 4, 2012, from http://www.reuters.com/article/2010/04/06/us-india-maoist-idUSTRE6350TV20100406

Library of Congress, Federal Research Division. (1995). *Country Studies: Turkey: Police System.* Retrieved June 22, 2010, from http://lcweb2.loc.gov/frd/cs/trtoc.html

Library of Congress, Federal Research Division. (2008). *Country Profile: Turkey.* Retrieved June 22, 2010, from http://lcweb2.loc.gov/frd/cs/profiles/Turkey.pdf

Loader, I. (2006). Policing, recognition, and belonging. *The Annals of the American Academy of Political and Social Science, 605*, 201–221.

Lum, C., Kennedy, L. W., & Sherley, A. (2006). Are counter-terrorism strategies effective? The results of the Campbell systematic review on counter-terrorism evaluation research. *Journal of Experimental Criminology, 2*, 489–516.

Martin, Andrew W., McCarthy, John D., & McPhail, Clark. (2009). Why targets matter: Toward a more inclusive model of collective violence. *American Sociological Review, 74*, 821–841.

Miller, C. D. (2010, April 8). Hutaree tapes: David Bryan Stone, Sr. rants against "new world order," say prosecutors. *CBS News*. Retrieved June 15, 2010, from http://www.cbsnews.com/8301-504083_162-20002051-504083.html

Miller, J. M. (2006). Bahrain. In Dilip K. Das (Ed.), *World police encyclopedia* (Vol. 1, pp. 66–68). New York: Routledge.

National Consortium for the Study of Terrorism and Responses to Terrorism. (2011, July). *Global Terrorism Database*. Retrieved July 29, 2011, from http://www.start.umd.edu/data/gtd/

National Consortium for the Study of Terrorism and Responses to Terrorism. (n.d.). *Global Terrorism Database: Data collection methodology*. Retrieved May 15, 2011, from http://www.start.umd.edu/gtd/using-gtd/

National Counterterrorism Center. (2009, April 30). *2008 report on terrorism*. Washington, DC: Author. Retrieved May 15, 2011, from http://www.fbi.gov/stats-services/publications/terror_08.pdf

Nussbaum, B. (2007). Protecting global cities: New York, London and the internationalization of municipal policing for counter terrorism. *Global Crime, 8*(3), 213–232.

Pape, R. A. (2003). The strategic logic of suicide terrorism. *The American Political Science Review, 97*(3), 343–361.

Pape, R. A. (2005). *Dying to win: The strategic logic of suicide terrorism*. New York: Random House Trade Paperbacks.

Pape, R. A., & Feldman, J. K. (2010). *Cutting the fuse: The explosion of global suicide terrorism and how to stop it*. Chicago: University of Chicago Press.

Pelfrey, W. V., Jr. (2007). Local law enforcement terrorism prevention efforts: A state level case study. *Journal of Criminal Justice, 35*, 313–321.

Perliger, A., Hasisi, B., & Pedahzur, A. (2009). Policing terrorism in Israel. *Criminal Justice and Behavior, 36*(12), 1279–1304.

Policía Nacional Estará Presente En Estaciones De Metro Y Autopistas De Caracas. (n.d.). Retrieved July 15, 2010, from http://www.el-nacional.com/www/site/p_contenido.php?q = nodo/140121/Comunidad/Policía-Nacional-estará-presente-en-estaciones-de-Metro-y-autopistas-de-Caracas.

Robbers, Monica. L. P., & Jenkins, Jonathan Mark. (2005). Symptomatology of posttraumatic stress disorder among first responders to the Pentagon on 9/11: A preliminary analysis of Arlington County police first responders. *Police Practice and Research, 6*(3), 235–249.

Rorie, M. L. (2008). *Communicating through violence: An application of rational choice theory to terrorist claims of responsibility*. Master's thesis, University of Maryland, College Park.

Salahuddin, Sayed. (2012, July 4). Afghan local police group deserts to Taliban-led insurgents. *The Washington Post*. Retrieved July 4, 2012, from http://www.washingtonpost.com/world/war-zones/afghan-local-police-group-deserts-to-taliban-led-insurgents/2012/07/04/gJQAzvNCNW_story.html?wpmk=MK0000200

Sandler, Todd, & Lapan, Harvey E. (1988). The calculus of dissent: An analysis of terrorists' choice of targets. *Synthese, 76*, 245–261.

Shkembi, H. (2006). Albania. In Dilip K. Das (Ed.), *World police encyclopedia* (Vol. 1, pp. 8–14). New York: Routledge.

Smith, Brent L. (1994). *Terrorism in America: Pipe bombs and pipe dreams* (SUNY series in new directions in criminal justice studies). Albany, NY: SUNY Press.

Weisburd, D., Feucht, T. E., Hakimi, I., Mock, L. F., & Perry, S. (Eds.). (2009). *To protect and serve: Policing in an age of terrorism.* New York: Springer.

Weisburd, D., Hasisi, B., Jonathan, T., & Aviv, G. (2010). Terrorist threats and police performance: A study of Israeli communities. *British Journal of Criminology, 50*(4), 725–747.

Weisburd, D., Jonathan, T., & Perry, S. (2009). The Israeli model for policing terrorism: Goals, strategies, and open questions. *Criminal Justice and Behavior, 36*(12), 1259–1278.

Policing Political Violence in Australia

16

STEVE JAMES

Contents

Introduction

Popular and scholarly commentary on the policing of political violence in recent years has been dominated understandably by concerns over terrorist activities (as attested in the current volume). This chapter, however, charts somewhat different terrain in that it seeks to review developments in Australia related to other forms of political violence. Such a review is warranted as it is clear that violent crime related to terrorist activities hardly exhausts the array of political violence, and a concentration on terrorist activities and their policing should not obscure serious abuses taking place in other contexts. At the same time, it is possible to connect concerns about terrorism and political violence directed at communities that have been linked in popular (and indeed academic) discourse with terrorism; the reported experiences of many Islamic communities around the world, for instance, have been replete with examples of harassment, discrimination, and violence in the wake of the September 11, 2001, bombing of the World Trade Center.

Australia has not experienced the kinds of right-wing extremism and violence that have so alarmed European and (to a lesser extent) North American observers since 1993 (Daily Mail, 2009; Merkl and Weinberg, 1997; Westervelt, 2009). While right-wing extremist organizations have existed in Australia for many decades, their influence on mainstream political process is generally thought to have been marginal, and their criminal activities episodic and relatively contained. While their recent incarnations share some source commonalities with Northern Hemisphere phenomena (working-class alienation in the wake of postindustrialization and globalization, the perpetuation of Jewish conspiracy theories, fears engendered by immigration), their political successes and their recruitment potential at the formal organizational level remain very modest.

However, despite Australia's reputation as a relatively safe and highly multicultural society, there are enduring concerns that beneath the affable surface there exist persistent racist and other forms of intolerance that provide the oxygen for selective violence. Australia's Islamic communities have not been free from the kinds of Islamophobic abuses that have taken place elsewhere (Poynting and Mason, 2007). The internationally reported "Cronulla riots" of 2005 (Abraham, 2005) contained intriguing elements of anti-Islamic sentiment and the involvement of right-wing extremist groups. Very recently, Australia has been subject to aggressive reportage by the Indian TV news over what it sees as a series of persistent and racially motivated attacks on Indian students studying in Melbourne and Sydney ("Attack on Indian Students," 2009; Verghis, 2009; Wade, 2009).

The central problems of the policing of violence born of intolerance and discrimination is that such violence is not always the responsibility of readily identifiable extremist groups, but rather it is diffused in everyday examples of intimidation and harassment and is often perpetrated by people who share no conscious ideology of the extreme right. Historically, police have been implicated themselves in such intimidation and harassment, have acted passively toward those so inclined, or have been singularly unsympathetic to victimization. The task of contemporary police planners and managers is to embrace conceptions of tolerance and victimization that transcend parochial preferences. Australian policing has made some gains in this area in recent years.

The chapter outlines acknowledged extreme right-wing organizations. It then broadens the discussion into the wider arena of "hate" crimes in Australia and sketches in recent events that have jeopardized Australia's reputation for tolerance and relative freedom from political violence. The role of police within the dynamic of hate crimes is described, and recent developments are outlined and assessed.

The Explicit Threats of the Extreme Right

The spear carriers of the extreme right since World War II have been embodied by the Australian League of Rights and various neo-Nazi parties. The national League of Rights was consolidated in 1960 following state branches first established in 1946 by the late Eric Butler, an anti-Semite who propagated in Australia the infamous Protocols of the Elders of Zion. The party embraces stereotypical far-right beliefs: the threat of international Jewish dominion; denial of the Holocaust; the supremacy of white Christian culture; the inferiority of Africans and Asians; and the danger of nonwhite immigration (Campbell, 1978). The league campaigned vigorously in the 1980s against Aboriginal land rights (which it saw as a communist plot) (Greason, 1997). The current strength of the league is unclear; Greason in 1997 estimated some 1,000 activist members nationally. Greason, a reformed adolescent fascist, considered the league to be politically marginalized: "It has no known parliamentary representation, and attracts unfavourable comment on the rare occasions that it stumbles into the public spotlight. ... It is highly unlikely ... that any MP with serious leadership aspirations would wish to be associated with the league" (Greason, 1997, p. 196). He argues as well that, unlike the neo-Nazi movements (see the following discussion), league activists are not violent: "The only thing its members are likely to bombard are the phone lines to a talkback radio program" (Greason, 1997, p. 189).

The *Report of the National Inquiry into Racist Violence* by the Human Rights and Equal Opportunity Commission (HREOC) (1991, p. 201) was not so sanguine:

> The League is particularly strong in rural areas, where its meetings can attract hundreds of people. In many respects the influence of the League may be more profound and dangerous than other extremist groups because it has assumed an image of "respectability" by espousing family values, patriotism and nationalism while covertly disseminating quite racist views. The league represents the acceptable face of racism. Its advocacy of traditional values may have won it mainstream support from people who are unaware of its racist and extremist ideals.

Neo-Nazi parties have captured the public's (or at least the media's) attention over the decades, arguably well out of proportion to their political importance. Greason (1997) describes them as developing since World War II in three broad waves: the explicitly nazi Nationalist Socialist Party of Australia (NSPA) in the 1960s; the less symbolically laden (that is, no swastikas) National Front of Australia and the Australian National Alliance during the 1970s and early 1980s; and National Action (NA) from the early 1980s onward. A return to explicit Nazi ideology and paraphernalia was evident in the NA breakaway group, the Australian Nationalists Movement (ANM), formed in 1984 because its leader believed that NA was insufficiently explicit in its anti-Semitism and neo-Nazism. The membership of these respective groups has never been particularly high; the National Inquiry into Racist Violence estimated in 1991 (HREOC, 1991, p. 198) that NA's membership in New South Wales, its core location, was about 20 activists. However, the propensity of the various groups to engage in violent crime has given them a prominence beyond their mere numbers. The ANM conducted a series of bombings of Chinese restaurants in Perth (Western Australia) in the late 1980s, and its leader, Jack Van Tongeren, was sentenced to jail for 18 years. Greason (1997) reported that NA activities in Sydney (New South Wales) during the late 1980s and early 1990s included firebombings and shotgun attacks on prominent antiracist commentators and raids on antiracist group functions. NA's leader, Jim Saleam, was sentenced to jail in 1992 for an attack on Australia's African National Congress representative, and both NA and ANM members have been sentenced to imprisonment for murder (usually of fellow members).

Saleam has since established a new political party—Australia First— which first fielded candidates in the 2010 federal election: "Australia First aims to become the far-right force in Australia and to emulate the British National party's electoral success in the European Parliament" (Bearup, 2009, p. 22). Saleam completed a PhD on Australia's far-right groups at Sydney University after his release from prison. Ironically, according to friends of the Saleam family in the rural area where he grew up, Saleam is of Lebanese or Syrian heritage (Bearup, 2009, p. 24; Fight dem back! 2009), rather than the Greek ancestry he has long claimed.

The criminal activities of the fascist groups throughout the 1980s and early 1990s have been alarming and well documented (see HREOC, 1991, for a detailed description of attacks to that year). The HREOC report cites the 1989–1990 annual report of the Australian Security Intelligence Organization (ASIO):

> The only discernible domestic threat of politically motivated violence comes from the racist right. This has suffered serious setbacks in the past year with the arrest of a large number of leading members of the two most danger- ous groups. Their capacity to recover from their setbacks is yet to be shown. However, they appear to have established themselves as fairly durable political entities and will probably persist for some time as sources of communal and politically motivated violence. (HREOC, 1991, p. 223)

The Jewish community in Australia arguably feels the greatest threat from right-wing extremist groups, given their consistent anti-Semite ideolo- gies. The Executive Council of Australian Jewry publishes a regular review of anti-Semitism activities in Australia. In its most recent report (Jones, 2008), a number of fascist and neo-Nazi groups in Australia that are explicitly anti-Semitic are identified. Besides the League of Rights, the ANM, and NA, the report lists the Adelaide Institute, organized by Holocaust revisionist Fredrick Toben (Toben was ordered by the federal court to remove Holocaust denial material from his website in September 2002 under the commonwealth racial vilification law; *The Law Report*, 2002); the Covenant Vision Ministry in Sydney's outer western suburbs; the Christian "identity" ministries of far north Queensland; and the Citizens Electoral Councils (CECs), based in Melbourne, which follow Lyndon LaRouche. Neo-Nazi groups include Ausi Freedom Society and the Invisible Australian Empire. Anti-Semitic websites have proliferated in recent years, from extremist "Christian" sites often based on U.S. parents (Revival Centers International, World Church of the Creator, Christian Separatist Church Society) to neo-Nazi (White Pride Coalition, Stormfront). The Jewish community acknowledges that these groups remain on the fringes of Australian politics, and that the web presence is often all that exists of a named group (Jones, 2008, p. 87). Nevertheless, the groups are held responsible for activities, including hate mail, leafleting, poster campaigns, and graffiti, that offend or intimidate Jewish Australians (Australia/ Israel and Jewish Affairs Council [AIJAC], 2001). Jones (2008, p. 18) reports:

> During the twelve months ending September 30, 2008, 652 reports were recorded of incidents defined by the Human Rights and Equal Opportunity Commission as "racist violence" against Jewish Australians. These incidents included physical assault, vandalism—including through arson attacks— threatening telephone calls, hate mail, graffiti, leaflets, posters and abusive and intimidatory electronic mail. This exceeded by 2% the previous highest total, recorded in the year ending September 30, 2007. It was more than twice the previous average annual total.

The impact of the incidents described on the Australian Jewish community needs to recognized and deeply regretted. However, it is fair to say that organized and systematic violence by extremist right-wing groups has not been particularly widespread, and its incidence in recent years (outside the Jewish community) appears to have declined. It would be wrong, however, to conclude from this that violence based on racist and other discriminatory beliefs does not constitute a problem in Australia and its law enforcement agencies.

Crimes of Hate

It is now orthodoxy to consider certain categories of violence and other offenses directed at specific groups of people as "hate crimes." Mason (1993, cited in Cunneen, Fraser, and Tomsen, 1997, p. 1) defines hate crimes "as crime, most commonly violence motivated by prejudice, bias or hatred

towards a particular group of which the victim is presumed to be a member."
Thus, it is a class of crime characterized by the motivations of the offender
rather than any distinction in the act itself and as such has not generally
been specified in criminal statutes (at least in Australia, with some limited
exceptions). That is, an act of violence directed toward a particular victim
as an act of hatred is not usually considered legally different from an act of
violence motivated by profit or revenge. There are specific legislative developments directed at aspects of expressed hatred, such as antidiscrimination,
racial vilification, and racial hatred legislation (Jones, 1997), but these tend to
be concerned with offenses of workplace bias and public incitements to racial
hatred rather than violence per se. In the Australian context, McNamara
(2002, p. 11) argues:

> Racial vilification does not involve physical violence (although it may be
> accompanied by actual or threatened violence). In addition, one of the most
> common arguments advanced in support of the legal regulation of racial
> vilification is that it may be a precursor to, or may incite, racist violence or
> "hate crimes." Nevertheless, it is important to recognise this point of distinc-
> tion between racial vilification and racist violence. Conduct falling into the
> second category is unquestionably unlawful as a crime against the person or
> property. Conduct falling into the first category will generally be considered
> lawful unless regulated by specific racial vilification legislation.

Nevertheless, if not a legally distinct class of crime, hate crimes certainly
have a self-evident motivational dimension that makes some common sense.
Bell (2002) does not even define *hate crime* in her volume *Policing Hatred: Law
Enforcement, Civil Rights and Hate Crime*, but clearly assumes it to mean crime
(particularly violent crime) based on racist sentiment. Indeed, racist violence
appears to be the obvious subtext in most discourses on hate crime. This is too
narrow a conception, but the connotations of hatred with racism are enduring.

The extent of hate crime in Australia is difficult to gauge. Australia has
no national monitoring system for such crimes (sometimes known as "bias
crimes") like the U.S. Federal Bureau of Investigation's (2002) *Hate Crime
Statistics*. The evidence is often anecdotal, and this has led some commentators
to critique allegations of the widespread nature of and rises in the occurrence
of the offenses (Mukherjee, 1999). HREOC (1991) made recommendations
for systematic gathering of information about racist violence, and De Rome
and Cunneen (1993) conducted a trial program for gathering such information within the New South Wales Police Service. But, to this date, I am not
aware of any developed and systematic collection of national hate crime data.
Nevertheless, while national reliable and representative data would be valuable
(although extraordinarily difficult to obtain), we can look elsewhere for evidence and be persuaded that hate crime exists and is a serious problem.

The landmark investigation of hate crime in Australia has been HREOC's (1991) National Inquiry into Racist Violence in Australia. The inquiry devoted a substantial proportion of its investigation and subsequent report to the violence directed at Aboriginal and Torres Strait Islander communities. While it recognized racist violence against other minority ethnic communities in Australia's distant and near past (for example, against Chinese immigrants in the 19th century and against southern and eastern European migrants in the 20th century), it concluded its report by emphasizing the persistent and consistent violent discrimination against Indigenous communities.

Violence against Indigenous people in Australia does not exhaust the extent of hate crime. In the edited volume *Faces of Hate: Hate Crime in Australia* (Cunneen et al., 1997), the contributors produce a sorrowful and deeply disturbing inventory of hate-related crimes against Asian and Islamic migrants, against gay and lesbian communities, and (as we have seen) against Jewish Australians.

Targeting Islamic Communities

International attention has been devoted to the "demonization" of Islamic communities throughout the world in the wake of the "first" Gulf War in 1990–1991; the bombing of the World Trade Center and the Pentagon on September 11, 2001; the toppling of the Taliban in Afghanistan in 2002; and the "second" Gulf War in 2003. Australia played logistically minor but symbolically important roles in each of the armed conflicts, especially in the U.S. invasion of Iraq in 2003. In October 2001, Middle Eastern asylum seekers were forced into the water after their vessel began to sink off the western coast of Australia. The Australian Navy effected a rescue, but video footage of women and children in the water was interpreted by the then-federal defense minister and the then-prime minister in the midst of a federal election campaign as evidence that the asylum seekers had "thrown their children overboard" in an attempt to force the Australian Navy to take them to Australian shores. Conservative politicians and media observers loudly proclaimed that "we do not want the kind of people who throw their children overboard as Australian citizens." The misrepresentation of the footage became a political scandal, and it was eventually made clear that the alleged event had not taken place (although it did the then government no harm at that election, in which it was comfortably returned) (Poynting, 2002). A further domestic incident was a series of gang rapes in Sydney (New South Wales) between 2000 and 2001, for which a number of young Muslim Lebanese men received very lengthy jail sentences amidst a dramatically hysterical media discourse on ethnicity and crime (Poynting, 2002).

The conflation of "terrorist" with Arab/Middle Eastern/Islamic communities and the development of a Western "Islamophobia" is not unique to Australia (see Fraser, Melhem, and Yacoub, 1997; Manne, 2002). But, when we add the simultaneous association between Islam and "unAustralian" criminality and between Islamic asylum seekers and unAustralian practices (such as throwing children overboard), Australia has experienced a combustible environment in which the robustness of the country's multicultural credentials has been put sorely to the test. The virulence of anti-Islamic sentiment has not been confined to the fringes of the right but has been played out in national and state parliaments and in the "respectable" mass media (Manne, 2002; Poynting, 2002; Stebbing, 2002; Zaman, 2002). The outcomes of the sentiment have been evident on the streets of Australian cities.

The National Inquiry into Racist Violence (HREOC, 1991) identified a number of criminal incidents directed at Arabic and other Islamic people before and after the first Gulf War. These included vandalism of Islamic society premises and mosques in Victoria and New South Wales, arson attacks on a Muslim primary school and on properties owned by Australians of Middle Eastern background in Western Australia, and the abuse of women wearing the hijab throughout Australia (see also the Committee on Discrimination against Arab Australians, 1992). Patterns of damage (including bombings) to Muslim places of worship and educational institutions and attacks on Muslim citizens (particularly women because of the hijab) persisted throughout the 1990s to the present day, reaching peaks after the various international and domestic incidents identified previously (Carbone, 2002; Poynting, 2002; Poynting and Mason, 2007).

The Cronulla Riots and Indian Assaults

In December 2005, some 5,000 young "Anglo" Australians gathered at the Sydney beachside suburb of Cronulla and set about attacking anyone identified as "Middle Eastern" in appearance. Draped in Australian flags, wearing T-shirts proclaiming their "Aussie pride" and awash with alcohol, the crowd sought to reclaim their beach from the young Lebanese Australian men who they had come to see as utterly un-Australian invaders of their sacred sand. The deep causes of the riot have been pondered (Johanson and Glow, 2007; Poynting, 2006), but the immediate trigger event was the assault by Lebanese Australian men of several lifeguards the previous weekend. Outrage whipped by tabloid media and shock-jock radio presenters at the initial assault led to an astonishing text message barrage that resulted in the gathering the following weekend. Perhaps the most famous text, reproduced in one of Sydney's tabloid papers, read: "Come to Cronulla this weekend to take revenge. This Sunday every Aussie in the Shire get down to North Cronulla to support Leb and wog bashing day" (Johanson and Glow, 2007, p. 37). Poynting (2006, p. 85) argues that the incident was not a "race riot" in the traditional sense, in which members of a repressed minority finally lose restraint and take to the streets; it was more akin to a pogrom: "a violent attack by members of a dominant ethnic group against a minority, in order to put them back in their place." Several media outlets reported the presence of neo-Nazi groups at Cronulla on the day of the main riot ("Neo-Nazis in Race Riots," 2005; Poynting, 2006), including Jim Saleam's Australian First, along with the Patriotic Youth League and Blood and Honour.

The southeastern state capital cities of Melbourne and Sydney are host to many thousands of Indian students completing tertiary study in Australia. From early 2009, a series of assaults on members of this group of visitors has received widespread publicity, especially in India. Some angry 2,000 students took to the streets of Melbourne in June (Millar and Doherty, 2009), amidst considerable concern among politicians and tertiary institutions that such adverse publicity might harm the very lucrative overseas student market. It remains unclear whether the students are being assaulted in numbers disproportionate to their population presence and to their exposure to risk (many are employed as late-night shift workers in taxis and 24-hour convenience stores and live in the poorer western suburbs with elevated crime rates). It is clear, however, that the students consistently describe racist abuse before and during assaults and have no doubt that they are being targeted for violence and street theft because they are Indian.

Law Enforcement Responses to Hate Crime

Crimes of violence motivated by extreme right-wing ideologies or other political sentiments usually are not specifically identified in the criminal codes of the commonwealth, the states, or the territories. They fall under general common law or criminal statute prohibitions against assaultive behavior. Specific legislative responses to hatred generally are contained in racial vilification legislation. For instance, the commonwealth enacted the Racial Discrimination Act in 1975; New South Wales followed with its *Anti*-Discrimination Act in 1977. Other relevant legislation includes the South Australian Racial Vilification Act (1996), the Queensland Anti-Discrimination Act (1991), and the Victorian Racial and Religious Tolerance Act (2001) (McNamara, 2002). With several exceptions, the legislation around the country does not use the criminal law as the primary means for regulation of racial and other forms of hatred. Civil human rights complaints processes are the most prominent regulatory mechanisms, while the South Australian act defines a statutory tort of racial vilification. To date, only two states use the criminal law. Under amendments to the Western Australian

Criminal Code (1913) made in 1990, four narrowly defined crimes concerned with publishing and displaying material that incites racial hatred were established. The amendment to the Criminal Code was an explicit response to the activities of the Australian Nationalist Movement, headed by Jack Van Tongeren, during the 1980s (McNamara, 2002).

Failure to abide by provisions of various vilification codes can result in criminal sanctions. Frederick Toben of the Adelaide Institute was jailed for 3 months in 2009 by the Australian Federal Court for numerous contempt of court offenses arising from his failure to remove Holocaust denial content from his website in defiance of court orders under the Racial Discrimination Act. It is clear, however, that the prison sentence was not primarily about vilification: "Federal Court Justice Jeffrey Spender today said the case was not about the Holocaust, but whether Toben had complied with court orders" (ABC News, 2009).

Victoria's Racial and Religious Tolerance Act (2001) creates criminal offenses concerned with racial and religious intolerance. In September 2009, in the wake of the massive publicity given to the attacks on Indian students, the Victorian State government amended the Sentencing Act to require judges to take into account hate motivation:

> The Sentencing Act 1991 will now explicitly list hatred and prejudice of people who share common characteristics as a factor that must be taken into account by a judge when sentencing. This means that where the motivation for a crime was hatred or prejudice, or victims are targeted by offenders because of the offender's prejudice, or their conduct indicated that prejudice was the motivation, the courts will specifically take that into account when sentencing. The Sentencing Act 1991 will now explicitly list hatred and prejudice of people who share common characteristics as a factor that must be taken into account by a judge when sentencing. This means that where the motivation for a crime was hatred or prejudice, or victims are targeted by offenders because of the offender's prejudice, or their conduct indicated that prejudice was the motivation, the courts will specifically take that into account when sentencing. (Victorian Premier's Office, 2009)

The warrant and effectiveness of racial vilification legislation have been hotly contested, not least on the grounds that they may jeopardize free speech (see McNamara, 2002, for a critique of Australia's regulatory responses to racial vilification). Assessment of the impact of Victoria's amendment to the Sentencing Act will take some time to be meaningful.

Thus, regular police agencies in Australia are not in general equipped with any express powers to deal with political violence and other crimes generated by hate. Three dimensions of the policing of these behaviors need to be addressed here. The first concerns the historical implication of police personnel themselves in the perpetration of violence and hate crime. The second concerns the somewhat more benign but arguably more enveloping critique that police have significantly misunderstood such crimes as a result of an unsophisticated grasp of the challenges faced by communities vulnerable to hate; as a consequence, there is "underpolicing" of hate crimes. The third concerns the growing awareness among police planners and managers that there needs to be a more vigorous and proactive set of responses to hate crime.

Intolerant and Violent Policing

While issues of discriminatory policing reach considerably further than singular groups in Australia (see Coady, James, Miller, and O'Keefe, 2000), the most prominent and systematically researched critique of police involvement in bias-related behavior concerns the treatment of Aboriginal people. The National Inquiry into Racist Violence (HREOC, 1991) devoted considerable attention to allegations of systematic violence by police against Aboriginal communities, especially in Western Australia, Queensland, the Northern Territory, and New South Wales. The inquiry was persuaded that a culture of intimidation and violence toward Aboriginal people was an endemic characteristic of Australian policing:

> The most common complaints made against police were the degree of force used in making arrests; the use of threat of physical violence when in custody (particularly with juveniles); and the provocative and disrespectful language and the rough handling of Aboriginal women by male police officers. (HREOC, 1991, p. 80)

The inquiry heard that racism was rife within policing, and that structurally, many Aboriginal communities were significantly overpoliced, with resultant hostility between police and Aboriginal people, a disproportionate number of public order offenses, and high rates of incarceration. More recent reviews and studies have added weight to the HREOC findings (see, for instance, Chan, 1997; Cunneen, 2001; Findlay, 2004). Richards (2009) notes that in 2007–2008, of young Indigenous people apprehended by police in New South Wales, 48% were sent to court compared with 21% of non-Indigenous young people; in Queensland, over 2006–2007, of young Indigenous people processed by police, 39% were arrested, compared with 17% of non-Indigenous young people.

Neglectful Policing

A more pervasive critique of policing and hate crime concerns the apparent indifference by police toward victims of such crimes. This is a complex area, usually associated with the traditional monocultural constitution of Australian police personnel (in the past, typically white Anglo-Celtic working class males), and their inability to forge sympathetic relationships with Indigenous, ethnic, and other minority groups. The perception of many members of such groups is that police do not treat their victimizations seriously enough. Jones (1997, p. 233) describes a submission by the Ethnic Communities Council of New South Wales to the New South Wales Ombudsman in his inquiry into race relations and the New South Wales police in 1995, which she paraphrases thus: "There is some disquiet at the failure of police to find the perpetrators of crimes that appear to arise out of ethnic conflicts and hatreds, such as attacks on the property of members of particular groups, or on churches, mosques and synagogues." From the police perspective, the problem is often explained as a reluctance by community members to cooperate fully with police in providing necessary information and evidence. This is a well-known cycle of distrust, inaction, and exacerbated antagonism. Fraser et al. assert:

> Arabic-speaking Australians are reluctant to report crimes in general, and hate-motivated crimes in particular to the police. ... The fact that Arab Australians who present themselves at the local police station when they are the victims of crime cannot communicate with police representatives in their own language and that they must necessarily see the police as hostile or at least foreign because they do not encounter police officers who share a similar cultural or linguistic heritage means they are reluctant to report incidents to police. (1997, p. 90)

A survey of a number of culturally and linguistically diverse communities in Victoria provides detailed and diverse support for the general problems outlined (Victorian Multicultural Commission, 2000). Many of the respondents (including members from Victoria's Vietnamese, Somali, Turkish, Iraqi, Italian, Albanian, Chinese, and Bosnian communities) reported high levels of what they perceived as racist intimidation and violence:

> Many participants had suffered verbal or physical abuse in the streets, which they identified as being largely motivated by their ethnic identity and physical appearance. These attacks appeared to be mostly on the women, particularly when the women looked different, wearing their hijab or observing particular cultural or religious dress codes, but the attacks were also on males in the community. Many times the racist attacks were from strangers on the streets, but sometimes, the attacks were from neighbours. Some people had also encountered racism and physical abuse by service providers in their local area, such as post office staff and bank staff. (Victorian Multicultural Commission, 2000, p. 43)

When asked about their contacts with local police and their willingness to report crimes to police, some predictable differences emerged. Respondents with limited English (generally older people) were most reluctant to report, while younger members with better English were more prepared. However, those with dissatisfying contact with police (often younger men, particularly from the Vietnamese community) would not report crime to police, and there was a litany of complaints about poor police responses to calls for service, often associated with linguistic difficulties as well as a concern that police engaged in clumsy ethnic stereotyping.

Even when police grasp the seriousness of crimes targeted at vulnerable groups in the community, they can be reluctant to acknowledge the presence (let alone the pervasiveness) of hate as a motivating force, especially hate based on racist sentiment. Arguably, this is because an acknowledgment that (for instance) race hatred is widely distributed undermines police conceptions of their control of public order and public values. This is especially likely to be the case if the expressions of racial sentiment are embodied in mainstream, majority communities. Poynting (2006, p. 86) records that the assistant commissioner of the New South Wales Police was reported in a newspaper in the week proceeding the riots in Cronulla as saying "that he grew up surfing at Cronulla, (and) instructed Telegraph readers on what was the 'Australian way' at the beach; something the front-page headline said he vowed to defend." The chief commissioner of the Victoria Police, in responding to the vociferous concerns of Indian students about attacks on them, provides a contorted account of the place of racism in the attacks (Overland, 2009):

> I understand that the Indian students believe that these crimes are race-based. Some of these crimes are racially motivated; however I also believe that many of the robberies and other crimes of violence are simply opportunistic.
>
> We know that a lot of international students work and study late at night and are often travelling home by themselves on trains, equipped with their laptops and phones. Unfortunately they are often just in the wrong place at the wrong time.
>
> Whatever the motivation, racism in any form is wrong and these crimes are wrong and Victoria Police has already dedicated a lot of time and effort to tackling this problem.

Recognizing the Gravity of Hate Crime

There have been at least two significant drivers in the development of law enforcement responses to violence and other crimes based on hate or ideology in Australia. The first of these concerns the threat to national security represented by organized groups with a radical change agenda. The second concerns the recognition that traditional policing responses to the victimizations experienced by a range of minority groups have been deficient, for the reasons sketched in the previous discussion.

The agency tasked with the major watching and investigation brief with regard to political violence is the ASIO. ASIO's mandate, inter alia, requires that it investigate "politically motivated violence" (PMV), a subset of which clearly is extremist right-wing violence.[1] The ASIO role is primarily preemptive; it is an intelligence-gathering exercise to enable the organization to alert the commonwealth attorney general to the likelihood and magnitude of threatened or perceived violence, especially if that threat appears related to national security. There is obviously some overlap in responsibility between ASIO and the state and territory police agencies whose job it is to investigate breaches of their respective criminal codes. However, it seems that ASIO loses some interest in PMV after it has actually occurred: The commonwealth attorney general's guidelines regarding the investigation of PMV appear to indicate that ASIO will pass on relevant intelligence information to police if they believe that it may assist in the investigation of the offenses, and that ASIO is not generally to investigate the offenses ex post facto.[2] Much of ASIO's work is classified, and there is no publicly accessible information regarding the extent to which it does pass on its intelligence regarding PMV to state and territory police.

ASIO has had an interest in extremist right-wing violence in the past, as evidenced in the ASIO Annual Report extract cited and drawn from the 1991 HREOC inquiry. But, recent reports make little or no explicit mention of such sources of violence. For instance, the ASIO 2007–2008 report to Parliament devotes the bulk of the section on "Threats to Australia" to terrorist activities under the auspices of the "Global Militant Jihad" and touches lightly on issues of espionage, foreign interference, and violent protest (this last falls under the rubric of PMV and is the only reference to PMV in the report); the report notes that there were no violent protests in Australia in 2007–2008 (ASIO, 2008, p. 70).

It is clear that ASIO has turned its attention increasingly away from domestic right-wing violence and toward intelligence gathering with regard to Islamic terrorism in the wake of recent international events. Indeed, in recent years ASIO has led a number of raids, in conjunction with the Australian Federal Police, against Arabic and other Muslim immigrants, raids that have outraged Muslim communities and civil libertarians. In late 2001, some 30 houses in Sydney were raided, ostensibly to identify Middle Eastern immigrants with affiliations to radical groups such as Al-gama Islamiya (Poynting, 2002). In late 2002, further raids across Australia took place, this time against members of the Indonesian community, again seeking evidence of affiliation with extremist groups, in this case Jemaah Islamiah (Forbes, 2002). The latter raids were condemned by the Australian Arabic Council, the Islamic Council of Victoria, Liberty Victoria, the Australian Council for Civil Liberties, and the New South Wales Council of Civil Liberties. Cameron Murphy of this last organization was reported to have said:

> ASIO had relied upon speculation, innuendo, rumour and conduct taken out of context. Raids had been conducted on the homes of ordinary citizens who, it seemed, had attracted suspicion for doing nothing more than attending Islamic faith meetings. (*West Australian*, 2002)

Bilal Cleland of the Islamic Council of Victoria "accused ASIO of using 'jack-boot tactics' and warned that Muslim communities could lose confidence in the intelligence organization" (*West Australian*, 2002). It would seem that ASIO has not been consolidating a reputation for being the watchdog against racist victimization.

I am unsure whether state and territory police departments continue to devote specific resources to the dedicated targeting and policing of right-wing extremist groups in Australia; police annual reports typically include no details of such targeted policing. Most Australian police agencies used to house "special branches" or similarly named departments whose mandate it was to surveil political groups in the community. Historically, however, the focus was on left-wing groups, Labor parliamentarians, union leaders, and so forth (Bryett and Harrison, 1993; Finnane, 1987; McCulloch, 2001). Most of these units were disbanded in the 1970s and 1980s when there was a succession of Labor Party elections to government. However, many of these units have been resurrected as "special intelligence units" or the like and continue to surveil and at times infiltrate community groups. While some of these infiltrations have been targeted at alleged terrorist cells, it seems that police concerns for left-wing and reformist agitation endure. In 2008, Melbourne's broadsheet daily, *The Age*, reported that an officer from the Victoria Police Security Intelligence Group had infiltrated Animal Liberation Victoria, Stop the War Coalition, Unity for Peace, and Socialist Alternative (Baker and McKenzie, 2008). Media reports are usually the only source of information about the activities of the intelligence units as there is no publicly accessible review of contemporary political intelligence units within state and territory police agencies.

Because the quantum of organized extremist violence is relatively slight compared to more diffuse crime generated by hate and intolerance, the bulk of the policing of such crimes falls to regular police units. The final concerns of the chapter lie with developments in this last domain, which is arguably the most important given its reach into the daily lives of so many communities.

While individual serving and ex-members of police services have at times publicly acknowledged the historical (and sometimes contemporary) racism of their organizations (see HREOC, 1991, p. 81), the organizations themselves have predictably been reluctant to make such acknowledgement. A somewhat easier concession has been that their relations with ethnic and other minority groups have not always been robust and need improving. The major institutional reflection, that Australian police departments have recognized the need to improve their understanding of and sensitivity toward non-Anglo communities, was the establishment in 1993 of the National Police Ethnic Advisory Board (NPEAB).[3] The board had representatives from all Australian police departments and from ethnic communities under the auspices of the Australian Multicultural Foundation and the Commonwealth Department of Immigration and Multicultural Affairs. The mission of the board was to provide professional responses to the challenges of Australia's cultural, religious, and linguistic diversity. This was achieved by the following:

- recommending to the Conference of Commissioners of Police, Australasia and the South West Pacific Region appropriate national policies, programs and initiatives
- coordinating national endeavours in the area of police management of cultural, religious and linguistic diversity and police/ethnic relations
- promoting and facilitating partnerships between Police Services and ethnic communities
- providing advice and assistance to Australian police jurisdictions (National Police Ethnic Advisory Board, 2001, p. 1).

In essence, the board promoted two mechanisms under the broad agenda of fostering better reciprocal relations with ethnic communities: the dissemination of cross-cultural training and guidelines for dealing responsively with ethnic communities throughout Australian police agencies (NPEAB, 2000, n.d.; NPEAB and Australian Institute of Jewish Affairs, 1997); and the recruitment of members of culturally and linguistically diverse communities into police service (Faelli, 2002; NPEAB and Australian Institute of Jewish Affairs, 1997). These mechanisms were designed to address a large number of problems that have existed between police and minority communities, but the issue of dealing effectively with hate crimes such as racist violence was one of the explicit drivers of the agenda (NPEAB, 2001).

At the same time, it has clearly been difficult for NPEAB to ignore persistent allegations of racism within policing itself, and while the sixth principle in its *Policing in a Culturally Diverse Australia: Governing Principles* (NPEAB, n.d.) does not actually acknowledge the existence of such sentiment, it spells out its noxiousness, as seen next.

Racism and Discrimination

> Police jurisdictions in Australia unequivocally reject all forms of racism, prejudice and bigotry and declare any racist behaviour by police members as professionally unacceptable.
>
> To this end every effort will be made to make clear in police standing orders or similar regulations the unacceptability of racially motivated conduct by police personnel and that such behaviour will be treated as a breach of instructions.
>
> Police jurisdictions in Australia are committed to do their utmost within legislative limits to combat racism and unlawful discrimination and to actively promote harmonious relations with all sections of Australian culturally diverse community. (NPEAB, n.d., p. 10)

There seems to be little doubt that Australian police at management level genuinely have identified the deficiencies in traditional law enforcement responses to the victimization of communities vulnerable to hate in Australia and have moved to redress those deficiencies through bodies such as NPEAB. The extent to which the propagation of cultural sensitivity training and the recruitment of police from those communities have made or will make a difference to the lived experiences of those communities remains a moot point, in the absence to date of detailed evaluation research. The extent to which these mechanisms are sufficient on their own is also moot. The successor body to the NPEAB, the Australian and New Zealand Policing Advisory Agency (ANZPAA), lists in its 2009–2010 strategic priorities, in reference to the policing of diverse communities, only an intention to upgrade the booklet *Religious Diversity Reference for Police* (ANZPAA, 2009). It is a concern that an expansion of sensibilities regarding the impacts of hate and other forms of politically motivated crime on vulnerable communities does not appear to be taking place at the federal level.

Improving the Policing of Hate

Australian police services are not alone internationally in facing formidable challenges in the development of effective responses to PMV and hate crime. Sociopolitical circumstances beyond their control, gaps in legislative provision and empowerment, and stubbornly entrenched deficiencies within their own structures and occupational cultures all collude to attenuate their capacities in this regard. A comprehensive response to these challenges is beyond the scope of the present chapter. Nevertheless, a broad agenda can be sketched here.

It can be argued that while all crime is an assault on rights and free-doms, crimes of violence and intimidation motivated by ideology or systematic hatred represent particularly insidious attacks on rights because they are based on explicit assumptions that some people's rights are less, or less important, than other people's. That is, the predations are functions of a characterization of the victims as a class of people who are less worthy, or indeed more blameworthy, than others. It is, of course, the traditional duty of policing agencies to protect rights. Yet, the history of modern policing has taught us that consideration of "rights" has occupied a problematic place in the policing enterprise. Systematic critiques of police conceptions of rights (for example, Goldstein, 1977; Skolnick, 1975) have led consistently to calls for a recommitment by police to democratic values. More recently, John Braithwaite (1992) has asserted that a "good" police service both maintains the rights (which he conceives of as "dominion" or republican liberty) of citizens from threats of crime and refrains from jeopardizing rights by prejudicial or partial policing.

The problem, however, has been to devise reform mechanisms that overturn the traditional police officer's conflation of rights with due process requirements or constitutional restrictions, which are seen as impediments to efficient law enforcement and the maintenance of order (Skolnick, 1975). When we add police cultural and external pressures toward defining certain groups as possessing lesser rights than others, the difficulties are manifest. Chan (1997) argues in her work on reform of policing within multicultural societies that the typical reformist agenda has been flawed because it pays insufficient attention to the need to shift in concert both the "habitus" (the cultures and "ways of doing things") and the "field" (or sociopolitical contexts and structural arrangements) of policing. While important as constituent parts of a broader reform program, the kinds of initiatives developed by NPEAB are doomed, Chan's work implies, if they stand alone.

The work of Neyroud and Beckley (2001) takes broadly into account the complexities outlined. These British police managers offer a comprehensive account of the transformations taking place in international policing, with a particular emphasis on European policing following the implementation of the European Convention on Human Rights (ECHR) and in the wake of Patten's (1999) blueprint for the reform of Northern Irish policing. The center of gravity for policing reform, according to Neyroud and Beckley (2001, p. 220) is the integration of enhanced professionalism, ethical decision making, and compliance with human rights obligations:

> [G]ood policing in the twenty-first century requires more than "good performance." It needs a renewal of the contract between police officer and the citizen, which in turn requires greater openness and scrutiny, continuously

improving professional standards and a new commitment to ethics at the core of policing.

The elegance of the blueprint offered by Neyroud and Beckley (2001) is reflected in their careful attention to the necessary synthesis between formulations of personal ethics, the ethical contexts of police performance management, operational and organizational ethics, human resource restructuring, and the establishment of human rights compliance mechanisms.

The ambit of the proposals by Neyroud and Beckley (2001) extends very much beyond the kinds of policing demands outlined in the present chapter. Nevertheless, their proposals contain much that is directly relevant to the policing of crimes motivated by ideology and hate. Besides the occupational, cultural, and structural reforms mandated by their proposals, their advocacy of a systematic ethical decision-making core to police operational policy and practice encourages a consistency in approach that transcends the situational imperative. At the same time, the human rights context of that decision making provides police with an articulated, formalized, and accountable rationale for consistent responses to crimes that jeopardize rights. In Chan's (1997) terms, Neyroud and Beckley (2001) have offered transformations in both habitus and field.

Conclusion

Australian legal responses to violence and other hate crimes directed at particular communities have been various. Three broad approaches can be identified: racial vilification legislation; targeting and investigation of extremist groups by the national security agency; and improvements in the regular policing of communities vulnerable to hate. The vilification legislation may well have an educative and exhortatory impact in the long term, but its regulatory strategies lie largely outside the criminal law and therefore are of little immediate relevance to police. The involvement of ASIO in the surveillance and investigation of extremist groups has been embroiled in recent controversy; the apparent shift in focus away from right-wing extremist groups and toward terrorist groups associated with Islam has resulted in dramatic interventions into Muslim communities, interventions that have clearly not advanced government–community relations.

In an everyday sense, then, the burden of preventing and dealing with victimization within communities vulnerable to hate falls on state and territory police. The dilemmas facing police in their shouldering of this burden are twofold. First, they have to redress a legacy within their own ranks of (at the least) neglect of and (at worst) complicity in such victimization. Second, they have to operate in a sociopolitical context in which intolerance toward certain groups, particularly Australian Muslims in recent years, is endorsed implicitly (and sometimes explicitly) in mainstream political, media, and community discourse.

It is a tired axiom in Australia that its police reflect the values and standards of the communities from which they are drawn, and if those communities harbor racist and other discriminatory sentiments, then so will police. We need to dispense with this reductionist chestnut and imagine and work toward police services that actively propagate the principles and practices of multiculturalism and respect for human rights. The application of a consistent, rights-based approach by police anchored in ethically informed strategies and practices would bring many rewards. One of the likely benefits of such an application is a policing system particularly intolerant of crimes born of hate and committed against the more vulnerable members of society. Another is a police service that leads by example and shapes public opinion, rather than one that is driven by populist sentiment and archaic cultural practices.

Notes

1. *Politically motivated violence* means:
   (a) acts or threats of violence or unlawful harm that are intended or likely to achieve a political objective, whether in Australia or elsewhere, including acts or threats carried on for the purpose of influencing the policy or acts of a government, whether in Australia or elsewhere;
   (b) acts that:
       (i) involve violence or are intended or are likely to involve or lead to violence (whether by the persons who carry on those acts or by other persons); and
       (ii) are directed to overthrowing or destroying, or assisting in the overthrow or destruction of, the government or the constitutional system of government of the Commonwealth or of a State or Territory;
   (c) acts that are offences punishable under the Crimes (Foreign Incursions and Recruitment) Act 1978, the Crimes (Hijacking of Aircraft) Act 1972 or the Crimes (Protection of Aircraft) Act 1973; or
   (d) acts that–
       (i) are offences punishable under the Crimes (Internationally Protected Persons) Act 1976; or
       (ii) threaten or endanger any person or class of persons specified by the Minister for the purposes of this sub-paragraph by notice in writing given to the Director-General. (Commonwealth Attorney-General, n.d.)
2. Intelligence gathered by ASIO in relation to PMV could be valuable in assisting a police force in preventing the commission of criminal offenses or in effectively resolving their investigations. Investigating criminal offenses after the event is, however, primarily a police function (Commonwealth Attorney-General, n.d.).
3. The organization changed its name some years ago to the Australasian Police Multicultural Advisory Bureau and in 2008 was swallowed by a new national body, the Australian and New Zealand Police Advisory Board, which has

absorbed what were called common police services, such as national research and forensic development units. This chapter persists with the old name as many of the source documents appear under that title.

References

ABC News. (2009, August 13). Toben jailed as appeal fails. Retrieved September 25, 2009, from http://www.abc.net.au/news/stories/2009/08/13/2655297.htm?section=justin

Abraham, Yvonne. (2005, December 25). On the beach: why the recent riots in Australia should surprise no one. *The Boston Globe*. Retrieved July 1, 2009, from http://www.boston.com/news/globe/ideas/articles/2005/12/25/on_the_beach/

Attack on Indian students. (2009, May 28). *Hindustan Times*. Retrieved June 17, 2009, from http://www.hindustantimes.com/News/world/Attack-on-Indian-students-ustralian-official-to-visit-India/Article1-415655.aspx

Australia/Israel and Jewish Affairs Council. (2001). *Report on Anti-Semitism in Australia: 1 October 2000–30 September 2001*. Retrieved June 5, 2009, from http://www.aijac.org.au/resources/reports/antisemitism-aus-2000-01.html

Australian and New Zealand Policing Advisory Agency (ANZPAA). (2009). *Religious Diversity Reference for Police*. Retrieved June 25, 2009, from http://www.apmab.gov.au/

Australian Security Intelligence Organisation. (2008). *Report to Parliament 2007–2008*, Canberra: Commonwealth of Australia.

Baker, M., and McKenzie, N. (2008, October 16). Police spying on activists revealed. *The Age*. Retrieved October 20, 2008, from http://www.theage.com.au/national/police-spying-on-activists-revealed-20081015-51k0.html?page=-1

Bearup, G. (2009, September 26). The audacity of hate. *Good Weekend*, pp. 22–29.

Bell, Jeannine. (2002). *Policing Hatred: Law Enforcement, Civil Rights and Hate Crime*. New York: New York University Press.

Braithwaite, J. (1992). Good and bad police services and how to pick them. In P. Moir and H. Eijkman (Eds.), *Policing Australia: Old Issues, New Perspectives*. South Melbourne, Victoria, Australia: Macmillan.

Bryett, K., and Harrison, A. (1993). *Policing in the Community*. Sydney: Butterworths.

Burke, K. (2002, November 25) Muslims bear brunt of racist comments on air. *The Age*, p. 2.

Campbell, A. (1978). *The Australian League of Rights*. Melbourne: Outback Press.

Carbone, S. (2002, May 29). Ten complaints under hate laws. *The Age*, p. 9.

Chan, J. (1997). *Changing Police Culture: Policing in a Multicultural Society*. Cambridge, UK: Cambridge University Press.

Coady, T., James, S., Miller, S. and O'Keefe, M. (Eds.). (2000). *Violence and Police Culture*. Melbourne: Melbourne University Press.

Committee on Discrimination against Arab Australians. (1992). *The Gulf in Australia: Racism, Arab and Muslim Australians and the War Against Iraq, Vol. 2: November 1990–July 1991*.

Commonwealth Attorney-General. (n.d.). *Guidelines in Relation to the Performance by the Australian Security Intelligence Organisation of Its Functions Relating to Politically Motivated Violence*. Retrieved August 6, 2003, from http://www.asio.gov.au/about/content/attorney.htm

Cunneen, C. (2001). *Conflict Politics and Crime, Aboriginal Communities and the Police.* Sydney: Allen & Unwin.

Cunneen, C., Fraser, D., and Tomsen, S. (Eds.). (1997). *Faces of Hate: Hate Crime in Australia.* Annandale, NSW, Australia: Hawkins Press.

Daily Mail. (2009, September 13). Labour minister: Anti-Islam extremists no better than Oswald Mosley's 1930s Fascists. Retrieved October 4, 2009, from http://www.dailymail.co.uk/news/article-1212831/Tensions-threaten-boil-right-wing-extremists-anti-fascist-protestors-clash-outside-London-mosque.html

De Rome, L. and Cunneen, C. (1993, June). *The Monitoring by the Police of Racist Violence in the Community.* Paper presented at the Second National Conference on Violence, Australian Institute of Criminology, Canberra, June.

Faelli, R. (2002). *A Qualitative Study of Police Officers from Culturally and Linguistically Diverse Backgrounds: Workplace Experiences and Perceptions and the Impact on Retention.* Melbourne: Australasian Police Multicultural Advisory Bureau.

Federal Bureau of Investigation. (2002). *Hate Crime Statistics, 2001.* Clarksburg, WV: Federal Bureau of Investigation Uniform Crime Reports, Program Support Section.

Fight dem back! (2009). *Fighting Race-Hate in Australia and New Zealand.* Retrieved October 4, 2009, from http://www.fightdemback.org/

Findlay, M. (2004). *Introducing Policing: Challenges for Police and Australian Communities.* South Melbourne, Victoria, Australia: Oxford University Press.

Finnane, M. (Ed.). (1987). *Policing in Australia: Historical Perspectives.* Kensington, NSW, Australia: University of New South Wales Press.

Forbes, M. (2002, November 1). Attacks inevitable, says security chief. *The Age,* p. 1.

Fraser, David, Melhem, M., and Yacoub, M. (1997). Violence against Arab Australians. In C. Cunneen, D. Fraser, and S. Tomsen (Eds.), *Faces of Hate: Hate Crime in Australia.* Annandale, NSW, Australia: Hawkins Press.

Goldstein, H. (1977). *Policing a Free Society.* Cambridge, MA: Ballinger.

Greason, D. (1997). Australia's racist far-right. In C. Cunneen, D. Fraser, and S. Tomsen (Eds.), *Faces of Hate: Hate Crime in Australia.* Annandale, NSW, Australia: Hawkins Press.

Human Rights and Equal Opportunity Commission (HREOC). (1991). *Racist Violence: Report of the National Inquiry into Racist Violence in Australia.* Canberra: Australian Government Printing Office.

Johanson, K., and Glow, H. (2007). Re-thinking multi-culturalism: Performing the Cronulla beach riot. *The International Journal of the Humanities,* 5, 37–43.

Jones, J. (2008). *Report on Antisemitism in Australia, 1 October 2007–30 September 2008.* Darlinghurst, NSW, Australia: Executive Council of Australian Jewry.

Jones, M. (1997). The legal response: Dealing with hatred—A user's guide. In C. Cunneen, D. Fraser, and S. Tomsen (Eds.), *Faces of Hate: Hate Crime in Australia.* Annandale, NSW, Australia: Hawkins Press.

Manne, R. (2002, September 16). Beware the new racism. *The Age,* p. 13.

Mason, G. (1993). *Violence against Lesbians and Gay Men* (Violence Prevention Series No. 2). Canberra: Australian Institute of Criminology.

McCulloch, J. (2001). *Blue Army.* Melbourne: Melbourne University Press.

McNamara, Luke. (2002). *Regulating Racism: Racial Vilification Laws in Australia.* Sydney: University of Sydney, Institute of Criminology.

Merkl, P., and Weinberg, L. (Eds.). (1997). *The Revival of Right-Wing Extremism in the Nineties.* London: Cass.

Millar, B., and Doherty, B. (2009, June 1). Indian anger boils over. *The Age.* Retrieved July 3, 2009, from http://www.theage.com.au/national/indian-anger-boils-over-20090531-brrm.html

Mukherjee, S. (1999). *Ethnicity and Crime: An Australian Research Study.* Canberra: Australian Institute of Criminology.

National Police Ethnic Advisory Board. (2000). *Culturally Competent Police Organisations: National Recruitment and Retention Strategic Framework.* Melbourne: Author.

National Police Ethnic Advisory Board. (2001). *Annual Report 2000–2001.* Melbourne: Author.

National Police Ethnic Advisory Board. (n.d.). *Policing in a Culturally Diverse Australia: Governing Principles.* Melbourne: Author.

National Police Ethnic Advisory Board and the Australian Institute of Jewish Affairs. (1997). *National Survey of Police and Ethnic Issues Report.* Melbourne: Authors.

Neo-Nazis in race riots: Police. (2005, December 12). *Sydney Morning Herald.* Retrieved May 24, 2009, from http://www.smh.com.au/articles/2005/12/12/1134235970427.html

Neyroud, P., and Beckley, A. (2001). *Policing, Ethics and Human Rights.* Cullumpton, UK: Willan.

Overland, S. (2009, June 2). *Chief Commissioner Discusses Assaults on Indian Students.* Press release, Victoria Police. Retrieved September 13, 2009, from http://www.vicpolicenews.com.au/our-say/547-our-say-chief-commissioner-discusses-assaults-on-indian-students.html

Patten, C. (1999). *A New Beginning: Policing in Northern Ireland: The Report of the Independent Commission on Policing for Northern Ireland.* London: HMSO.

Poynting, S. (2002). "Bin Laden in the Suburbs": Attacks on Arab and Muslim Australians before and after 11 September. *Current Issues in Criminal Justice, 14,* 43–64.

Poynting, S. (2006). What caused the Cronulla Riots? *Race and Class, 48,* 85–92.

Poynting, S., and Mason, V. (2007). The resistable rise of Islamophobia: Anti-Muslim racism in the UK and Australian before 11 September 2001. *Journal of Sociology, 43,* 61–86.

Richards, K. (2009). *Juveniles' Contact with the Criminal Justice System in Australia* (Monitoring Reports 07). Canberra: Australian Institute of Criminology.

Skolnick, J. (1975). *Justice without Trial* (2nd ed.). New York: Wiley.

Stebbing, L. (2002, November 6). Our distorted image of Muslim world. *The Age,* p. 7.

The Law Report. (2002, September 24). Retrieved July 14, 2003, from http://www.abc.net.au/rn/talks/8.30/lawrpt/stories/s683070.htm

Victorian Multicultural Commission. (2000). *Multicultural Perspectives on Crime and Safety.* Melbourne: Crime Prevention Victoria.

Victorian Premier's Office. (2009, September 15). *Sentencing Act to Recognise Impact of Hate Crimes.* Retrieved September 21, 2009, from http://www.premier.vic.gov.au/attorney-general/sentencing-act-to-recognise-impact-of-hate-crimes.html

Wade, M. (2009, September 17). Uproar in India over latest student attacks in Melbourne. *The Canberra Times*. Retrieved October 4, 2009, from http://www. canberratimes.com.au/news/world/world/general/uproar-in-india-over-latest-student-attack-in-melbourne/1626087.aspx

Westervelt, E. (2009, September 2). Wave of violence strikes Eastern Europe's Gypsies. *National Public Radio*. Retrieved September 4, 2009, from http://www.npr.org/templates/story/story.php?storyId=112460670

Verghis, S. (2009, September 10). Australia: Attacks on Indian students raise racism cries. *Time*. Retrieved September 11, 2009, from http://www.time.com/time/world/article/0,8599,1921482,00.html

Zaman, Y. (2002, November 11). Australian Muslims have no case to answer. *The Age*, p. 15.

Concluding Observations

In this volume are selected studies of governments' efforts to counter those who have challenged their authority. Challenges to authority are enacted as conflicts between and among parties varying in the power resources they have and can mobilize. Power resources include—first and foremost—the means of violence, plus economic, political, ideological, and diversionary forms of social control. Economic power is control of the production and distribution of financial and other goods and services. Political power is control of decision making, including the making of laws. Ideological power is the capacity to influence what people know and believe. Diversionary power is the ability to substitute entertainment or exhortation for real information on the distribution and mobilization of the other power resources—for example, speeches, sermons, or writings by charismatic political or religious figures (Turk, 1982, p. 14–15).

The contributors emphasize the historical and cultural contexts in which governments have tried to counter terrorism and insurgencies. Overall, it is made clear that violent political conflict is a complex process marked by shifting blends of resources as the participants try to increase their relative power. Although political conflicts may in principle be resolved short of violence, contemporary developments suggest that in unstable nations such conflicts are increasingly likely to escalate to violence—initially aimed at coercing the opposition to negotiate but tending rather quickly to be characterized by more injurious and eventually destructive forms of violence, specifically terrorism and war (Turk, 2002).

Despite the likelihood of violence, both against and in defense of governmental authority, the strategies employed by governments include conciliatory as well as repressive countermeasures. These case studies show that the proportion of conciliatory relative to repressive measures varies greatly among countries and time periods, depending on both internal and international political and economic circumstances.

No consensus yet exists regarding what measures are effective under what conditions in reducing political violence. Repression seems most probably to increase oppositional violence but also may so weaken the opposition that only acquiescence or retreat are left as tactical options. Destruction of leadership, communications, supplies, and support conduits can make it impossible for terrorist or insurgent groups to carry on the fight. On the other hand, conciliation offering rewards for desisting from violence not only can reduce violence but also can dissolve its sources. But, it also seems that the more ideologically extreme the motivation of challengers, the less likely are conciliatory policies to succeed. Clearly, some combination and sequence of countermeasures work in particular instances, but specifying what succeeds is still very much a work in progress.

Before noting the major issues raised by the contributions and to which readers should be especially alert, it should be recognized that there is a long and ongoing discussion about the relative merits of case studies and quantitative analyses of statistical data (Laqueur, 1977, pp. 226–227, 1999; LaFree and Dugan, 2009, pp. 414–415).

Our view is that the methods are complementary. In addition to their informative value, case analyses provide an essential variety of perspectives from which to address basic issues. They contribute to the quest for theoretical understanding, as well as operational criteria for preventing and reducing political violence in particular circumstances. Theoretical work is characterized by refining research questions rather than providing definitive answers, which means there is always some tension between theoretical reluctance to end the process of knowledge seeking and the operational need to suspend the process at some point to undertake timely actions. Both long-term theoretical work and timely operational research are necessary to address the issues discussed next.

When and where have countermeasures been effective? A priority is to develop measures of effectiveness independent of political or media assumptions (Zimmermann, 1983, pp. 142–150). Ending or decreasing oppositional violence is the objective, but reports of success are often belied by later events. For examples, the Irish peace has been at least strained by subsequent instances of extremist violence, Sri Lankan truces with the Tamil Tigers have proven shaky, and the Israeli–Palestinian conflict features a succession of intifadas and peace accords. Given that final solutions appear to be rare, a more modest measure of success may well be the stabilization of political accommodations without expecting them to be permanent. The "two-state solution" would exemplify this kind of measure in the Israeli–Palestinian case.

In what contexts are opponents motivated? When do political actors come to see others as enemies? One of the common themes in reports of ethnic cleansing has been that people who were once friends and neighbors have quickly shifted their perceptions of one another from friends to enemies. Case studies provide the historical and cultural specificity needed to understand this phenomenon, which may be an eruption of unresolved conflicts papered over by long subjugation of the parties to external powers (e.g., European imperial conquests in Africa, the Middle East, and elsewhere) or the loss of overwhelming power by one party over others (e.g., post-Yugoslavia Bosnia, the Rwanda genocide). Where lines of cultural, especially religious, cleavage exist, power shifts provide the opportunity for earnest or merely ambitious leaders of a population to disseminate arguments for the need to expel or exterminate outsiders. Such arguments may well be persuasive in the face of real or perceived competition for scarce resources, when local disputes have long existed without resolution, when the outsiders are seen as having collaborated with external masters to gain advantages in an imposed political order, or where the outsider population is becoming what is perceived as a potentially threatening majority.

Is the escalation process reversible? Can terrorism and other forms of political violence be countered without resorting to destruction of the enemy? In principle, conflict resolution is always possible. Diplomats do often manage to negotiate working agreements among opposing states or other established organizations. Specialists in interpersonal or intergroup conflict such as psychiatrists and labor mediators frequently are able to bring opposing parties to understand the bases of their antagonism or dispute. Nonetheless, it seems to be exceptionally difficult to reverse the process when one or more of the opponents is highly committed to an uncompromising struggle, especially when the motivation stems from religious or other ideological absolutism (Juergensmeyer, 2000).

Of particular relevance here is determining the relative significance of material and political inequities in generating or exacerbating cultural conflicts. Although it is well established that class differentials alone do not account for social conflicts, material inequalities felt as illegitimate and potentially changeable clearly have some impact in helping to produce an audience receptive to exhortations to "rise up" against the socially advantaged and politically dominant. Combined with ideological justifications extolling the virtues of the challengers and the moral deficiencies of their opponents, a history of real and perceived material deprivations has been shown in myriad studies to be a significant factor in the causal dynamics of political violence in many specific times and places (Zimmermann, 1983, passim).

Whether escalation in conflicts with the truly committed can be reversed may be doubtful, but relieving the material distress of their supporters and potential recruits does appear to be a key element in a strategy with promise for curtailing political violence short of its total destruction end stage. Indeed, counterinsurgency doctrine (and counterterrorism strategies, to a lesser degree so far) gives increasing weight to operations designed to help local economies by building roads, schools, and other parts of the infrastructures required for socioeconomic development and political stabilization (Petraeus, 2006). Material assistance can at least help to make a hostile or indifferent population more amenable to efforts to persuade them of the legitimacy and uses of governance in a polity in which they are participants.

Can terrorism and other destructive political violence be countered without sacrificing the rule of law? In the aftermath of the September 11,

2001, attacks on New York, Washington, D.C., and Pennsylvania, the United States launched a "war on terrorism" characterized, as is increasingly evident, by an unprecedented disregard for constitutional, statutory, and judicial legal norms. It was assumed that the threat of international terrorism posed especially by Al Qaeda was so imminently grave that legal processes had to be bypassed to mount an effective response. It is now being realized that the response itself has contributed to weakening both the internal and external legitimacy of the American nation. The policy makers gave credence to those who reject America's claims to represent the highest stage of democratic political order, to be the leader of free nations founded on the premise that each person has moral value, with the absolute right to "life, liberty, and the pursuit of happiness."

Strong actions against terrorism must indeed be continued, but not at the cost of the democratic values that they are intended to defend. The mandate is to preserve the rule of law while dealing with lawless enemies, or else government of, by, and for the people will eventually perish. Some guidelines are found in a cogent study by Philip Bobbitt (2008), who uniquely combines scholarly and policy-making expertise in geopolitical strategic analysis, international law and security issues, and military history.

Compelling arguments are offered that operational strategies must be in accord with law. In practice, this means that decisions must be reviewable, and those responsible must be accountable. Secret procedures should be minimized and exposed as soon as possible to scrutiny by the people's representatives and ultimately by the general public. Despite the risks of disclosures, consultation among allied nations should be made routine to retain trust and ensure cooperation and coordination. Similarly, interagency rivalries among investigative and enforcement agencies, at and between levels of government from local to national, must be replaced by institutional mechanisms ensuring the sharing of information and cooperation in investigating and countering groups and individuals engaged in political violence.

Apprehending, detaining, and interrogating individuals must not contravene legal restrictions. Decisions regarding each stage must be in accord with law, with the clear implication that such decisions and their implementation can be secret only under extraordinary circumstances specified in law and ultimately made public as mandated by law. Plainly stated, kidnapping, indefinite and inhumane imprisonment, and torture cannot be made legal. Severe measures, most notably assassination, must be defined in law as exceptional and extraordinary, with those responsible being publicly accountable for their decisions. Secret courts should be abandoned in favor of open reviews by juries, not judges, to maximize the capacity of the people to know and assess what is being done to counter threats to their safety and well-being.

It is imperative that the citizenry understand not only that security policies and operations are legal but also that the law must be periodically reviewed and changed in light of experience. Flexibility under law must be maintained to adjust countermeasures against violence to the realities of fighting a war without boundaries against a clandestine though ubiquitous enemy unrestrained by any rules of combat. And, people must learn that there are costs, for example, in the lessening of private space resulting from enhanced surveillance and decreasing tolerance, meaning more severe penalties, for citizens who join or assist the enemy.

As a final concluding observation, the contributors to this volume have provided a wealth of informed thinking about what has happened in a variety of settings, how to understand the events and situations observed, and what has been tried with what outcomes to deal with the problems of developing and implementing effective countermeasures against oppositional political violence. They have done us all a service.

References

Bobbitt, Philip. *Terror and Consent: The Wars for the Twenty-First Century*. New York: Knopf, 2008.

Juergensmeyer, Mark. *Terror in the Mind of God: The Global Rise of Religious Violence*. Berkeley: University of California Press, 2000.

LaFree, Gary, and Dugan, Laura. Research on terrorism and countering terrorism. In *Crime and Justice: A Review of Research*, ed. Michael Tonry. Chicago: University of Chicago Press, 2009, volume 38: 417–477.

Laqueur, Walter. *Terrorism: A Study of National and International Political Violence*. Boston: Little, Brown, 1977.

Laqueur, Walter. *The New Terrorism: Fanaticism and the Arms of Mass Destruction*. New York: Oxford University Press, 1999.

Petraeus, David. *Counterinsurgency: Field Manual 3-24*. Headquarters, Department of the Army, 2006.

Turk, Austin T. *Political Criminality: The Defiance and Defense of Authority*. Beverly Hills, CA: Sage, 1982.

Turk, Austin T. Political violence: Patterns and trends. In *Crime and Justice at the Millennium: Essays by and in Honor of Marvin E. Wolfgang*, ed. Robert A. Silverman, Terence P. Thornberry, and Barry Krisberg. Norwell, MA: Kluwer Academic, 2002: 31–44.

Zimmermann, Ekkart. *Political Violence, Crises, and Revolutions: Theories and Research*. Cambridge, MA: Schenkman, 1983.

A Call for Authors

Advances in Police Theory and Practice

AIMS AND SCOPE:

This cutting-edge series is designed to promote publication of books on contemporary advances in police theory and practice. We are especially interested in volumes that focus on the nexus between research and practice, with the end goal of disseminating innovations in policing. We will consider collections of expert contributions as well as individually authored works. Books in this series will be marketed internationally to both academic and professional audiences. This series also seeks to —

- Bridge the gap in knowledge about advances in theory and practice regarding who the police are, what they do, and how they maintain order, administer laws, and serve their communities
- Improve cooperation between those who are active in the field and those who are involved in academic research so as to facilitate the application of innovative advances in theory and practice

The series especially encourages the contribution of works coauthored by police practitioners and researchers. We are also interested in works comparing policing approaches and methods globally, examining such areas as the policing of transitional states, democratic policing, policing and minorities, preventive policing, investigation, patrolling and response, terrorism, organized crime and drug enforcement. In fact, every aspect of policing, public safety, and security, as well as public order is relevant for the series. Manuscripts should be between 300 and 600 printed pages. If you have a proposal for an original work or for a contributed volume, please be in touch.

Series Editor
Dilip Das, Ph.D., Ph: 802-598-3680
E-mail: dilipkd@aol.com

Dr. Das is a professor of criminal justice and Human Rights Consultant to the United Nations. He is a former chief of police, and founding president of the International Police Executive Symposium, IPES, www.ipes.info. He is also founding editor-in-chief of *Police Practice and Research: An International Journal* (PPR), (Routledge/Taylor & Francis), www.tandf.co.uk/journals. In addition to editing the *World Police Encyclopedia* (Taylor & Francis, 2006), Dr. Das has published numerous books and articles during his many years of involvement in police practice, research, writing, and education.

Proposals for the series may be submitted to the series editor or directly to –
Carolyn Spence
Senior Editor • CRC Press / Taylor & Francis Group
561-317-9574 • 561-997-7249 (fax)
carolyn.spence@taylorandfrancis.com • www.crcpress.com
6000 Broken Sound Parkway NW, Suite 300, Boca Raton, FL 33487

International
Police Executive
Symposium (IPES)

The *International Police Executive Symposium* (IPES)* was founded in 1994. The aims and objectives of the IPES are to provide a forum to foster closer relationships among police researchers and practitioners globally; to facilitate cross-cultural, international, and interdisciplinary exchanges for the enrichment of the law enforcement profession; and to encourage discussion and published research on challenging and contemporary topics related to the profession.

One of the most important activities of the IPES is the organization of an annual meeting under the auspices of a police or educational institution. To date, meetings have been hosted by the Canton Police of Geneva, Switzerland (Police Challenges and Strategies, 1994); the International Institute of the Sociology of Law in Onati, Spain (Challenges of Policing Democracies, 1995); Kanagawa University in Yokohama, Japan (Organized Crime, 1996); the Federal Police in Vienna, Austria (International Police Cooperation, 1997); the Dutch Police and Europol in The Hague, The Netherlands (Crime Prevention, 1998); Andhra Pradesh Police in Hyderabad, India (Policing of Public Order, 1999); and the Center for Public Safety, Northwestern University, Evanston, Illinois, USA (Traffic Policing, 2000). A special meeting was cohosted by the Bavarian Police Academy of Continuing Education in Ainring, Germany, University of Passau, Germany, and State University of New York, Plattsburgh, USA, to discuss the issues endorsed by the IPES in April 2000. The police of Poland hosted

* www.ipes.info

the next meeting in May 2001 (Corruption: A Threat to World Order), and thereafter the annual meeting was hosted by the police of Turkey in May 2002 (Police Education and Training). The Kingdom of Bahrain hosted the annual meeting in October 2003 (Police and the Community).

The 2004 meeting in May of that year (Criminal Exploitation of Women and Children) took place in Chilliwack, British Columbia, Canada, and it was cohosted by the University College of the Fraser Valley, Abbotsford Police Department, Royal Canadian Mounted Police, the Vancouver Police Department, the Justice Institute of British Columbia, Canadian Police College, and the International Centre for Criminal Law Reform and Criminal Justice Policy. The next meeting (Challenges of Policing in the 21st Century) took place in September 2005 in Prague, Czech Republic. The Turkish National Police hosted the meeting in 2006 (Local Linkages to Global Security and Crime). The 14th IPES was held in Dubai on April 8–12, 2007 (Urbanization and Security). The 15th annual meeting (Police without Borders: The Fading Distinction between Local and Global) was hosted on May 12–16 in Cincinnati, Ohio, by the City of Cincinnati Police and the Ohio Association of Chiefs of Police. The Republic of Macedonia hosted the 2009 meeting (Tourism, Strategic Locations, and Major Events: Policing in an Age of Mobility, Mass Movement and Migration) in Ohrid, Macedonia, on June 9–14. A Special Meeting of IPES was held in 2010 (November 2–6) on the theme of Community Policing. In the following year (June 26–July 1, 2011) the city of Buenos Aires, Argentina, hosted the 18th (20th with two Special Meetings included) Annual Meeting on the topic of Mass Action, Violence, and Crime: Policing Disorder and Discontent. The last annual meetings were hosted in the United Nations in New York on the theme of Armed Violence and Economic Development (August 4–8, 2012) and in Budapest on Contemporary Global Issues in Policing (August 5–9, 2013).

The majority of participants of the annual meetings are usually directly involved in the police profession. In addition, scholars and researchers in the field participate. The meetings comprise both structured and informal sessions to maximize dialog and exchange of views and information. The executive summary of each meeting is distributed to participants as well as to a wide range of other interested police professionals and scholars. In addition, a book of selected papers from each annual meeting is published through CRC Press/Taylor & Francis Group, Prentice Hall, Lexington Books, and other reputed publishers.

The IPES fulfills its mission with the cooperation of a global network of institutional supporters.

IPES Institutional Supporters

APCOF, The African Policing Civilian Oversight Forum (contact Sean Tait), 2nd Floor, The Armoury, Buchanan Square, 160 Sir Lowry Road, Woodstock Cape Town, 8000 South Africa. E-mail: sean@apcof.org.za

Australian Institute of Police Management (contact Connie Coniglio), Collins Beach Road, Manly, NSW 2095, Australia. E-mail: cconiglio@aipm.gov.au

Cliff Roberson, *Police Practice and Research: An International Journal*, managing editor: e-mail: managingeditorppr@gmail.com

Cyber Defense and Research Initiatives, LLC (contact James Lewis), P.O. Box 86, Leslie, MI 49251, USA. Tel: 517-242-6730. E-mail: lewisja@cyberdefenseresearch.com

Defendology Center for Security, Sociology and Criminology Research (Valibor Lalic), Srpska Street 63,78000 Banja Luka, Bosnia and Herzegovina. Tel and Fax: 387-51-308-914. E-mail: lalicv@teol.net

Department of Criminal Justice (Dr. Harvey L. McMurray, Chair), North Carolina Central University, 301 Whiting Criminal Justice Building, Durham, NC 27707, USA. Tel: 919-530-5204, 919-530-7909; Fax: 919-530-5195. E-mail: hmcmurray@nccu.edu

Department of Psychology (Stephen Perrott), Mount Saint Vincent University, 166 Bedford Highway, Halifax, Nova Scotia, Canada. E-mail: Stephen.perrott@mvsu.ca

Edmundo Oliveira, Prof., PhD., 1 Irving Place, University Tower Apt. U-7-A, Manhattan, New York, New York 10003-9723, USA. Tel: 407-342-2473. E-mail: edmundooliveira@cfl.rr.com

Faculty of Criminal Justice and Security (Dr. Gorazd Mesko), University of Maribor, Kotnikova 8, 1000 Ljubljana, Slovenia. Tel: 386-1-300-83-39; Fax: 386-1-2302-687. E-mail: gorazd.mesko@fvv.uni-mb.si

Fayetteville State University (Dr. David E. Barlow, Professor and Dean), College of Basic and Applied Sciences, 130 Chick Building, 1200 Murchison Road, Fayetteville, North Carolina 28301, USA. Tel: 910-672-1659; Fax: 910-672-1083. E-mail: dbarlow@uncfsu.edu

International Council on Security and Development (ICOS) (Andre Souza, Senior Researcher), Visconde de Piraja 577/605, Ipanema, Rio de Janeiro 22410-003, Brazil. Tel: (+55) 21-3186-5444. E-mail: asouza@icosgroup.net

Justice Studies Department (Mark E. Correia, Ph.D, Chair and Associate Professor), San José State University, 1 Washington Square, San José, CA 95192-0050, USA. Tel: 408-924-1350. E-mail: mcorreia@casa.sjsu.edu

Kerala Police (Jacob Punnoose, Director General of Police), Police Headquarters, Trivandrum, Kerala, India. E-mail: JPunnoose@gmail.com

Liverpool John Moores University Law School (Dr. David Lowe), Redmonds Building, Brownlow Hill, Liverpool L3 5UG, United Kingdom Tel: 0151 231 3918 email: D.Lowe@ljmu.ac.uk

Molloy College, Department of Criminal Justice (contact Dr. John A. Eterno, NYPD Captain-Retired), 1000 Hempstead Avenue, P.O. Box 5002, Rockville Center, NY 11571-5002, USA. Tel: 516-678-5000, Ext. 6135; Fax: 516-256-2289. E-mail: jeterno@molloy.edu

National Institute of Criminology and Forensic Science (Mr. Kamalendra Prasad, Inspector General of Police), MHA, Outer Ring Road, Sector 3, Rohini, Delhi 110085, India. Tel: 91-11-275-2-5095; Fax: 91-11-275-1-0586. E-mail: director.nicfs@nic.in

National Police Academy, Japan (Suzuki Kunio, Assistant Director), Police Policy Research Center, Zip 183-8558: 3-12-1 Asahi-cho Fuchu-city, Tokyo, Japan. Tel: 81-42-354-3550; Fax: 81-42-330-1308. E-mail: PPRC@npa.go.jp

Royal Canadian Mounted Police (Helen Darbyshire, Executive Assistant), 657 West 37th Avenue, Vancouver, BC V5Z 1K6, Canada. Tel: 604-264-2003; Fax: 604-264-3547. E-mail: helen.darbyshire@rcmp-grc.gc.ca

School of Psychology and Social Science, Head, Social Justice Research Centre (Prof. S. Caroline Taylor, Foundation Chair in Social Justice), Edith Cowan University, 270 Joondalup Drive, Joondalup, WA 6027, Australia. E-mail: c.taylor@ecu.edu.au

South Australia Police (Commissioner Mal Hyde), Office of the Commissioner, South Australia Police, 30 Flinders Street, Adelaide, SA 5000, Australia. E-mail: mal.hyde@police.sa.gov.au

UNISA, Department of Police Practice (Setlhomamaru Dintwe), Florida Campus, Cnr. Christiaan De Wet and Pioneer Avenues, Private Bag X6, Florida, 1710 South Africa. Tel: 011-471-2116; Cell: 083-581-6102; Fax: 011-471-2255. Email: Dintwsi@unisa.ac.za

University of Maine at Augusta, College of Natural and Social Sciences (Mary Louis Davitt, Professor of Legal Technology), 46 University Drive, Augusta, ME 04330-9410, USA. E-mail: mldavitt@maine.edu

University of New Haven (Dr. Richard Ward, School of Criminal Justice and Forensic Science), 300 Boston Post Road, West Haven, CT 06516, USA. Tel: 203-932-7260. E-mail: rward@newhaven.edu

University of South Africa, College of Law (Professor Kris Pillay, School of Criminal Justice, Director), Preller Street, Muckleneuk, Pretoria, South Africa. E-mail: cpillay@unisa.ac.za

University of the Fraser Valley (Dr. Darryl Plecas), Department of Criminology and Criminal Justice, 33844 King Road, Abbotsford, British Columbia V2 S7 M9, Canada. Tel: 604-853-7441; Fax: 604-853-9990. E-mail: Darryl.plecas@ufv.ca

Index